To Dicky!

Me and Th[e]

[signature]

Peter McDonagh

The Tales of a Cold War Freelance Spy

Thanks so much for taking on the nicest broadcasting station & network on the planet! (And winning!)

xxx

2014

07/10/2014

i

SYNOPSIS

The book opens in the shadowy underworld of a cold and snow-bound West Berlin in the late sixties - a world where espionage is king, and where the permanent threat of a Soviet attack by the 21 Russian Armoured Divisions within 24 hours drive of the city is a permanent reality.

Against this doom-laden scenario, a callow teenage youth sways nonchalantly on a pavement by the bus-stop outside a rather seedy 'Kneipe' (pub) in West Berlin's Charlottenburg district. He, and only 13 British tanks, are in fact Cold War warriors. Although unarmed, our hero will frustrate the bellicose intentions of the Russian Bear between 1948 and 1970, returning several times after that date to check on the Final Plan - and ultimate victory - in 1994

This book charts his progress as subversive, saboteur, soubrette, and star, from his first stage appearance at nursery school, all the way through a copper-bottomed education at Reading School and St. John's College, Oxford. It records his recruitment by Forces Radio - BFBS - and becoming the Malta end of BBC Radio Two's 'Family Favourites', and the BBC Radio One Roadshow in Germany during 1987 with Steve Wright and Samantha Fox, as well as appearing with the late Sir David Hatch in a world-wide cabaret entitled "Fat Bastards On Tour".

We leave him as he reminisces from his Estate in the Far North of Scotland ('all we could afford, old boy!' He chirrups) as he struggles to be a 'gentleman farmer' (!) and senile delinquent, trying to remember the events of a not altogether boring life. We hope you will agree!

To the wonderful Moo McD, who for more than 40 years has endured the ups and downs of an itinerant bog-trotter with delusions of competence. You are loveliness itself, and deserving of far more than my eternal gratitude for your love, your laughter, and your patience. Thanks in particular for turning a tin ear to all the "F" noises coming out of my study while I was getting all this down!

FOREWORD

BY

RICHARD ASTBURY MBE

The mind of the man! What *is* Peter McDonagh on? From Cold War to Gulf War; maverick to manager; alcoholic to workaholic…

As PMcD worked his way around the world with BFBS Radio, he created concepts and ideas that had never been done or even dreamt of before. Yes, some people have mentioned the word 'eccentric' in connection with him and his schemes, but with that eccentricity came constant creativity.

I first met PMcD in 1972. We were young, keen and green presenters at the bottom of a pile of established broadcasters and producers at BFBS (formerly BFN) Cologne, a station best known for its role at the overseas end of that perennial radio favourite, Family Favourites. Quirky, charismatic and chaotic, PMcD was a breath of fresh air in a stuffy old MOD-based institution. I didn't know it at the time – nobody knew it at the time – but he would be the man to lead BFBS into a new era of Forces' broadcasting.

That was years away, though. In the meantime, he had some pioneering presentation to do. His first piece of brilliance was a three-hour slot on a Saturday morning called 'The Great North Rhine West Phailure'. It was a sign of what was to come. Management hated it.

We moonlighted on a gig with ABBA before they became household names. International stars came to our Cologne studios first. We worked hard and drank hard before being separated by postings to pastures new. But we stayed in constant touch.

The demon drink was to take its toll on PMcD in Cyprus, but not before bad press involving Ken Livingston and Northern Ireland almost ended his BFBS career. He recovered and went on to lead BFBS into the satellite age, shaking up programmes, presenters and policies, stopping off in the Falklands, the Gulf and many places in-between, before ending his BFBS career at the top, as Director of Broadcasting.

This memoir is about Forces' broadcasting, the many colourful characters of the BFBS staff and audience, and postings to exotic former colonial outposts. Of course, it's also about that man McDonagh and his creative coat of many colours! I admire him greatly and long may he be a close friend.

Acknowledgements

To the late A. Hitler of Linz, without whose historical input this book could not have been written. Dad and I reckon we owe you one, you 'orrid little strutting Lance-Corporal! To MI5 and its baby brother, BSSO Berlin, who put money into my father's pocket from 1946 – 1979. And made sure he didn't have to do a full days work. To all my friends, acquaintances, employers, enemies, warders, wardens, doctors, psychiatric nurses, HM Forces and others who kept me nearly always on the straight and narrow. To the British Forces Broadcasting Service (BFBS) who employed me, sometimes with no pay, and sometimes with far too much for thirty electrifying and never – boring years of playing my kind of music for the lads and the lasses in the trenches.

For a book to be able to convey my story, I needed more than text, in other words photographs. Many of the photographs came from my own collection, whilst others were taken from the BFBS Archive. Sometimes, we were unable to track down the original source of a few photographs.

To Moo – the Memsahib – for patiently being part of the McD machine – as were daughter Mandy, and sons Olly, Alex and Paddy. Love and smiles to you all.

To Damian Watson, who burnt the midnight oil getting rid of a huge number of faux pas, spelling idiosyncrasies, anthropomorphisms, and infelicitous thoughts.

And last but not least, a huge bouquet and a bucket of gratitude to Alan and June Grace who collated, refined, discovered the art of the possible, prevented me from spending a fortune on leather-bound, gold-blocked, vellum-paged tomes at £200 a pop, and gave me the great blessings, hope, and a final ambition.

BIOGRAPHICAL NOTE

Peter McDonagh (hereafter known as 'PMcD' or 'Hey You!') was born during the Berlin Airlift of 1948-1949 at BMH Spandau in West Berlin, where he grew up in a family whose father was licensed to kill with knife, gun, and paper-clip as an employee of the British Services Security Organisation - a sub-set of MI 5. Over the years the young McD learnt how to drink Schultheiss (Berlin beer), speak German with a Berlin patois, and 'Jinglish', too, and become subversive like his father.

After a few years of primary schooling at the British military school in Charlottenburg, he was despatched to Reading School, where he added mild and bitter to his repertoire, and plenty of drama on and off stage. He also learnt how to be clumsy in matters romantic. After years of training at one of the UK's biggest and best GCE 'A' level factories, McD magicked up 3 top grades which propelled him into St. John's College, Oxford, where he excelled at punting, the best vintages for Bernkasteler Riesling, and falling over.

This qualified him for a 'gentleman's third' and a wonderful new life -eventually - as a pop-jockey with BFBS where he bemused entire nations in Singapore, Germany, Cyprus, Malta, Hong Kong, the Falklands, the Gulf and London, as well as whistle stop visits to Belize, Brunei, Gibraltar, Kathmandu, Brunnsum, and Las Vegas. He took an early bath in 1999 at the age of 50 to become a shelf-stacker at High Wycombe M&S, and then did 5 years as a lecturer in radio production at Amersham & Wycombe College. In 2010 he finally retired from paid employment to become a gentleman farmer (!) in the far north of Scotland, where he has enough lebensraum to play the Dead Kennedys at 11, and declaim poetry to the sheep right on the shores of the Moray Firth. Which accounts for a lot of beached marine mammals.

As we go to press, McD is celebrating his own swan song - cruel fate has interrupted his flow with a dose of terminal cancer, with the show heading towards the end of its run. McD is sanguine, as he's convinced the Big Man will gather him up, and put him with his chums where he can sup on a celestial Myers's rum and coke alongside the Choir Invisibule, happy with   his bunch of mates who have also 'gorn before'.

Contents

Foreword	By Richard Astbury MBE
Acknowledgements	
Chapter 1	Living On The Frontline
Chapter 2	Gaudy Arms And All That
Chapter 3	High On The Hog
Chapter 4	In At The Deep End
Chapter 5	The Calm Before The Storm
Chapter 6	Let's Limbo Some More
Chapter 7	Far East, Baby!
Chapter 8	World Record!
Chapter 9	The Golden Days
Chapter 10	The Home Front
Chapter 11	Folk In The Round
Chapter 12	Malteasers
Chapter 13	Formatt 77 And Beyond
Chapter 14	Odour Cologne
Chapter 15	Bodies, Booze and Boo Boos

Chapter 16		Guests And The Best
Chapter 17		Red Ken And A Sunset
Chapter 18		Aphrodite's Isle
Chapter 19		Vultures To Penguins
Chapter 20		The Governor's Taxi
Chapter 21		The Alkie Ward
Chapter 22		The Power Of Nefertiti
Chapter 23		The Greasy Pole
Chapter 24		Jackpot
Chapter 25		We Go To War
Chapter 26		The Big Five Oh
Chapter 27		For You The War Is Over
Chapter 28		All Good Things...

Epilogue

Chapter One:

Living On The Front Line

Hannelore sat glumly on the corner of the bench, which fitted three more like her. She was, like the others, fairly attractive, dressed in top, tights, mini and boots, which meant it must be the sixties. She tapped her foot to the English music that pulsed from the beer-soaked speakers of the squaddies'cellar bar in the Berlin Summit House NAAFI. She sipped a lady-like pint of Schultheiss beer – only 8d in 'BAFFS' (British Armed Forces Special vouchers) notes.

She was on two missions. The most important from her Mum's point of view was to get hold of some duty-free fags and vodka from one of the increasingly generous squaddies who packed the bar.

The second was rather darker. She had missed a period and her boyfriend had done a runner courtesy of Her Majesty. Yes, he'd been posted back to UK and, as far as she was concerned, to oblivion. So, there she was, up the duff, a bit miz, but bright enough to realise she still had a window of opportunity. All she needed was to catch the eye of one of the squaddies at the bar, maybe exchange a few words of each others' language and, who knows, both goals might be achieved at the same time. One bird, two stones. Ah well, it would be nice if that Pete turned up. He could speak German *and* English, and of course he could be trusted.

Brian was an Infantryman, stationed up in Spandau's Brooke Barracks. Like most of the lads, he'd really taken a shine to the Berlin posting. Light on square-bashing and training, plenty of spare time, and if the Soviets actually attacked, well, it was goodnight Vienna, and indeed the world. So, no probs fill yer boots, get 'em down. And look around for a bit of skirt. Like that one over there in the corner, on the bench...

I blinked behind my thick specs and wiped some of the beery fog off them. I peered into the gloom of the keller bar, and edged through the crowd to the bar. Showtime.Albrecht, the barman, gave me a quizzical look, and machine-gunned me in Berlin dialect.
 'Na Junge – was soll's sein?' ('What you having, mate?')
 'Also – Myers und Cola, bitte! Kreigst du wat?' ('Rum and coke, please. Something for you?')
 'I'll get this'. Brian the squaddie joins in. Bit curious. Obviously I'm a Brit. Teenager. Service brat. Bit specky four eyes. But he talks Boxhead. Could be handy.
Brian nods in greeting. 'Brian' he says. 'I'm up in Spandau. You?'
 'Pete. I'm working in the NAAFI stores right now. Back to school in September.'

Some chat and a bevvy or three later, Brian goes for the kill.

'You see them tarts on the bench over there? German, ain't they?'

'Yeah, they like coming down here. Especially if there's any chance of duty-frees for Mutti and Vati.'

'You reckon any of 'em'd be good to take out? Could do with a bit of fun?'

'Usually OK. Anyone you fancy?'

'The one on the end, the blonde with the red lipstick.'

'Oh, Hannelore! Good choice, mate!'

'You *know* her?' (Bit of respect, for the first time.)

'Yeah, I know her.'

'Don't suppose you could do us a favour, what with you knowing German and that. Go over and tell her I love her, an' I wanna buy her a drink.' (Tries to look cool, still looks like a pissed squaddie.)

'Sure.'I slid off my bar stool, and went over to Hannelore. She smiled in recognition.

'Abend,'I said, about to start the night's work. 'Bloke at the bar, Brian. Says he fancies you. Wants to buy you a drink.'

She peers round Pete to examine Brian, who is grinning inanely at her, his late teenage spots providing a facial cabaret.

'OK, Pete. Ich hätte gern ein Vodka Tonik.' (Work it out.)

It was the work of a moment to get Brian to buy Hannelore a drink, call in a favour, and find a table for two for them in an even more intimate recess of the keller bar, where the dim lighting and acrid smell mixed with the booze to create a very false romantic atmosphere. I now kept a weather eye on them, translating rather sordid requests from time to time, while repeating my other 'introduction' routine for the rest of the girls on what I (and the girls) know is called 'the preggie bench'.

The usual outcome was that the forlorn squaddie and preggie girl got it on, and slipped the ring on before the bump became too obvious. And then they would live, just like the fairy tales, happily ever after, while Brian and his muckers provided enough duty frees to win the affections of the girl's parents.

Well, nearly. Once the wedding was over, the blushing bride suddenly stopped being fluttery and winsome, and became like her very strict and stern mother, who insisted the new couple would take an apartment directly next to hers - after he'd bought himself out of the army. He needed to do this because when he was posted the girl and baby would not go to the UK because the climate was "too damp". He'd work in a menial job. He'd lose duty free privileges but still trade on the black market. And he'd watch Hannelore turn slowly, horribly, into her Mum.

And what was in it for me? A regular clientele, always a new stock of squaddies and girlies who'd already been a bit naughty, all the drinks I could neck and quite a few good evenings for a 17-year-old geek still at school for most of the year.

But all good things come to an end and at the end of a productive evening it would be back out on the streets – either across the road from Theodor-Heuss-Platz to the 'Zum Lindenwirtin' – the after hours place that sold draught Guinness, or 'Ozzie's Funk Eck'- on the corner of Leistikowstrasse or, more usually, the little Berliner Kindl 'Kneipe', warm as an armpit, which sold 'curry pommes frites' – curried bratwurst and chips, compulsory in a Berlin winter.

*****

One night I was coming home from the Keller Bar and had just crossed the road to the BK when a Number 94 double-decker pulled up. A British squaddie had started a fight and taken a swing at the bus conductor. A crowd gathered in the snow. I recognised a mate of mine, Richard Glyn-Jones, and we two Brits (who both spoke German) waited to see what was going to happen.

(Point of order: when the Allied Forces first occupied Berlin they were called simply the 'Besatzungsmacht' – the occupying power. After the Berlin airlift, when the Americans and British effectively saved Berlin from starvation, the Allies rejoiced in a new name: the 'Alliierten Streitkräfte', or Allied Forces. The only lot outside the wire were the continuing bogeymen, the Russians, who lived 'drüben' ('over there') and were hated after their rape, pillage and murder in 1945.)

So the argument on the pavement with the Berliners was 'stupid squaddie, bad form to get drunk' and/or 'poor young man, miles from home, Christmas coming, missing his loved ones, few too many, put him in a taxi and get him back to barracks'. Some emphasised the latter point with 'Aber wenn die Ivans kämen?' – 'What if the Russians had come here instead?')

I detected some icy breathing next to me. There stood an elderly Berliner, wearing a rather sinister full-length black leather overcoat, a trilby set low on his head. In the street lamps his gold-framed spectacles reflected much of the light. Behind them, the eyes were older, and hollow, and the lines on the face spoke of tragic times and great sadness.

'Wenn die Ivans kämen!' he almost whispered. I answered him, in Berlin dialect.

'Na, wie war es ei'nt'lik?' – 'What actually happened?'He looked me up and down. Here was I, young, about 17, clearly wet behind the ears. I was about to be chosen to receive a harsh lesson of history.

'It was in the last days of the war,' he started, slowly and deliberately. 'There were twelve of us in our unit and we had been cut off from the remaining body of the militia, retreating towards the city centre. Eventually we realised we were trapped in a dead end street. We broke into a building and found a cellar that could be secured. We effectively bricked ourselves in and waited for the end. Above us, huge explosions, shouting voices, day in, day out, more bombs, guns, and the crash of buildings lurching to the ground. We had no idea of time. We were in hell and we were finished.' He paused, and looked into the distance. There was a glazed look in his eyes as he remembered things that no man should ever have reason to know.

Strangely enough, I felt a huge wave of sympathy for him even though, by his demeanour and speech, I'd 'worked out' that he had been an officer - maybe even a Gestapo official.

However, it was his answer to my next questions that unseated me completely.

'There were twelve of you effectively cornered and bricked up in a cellar for a good few days. What was it like down there? What did you have to eat and drink?'
"Water was not that much of a problem. There was enough with puddles, a wet cellar and some rainfall to keep us going.'
'And food?'
'We had taken no rations with us.'
'So?'

'Twelve of us went down into that cellar. Nine of us returned to the surface.'

The face that had seen hell was telling the truth. If the Russians had come... He wandered off into the night, taking with him indelible and searing memories.

*****

Not all memories were as hateful, or as evil, as his. While I was growing up, Mum and Dad liked to go out to the Civvie Mess a few evenings a week, to drink and dance with the other Great Liberators (!) of Nazi Germany. Life as a victor had its advantages. They would leave me in the tender care of our 'Putzfrau' (cleaning lady – one, for the use of, came with the Married Quarter, paid for out of occupation costs by the Berlin Senat budget). Frau Freitag, or 'Tante Martha' ('Auntie Martha', as I knew her), loved to come to our first flat in Plönerstraße in Berlins Grünewald district, as a). our apartment had a working roof, central heating, and running water, unlike hers and b). she got to enjoy a hot meal, a bath, and some comfort. She taught me German – well, Berlin dialect, which enjoyed the same cachet as Sarf Lunnun talk in polite society. But I had an ear for it and was soon able to rabbit along 'auf Deutsch'.

After a while, the authorities repaired her roof, gave grants to install heating and double glazing (a huge improvement on cardboard) and one day Tante Martha asked my folks if they were going out on the Friday and, if so, could Peter come round to her flat and stay over for the night? She would really appreciate the opportunity to repay my folks' hospitality.

There was a bit of humming and hahing from my parents but eventually they agreed and I travelled with Tante Martha on the Straßenbahn (tram) to her place in Goebenstrasse in the district of Schöneberg. Her building was shabby but imposing, a ten storey block with a huge inner courtyard/garden. Needless to say, Tante Martha lived on the top floor (that's why she noticed the lack of a roof), up endless flights of creaking, rickety stairs.

The flat itself – two rooms and a kitchen and toilet - was beautifully kept, with display cabinets, heavy furniture from a different age, and cloths and drapes everywhere. A huge brick and tile oven gave off plenty of reassuring heat. Tante Lange, a distant and elderly relative, shared the flat with Martha and the pair of them enjoyed fussing over this rather owlish English boy, son of a former enemy.

After some card games, a German supper of ham and cheese and a little conversation, we all retired early. Tante Lange slept in the big room. Tante Martha and I decamped to her room, where I joined her in the biggest featherbed I'd ever seen, complete with bolsters that I swear were as big as I was. I was so tired that I hardly took in my surroundings. Within minutes I was away with the fairies.

When I woke up the next morning the sun was poking in through the lace curtains. Tante Martha was already next door, brewing up the breakfast coffee. I opened my eyes and looked at her bedside locker. In a large silver-coloured frame there was a black and white photograph of a soldier in uniform. A German soldier. I decided I would not mention this to Frau Freitag but it played on my mind all the way home. As soon as Tante Martha had dropped me off, I told Dad what I had seen. 'A framed picture of a German soldier. In uniform. The enemy, Dad. The ones you fought against in the war. Why has she got a picture in her room Dad?'

My father explained to me that the portrait was of her husband. He had been killed at Stalingrad, on the Eastern Front. He was not the enemy. He was a man, like Dad, who had been given a gun and told to fight for his country. He was not to be hated. He was a human being, in the wrong place, at the wrong time.

What a perfect lesson.

Strangely enough, about ten years later, when I was a student, it was Tante Martha's flat that provided another great lesson in life. It was 1966, I was 18, the Berlin Wall had been with us for about five years and the East Berlin authorities had allowed elderly relatives in the Russian Zone to visit family in West Berlin (just for a day or so). And thus it was I came to meet Frau Klara. She looked almost Victorian, dressed completely in black, with an angular, almost aristocratic face, but a wonderful twinkle in her eye. I was a pushy, slightly lefty student, keen to know about how humans work, without the hard work of actually experiencing life.

'Tell me, Frau Klara,' I started, after the coffee and cakes. 'What's it like living – drüben?'

'*Young man!*' she barked, as she focused on the callow youth from some other country. 'You want to know what life is like in the East? I will tell you'. She smiled icily. She had clearly rehearsed this answer and it was a cracker.

'First,' she said, 'there was the Kaiser. And we had no oranges.'

'Next came the Weimar Republic of the 1920s. Hyperinflation – and, of course, no oranges.'

'Before long, Adolf Hitler arrived with the Nazis. Everything was possible. Except oranges.'

'Then the War, rationing, shortages and – you can imagine – no sign of an orange.'

'Finally, the glorious German Democratic Republic, with our new Leader, Walter Ulbricht! Democracy, education and work for all in the first workers' and peasants' state. I scarcely have to tell you – *still* no oranges. And that, young man, is what it is like living "drüben"!'

We both cracked up at the idiocy of the political classes.

What I really loved in Berlin was the fact that it was a city of contrasts. As the hub of the Nazi regime it had also harboured the White Rose anti-Nazi underground movement. As a landlocked city, it has more coastline than the South of France, thanks to its incredible panorama of lakes, rivers and canals. Again, it is one of the few cities to be built on sand and thus some of the bigger lakes – Wannsee, in particular - have sandy beaches. Still, enough of the picture postcards. Let's go back to the harsh reality of life on the front line.

I soon realised that, not having a gun or even a uniform, my job as a Cold War warrior would have to take a different direction. First, I looked at the French occupiers. All they did was to annexe part of Berlin and turn it into part of France, a jolly French frog leg ghetto with hot and cold running Burgundy. They pretended to be soldiers and the West Berliners pretended to let them. Sales of white flags were not seriously impaired by their presence. They mainly had masters' degrees in expostulation and outrage.

Then we had the Americans. God, they took themselves *so* seriously. They turned their sector into a 'Little America'. They were actually awarded a medal for serving in West Berlin, which on AFN Radio they insisted on calling 'Freedom's Fortress' or 'The Divided City'. Mind you, they were also awarded a medal for crossing the Atlantic. British squaddies used to joke about them getting medals for tying up bootlaces... As for the Brits? Well, they felt a bit embarrassed being conquerors of a whole nation, even one led by that beastly little man with the shouty voice. They became incredibly nice very quickly to the Germans and treated them with, at first, a distant charm that led, once trust had been established, to a fine relationship.

There was one quiet activity that I found out about when I was working in the NAAFI at Summit House. Every summer the GOC (General Officer Commanding) would take tea, unreported and very discreetly, with a group of women known as the 'British Ladies'. It was a very good afternoon tea, much appreciated in hard times, and remained as a tradition when times improved. I asked some questions and it turned out that the "British Ladies" were British citizens who had moved to Germany before the war and married Germans – nearly all of them military officers and NCOs. Each of them had been widowed and the General's gesture was one of recognition: although they had, in effect, consorted with the enemy, they had done so from motives of love, not treachery, and so were to be received humanely and with kindness. It left a nice warm feeling.

Dad used to work for a subset of MI5, called the British Services Security Organisation, based at the Olympic Stadium in Berlin. His was a front-line role, openly being chauffeured around Berlin, dropping off documents at the individual Allied Powers Headquarters, as well as the Allied Kommandatura, and the British Air Safety Centre. His pass had a red background, which seemed to open a lot of doors. As this task could be done in three hours a week, the rest of his time was spent sipping Schultheiss beer in West Berlin's delightful boulevard cafes, people watching, while his driver waited round the back in a big blowzy old Ford Kapitän. What a life. Dad said that the reason he enjoyed the job – and stayed in it for thirty three years – was the knowledge that the Berlin Senat, which paid *all* Occupation Costs, was paying his salary and overseas allowances, our accommodation, my education and all incidental expenses along the way...

I didn't find out what he did until one awesome night when I was fifteen. Father had come home and he'd clearly had a bad day. He flumped down in his chair and called for a beer. He took a long slug. I looked at him. He looked at me.

'The prysh of budder in Leipshig,' he slurred. Clearly, the boulevard cafes had taken a hit that day.

'The price of butter in Leipzig?' I encouraged.

"Thass was iss all about. We keep an eye on the prysh of budder in Leipshig, shampoo in Dreshden, TV shows and magazinesh, whasson sale an' all that.' His treachery and breach of the Official Secrets Act would no doubt have continued had he not fallen into a beery sleep, after which his job was never mentioned again.

From this I surmised that BSSO was in the game of gathering low level economic intelligence to assess consumerism in the GDR, its effects upon morale, loyalty to the State and the potential for subversion by black, white, or grey propaganda. Later in my career, I discussed this with Chapman Pincher, former agent and author of *Their Trade is Treachery*, and he agreed that this was close to the mark. So, I was the son of a spook!

I said that his job was never mentioned again. He did tell me one story, which, whether true or apocryphal, makes the room rather dusty whenever I tell it.
A West Berlin policeman was doing his rounds up by the Berlin Wall in the British Sector late one night when suddenly there was a low 'pop-scoooosh' and he noticed, just centimetres away from his boots, an implosion of Berlin's famous sand. A little hole appeared. A pork pie hat appeared to rise above the surface, accompanied by the bespectacled face of a pensioner blinking in the glare of the border lights.

The policeman gave the pensioner a leg up and waited a moment with polite patience while the elderly gentleman composed himself.
'Good evening,' said the pensioner. 'Am I in West Berlin?'
'You are - and you're welcome,' said the policeman. 'Now, this is what will happen. I need to call for the British Military Police, as they will want to inspect your tunnel. Once you have been cleared, you will be driven to the Marienfelde Refugee Centre, where you will get some food and drink, fresh clothes, and transit accommodation. Once the authorities have had a chat with you, you'll be given West Berlin identity papers, some interim allowances and a place to live independently.'

The old man heard all of this and nodded his thanks.
'That's very kind,' he said, 'but I have eleven others waiting below. May they come up now?'
'But of course!' said the policeman kindly and helped the entire party of elderly men and women to the surface. Within minutes the Royal Military Police and other British officials arrived. In next to no time the hole was being inspected.
The tunnel was very long and was boarded carefully throughout; once again, the soft sand of Berlin could be a hindrance here. There was even a string of low power light bulbs disappearing back into the distance. The investigating officer was concerned. Something wasn't right. He climbed to the surface and looked at the party of twelve. They were all, in effect, dressed in their Sunday best: suits, well cut-dresses, all very chic and middle-class.

He suddenly hit on the answer. He knew what was wrong with the tunnel. Most tunnels are low because the less dirt you have to remove, the quicker and easier it is to escape. But this tunnel was nearly two metres high!

He turned to the party's spokesman. 'I must ask you,' he said: 'Why did you dig this tunnel nearly two metres high?'

The pensioner's eyes lit up with a pride that only exists in the finest of people.

'We dug the tunnel so high because we wanted to walk to freedom like people, not crawl like animals.'

As I said, the room gets very dusty whenever this tale is told.

*****

This was life on the front line. Boarding school pupil Pete (that's me, by the way!) was already finding out about more than the birds and the bees and, apart from a NAAFI Stores job, which was temporary, becoming a Cold War warrior – unarmed – working in West Berlin in the late 60s as an undercover pimp. From 1948, when I was born in Spandau British Military Hospital, until 1970, West Berlin was *my* patch and I guarded it with might and main even after I left for other parts in 1970. I was born during the Berlin airlift in 1948, was there when the infamous Berlin Wall went up on 13th August 1961 and again on 3rd October 1989, when it was effectively pulled down. Then, after the Russians left in 1994, I closed down the British Forces Broadcasting Service, Berlin, operation with a cheery 'Tschüss!' ('Cheerio!') from the new studios in Spandau.

But we've got some history and some oddities to sniff before we get there. Time for a wobble of the opaquometer, indicating a time shift, back to the post-war period. Europe is shattered. Whole cities are derelict. Millions have died. Luckily, the human spirit rises above it all and the great reconstruction is underway.

The Soviets had not been kind. They waited until my Dad had finished with his walk-on part in World War Two, got himself demobbed and found a nice gig as a low-level spook in West Berlin. Then they sealed off West Berlin by land and water, which meant a city of more than 2 million people was besieged by the pesky Rooskies and their nasty Commie 'Democratic' East Germans for more than a year. Everything from food to coal was shuttled in on flights, which landed every 30 seconds; so tight was the schedule that if the pilots missed their landing slots they turned back with a full load in order to wait for a second go.

One of the pilots flying Hastings aircraft was a little, smart and very skilled RAF flier called Bill Bailey. As well as flying in food for adults, he and his fellow pilots were responsible for flying in the drugs that I needed to stay alive: 'National' NHS dried milk and little bottles of 'National' orange juice concentrate. Many years after Bill had been kind enough to keep me alive, he became my number two boss when he was Assistant Managing Director of the Services Sound and Vision Corporation and I was Director of Broadcasting. Once I'd jogged his memory, we both agreed that he might well have flown these goods into West Berlin and, as a consequence, saved my life. From that moment on, whenever we went to functions together, Air Vice-Marshal Bill would always introduce me to his RAF chums as 'Peter, our Director of Broadcasting. I once saved his life, you know!' He was a proper gent – old school, and time off for the Cheltenham races...

Dad, on the other hand, didn't have quite as jolly a jump into Civvie Street. The silly bugger joined up on 3rdSeptember 1936, for a three year spell, because his Dad had done a moonlight flit to the USA, leaving my grandmother Mary scrubbing *other* people's doorsteps in Middlesbrough. Dad had to leave college to earn a crust and keep a roof over Mary's head. Well, how blue was the air when, as Dad was celebrating by burning his puttees after three years before the colours, that horrid little scrote Neville Chamberlain came on the wireless to announce that Mr Hitler was being a pain, that Father could stop burning his puttees, put them on again for the duration and receive an open ticket for World War part two.

My Dad was one part worrier, one part Pollyanna and one part (his interpretation!) state registered coward, so he was a little peeved when he ended up in Dunkirk. His footwear on returning on HMS Marlborough was a pair of ballet pumps (as well as some uniform; don't snigger). After Dunkirk he succumbed to the charms of my Hampshire-born Mum, Rene. In 1941 they were married but family was immediately put on hold as Dad was further invited to tour Iraq, North Africa, Italy and the deep delights of Monte Cassino. It was there that he single-handedly failed to capture an entire platoon of the Wehrmacht. As a wireless operator with the Royal Artillery, one beautiful sunny day Dad found himself in sole command of a trench, a radio, a bottle of vino collapso and a bunch of fresh, cool cherries. He was listening to some music station or other, not a care in the world, when he felt a tap on his shoulder. Turning round, he looked into the eyes of a rather battle-weary Wehrmacht officer.

'Ve Vish,' said the officer, with great formality, 'to surrender to you.'

'Ve?' – 'We?' said Dad, not unkindly. He had always thought it was politicians who caused wars, not ordinary people.

'Ve,' repeated the officer, and stood back to reveal a bedraggled platoon of some thirty souls.

'Ah,' said Dad, as he stalled for the right answer. 'I'm sorry but as I am not an officer I cannot accept your surrender. You will have to go up the lines over there.' He gestured to a point somewhere – anywhere – up country.

'Nein!' said Hermann, with some horror. 'Up zere are die Amerikaner and ve cannot surrender to zem because they eat zere prisoners.' Obviously the Yanks had put out some fine black propaganda! 'Hier,' he said, and put a huge pocket watch on Dad's wireless table. 'For you, venn you make us prisoner!'

'I can't do that!' said Dad. Next to appear was a bronze two-foot tall classical statuette of a Greek god – still in our drawing room to this very day – and a Voigtländer Bessa bellows camera, on which I later learned to take my first photos.

Dad was still not impressed. Prisoners meant admin, which has been hated by the McDonaghs from the dawn of time. It also meant forms, hassle, no more cherries or music and a sunny day spoilt. Then he had a bright idea. He radioed HQ to tell them some Germans wouldn't mind surrendering, if somebody could tool along with a 3-tonner and pick the blighters up. Peace and honour was restored, the Germans went away to a gentler captivity than they would have got on the Eastern Front and Dad went back to music, cherries and admiring his new prezzies.

Chapter Two:

Gaudy Arms And All That

Ah, schooldays. My generation enjoyed the time before teaching became the educracy it is today, with government and experts taking it in turns to change the syllabus and structure once a whim, leaving behind both employers and kids totally confused as to what these ever-changing qualifications actually mean.

Sorry, bit of a rant. Like many others, I was brought up by hand. (Joe Grundy, are you still there?)

It all started with Davoserstraße Nursery School, a little oasis of tantrum-filled British egos in a sea of Teutonic bourgeoisie in West Berlin's leafy Grünewald district. Here we played in the biggest sandpit in the world and here it was that I was to give my first performance, my first starring role, in the world premiere of 'I'm A Little Teapot', in which I was called upon to give my heart and soul, but also to sing out loud in front of a bunch of parents who couldn't wait for it all to be over so they could get over to the mess and sink a few.

My motivation, as I remember, was that if I successfully essayed the role I would get a gold star (awarded liberally for just not being an arsewipe). My fellow thespian was a good friend, Donald Tricker, who would be playing the part of a large teacup to my juvenile lead role as a giant teapot. To emphasise the status of the role, I was to stand on a table, the better to express the motion of pouring at the critical moment, the denouement of the piece.

The great day arrived. The performance was held in the large hallway of the mansion in which the kindergarten was located. Rows of seats accommodated dyspeptic but acquiescent parents and other masochists. Now it has to be admitted that there *were* other pieces in this cabaret, but I think we were all agreed that 'I'm A Little Teapot' would be the highlight of the afternoon and was thus rightfully placed at the end of the proceedings.The other tawdry 'turns' had their moment of plastic glory in front of sixty drooping eyelids: surely my piece de resistance was about to knock them dead? I strapped on my very large and cumbersome cardboard cut-out teapot and took up my position on the table. I should perhaps have taken note of the shiny tablecloth but first night nerves conquered all other thoughts. Donald took up position on the floor beside me, engulfed in an equally large cardboard teacup.

It was clear that the moment of truth had arrived. I had my motivation. I had my costume. I had my lights and indeed my audience. It was time to gather,   breathe, and launch.

'I'm a little teapot,' I ventured. Confidence welled inside me, as I noticed my audience was hanging on my every word.

'Short and stout. Here's my handle. Here's my spout. When I get my steam up, hear me shout...'

I leant backwards for maximum effect. I had my audience sitting on the edges of their seat:

'Tip me up and pour me out!'

Well, I guess it had to happen. Pride comes before a fall. But what a fall. Suddenly the audience became animated. They, rather cruelly, I thought, collapsed with laughter. I had given them a reward for their righteous parental behaviour. An unexpected pratfall. Deep joy.

Subconsciously, I filed this event away for future reference. It seemed that if you gave people a reason or even an excuse to laugh, they'd love it.

My next performance left little room for manoeuvre. I had achieved primary school and was rewarded with the lovely Miss Phillips, a sweet but stern schoolmistress of the old order: prim and precise, but if you looked closely enough you could see the twinkle.

We were in class one sunny day, reading out loud. I quite enjoyed this (already beginning to like the sound of my own voice!) and we were being called upon to declaim a poem.

I thought I had located an excellent platform on which to display my talents - a short piece from the North East of England called 'Dance to your Daddy', in which the action centred on a mother's bribing of her son. Should the boy interpret the terpsichorean muse for his father, he would be rewarded by a piece of fish on a small plate.

I know: I would rather have gone for a Mars bar. But this was not the time for a debate.

I stood. I held the book away from me. I adopted a dramatic pose. I declaimed:-

'Dance to your daddy, my little laddy. Dance to your daddy, my little lamb. You shall have a fishy on a little dishy. You shall have a fishy, when the boat comes in.'

No. Although I'd read it 'nicely', there was no pizzazz there to 'lift' it.

Miss Phillips, however, had been impressed. 'Come with me,' she said. 'Jane, you're in charge. Everybody, read your books *quietly*.' Nobody would make a noise.

She took me out of the huge classroom that had been the drawing room of another Berlin mansion, across the huge flag-stoned hall and up three flights of stairs to the Headmaster's office, where one Mr J. Uren held court and decided the fates of his charges on a daily basis.

'Mr Uren,' said Miss Phillips. 'I have brought Peter to read his poem to you.'

J. Uren was an administrator rather than an educator. His struggle was with budgets rather than brains. However, he had the savvy to realise that happy teachers and happy pupils made his job a lot easier. He turned completely to face me. He was a severe looking man in a funeral suit, about twenty feet tall, with the hooded presence of a vulture. His dark brown voice put me not at all at ease.'Well, young man. You're going to read me a poem. Off you go, then.'

I read the poem. I thought I would add something to the reading. It was then I discovered I could move my eyebrows independently. As I read, randomly lifting each eyebrow in turn, then both together, then in reverse, I heard a choking sound coming from the direction of the great man.

I finished and looked up to see Mr Uren with a handkerchief, dabbing his eyes. He put his glasses back on and smiled thinly.

'That was very good, Peter,' he said. "Now run along!'

It was years later that I found out the cabaret with the eyebrows had given him a fit of the giggles. It had brightened up his day no end. More importantly, I'd been spotted.

Halfway through my primary school education at the palatial Herthastrasse School, the authorities had come up with the idea that an effective British Forces 'village' could be built fairly close to the Olympic Stadium in the Neu Westend quarter of the city. It was bright, leafy and otherwise unspoilt. The Berlin Senat was very happy to build untold new streets, a custom built primary school and acres of sculpted parklands, lawns and trees.

The new Charlottenburg School was the centrepiece, the jewel in the crown of the British Families

Education Service. It had a wonderfully large and airy assembly hall, with a first class stage. I was mortified that its very first production, the tried and tested nativity play, was cast and rehearsed before I knew about it.

Tragedy duly struck. One of the three wise 'Maggies', as we called them, was taken ill and the search was on for a new Melchior, with only one week till curtain up. Who could step into the breach? Who could give a profound and wise Melchior at the age of ten?

Step forward, young Peter. With recommendations from no less than Miss Phillips (and the headmaster) it was a done deal. A purple robe with white rabbit trim, a cardboard crown and an old shoebox done up with festive wrapping, and there we had it: one Melchior. All I had to do was learn the lines.

And I just can't remember lines without my brain nearly bleeding – one of the reasons I never considered the stage as a profession.

Miss King, the de facto scriptwriter of the nativity play, turned out to be something of a wit and placed quite a few topical references in the script. As luck would have it, she gave me the best line in the play. Something in me recognised this and I was determined to squeeze the most out of it on the night.

Showtime. And I knew I had the killer line. Both eyebrows would be deployed by this. The play trundled on, with only Miss King's script rescuing leaden and halting performances from my fellow thesps.

We came to the scene at the inn. The blessed couple were turned away, of course, but the innkeeper offered a packet of NAAFI tea as a kind of consolation prize, for which he wanted one and six in old money. (NAAFI had just announced swingeing price increases.)

As one of the wise men, standing by in the manner of a Greek chorus at this stage, I proceeded to hit the audience with Miss King's finest line:-

'One and six a packet? That's just another NAAFI racket!'

There was cheering in the hall. Howls of laughter. Melchior had deployed the eyebrows at the same time as the line, and the result was a winner. From wise man to wise guy in one easy stroke. My goodness, I *liked* this performing lark!

Secondary school brought new challenges. Dad decided his only son might do well at Reading School, notable as a leading grammar school with a shiny track record and very cheap boarding fees. I was duly despatched, eyes suitably moist, soon forgot about home and led the nearest thing to a Greyfriars existence that it was possible to have in the sixties. We did all kinds of naughty things from the first year. By the time we were in the fourth year, hopping over the school wall to go to parties or the Excel all-night bowl was de rigueur, but the school did have some funny customs.

The most eccentric (at first sight) was the annual Gilbert & Sullivan thrash. Frank Terry, the history master, was officer i/c G&S, and every year he would launch one of these on an unsuspecting public. I started as a young maid in 'Trial by Jury'. I was a very good young maid. In fact, I looked dangerously *like* a very good young maid. Thank goodness those days were still innocent! The following year I thought my voice was about to break but it didn't and once again I was a bloody young maid in 'The Pirates of Penzance'. The next year I yearned to play somebody in trousers – even the chorus would have been smashing. But Frank pointed his finger at me and smiled with that dedicated resolve of a producer who knows what he wants:

'McDonagh!' he barked, from below the apron of the Big School stage where we G&S hopefuls had assembled.

'Yes, sir?' I tried to sound as butch as I could. My voice was on a knife-edge. I could even yodel. But my basso profundo was rather less grand than it might have been.

'Are you in good voice, McDonagh?' He was being pleasant. He was toying with me. I knew we were seconds away from the kill.

'Yes *sir!*' I snapped back, as confidently as I could but with all the shit-scared venom of a raw US marine confronted by a drill sergeant. I must have been nervous, as my voice now went up about three octaves. I sounded like a young maid. Oh no!

'Just the part for you, McDonagh. Lady Saphir. Here's your copy.'

There was no argument. On with the motley, on with the Leichner 5 & 9. On with the misery of wanting to be going out with *girls* but having to play one instead.

I sulked through three months of rehearsals. My only consolation was that my oppo, the Lady Angela, was being played by one of my dorm-mates, one imaginatively named Roderick Alexander Siegfried Stuart

McKitrick, who was later to go to Sandhurst and become a very butch colonel. Between us, we knocked 'em dead.

We did five days of performances and with each show the knife dug deeper and deeper into my heart. Saturday night was the big night, when not only the headmaster attended, but also the mayor of Reading himself! We all went up a gear, and even Frank Terry was clearly pleased with our efforts. Instead of guiding us from the wings, in the last half he joined the mayoral party in the posh seats at the front. This was not as good as it might have been, as directly in front was the school band, who gave new resonance to the phrase 'orchestra pit'. It would have been a kindness to call them dreadful, or even a band. Fourteen individual instrumentalists in a forlorn search for some notes in common…

And so to the finale. Principals and chorus assembled on stage for the mandatory encore and bows. Having squeezed the last pustule of unremitting joy out of this Victorian confection, it was now time to sing the national anthem.

I was in the centre, at the front, directly facing the headmaster, the mayor and Mr Terry. My thespian eyebrows danced their own tarantella as my broken voice boomed out in a hearty baritone our song of loyalty to Her Majesty. Under normal circumstances, this would have gone unnoticed apart from two things:-

a).   I was singing very, very loudly.

b).   I was still dressed and made up as a rather beautiful Victorian aristocratic young lady.OK. I admit it. It was deliberate. At the interview without coffee, which followed the next Monday, I pleaded forgetfulness and was more or less pardoned, but it was the last Gilbert & Sullivan I was allowed to take part in.

In amongst A levels, smoking, pints of mild in the Eldon Arms and the first onset of *girls* (God, I was bad at that), I carried on as a subversive actor and, while I was sitting my Oxford entrance exam in the Autumn term of 1966, I also decided to have a bash at the annual school play, the rather lugubrious and textually overstuffed 'Richard III'.

It turned out there were two of us auditioning for the role of the hunchbacked king. One was a genuine and very good actor called David Something (I call him that merely to hack him off; you'll see why later) and the other one was me. An English master, the late John Periton, was an able and skilled producer. We rehearsed on a row of chairs in Big School. Of course, lah-di-dah David went for the usual 'Now is the winter of our discontent' opening. I have to say he made it sound really good.

But I'd got the devil in me, and a bit of gum disease. And the two combined with my memorising a chunk of Richard's part so that I could actually *act* the audition. I pulled three chairs together, and explained that I was lying on a palliasse in my tent at the Battle of Bosworth. I knew in my heart I was about to die but I was still evilly powerful. So, with great venom, I spat out the lines. With a difference.

It started with a low moan and my head jerking back as though I was having a fit. 'Bring me another horse!' A long pause and some jerking of the padded shoulder and withered arm. Then, bolt upright: 'Bind up my wounds!' At this point, I sucked my gums and produced a trickle of real blood which I allowed to run out of the corner of my mouth. 'Have mercy, Jesu!' Then a collapse. 'Soft, I did but dream…'

John Periton was seriously worried. 'Are you alright, McDonagh?' 'Oh, yes, Sir – just got a bit carried away'.

David Something just glared at me. He knew he was beaten. He would be offered the role of Duke of Buckingham, where he would commit an act of treachery outside the 'Little O' of the theatre. I was given the part, and spent a whole term learning the lines. I've already mentioned that I hated learning lines, one of the two reasons I never became an actor. (The second was doing the same thing night after night for long periods of time).

The show lasted for a week in December and went well. I, and many of the cast and production team, got great write-ups in the Reading Chronicle. I heard through the grapevine that the joke in the staff room was that someone had accused John Periton of typecasting by giving me the part of Richard. I took it as a compliment.

I mentioned treachery. David Something, who thought I had effectively stolen the part of King Richard from him, went to Periton to ask that the annual Boulting Brothers drama medal should not be awarded that year, as the play was so obviously constructed to make sure Richard came out as top dog – or poisonous, bunch-back'd toad! The Boulting Brothers of British film fame were old boys of the school (they'd been expelled for pacifism, but time heals when you're famous) and they had endowed this annual prestigious silver medal for best performance in a school drama.

Periton thought long and hard about David Something's request and indulged him in a sanitised version of the request which normally involves sex and travel. So, drama in the house! McD get de gong! Much cider broken out at the provisional wing of the Drama Society's after-show party. Sadly, David Something couldn't be there.

And that really was the end of my drama career. Learning the part of Richard killed it for me and since that day I've been incapable of learning lines. So I've been writing them instead, or extemporising with after-dinner speeches and the like.

*****

Of course, there was another side to school as well: the academic bit. Because I'd been brought up as an only child, I learnt how to make a virtue out of my own company and enjoy a great degree of solitude. Until I was about sixteen, I wasn't really allowed out to play. It was usually the voice that got me through.

Even at primary school I learned, as many kids do, how to speak three languages. The formal language of the classroom, the natural but guarded language of the home, and the much more slangy, slanderous language of the playground.

But there was an extra dimension in Berlin. Every two years, a new UK battalion was posted in, and they came from absolutely everywhere. So the playground would ring to the sounds of the King's Own Scottish Borderers, the Somerset and Cornwall Light Infantry or the Inniskilling Fusiliers. If you're a skinny specky four-eyes with not much going on in the fighting department, you need to adapt to survive.

And so, with me, it was dialect and humour. With German, I'd found I had an ear for the music of the language and it was the same with UK dialects. I had a ball. You didn't even have to say funny things – just say things funnily. Gradually, I picked up on some key stories and started to build a repertoire. Before long I was able to fit a story in a specific dialect to a given event. It sounded witty, but relied on what I later learned was a kind of 'mind-map'.

The next part was stringing the pieces together – a kind of 'act' – which in time became the basis for after-dinner speaking. I would arrive at the venue without any notes, join in the socialising to pick up on key characters and events around that evening's dinner and then combine that input with a tailored selection of 'prepacked' stories, which would later be delivered as a complete whole. If you looked at my crib sheet (prepared ten minutes on a table napkin or an old envelope before standing up and spouting) you might have seen something like:- 'Playground chat'MD golf – Geoff Chisholm – 'microphones left on' Bill Nantwich – company joker – beer – 'soldiers and their slang' - Liz Machin – company outing – goat – 'rice pudding' –

canteen's finest – turkey twizzlers – 'folk music' – Fred Wedlock & the closing of the bar – 'reindeer joke' –' Christmas bonus for staff…. or else?'

That little skeleton could easily turn into a seamless ten-minute after-dinner speech. People love hearing about themselves, so make sure your audience is included.

The wobbly curtain of flashback now takes us back to school and those "A" levels.

For some reason, I work in 'jags' of about a year, where I do nothing else. Otherwise, I am a lounge lizard, a boulevardier, a flâneur, a drone – or, to put it simply bone idle. The other thing about the work 'jag' is that I can't call it up. It arrives when it wants to and leaves the same way. With my 'A' levels the 'jag' started at the beginning and left when the results were announced.

Our Upper Sixth form – seventh year – was deliciously different, but only for the 'arts' side. "Gunner" Lewis, the 'arts' sixth form head, was a rubicund Welshman with an almost sacred aura about him and was the grand master of cool. The 'science' side had "Toad" Liddington, a pooteresque martinet who still believed in desks, rows, and detentions. Gunner had easy chairs with soft cushions, a radio and a round table where we just sat, chatting and where we could brew our own coffee in the classroom/salon itself. No register was ever called and pupils, or 'gentlemen' in Gunner's lingo, just popped in and read, chatted, or thought.

And this was where I wanted to be. Which meant arts 'A' levels - in my case, English (because I already spoke it), German (because I could speak at least a Berlin dialect) and French (I found I could read it, and it was dead sexy). My work 'jag' had me turning out essays like a sausage factory, all twice as long as they needed to be, and I learned quickly from the red ink in the margins (green ink for 'Gunner') where I was going wrong and what I needed to do to put it right. I reckon I did three times more work than anyone else and that was while sneaking out to the pub, going over the walls for parties, and getting involved in toxic 'relationships' with the local girls.

Cometh the hour, cometh the geek. My industry paid off in the end. Three grade As in English, French and German – and a distinction in the Special Paper. I failed the French Special Paper, and the old Irish black dog held this to be a dismal failure and the end of the world as we know it. Looking back – what a plonker. Anyway, I had made it to 'Gunner's Sanctuary', which meant an easy ride until December, when I would take the Oxford entrance exam and hopefully trickle off to the dreaming spires with a hey and a ho and a hey nonny no. Oh, and I had to learn the title role of 'Richard III'.

*****

I suppose the one good thing about the total term-long panic of trying to remember lines for the play was that I didn't give Oxford entrance a thought. I knocked off a few exam papers and waited for a call for interview. My college, St. John's, was chosen by the School, as one of Reading's old boys was a certain Archbishop Laud, who was a big wig there. Anyway, I read up on it and it seemed a good place to go: not too posh, and with a bit of a track record.

Would they have me, though? That was something else. I had first decided Oxford was a good thing when I was reading 'The Big Boys' Book About Everything' at the age of fourteen in the school library. The book showed a comic strip of what happened when you were an Oxford student, and I really took to the idea of punts, your own study with two doors, 'sporting your oak', May Balls, lots of beer and pretty girls. Oh, and some pretty clued-up professors to teach you.

Well, at last the invitation came and I made ready for a night in a room on a staircase in the college itself, followed by a morning interview. I had to report to 'The Beehive' in the North Quad and would be seen by a Dr. Carey. Butterflies. I sorted out my room, found one or two kindred spirits and we popped next door to 'The Lamb and Flag', where much beer was quaffed and we all tried to be cool about the forthcoming life-changing interviews. We crawled into college, just before the curfew, and I can almost remember climbing into bed.

I knew when I awoke that a). I should have packed an alarm clock, b). listened to the little man who stuck his head round the door to tell me 'seven o'clock, sir!' and c). remembered that panic is one of the least attractive images to project to an interviewer.

I ran over to the Beehive – easy to spot, a hexagonal segmented building that didn't quite fit in with the sixteenth century surroundings – and ran up to the second floor, where I could see the nameplate for Dr. Carey's rooms. Unfortunately, ahead of me was a four-square northerner with thick spectacles and a rather forbidding exterior. Without giving my next action too much thought, I persuaded him that I was next and that he should come back in an hour's time, which was completely wrong. Martin Blocksidge was indeed ahead of me but, fortunately, was incredibly polite. (Martin is now a noted academic author.)

It was twelve o'clock. No intelligence from inside the room. Obviously an initiative test. I knocked as confidently as a man about to be hung can. A lazy voice invited, 'Come!'

I'd never seen a room decorated entirely with books, and only books. Floor to ceiling, on five of six walls. The other was a huge picture window, which threw light on a much-used desk. Dr. Carey indicated a comfy chair, which I occupied. Another chair contained a younger lecturer called Ian Jacobs, who looked intense, scholarly, and wouldn't have lasted five minutes in any school playground.

Once we were all settled, John Carey asked me if I'd had a good journey from Oop North. They thought I was Martin Blocksidge. Oh shit. I confessed I'd sent him away and I was McDonagh. There was a general darkening of brows. In my mind's eye I could see John making up the black spot to finish my university career there and then. But no, the man upstairs had a different plot for me today.

John started to smile and clearly thought it was very odd that I'd managed to persuade another keen-as-mustard hopeful to go away. He and Ian made a little cabaret about it and eventually I joined in.

Then it would of course be the time to cut the niceties and get on with the interview.

In my head, oodles of Shakespeare and Chaucer and Milton and poetry from through the ages and some top opinions from the best critics bubbled away, beautifully prepared. What I should have remembered was that Oxford entrance interviews make 'Alice Through The Looking Glass' seem completely commonplace. These guys spent all day every day banging on about the giants of English Literature. These guys wanted some fun.

The next forty minutes became a general discussion on the sado-masochistic episodes in Ian Fleming's 'James Bond' books and how sex, drugs, violence and criminality played out. Nerves disappeared. I was a great James Bond fan and the conversation just got better and better as we each tried to make the other two blush.

(By the way, you're right. It is *that* John Carey: English professor, Sunday Times contributor, generally considered number one honcho in the world of Eng. Lit. and the man who writes scholarly works that race along like detective novels. He has a brain the size of a planet and, if I was lucky, he was going to be my tutor.

After the interview, it was hair of the dog at the 'Lamb and Flag' and then back to London, the BEA terminal at West Cromwell Road, the coach to Heathrow and the BEA Viscount to West Berlin. I got my usual job at the Olympic Stadium as a lifeguard - well, 'attendant', as it said on the shirt - where I vacuumed the huge 1936 Olympics outdoor pool with a machine twice as big as me and went swimming in the warmer waters of the indoor pool.

I was waiting for a telegram that would tell me my future. And knocking 'em back at night. Latest drink of choice was Myers's rum and coke. Not good for early shifts.

One day, Dad came home for lunch. I noticed he was a little withdrawn. Eventually, after lunch, he produced a telegram from the President of St. John's College, Dr. John Mabbott, inviting me to take up a place at the college and to be so kind as to let him know if I wished to take up the offer. My insides did the rumba and my brain turned to rum baba.

Dad, being a northerner, contented himself with 'I see you didn't get a scholarship, then', which even upset Mum, who was baffled by GCEs, let alone golden tickets to the UK's number one palace of learning, but who had figured that a tick in the box from Oxford was very nice.

I learnt later from one of Dad's colleagues that when he'd opened the telegram and read the contents, he cried with pride and happiness. Strange Dad.

My thoughts were up with the angels that day. But to celebrate? Only one place to go - and no, it wasn't the Squaddie's Bierkeller, the Lindenwerder, or the Berliner Kindl Kneipe. We had bigger fish to fry, or nicer drinks to drink, at the Berlin British Officers' Club, behind the imposing skyscraper called Edinburgh House, the British Transit Hotel on Theodor-Heuss-Platz. The Club became my Berlin 'office' for the next three years.

Chapter Three:

High On The Hog

The bad old days of Squaddie Bars needed to be left behind. They were dangerous places and although I had learnt how to do a swerve whenever danger presented itself, I seemed to have had a common sense injection. Sure, I could carry on drinking, but I needed better surroundings.

Things changed when I started going to the famous cellar parties. These happened in officers' married quarters, where mummy and daddy would take their lives in their hands and go out for the night, leaving the huge cellars of these houses as drinking and dancing dens for the local teenagers.

This was not as perilous as it might have been. Guests were drawn from known families at known addresses. The military intelligence system was easily able to find out who was OK to invite, as any troublemakers were usually simply sent back to the UK, without formal proceedings and along the following lines:

'Captain Pole-Squatting, your son Justin has been chasing Major Fazakerley's daughter Laetitia and subjecting her to less than gentlemanly advances. Justin will be on the next air trooper to Luton, understood?'

The understanding was that if Captain Pole-Squatting *didn't* understand, he would very soon be on the air trooper himself. And maybe not as *Captain* Pole-Squatting anymore! The military is a jealous god, and pretty good at smiting…

Suffice it to say that the guest list would be duly scanned for 'unsuitables' and about thirty shiny faces would appear in party frocks and suits, nod a polite 'hello' to the parents, and then disappear into the cellars for the night's entertainment, which would typically run from 2000 to 0100 hours military (8pm – 1am). Once below, the lights would be switched to 'smooch', the volume on the

radiogram turned to 11, and the sounds of 1967/8/9 - surely the most brilliant time for bubblegum and mainstream pop? – would resound along the corridors and rooms of the cellar complex.

The décor tended to be 'off limits night club'. The best I ever saw was a real bar made out of wooden packing crates and decorated with black and purple taffeta, with the whole range of duty free spirits bottles plus optics mounted on a mahogany board. Paper lampshades covered the rather stark bulkhead ceiling fixtures, walls were painted black and covered with the usual posters and pin up photos and the ceiling was a riot of tinfoil covered papier maché, crumpled to give a thousand little rays of light, cutting through the gloom to the comparative darkness of the floor, which was edged around the room by old mattresses covered with throws.

There were some simple house rules for parties. Smoking and drinking were compulsory. Dancing and reasonable groping between willing participants were encouraged. Nobody would break away from the main group. If any couple wished to take things further along Cupid's way, they could bloody well do it in private somewhere else and sometime other – *not* on party nights!

Further 'unwritten laws' included never going into the rest of the house, apart from the downstairs loo. Never throwing up anywhere except same. Never trying to nick somebody else's boy/girlfriend during the party itself.

And of course, what happened at a cellar party stayed at a cellar party.

Frankly, most of it was just drink-fuelled high jinks, including the weekly ritual of La Bamba, which was a huge circle of partygoers with one in the middle who had to bring in the next centrepiece with a snog. This tended to break the ice among newcomers and this is how I was introduced as a kind of 'honorary member'.

I say 'honorary' because my Dad was not of officer status. This was a huge social divide and actually dictated everything on the Garrison. When I was a kiddie, even in the NAAFI Ballroom inSummit House there were signs for 'officers and their ladies', 'NCOs and their wives' and 'other ranks and their women'. Officers lived in houses, not apartments; they lived in their own landscaped areas, had bigger staff cars and, from about the rank of Major, the wives got to chug around to the NAAFI and the tennis club in their old man's duty car, complete with driver.

I guess it was because I wore glasses, spoke proper English and went to a real boarding School in the UK that I was accepted onto the social list by the parents' committee. By that time our family had been in Berlin for more than twenty years anyway and my father's rank and status were fogged a little because he worked (hah!) for the 'security services' – the sneaky beakies.

Also, I seemed to get on quite well with my fellow teens themselves, who came from both UK schools, and a significant group from Prince Rupert's School in Wilhelmshaven, on West Germany's rugged north coast. (PRS was also known as 'Pros' Reform School' and it has to be said that in the days of the mini-skirt, PRS girls were given to favour the rather intimidating 'pussy pelmet'.) There was also a great tradition of 'crush pins', which were colour-headed dressmakers' pins, worn on the lapel to indicate status (social and sexual) and current availability. Red, white and blue marked out your boarding house, whilst at the other end of the spectrum orange and purple gave out signals of pregnancy, multiple birth, or interesting ailments. It seemed to work.

I had fallen in with a good crowd, as far as party nights were concerned. But what of ordinary evenings, and indeed the long vacation days when I wasn't working at the Stadium or the NAAFI?

One day, fairly early on, I found out. A group of partygoers international took me to the Berlin British Officers' Club in Thüringerallee, behind the Churchill House civilian accommodation towers and the imposing Edinburgh House British transit hotel.

The Club was a two storey lush and louche building approached by a long drive, an entrance barrier and guard post, a sprinkling of tennis courts behind large, rolling grassy berms, an outside sun-shaded bar-terrace and a beautifully kept twenty-five metre swimming pool with a wide walkway complete with poolside loungers, easy chairs and a modern suite of changing rooms. This was paradise by day and night: it was duty-free, and its dining room was overlooked by the inside upper bar gallery.

The Club was managed by Herr Wiezorek, who ran a tight ship very tightly indeed. In fact, sometimes it was an utter wonder he could stand. He certainly had hollow legs and was the subject of much admiration. The drinking culture amongst the British in West Berlin was legend: it was a matter of honour to be seen with a rapidly-emptying glass at all times of the day or night; the red nose was a mark of honour and accomplishment and lives were measured in bottles consumed. You also need to remember that smoking was almost compulsory. Sex was very British. It was there, if sporadic; if you were good at it, all very well - as long as you didn't fart in church or frighten the horses, you could do most things. Even the lavender brigade were loosely tolerated, as long as they were utterly discreet or, strangely enough, mad queens and divas as camp as a row of pink tents. All human life was there.

The club was actually overseen by a military committee, which was headed by the RMP Provost-Marshal, on the grounds that if anyone argued the toss, the Provost Marshal as president of the mess committee could give a definitive answer on the spot. Justice was rough, arbitrary, and generally fair.

And it sometimes worked in mysterious ways, as is so often the case with the military.

We flash forward to 1977, the year of the Queen's Silver Jubilee. I had come to Berlin from Malta to visit my folks in Churchill House and I discovered this amazing tale.

The 'doorkeeper' at the Officers' Club was an ancient German civilian, Herr Stennart. He was eighty-three years old but still had the upright bearing of one who had served his country. He had also served our country in a variety of roles, having been employed by Berlin British Brigade since 1945. For this, he had been appointed BEM (holder of the British Empire Medal). This was an unusual honour for a German and Herr Stennart was very proud to have been recognised in this way.

For the Queen's silver jubilee, it had been decided that the Club would honour the occasion with a drinks party in the upper bar, with dancing and dinner in the restaurant and terraces. The guest list would be drawn from Berlin's glitterati, senior allied officers and their ladies and anyone else of significance. In British military eyes, this was an 'A' list event. The PMC himself briefed the staff on the need for protocol to be observed to the letter and finest detail on this night of nights.

And then he came to the 'any questions?' bit.

Herr Stennart, tall, upright, in spite of his years, and with something of a presence, quietly asked if it would be in order to wear 'my decorations'.

'Decorations?' said the Provost Marshal. 'I remember now – you've got a BEM. Of course you should wear that. You are entitled to wear it.'

A short pause. Herr Stennart cleared his throat, then went on: 'Yes, Colonel, of course I will be honoured to wear the BEM. I was thinking of my other decoration'.

Immediately thoughts turned to the Iron Cross, Hitler, and the evil Nazi era. Herr Stannart immediately stopped those thoughts at the pass.

'Please do not think I was referring to our shameful times,' he said. 'I was referring to a particular decoration I received during the First Great War.'

The Provost Marshal was genuinely relieved and there was a friendly tone to his next question.

'I think that may be in order, Herr Stennart. What is the decoration, by the way?'

'Ah, Colonel. I was lucky enough to be awarded the Golden Military Merit Cross after a cavalry charge when I was a young officer in the Uhlans in 1916.'

There was the kind of silence that requires a very, very special and rare form of words.

Never mind the correct protocol. The Provost Marshal snapped to attention and delivered the most emphatic and heartfelt salute of his military career. He then walked over to Herr Stennart and put his hand on the old veteran's shoulder.

'Of course you may wear your decoration, Herr Stennart - and on behalf of the Berlin Brigade I insist that you wear your Golden Military Merit Cross in precedence to your BEM.'

Brothers in arms, you see? The military have their own code and it seems to work well.

*****

I had a slight problem with going to the Officers' Club at first. When I told Dad I had visited he went into 'northern working class' mode, muttering darkly about 'lah-di-dahs' and chinless wonders ripping crusts from the gaping mouths of starving widows and orphans while choking on the silver spoons wrenched from the deserving clutches of a drowning sea of workers.

I must have been a bit braver than I had been previously and I joshed back in a cut glass accent, 'Oh, come on, Pater, you sent me to a posh (?) school. What did you expect?' But I was still getting the steelworker's eye. It seemed that when he first came to Berlin, he was invited by a colleague to the Officers' Club and was outraged to see the laid-back lifestyle of the senior military, compared to the six years of mud, shit, bullets and crawling around he'd had to go through. He was not impressed at all. 'No son of mine…' etc.

Eventually I wore him down, with Mum's help, and one day he came home for lunch bearing a little blue oblong folded card – an associate membership card for the Club! No more waiting forsomeone to sign me in. But how had he done it? He was still officially of non-officer status. He smiled in a George Smiley way. This was the man who used to walk to work from Platanenallee to the Olympic stadium HQ with double agent George Blake. Hey, this is Berlin and anything goes! The land of British Chinese radio specialist Peter Hammond, who always ordered a 'vokda tonlik' at   the bar, and poor old Bert Barrow, a copious toper, who had been locked in his room at Number 6 Mess to sober up. There was a crate of Angostura bitters stored under the bed. When they tried to revive him the following morning, it was too late. He had become the stiffest, greatest and latest 'pinker' in the world. It is rumoured there was a broad smile on the deceased's face...

And so now I had fast track into the Officers' Club, complete with my little blue membership card. The next years would give me access to a whole new world of people and ideas - of cabaret, of romance and indeed a completely new career. I joined the club as a boy and left as a man.

The first cabaret was the night of the A-level results. I had got my 3 'A' grades in English French and German. I needed to *party*! I called up all my teenage chums and we met poolside for a steak sandwich and a few wets before hitting the town and the clubs for a good night out. I remember wearing a very cheap suit (DM 68 – less than a tenner) and deciding to dive into the pool from the springboard. In I went, fully clothed and partially pissed. It then seemed a good idea for all of us to order more drinks, get changed into cozzies, pull a few white-painted aluminium chairs and tables into the shallow end of the pool and have an early evening pool party. A slightly swaying Herr Wiezorek chased us off, so we climbed back into our party gear (in my case, still mildly moist, but the evening sun had dried it out a bit) and moseyed on upstairs to sink a few more and listen to the mellifluous tones of the house band.

This was a small group of German musicians – a quartet of piano, strings, drums and vocal that regularly and relentlessly murdered a middle of the road repertoire of the same songs every evening, six nights a week, in the manner of a between-the-wars bad Berlin cabaret turn. Their most requested number (after 'Be quiet! I'm trying to eat my cutlet!') was 'The Last Waltz', which required the oily vocalist to get his tonsils around 'Ahyee head der Larst Vorltse viss *you* – two lonelee peeples togezzer.' Engelbert Humperdinck he most certainly was not. The drummer employed a very modern technique (imagine a 'Kraftwerk' monotonic beat set to 'max-techno-hypno-rhythmus' and you've got the idea). He was further hindered by his only recent return from a slave labour camp in Siberia, where he had been interned by the Russians since the end of the last lot. The string section (fiddles of varying sizes) enjoyed his drink, especially in A flat, A sharp, or A tumbler.

But they were *our* awful band, dammit. And woe betide anyone who tried to do them harm. More of that later.

So, there we were: tomorrow's young bright things, knocking back the duty free and getting ready to do the town. I won't mention them all by name but there was a whole happy tribe of Sally, Siggie, John, Big

John, Mick, Scotty, Audrey, Mags, Jane, Lyn, Ray, Tony, Sue, Julian, Irene, Lyndsay, Neil, Heather, Julia, The Other Neil, Linda and many, many others who drifted in and out of party international by virtue of postings and accidents of family fortune.

You will notice we were particularly strong in one area. 'We' refers to the A-level and Uni students. We had girls. The enemy were actually the military – and here is the great revelation – because the military only ever used the club for formal events; otherwise they were utterly discouraged from going there, both by their seniors and by the other members, who included all the BEA and Pan Am pilots, civilian attached members and various diplomatic, consular, and press people. Anyone turning up in a uniform was ignored and that tended to include being passed over by the very cosmopolitan bar staff.

Although discouraged, the only military who wouldn't listen to reason were the universally loathed new 2nd Lieutenants, or 'subbies', as we members of the provisional student wing used to call them (as in 'subalterns'). They brayed a lot and waved large denomination notes all over the place. They also tried so very hard and often to get off with 'our' young ladies, but the girls tended to be very loyal and would hoover up a few free subby drinks and then obviously return to the fold.

One night the subbies went just that step too far. They upended tables over the balcony on to the dining area below and a chair bounced off the head of one of Herman and the Germans, causing a bloody wound. (Remember, they were not that good, but they were *our* band.) The resulting melée resolved itself when the paddywagon appeared and the chinless wonders were carried off to cool their heels in the nearest guardroom. Shaken but not stirred, we returned to our drinks and made ready to shoot off to the bright lights.

On to the U Bahn underground at Theodor-Heuss-Platz, off at Kurfürstendamm and a quick dive round the corner to the Big Apple, one of West Berlin's newest and finest discos, complete with swirly lights and a really light and fun atmosphere. Then we'd usually end up in 'The Riverboat' – Atlantic soul and Tamla Motown till the wee small hours - then back to base. Did we really manage all of that *and* pass exams along the way…?

Our clique was made simple by the 'one for all and all for one' party mentality but tended to get a wee bit unstuck when it came to the romantic side. I know nothing about girls but, throughout my teenage years, had managed to hold hands and attempt the odd misdirected kiss in the general direction of a few sympathetic females. This plan of action bore no resemblance to what all my friends said they were up to but even at that stage the difference between the telling and the doing had become a bit obvious.   So I did what I always did: made a joke of it all. And that turned out to be the key. Up to a certain point, girls like a sense of humour, a twinkle and a ready wit and although I didn't do butch, muscles, or big boy bullshit, I was OK in the laughter stakes.

Eventually this hooked me the nearly undivided attentions of Sally, who more or less explained to me what it was all about. I was a keen but often bemused student. It got even stranger when attitudes and moods came into it and I'm still more at home today with a Bratislavan book of differential calculus tables than I am with the female of the species.

But Sally was fun, flamboyant, a flaunter of floaty frocks and a great partygoer. So much so, we used to split up and flirt with loads of other people. Well, Sally would flirt, and I would drink myself stupid and talk bollocks at uncomprehending girls' bosoms. Then at the end of the evening, we'd compare notes.

Eventually my attentions were rewarded in the Sally area and she deigned to give me a special present just before I shot off to Oxford: a beautiful tie. It looked like it had been designed by Jackson Pollock while having a fit in a paint factory. Turquoise and ochre blobby stripes were enhanced with shapeless black, orange and olive green blobs. I could have spilt any food or drink down it and it would not have disturbed the pattern one bit.

Of course, it was not a tie at all. It was a gift of lurve - of love even - from a steady girlfriend - a companion who didn't actually wince if you were seen together in public. This tie was an enduring example. I just loved the way her Mum and Dad smiled at each other whenever I wore it in my girlfriend's honour. I loved the way all three of them would leave the room whenever I started fiddling with it.

I only found out many years later that the tie had been a joke, a bet, right from the start. It had been chosen to be as ugly and horrible as a tie could possibly be. Again, Quasimodo had been dealt a killer blow by Esmerelda. From the distance of years, it *was* a joke. Had I rumbled it at the time, I think I might have joined the gay community

Back to the Club. The subbies were about to meet their nemesis. After the business of chucking bar furniture over the balcony, their next outrage was to throw an RMP short-service commission officer, Chris Farley, into the pool while wearing his brand new suit. This was an act of bullying. And Chris was our friend, the only army officer ever allowed to join the students as an honorary and honoured member. (As a Royal Military Police officer, he couldn't mix with ordinary army officers.) Using the power of our fathers and their interlocking offices, we managed to draw a bead on the ringleader of this group of chinless and brainless hotheads. Before the powers could swoop in revenge of Chris and his suit, the ringleader rather blotted his own copybook by burning down the dining room of his regimental officers' mess in Spandau, which took with it centuries of mess silver, melted in the fire.

In military terms, this was one down from goosing Her Majesty and accordingly required the full might of military law. Suffice it to say, he received an invitation to resign his commission, which was much better than the other unspoken offer: of having his meat and two veg sawn off with a rusty bayonet and sewn into his mouth. It took only two days to get him out forever. High spirits is one thing…

There was one last episode involving the subbies. I had popped along one early evening to sink a few Myers's and cokes and just see on spec who might turn up. While I was sitting on my own at the twenty-foot curving bar which took up one wall, I noticed in the mirror a chap in civvies, about ten feet away, also having a quiet one. Where we differed was in his next action. He picked up an ashtray from the bar and placed it in his pocket.

I peered carefully at the mirror. Yes, an ashtray had definitely gone. And – yes – this fellow was one of that vile gang of subbies. My move, I thought.

I piped up to the barman, polishing glasses at the far end of the bar: 'Günther!' The elegant German-Swiss head barman turned to look at me down his nose, as he did with everybody. 'Yes, sir?' he smoothed, as he glided towards me.

I indicated our besuited subby friend halfway down the bar with a dramatic sweep of my arm. 'This gentleman has just stuck one of the bar's ashtrays in his jacket pocket,' I revealed. 'Günther, would you be so kind as to add it to his club bill?'

There came a very plosive sound from the depths of our hapless kleptomaniac, accompanied by a very public school ruddying of cheeks and, finally, an observation.

He peered at me with pure hatred. Alas, his speech impediment reduced the potency of his statement to render it ridiculous.

'How *dare* you!' he hissed. 'You…you've got no *bweeding*!'

And off he flounced. He was the last of the phew.

So: romance and battles joined and won. I mentioned career. This happened in the same bar, just before my third year at Oxford. I had got to the stage where autopilot was wearing out. I went to primary school because it was the law and they told me to. The same for secondary school. At the end of secondary school I was told to take A levels, so I did, and I seemed to be good at them, so I was told to apply for Oxford, and I got in because they told me I could, and so I did and that was that then, wasn't it?

Well, maybe. But there was something wrong here. Nobody, but nobody, was telling me what I was supposed to do in eight months' time. What was even worse, I had been expecting them to, as usual. Not only that, I myself had no idea whatsoever what I wanted to do. There was some vague background noise about getting a job and living on my own, but it was almost inaudible.

And then it happened. I was having a natter with Mick, John and Charlie, the Pan Am pilot, when I became aware of a rather charismatic figure standing next to me at the bar, complete with a striking, loud, Irish lady clearly completing the most elegant couple I had seen in the club. The man nodded around what was clearly a wide circle of acquaintance, then looked at Günther, who

had magically appeared from nowhere. 'Two Campari and Soda, please Günther, and one for yourself.' The voice was honey over rocks – dark brown and so reminiscent of the best voice-overs of the age. The voice of a storyteller, who could weave words to make them mean anything. I was very impressed.

Not only that, this man wore his clothes, not the other way round. Shot silk and finest cottons, lightweight but totally uncreased. This man exuded calm, and, more importantly, cool. James Bond could just about have played him. He turned to the lady and they fell into a low hum of conversation. Well, he did. She had a voice like a corncrake with a sore throat, and was clearly totally unafraid of the power of expletives, which peppered her chat like barbs on trench wire. This was Pam, a former 'Vogue' model and generally regarded as extremely dangerous.

I had to find out. I turned to Mick. 'Who's *that*?' I hissed. Mick looked knowingly, as only a streetwise master criminal can. (It was Mick who stole a pair of Rudolf Hess's pyjamas to sell on the black market whilst working as a medical orderly in the war criminal's private suite at the British Military Hospital in Dickensweg.)

'That's Dick Norton. He's the Berlin Representative from BFBS (British Forces Broadcasting Service). Do you want me to introduce you to him? He lives just down the road from us.'

Gosh. He's on the radio. On BFBS. He's famous. Yes, and I *do* recognise the voice. Oooh, I hope we get on…

'Er, Dick'. A tap on the shoulder from Mick. 'Got a moment?'

'Er – yah – cool,' said the great man. He turned to face us both. 'Hi, Mick.' He looked at me in a neutral, but slightly superior way.

'This is McD,' said Mick. 'Peter McDonagh. A mate of mine.'

'Hi, there Pete, What do you do?' 'I'm a student'. I remembered to look him in the eye. Maybe it was a little aggressive, to make up for the jelly legs.

'I can't stand students,' deadpanned Dick, with all the finality of a grumpy vicar ending a burial service. I didn't understand this kind of humour and was stung by what I thought was a gratuitous put-down. (A little residual Irish blood runs through my veins.)

'And what do *you* do?' I said, against every warning beacon of common sense.

'I'm Dick Norton,' he said. As in 'Bond - James Bond.' A brand name.

'Great.' I tried again. He was going to tell me. 'And what do you *do*, Dick?'

'I said, I'm Dick Norton.'

No going back. 'I've got that, Dick. Just wanted to know what *job* you do?'

This one had clearly run its course. He broke into a disarming smile. 'I'm the BFBS Berlin Representative. I do stories and features for the network based in Cologne.'

I kept a straightish face. Two could play at this one. 'Oh, BFBS. Broadcasting.' I made it sound like a social disease. 'Surely *anyone* can do that?'

I swear there was just the trace of annoyance in his eyes. But the smile returned – the thin, killer smile of someone who knows he will win in the end. 'Well, if you want to try it out, come up to the studios tomorrow afternoon and you can read out the   local announcements before the six o'clock news.'

I ran his last statement back in my mind. Yes, this man was offering me the chance to go on the radio, alone, and talk to an audience of thousands. Of course, I'd had years of training. Reading

aloud in class, school plays, Gilbert and Sullivan... It couldn't be that hard. Just because you were effectively locked in a small room and talking not to a live audience, but to a black stick and had no idea of what people were thinking when they heard you... Then again, what if you froze, or said something stupid, or lost your place, or the studio caught fire? It didn't take too long for the panic to set in, the little heart to start beating faster... and then I remembered.

Flashback - I am in our luxury apartment in Kastanienallee, off the Reichstraße, in the district of Charlottenburg. Next door to the propaganda-broadcasting traitor Lord Haw Haw's Berlin residence. I am a child, sitting in a full-sized wooden tea chest. I have drawn dials and meters on the inside walls. I am holding a hairbrush. For some reason I am talking. 'This is the American Forces Network and the time is ten o'clock and here is the news from AP, UP and INS. There has been nobody killed today and nothing bad has happened and that is the end of the news and so let us play some more music for you at home...'

OK wrong station. But as I panicked in the Club, I remembered my Mum telling me about this scene from my childhood (she overheard me debuting at this radio lark) and my resolve suddenly cut in. I may be bricking it, I may be shit scared, but I was meant to do this. Radio studio? Spandau? Tomorrow? Bring it on!

Chapter Four:

In At The Deep End

I woke up a bit late the next day. The usual slightly throbbing head from the drinks and smokes at the club the previous night and the usual late night fry-up of Danish bacon, eggs, fried bread, and a giant glass of milk. Time to kick start the day.

Then I remembered. Dick Norton. BFBS. Local announcements. Spandau. Today. A bit of me was a bit annoyed. I thought I'd have the full day to go up the Stadium for a swim but now I'd have to think about getting ready, what to wear and how to get there.

But where? I suddenly realised I had no idea where the BFBS Berlin studios were. Panic. Flapping. Eventually, I went up the WRVS office at Summit House and they told me the studios were on the top floor of Brooke Barracks in Spandau, part of No. 46 Army Education Centre – where the library was.

Good. I'd been to the library with Dad so I had a picture of where the studios might be. I stopped off in the NAAFI cafeteria (where Herman and the Germans played most late mornings) and enjoyed a visceral sausage roll and a coke. Home for lunch and set off nice and early on the 94 bus from Theodor-Heuss-Platz at the end of our road. I found the barracks, flashed my ID card and soon I was on the 5th floor, standing in front of a sign that declared 'BFBS Berlin'.

I knocked, and walked in. Wow, shedloads of kit here. Huge Telefunken reel-to-reel tape recorders standing in cabinets in a row, with giant speakers playing an interview between Dick Norton and Dave Brubeck, who'd recently visited Berlin. I was already quite impressed.

Dick was standing in front of a tape deck, editing the tape, which was stopping and starting as he went about his craft. Tape over the playback head to the edit point, press the button for a purple line on the back of the tape, move it along to the editing head, snip it, pull the tape behind along to the second edit point, purple mark, snip, put the tail and the new head together in a customised chrome plate former, take 2cm of sticky white editing tape and smooth it over, sealing the two ends together - then run back the tape for a few seconds, and listen to a clean edit going through the gate.

I was impressed. Dick knew I would be impressed. The broadcasting environment of the sixties was bound to impress the newcomer.

'So you found it then,' said Dick, without further introduction. He was relaxed, nonchalant and pleasantly at ease. 'Oh – your announcements are over there. They need to be re-written, in English.'

There was a quick nervous start. 'Why?" I said "Are they in German?'

Dick chuckled. 'German? Noooo. Much harder than that – military.'

I didn't understand and my face told Dick so. 'Military?'

'Look at this one here,' said Dick, kindly. 'A bingo night is to be held at the Summit House ballroom commencing at 2000 hours on the evening of Saturday 14th August. All military personnel and UK based civilians and their dependants are invited to attend and tickets may be obtained by telephoning Sgt George Striker, RASC, on Berlin Military 9246. The jackpot this week is currently standing at £75 pounds.'

'Yes,' I said – 'That – that's a bit formal, isn't it?'

'You got it!' Dick seemed genuinely pleased. 'We need to re-write it so it sounds like you're telling somebody about the bingo, not reading out routine orders. Here, have a go!'

He showed me to a typewriter and handed me the raw script. After a few minutes I'd knocked something out. Got rid of the passives, shortened the 'militarese' and made a selling point of the most interesting bit of information.'Fancy winning £75? Well, that's the Jackpot Prize at the Summit House bingo this Saturday evening. It all kicks off at 8 o'clock in the ballroom and the organisers are really looking forward to seeing you – that's if you're entitled military or UKBC. Make sure *you're* in the running to pick up that Jackpot Prize of £75. More info from Sgt George Striker on Berlin Military 9246.'

'OK.' said Dick. "Sounds more like you're telling the tale. Now, here's another ten announcements. Turn *these* into individual items.'

It was really tough going. Nearly all the annos used the same phrases, tenses and vocabulary. The trick was to make each one sound fresh, new and different. I got my head down, wrote each one in English, then read it out loud to see if it sounded like somebody telling somebody something. After a while, it got a little easier, but needed a lot of concentration. By the time I'd finished it was gone a quarter to six.

'When do I read them out?' I asked. I thought by Dick's laid-back attitude I still had some time to go.

'Oh, you'll need the weather first, from the Met office – 9675 – give them a quick buzz, write down the figures in the right places on this form and you're ready to shoot. About nine minutes to go...'

Nine minutes? I couldn't do this. And I still had to get the weather. I raced for the phone, took down the numbers from the slowest West Country metman I'd ever heard, put the weather at the back of the ten or so local annos and walked through the soundproof door into the studio for the very first time.

The silence was tangible. If I listened very hard, I could just make out the sound of the studio clock swishing away the seconds. Three minutes to go. Dick came in and very quickly went into instructor mode. 'At six seconds before five minutes to six enable the Berlin studio to join the Cologne network by pressing the red button – here – you'll see it light up. You're now ready to go. Push up the fader at the end – that's your microphone fader – all the way to the top, before you start speaking, and leave it open until just after you've stopped. Can you just say a few words from the first anno so I can check your voice level?' I spoke, and I could hear my own voice coming – strangely - back to me through the heavy Sennheiser headphones I was wearing. Was I going out on air already?

'Don't worry, that's called pre-fade listen – it checks your voice, but your mic isn't open till the fader goes up. Now, read your annos till about thirty seconds to six, then read the weather, and make sure you're finished by seven seconds to six. One second later you'll hear the pips. Close your mic fader and, after the last pip, disable the studio from the network by pressing the red button. Got all that?'

I nodded the nod of a condemned man. Yes, I'd heard what he said. But would I remember everything? I looked at the clock. Thirty seconds to go. Dick was outside, working at his desk. At least he wasn't looking at me.

Suddenly it all happened. Red button, clock second hand, fader up - deep breath...'Good evening. You're listening to BFBS Berlin. I'm Peter McDonagh with tonight's local announcements and weather forecast.'

The next five minutes were a complete blur. Only two parts of me – my voice and my brain – were somehow functioning. My legs had turned to jelly and one of them started shaking violently. I let my arms hang loose while I was reading the annos, so as not to shuffle them; perspiration was running off the ends of my fingers. A very low but insistent "lub *dub* lub *dub* lub *dub*" told me I was about to have a massive heart attack.

I had honestly never been so scared in my entire life. And then, to add to it all, I started thinking about the thousands listening to me – the equivalent of a man looking over the edge of the Grand Canyon.

Somehow I made it to the end. I even managed to get all the right buttons and faders in the right places at the right time. I just sat there for a couple of minutes. Dick was still bent over his work. I was glad he couldn't see the gibbering wreck behind the microphone.

Eventually I tried to leave the studio with some degree of nonchalance. It was a disaster. Anyone could see I was still a gibbering wreck. Dick looked up, with a grin this time, and quoted my remark from the club the previous night. 'Oh, broadcasting. *Anyone* could do that!' I smiled ruefully. Game set and match.

'Well', smiled Dick, 'do you want to do it again?'

He never gave me a critique; he never told me to go faster, slower, put more or less emphasis on certain bits. I had just received my first major piece of Dick Norton code, though it took a while to understand it. By saying 'Do you want to do it again?' he was really saying 'Congratulations! You've passed the voice test and your scripting and vocal skills are exactly what we need. Report here every Monday, Wednesday and Friday at 5pm – oh, and you can use the studios for practice and DJ dummy runs whenever you like.'

*****

As I walked back from the studios that night, on a beautiful Berlin summer evening, I knew I had finally found what I wanted to do. I wanted to be a radio broadcaster. Nothing else would do. From now on, until I got the job, I would be a radio presenter waiting for the big break. I smiled a lot that evening, as I headed for the club and a celebratory rum and coke. Nobody could quite understand why McD was quite so animated and full of plans, ideas and schemes. I would devote myself to broadcasting. I would give myself seven years to learn the craft and then I would be a professional. Yes, I had a lot to learn but – and here I quoted my dear old Dad, who was soon to become villain of the piece, 'Everybody starts by knowing nothing'.

Within a few weeks, before I went back to Oxford for my final year, I started learning the trade. When Dick wasn't around, I spent hours in the presentation studio, playing out record programmes from a stash of record company freebies, which came for Dick every day. I learnt how to check levels, use the mic properly, do voiceovers, edit speech and do basic interviews

'*Open* questions, McDonagh.' (Dick could be a little cod-magisterial at times) 'Who, what, why, when, where, how?' *Not* 'did your trip take longer than an hour? You want *full* answers so don't ask questions where they can only say yes or no.' And so it went on.

Based on my knowledge of today's radio courses, I think with the one-on-one I got from Dick and the practical work I did in the field – much of which was broadcast – I did the equivalent of a degree course in three vacations. And I didn't have to pay a penny, or indeed a pfennig.

Actually that was not strictly true and was the cause one of the two ruckuses which nearly ended my career before it had begun.

The first concerned my 'expenses'. I had long since understood that my apprenticeship was more of an internship than anything else and I was content that I was being taught a unique and rewarding course for nothing. But I still had to catch the 94 bus and the 76 tram to get to most interview locations, once I'd been shown the ropes, and I was paying quite a few Deutschmarks every week on public transport – and indeed the occasional taxi, if it was late at night.

And there were no 'expenses' heading my way from the BFBS Berlin budget. So Dick came up with a master plan. He would employ me as the toilet cleaner. In exchange for stuffing a

weekly bog brush down the station lavvy and changing the toilet rolls, I would receive enough not only for my exes, but also plenty left over for booze and fags. Everyone a winner.

I rushed home to tell my folks of my good fortune. I guess I could have explained it all a bit better. 'Dad!' I enthused. 'Dick's offered me a job as a toilet cleaner!'

I watched the various negative emotions galloping across my stern northern father's features. He poured more Schultheiss, took a magisterial swig, and pronounced.

It was the black cap. 'Ah've never 'eard anything lahk it,' said the man entrenched in pre-war industrial practices. 'Noo soon of mine, wi' all that education, is gooin' down the toilets. And that's the end of it.'

Discretion was the better part of valour. There was no point in defying him, and no point taking the job on the sly, as it all had to go through a vetting unit inside Dad's own offices and he'd know if I accepted it.

Dick was kind. From time to time he'd buy me an extra drink at the club to offset the tram fares, but I could have kicked myself for being so direct with Dad.

But it was the next fracas that nearly ended my BFBS career, even before I officially joined. I was still practising voice technique and one exercise I did was to use different ambiences to change voice quality – in this case, in my bedroom, with one voice above and the other voice below the sheets. Transitional moves could be cut by tight editing. And that was how the 'German Beer Drinkers' Federation' interview came into being.

It was a coming together of many events, leading to an international incident. First, Dick had been taken ill and rising star Sandi Jones had flown down to Cologne to stand in as acting rep. For three magic days, I found myself in that amazing position, with lots of help on the end of a telephone from sick Dick's bed of pain. I was quite relieved when Sandi – who went on to do Two-Way Family Favourites for a time – rolled up, showed she had a robust sense of humour and got down to work.

It was at this time I had completed and edited a four-minute spoof interview with 'Klaus-Dietrich Olk, President of the German Beer-Drinking Federation', which purported to be an interview in which this fictitious gentleman insisted that women were taking over the world and that the only sanctuary the red-blooded German husband had was to go to his local and get rat-arsed. Yup, it was about a subtle as that. Utterly toxic. Taking the mick out of the Germans. And women. And decent behaviour.

I wince when I remember some of the taped interchanges. 'But why do you need to go out and get drunk, Herr Olk?'

'It is so. Venn you are from vork coming, and you are into the flat going, and there sits your vife and Auntie Flickenstein from round the corner, and zey make of hats and clothes all day nonsense talking, then must the man direct to the bierhaus go, and have many, many litres until ze vorld iss a nice place again, and zennare the vommens in zair place put.'

Oh dear. But it got worse. When I had finished editing the interview, having transferred it to a broadcasting 'bobby' or open spool, I topped and tailed it properly with leader tape, and even wrote a pukka cue sheet, with cue material, tape cue in, tape cue out and back-anno.

Now it looked authentic. Why I put it in the in tray on Sandi's desk I will never know. I said nothing to her about it and went home to have a bite before club time.

Once back home I was halfway through a light supper. BFBS Radio was on in the dining room, courtesy of our lovely little Phillips Philetta. I was listening to the magazine programme, 'Time Out', when I suddenly realised it was time for one of the usual Berlin spots and I remember wondering what Sandi had sent down the line to Cologne as her first piece. I heard the Cologne presenter back-anno a record and then launch into the Berlin item cue.

'Thousands of Berlin men, husbands and boyfriends have reached breaking point. They are being nagged to death by their wives and girlfriends. But now they've had enough and have started the great fight back. And they're using beer as their weapon of choice. Our reporter, Peter McDonagh, caught up with Herr Klaus-Dietrich Olk, President of the German Beer-Drinking Federation, and asked him how he had come up with the idea...'

'Ah, Peter, yes, zis is a good qvestion. For too many years...etc...etc...' They didn't even pull the plug. Over four minutes of utterly unforgiving bollocks was transmitted, not just to hundreds of thousands of entitled Forces listeners, but also to a few million English-speaking Germans.

Including some German members of parliament, senior British officers and the British Embassy.

I gather all was not well at the BFBS Cologne as brickbats, telexes, outraged phone calls and general expressions of utter malevolence began to arrive. (I found out later that quite a few thought it was hilarious but even they had to go through the motions of disapproval.)

The giant turd landed at the feet of the very spiky John Russell, BFBS Germany's Senior Programme Organiser. He conducted the inevitable enquiry at breakneck speed and was able to pin the blame and the offence entirely on me.

Sadly, as he wasn't paying me, he couldn't sack me. I laid low and waited till Dick came back.

Dick was really quite laid back about it. 'See you managed to upset Cologne while I was ill,' he observed. I was still wincing like a cornered puppy dog. 'Don't worry," he said. 'You can still do local stuff. Just make sure *nothing* goes down the line again.'

Phew. I'd kind of got away with it. It was only years later that I saw the letter John Russell had written to Dick straight after the incident: 'Under *no* circumstances is McDonagh ever to broadcast on the BFBS airwaves again!' was the burden of his drift.

The gods, however, continued to play with us. A few months later John Russell was posted to Cyprus and Dick quietly made sure some of my proper pieces got a network airing. The last chance saloon had called extra time yet again.

*****

As the weeks of that long hot summer of 1969 drifted past, I did more and more interviews, leaving Dick to do his favourites, which seemed to involve him spending long relaxed lunches in the Berlin Hilton, and interviewing the jazz greats – including George Shearing, Oscar Peterson, Dave Brubeck, Count Basie and many other denizens of that crazy world. He rarely interviewed anyone in the military and didn't have too much time for people in uniform. That became my department and soon I was reasonably at ease with the portable Uher tape recorder. There were always two ready to roll at the station. All you needed was a handful of batteries and, from then on, a 50-50 chance you'd get a successful interview. Our Uhers were always breaking down and when they did there was little chance of recovering the content.

One day Dick let me play with the Nagra, the Swiss-engineered portable tape recorder recognised as the Rolls-Royce of the trade. If Dick was doing interviews on his portable, this was the one he would take. It was sleek, made of precision-brushed and shiny aluminium and weighed a ton. Once you had this on your shoulder, you began very soon to feel like Quasimodo.

As usual, I was dead keen to do the basics – make it record, look at the levels, play back the tape – and I wasn't quite listening to a lot of the other technical information Dick was passing on.

The idea was to go down to the Brandenburg Gate and do an atmospheric commentary on a 'Changing of the Guard' ceremony to be performed by Her Majesty's Life Guards, complete with horses, bugles, drums and full ceremonial uniform. I found a good spot in the Press area and decided to look the complete part and wear the headphones.

Problem. Two headphone sockets - and the 'show' was about to begin. A German reporter from Sender Freies Berlin spotted my predicament and very 'kindly' plugged me in so I could hear the balance of my voice against the equestrian backdrop.

Big problem. The SFB radio journalist had hastened away after plugging me in - and I soon found out why. He'd plugged my cans into the playback socket on the Nagra. In other words, there was about a half-second delay from the point I was saying anything to the point when the recorded tape reached the playback head. If you ever try it, you'll know it's the kiss of death. You hear what you said just after you've said it, but you're saying something new at the same time.

What happens in real life is that your voice slows down and juuuussst ggrrriiinnndds toooo aaa haaaaaallllllllllllttttttt.

What finally happens, when you've stopped swearing, is that you then record as much 'wildtrack' (background location sound) as possible, spend hours editing it in with a new voice-over and curse yourself for not having had the patience to listen to The Master.

Berlin at this stage was dying to be taken seriously as a centre of youth culture; the hippie movement and progressive rock had been sniffed at but there had, as yet, never been a major Rockfest West Berlin. The City decided it was high time, so they announced what was perhaps *the* line up of all time, to play Hitler's old stamping ground, the legendary Sportpalast, a vast theatre in whose arena Hanna Reitsch, the Nazi aviatrix, had actually piloted her autogyro.

As we were in the publicity loop, I watched the press releases with interest. First, Fleetwood Mac. Then the Nice, as bill toppers. Spencer Davis – and Deep Purple. My knowledge of 'Prog Rock' was pretty thin, but I knew this was going to be some spectacle.

Dick was more than happy for me to cover the all-day event (the city was a bit nervous about letting the long-hairs out to play after dark, so this would be a daytime concert) and so, a few days later, I set off on public transport for the greatest day of my broadcasting life.

I was well prepared. A brand new Uher, loads of batteries and tapes and a huge briefcase, which contained a giant thermos of coffee, a bottle of Cinzano nicked from our drinks cabinet at home and a beautiful sign, lettered lovingly by me in hippie style letters, man…

> 'BFBS BERLIN – RADIO FOR THE BRITISH FORCES
>
> COME IN AND BE INTERVIEWED
>
> FREE COFFEE AND/OR CINZANO'

As this was West Berlin's very first rock concert, nobody had any idea of protocol and their idea of security was an iron ring of police cars, bikes, water cannon, riot vehicles, plain-clothed policemen and hundreds of ordinary plods. Using my ordinary British military dependant's identity card, I swanned in with no problem through the front door, straight into a major drama. It was 11am – about two hours to kick-off.

Standing in front of me (I didn't recognise him) was Keith Emerson, keyboard player with 'The Nice' and later of Emerson, Lake and Palmer. He was arguing with a German uniformed jobsworth, who wasn't taking any crap from this long-haired freak. Their argument was made all the more noisy and pointless because Keith didn't speak German and the jobsworth couldn't speak English.

I was going to enjoy this. Guess who could speak English *and* not only German, but Berlin dialect?

I walked up to Keith and said. 'Wonder if I could help? I speak German.'

Keith gave me the old one-two. 'Nothing ventured…' I could hear him thinking.

'Yeah, would you mate? I just told this bloke we needed a concert grand for our act but he keeps pointing at that upright over there, which I guess is going to go on stage. I can't play on one of them.' His eyes flashed and I was just a bit spooked by the intensity of a muso not getting his way. 'Can you tell him if he doesn't get a concert grand - a Steinway or a Bechstein - up on stage within the hour, we ain't playing?'

Gosh. This was serious. And Keith was the star turn. And this was an official Berlin city function. There could be an international incident and, when that happened in Berlin, it tended to have repercussions. Like when they put up a wall in August 1961…

I focused hard on the jobsworth, my credibility, my use of the German language and some good old-fashioned flattery.

My spiel more or less praised him for the difficulties of the task I knew he had to carry out, especially when it was for something as strange as this. But the honour of the city of West Berlin was at stake and he had it within his gift to pour oil on troubled waters. Did he have such a thing as a concert grand on the premises. Yes, he did, but surely, that long-haired…

We spoke animatedly but with increasing communication and amity, watched by Keith Emerson, who, although he didn't quite yet know it, was about to be rewarded by getting a concert grand piano on stage within a very few minutes. I spoke my ace, pumped the jobsworth by the hand and we gave each other a proper bear hug.

As he disappeared to arrange for the Steinway to be on stage, Keith asked me how I'd clinched it.

I told him the broad outline but saved the best to last.

'And while he was thinking that he might just be able to help out, I told him that your Dad had been a raisin bomber?'

'A raisin bomber?'

(This was a nickname given to Allied pilots who had landed vital food and coal supplies straight into the heart of West Berlin during the great airlift of 1948-1949. Some of the pilots, mainly the Americans, used to drop little packets of chocolate and raisins to crowds of children gathered below just before they landed. These pilots were seen as the nearest thing to angels and were fêted wherever they went.

OK, so it was a white lie. But Keith was doing the same thing: bringing joy to a whole young generation of Berlin's youth. 'You don't half bullshit!' said Keith. 'Anything we can do for you?'

'I'm going to ask Jobsworth for a spare dressing room backstage. If you get a mo, can you come in and do an interview for BFBS?'

'Sure, I'll do it. I don't usually do interviews, but you've done us proud. Shall I have a word with the other bands?'

'That'd be great.' I pulled my sign out and waved it under Keith's nose. He laughed, I laughed. Then he went off to find his posh joanna and I sought out Jobsworth to fix a very fine dressing room in exchange for a few slugs of Cinzano.

I put my notice on the door and waited.

Keith was first to arrive, very relaxed, and did a chat for the radio. Mick Fleetwood – the Mac had the dressing room directly opposite mine - came in and did likewise. Then the concert started

– no chance of doing interviews, because the building was rocking like it had never rocked before – and then at one of the intervals Ian Gillan from Deep Purple poked his head round the door, as did Spencer

Davis. I'd only gone and got some of the biggest names in rock and pop for the price of two tram fares, a stolen bottle of Cinzano and a thermos of coffee.

I went home with my prizes and then went to see Dick at the station. I enthused wildly about the Sportpalast, the performers and the gig.

Now, had I said 'Oscar Peterson' it might just have registered on the Dick Nortonometer. As it was, I could see by his body language that he could scarcely contain his indifference. 'That's nice,' he muttered, then went back to his paper. 'See you down the club, later?'

He did. By which time I was away with the fairies and telling all of my student mates about the great rock stars I'd been mixing with all day. I still don't think they believed me...

*****

And so the end of summer crept up on us. I had jumped in at the deep end, interviewed the famous, the rich and the strange. I'd even done an interview with a bunch of semi-naked hippies in a warehouse squat in the infamous district of Wedding, where they'd taken great exception to me offering them vodka. To them it was on the scale of offering pork scratchings to Jews. Considering they were supposed to be hippies, they weren't really into peace and love, man, and I escaped with little dignity and without the bottle of vodka (which I'm sure they necked once I'd escaped down the metal staircase).

In the meantime, reality was kicking in and I realised that for the next few months I'd need to knuckle down to my studies to get the degree I no longer really needed because I now knew what I wanted to do. It was a dangerous attitude but I was so in love with the idea of broadcasting that I knew I could make it all come true if I really, really believed.

There were two major obstacles. The first was my age. Dick, at about forty years old, was not too far away from the median age of a BFBS presenter. That's why he knew nothing about pop or rock music and that's why there was so little of it on BFBS Cologne. The presenters were not given to use their names: they were 'announcers' and they 'announced' programmes with amazing titles such as 'For You at Home', 'Ask For Another', 'Roundabout' and 'Kinder Club', with about as much enthusiasm as a shut pub.

Programmes were grindingly boring for the mainstream audience. This was because the network was run by old former soldiers with limited vision and a huge enduring love of tradition, Vera Lynn and 'keeping up morale' merely by being artificially cheerful. The second problem was frustrated impatience. I wanted to start *now*. There was so much to be done. And I had to go back to Oxford, do my finals, swot and try and earn a few pennies - and only then could I apply, when they'd turn me down because of my age.

Oh, come on. I was nineteen, spotty, drinking like a fish, with a partially interested girlfriend, a crowd of distracting boozing buddies and the self-regard of a slug. In short, a teenager.

Chapter Five:

The Calm Before The Storm

'Back in the jug, agane,' as Molesworth might have said. On the balance sheet, two years of Oxford behind me. I'd passed the internal mid-course moderation exams in the fourth term and so I had a ticket to ride to the bitter end. I knew I was no academic, although I honestly enjoyed the reading part. But I also enjoyed punting, Bernkasteler Riesling 1964, going to the cinema and long evenings in the junior common room and the nearby pubs.

There is a truth well recognised by those who drink and smoke that unless you want to be shunned by your fellows, you need cash in your pocket to make it all work. So it was necessary to get a job during term time. Not really approved of, but needs must. I gravitated to the Royal Oak in Woodstock Road and, after a bit of selling myself (the landlord said later I sounded like a prat but he'd employed me out of curiosity), I became a pot boy, sentenced to permanent washing up, cleaning tables, and changing barrels

The Royal Oak's cellar was very well kept, at 52 degrees Fahrenheit, and sold a variety of good beers which the landlord ensured were served in clear pipes, clean glasses and with proper eye contact. It was he who taught me about a barman's 'radar', which has been a valuable weapon in the game of life ever since. 'Radar' is a barman scanning the length and depth of a crowded bar, reassuring even the most distant customer that he's been spotted, and that he will be served as soon as possible: it is the art of recognising the order in which customers get served by when they arrived, not by their size, charisma or amount of noise they make; and it is above all the ability to listen to, and to provide, the correct order and give the right change. On a quiet night, of course, it also meant listening sympathetically to a whole heap of slightly sloshed hard-luck stories and being the customer's occasional 'besht frien'' who can, in just one breath, become the person invited 'outshide' for a thrashing…

The potential for disaster is always there. There are egos, postures, imagined slights, chips on shoulders, the anger built up after a long drive or a crap day at work and, of course, during the course of the session, possible drunkenness. The only remedies are good eye contact, a clear voice, confidence and a very good sense of humour. Len the landlord gave me all of that and so good was his tutoring that it was only a few weeks before I became a regular barman.

There I learnt to respect some of the old boys who shuffled in. One, in particular, who had his own bar stool, was a WW1 Royal Flying Corps pilot who had seen action over the trenches in France and had been shot down twice. Len the landlord himself had a rare tale to tell: up in his attic was a giant bullet-perforated Swastika flag he had personally taken in the assault on Düsseldorf Rathaus, where a rather dedicated bunch of diehard Nazis was holding out.

The pub work told me a lot about human nature – its strong and weak points; its occasional unpredictability; its capacity to like and dislike, love and loathe, with or without justification; how drink brings out the best or worst in people and how some of the best tales ever told are constructed. Apart from the boozy buzz, there was a whole new world of education to be found in just one pub – infinite riches in a little room.

One snapshot just after I started. I'd bottled up, cleaned the pipes, set the barrels, checked the shelves, got my float sorted, opened the front door which led on directly to my tiny serving hatch – before branching off on both sides to go to the bar. Suddenly, blocking the sun, two roughly dressed giants walked slowly in and parked themselves foursquare in front of me. We were separated by two feet of bar-top. With a sweep of his shovel-sized hand the spokesman removed his cap with a slow but deliberate gesture and, with the most frightening of ruddy faces ever to have toiled in the blazing sun, leant in towards me, towering over my insignificant body like a vulture examining his prey.

He spoke, with a voice that seemed to come from the grave. It was a low, musical but harsh basso profundo - sulphuric acid coursing over gravel.

'Is it alright, Sorr, for us to be comin' in here, what with the workin' clothes an' boots?' he asked as politely as a Sunday school student.

I grinned broadly. The answer to this one was *so* easy. 'Of course it is,' I smiled confidently. 'You'll be having the Guinness?'

My radar was working brilliantly. Paddy looked at me as though he was looking at the man who had found the holy grail. 'That's roight,' he said in a voice full of wonder. 'And you'll be after havin' one yerself?'

I would. I did. And it was one of the best drinks I'd ever had.

I worked at the Royal Oak for the first two terms but had to hand my notice in as I was shooting off to Berlin for my last vacation before finals. Before that, there was a shed load of work to do.

Traditionally, I had cut my workload down, so that my academic pursuits didn't get in the way of drinking time. To start with, the assumption was that an honours degree in English language and literature required not only the reading and understanding of thousands of books from Anglo-Saxon times to the present day, but also a host of dusty tomes and learned monographs by assorted critics about all of these great works.

Well, that wouldn't do. I started by cutting out lectures, which appeared to be demonstrations of braggadocio by mumbling scholars who needed some cash. I did, in the end, go to five whole lectures in three years – but only because they were given by Lord David Cecil, who was known to be a star (he was one of the few people who could actually bring Jane Austen as an author to life) and because he would always stop for a chat with his old mucker from the Bird and Bastard, one J.R.R. Tolkien. Seeing those two together was the *real* Oxford!Next, I needed to do something about the reading list. Eventually I got it down to fifty books. A sprinkling of the greats throughout the ages with an extra helping of Shakespeare, who warranted eight plays: one I'd done at 'O' level ('Romeo and Juliet'); one at 'A' level ('Macbeth'); one for moderations ('King Lear'); one I'd performed in on stage ('Richard III'); and three I'd seen at the cinema or on the telly ('The Tempest', 'Othello' and 'The Taming of the Shrew'). The last of the eight I'd seen in German at the now defunct Schiller-Theater in Berlin ('Twelfth Night'). I particularly remember the Teutonic Malvolio, as evil and as wraith-like as Josef Goebbels himself…

So, all I had to do was revise fifty works and I'd be hot to trot. Oh yes - and there was the business of tutorials. I had one a week with Martin Blocksidge riding shotgun, in the presence of John Carey (all kneel), and allegedly one a week, along with the whole St. John's English Lit group – six of us - with Ian Jacobs. I stopped going to those fairly early on. He didn't even notice.

The snag was writing the weekly essay. After doing nothing except have fun from Friday to Wednesday, Thursday always dawned in a dark and forbidding manner. This week, we *would* start early and finish before bedtime. Books and papers had to be assembled, writing paper, pens and other implements of construction found, food and drink to corralled and then, once my writing partner, JK (Wheeler), had joined me, we would plod through the day and nearly always the night.

The whole thing was an exercise in procrastination. If done properly, it was an eight-hour slog to get the words out of the head, via the books, and on to the paper. We were both pretty good at this. But our timetable wasn't. A typical Thursday would read like this:

1100 – Assemble. Organise papers in study. Chat about social life.

1200 - Junior Common Room open. Subsidised bitter, very cheap. Maybe a bread roll.

1400 – Leave JCR with a couple of prisoners. Good film at the Scala. Troop down to cinema. 1600 – Film ends. High-tail it to 'Lamb and Flag' in St Giles. (Plan B: 'Bird and Bastard' - officially the 'Eagle and Child'- on the other side of the road.)

1800 – Back to JCR to grab a sandwich and maybe have a beer or two.

2000 – Back to the study. Make tinfoil bombs with match heads to explode over lit candles.

2100 – Frowns of concentration. Open books. Look blankly at essay titles. (We can't be of much use to each other: JK is reading History and I'm trying to read English.)

2120 - Sod it. Back to the 'Lamb and Flag' for a nightcap.

2240 - We finally begin. For more than eight solid hours we slowly write ourselves sober. Bits of paper fly into the bin until some degree of fluency is established. There is an occasional grunt. A few minutes with a ciggie in the quad. Some mild swearing. More writing.

0700- The deed is done. Thirteen handwritten quarto pages of close-written literary criticism shine forth. It's now time to hit the refectory and have a well-earned breakfast.

1000 – I meet up with Martin, who has been a good boy and done his homework properly.

1030 – We knock on John Carey's door and the tutorial begins. I very kindly let Martin go first. I still have a full English to digest. Martin reads out his essay. John Carey comments.

1100 – Now it's my turn. I have an advantage. Martin is bright, but has a flat northern monotone. I am a thesp. My words, although not so bright, fly off the page as I imbue them with life, vigour and the occasional arched eyebrow. It is enough to keep John amused, if not impressed. We've both sussed each other out and there is an innate contract between us. As long as I turn up and sound vaguely entertaining, he won't tell me I'm as thick as a St. Hilda's ankle. We end on promises and vows to do better and I stagger off in the direction of my pit. It is time to sleep the sleep of the wicked and I leave instructions for my scout to wake me at teatime. Scout? Oh, I'd better explain. Jim, my scout, came with the rooms. He was bed maker, mentor, confidant, pimp and protector. All this for a nice round tip of about £5 at the end of each term. Services provided by Jim included bringing me a bottle of Bernkasteler Riesling 1964 at 10am precisely each morning, ensuring there was always a crate of Bulmers's Cider in my wardrobe for visitors, organising my laundry, buying the odd item when I was taken busy or drunk, putting me back on the bed if I was cluttering up the room, cleaning the rooms and - the most impressive service of all – he would provide a champagne breakfast for two, served on a silver salver with a rose in a bud vase, wearing his number one white jacket with the polished buttons, on a Sunday morning, for the sum of thirty shillings, cash only. His discretion was second to none and his loyalty absolute. He was the dream topping to my halcyon days...

As far as the distaff side was concerned, I look back with much amusement on how terrible I was at this lurve business. I finally got the hang of it, but with such a level of immaturity that I always wanted to get back to the lads for some more carousing once the dark deed had been done. Anyway, you can take the rest as read. There's a bit of me that has much admiration for a WW1 Major of no great distinction, who made this curt note in his memoir:

'Tried this sex business last night with a young French lady in a local estaminet frequented by brother officers. Very messy. Never bothered again.' I wasn't quite at that stage, but occasionally I did see his point.

*****

My love of music was a constant through these golden days. I was always filling up the jukebox in the Gardener's Arms in North Parade, where mine host Cyril, a contender for the rudest landlord in Oxford, kept court. And kept people he didn't like out on the pavement.

We all loved our tunes in that pub. Many a lunchtime was spent to the sound of 'All Right Now' and the like. If you put the wrong tune on Cyril pulled the plug out, so you needed to have 'the ear'.

The Gardener's Arms was actually run by a management committee, only one of whom I had been introduced to. In Oxford terms, he was the University Professor of Arabic and St. Johns' principal tutor for admissions, which meant he glowed in the dark. He cut an imposing figure and when I knew him he must have been in his late fifties. He had shoulder-length white hair that he wore like a lion's mane and he favoured a very streetwise black leather rocker's jacket, with studs, which made him look, with his robust glasses, like a nightclub bouncer. Freddie Beeston was his name. He loved his pint, his shorts and the craic. His laughter, with head thrown back, was enough to improve morale in hell.

His number one sidekick was a senior consultant at the Radcliffe Infirmary just down the road. All I remember was that his name was John and he was paper thin, absolutely perfectly dressed in a three-piece morning suit, with striped trousers, bowler hat, and a vicious umbrella with a duck-headed handle. Totally aristocratic in speech and demeanour (as was Freddie), they made an unlikely couple. Until you saw the third member of the gang. Because it *was* a gang.

Tony, or 'Tone' if you wanted to lower it, would have been a spiv during the war, a Soho pimp in the fifties, or a biker boy in the sixties. But he'd gone a bit legit, apart from the duckin' an' divin', and now had a fat wallet and a Lotus sports car parked outside. Tone, John and Freddie were the 'A' listers but occasionally we were allowed to play too.

One lunchtime, two oafs came in and started being rude to Consultant John, aping his accent and pushing him at the bar. From behind the bar, Cyril told them to stop. They carried on, nudging John's elbow every time he tried to lift his glass. One of them went over to the jukebox in the corner. The scene was set for something quite horrid. When it came, it came out of nowhere. The duck-headed umbrella hit oaf number one on the head at the same time rocker Tone stuck his steel-capped winkle-picker Cuban boot toe right in matey boy's nuts and, with a howl, oaf number one hit the deck in some agony, which was prolonged by Consultant John jabbing tender bits of him with the point of the umbrella.

Meanwhile, Freddie had not been backward in coming forward. He simply picked up oaf number two, inverted him and smacked his head very hard against the glass cover of the jukebox. Luckily, Mr Wurlitzer had anticipated such occasional events, and so had fashioned the lid out of bullet-proof unbreakable glass.

Which meant bad news for oaf number two. *His* head was made out of very breakable meat, and soon he was looking at the world through a curtain of blood. The three unlikely musketeers then shooed off the damaged oafs and repaired to the bar for a quiet drink.

It was generally agreed that none of us had seen anything. But in those days, before victimhood became a means of income, oafs actually understood that it was tough out there and indeed a dog-eat-dog world.

It was about this time that I realised that some serious remedial work needed to be done if I was even to squeeze past the finishing post. I tried the college library, once populated by such exotic figures as Philip Larkin and Kingsley Amis, had a bash at the legendary Bodleian, but felt the aura of death in there and never bothered again. Finally, I took my books down to the Turf Tavern and felt very much at home.

The Turf was a legendary pub with a legendary Landlord. Wally Else was a proper tenant, not a manager, and he ruled the entire operation with a fist of vodka. He really enjoyed his pop and measured his life in successfully terminated bottles. Wally switched moods quite often, was a gruff northerner and called a spade a fucking spade. He hated his customers to a man and when occasionally he came downstairs he would start a huge argument with any professor, policeman, student or businessman who even looked at him the wrong way. Luckily, he was so unfit, and usually so pissed, that he would either fall over at the hitting stage, shamble off, or suddenly break into a grin, stick his arm round the bloke he was going to batter and buy him drinks all evening.

For all that, Wally had two reality checks every Sunday morning. The first was to enter the nest of pub toilets, male and female, and clean them till they sparkled. And his bare hands went everywhere. Pipes, bends, nooks, crannies, cleaning every nasty thing he could find.

As soon as he'd done that it was straight across the passageway to the huge mixing bowl, where he would mix the ingredients for a massive Yorkshire pudding. Yes, with those same bare hands. He lost his diamond wedding ring in the huge bowl of batter one week and started a cabaret of rage still talked about by Turf veterans.

Opening time was usually good for a laugh on Sundays. Wally always liked a joke, and on one Sunday he put a recently slaughtered pig's head on the bar top, facing the front door, and waited for the customers' reactions. (On Sunday at midday, the clientele was mainly professors, tourists and a slowly-emerging bunch of students heavily damaged from Saturday night party time.)

Such is the English way of dealing with things that the punters steadfastly refused to take offence at, comment on, or even acknowledge that there was a dead pig's head on the bar top. Wally was livid. He thought he'd get a right buzz from the probable outrage and disgust. When this failed to materialise, he did no more than to waddle round to the front of the bar and shepherd all the customers out of the front door, into the tiny courtyard, while yelling at them to 'fuck off!'. Which they did, until the next time, because Wally was part of the Turf experience.

What made the Turf heaven on earth for me was that Wally was a brilliant keeper of the peoples' ales. His pipes were as spotless as his hands were filthy, his beers were brilliant and even Old Hooky (Hook Norton) lost its muddy gloom and perked up with Wally's careful treatment. Also, the Turf itself was a secret enclave, just past Hertford College's Bridge of Sighs, then a sharp left turn down a tiny alleyway less than a yard wide, which looked like it came to a dead end after fifteen feet, but then a sharp right turn down another narrow alley, until you came to the little courtyard in the shadow of the high New College walls and the low-slung façade of this 15th Century alehouse. Inside was a maze of little bars, nooks and crannies where secrets and trysts were exchanged and took place and many a wet afternoon was spent just crouched on a bar stool in front of a blazing fire. This was paradise. One day I found myself talking to Wally, who was pleasantly in neutral. I think he was a bit impressed that I offered to buy him a large vodka (my very last grant cheque had come through, and it tended not to last long). Well. It was a quiet lunchtime and with a few drinks inside neither of us really wanted to call it a day. The result was that we tottered up to Wally's quarters above the shop after last orders and had a couple more. I didn't know about his darker side at the time, so all was well in the best of all possible worlds.

I clearly had enough of my Dad's northern blood and habits inside me to be able to speak and understand Wally as a human and as a language and we got on like a house on fire. I must have stayed well into the afternoon. I can remember, head throbbing, making my way down the stairs, with Wally grinning and waving at me. As I turned the corner, I heard his final words, 'Ah'll see you t'morrow evenin' then, Pete. About five'll be fine.' I shouted my agreement and staggered off back to my digs in Park Town.

It was only halfway up the road that I played back our conversation on my imaginary tape recorder. Had I really told him about my time at the Royal Oak as a barman? Had he really suggested I might like to do a few shifts at the Turf because he'd sacked a barman only earlier that day? Had I really agreed to work at the hallowed Turf Tavern?

It seems I had, starting the next day. 'Ah well', I thought, and mentally quoted my favourite author of the time, Kurt Vonnegut: 'Peculiar travel suggestions are dancing lessons from God.' Back at the ranch, I told JK and his girlfriend Boo Boo the good news. They looked very worried, as they usually did when the subject of me and anything to do with alcohol came up.

At 5'o'clock the next evening, I went down to the Turf, as directed. The place was locked tight shut. After a few minutes knocking, an incandescent Wally stuck his head out of an upstairs window and told me to fuck off. I explained why I wasn't going to and eventually he staggered down and let me in, muttering darkly in a northern kind of way. He'd had the mother of all rows with the missus (a rather brassy lady who nagged him and hid his vodka bottles), with the result that she had flounced out back to her parents in Brighton, leaving Wally without his adjutant. Somehow, we had to get the place shipshape for a 6pm opening. We were joined by Bob, another barman, and the three of us cleared away the lunchtime session, did the washing up, bottled up, and put a bit of polish on the tables in the posh bar. And then all hell broke loose. The Turf was very popular and the next few hours flew by in a flurry of bottles, glasses, cash, chat, jokes, atmosphere and that all-embracing warm feeling of folks having fun. The jokes were racy, the girls were flirty, the lads were chancy, the beer and wine flowed and the buzz was the best I'd seen in a long time. Please God, could this be my new spiritual home until the end of term and the last of my Finals?

It could - and it was. I even broke the ultimate rule at the end. Finals week finally came, bringing with it many learned papers on English Literature through the ages. Nemesis. I was as prepared as a person who'd read ten percent of the syllabus could be. Each day I would droop into Halls, my impotent little sub-fusc uniform of flappy short-arsed Commoners' gown, white bow tie and mortar board (officially a "square") making me look even more of a twat than I felt.

I should at this point tell you the magic secret of Oxford. Their exams are anything you want them to be. Let me explain. At various levels the questions become more general, thus:

a) GCE 'O' Level – 'Explain (using diagrams and hand signals) why Romeo is breaking with tradition in pursuing Juliet and why tensions between the two families are bound to have a tragic outcome.'

b) GCE "A" Level – 'Discuss the concept of guilt and its consequences in "Macbeth.'

c) Oxford Entrance – 'Shakespeare's comedies are rarely funny. Why?'

d) Oxford Finals – 'Shakespeare – overrated?'

The good news was the breadth of the question. At the more advanced level, you weren't tied down to pettifogging quasi-forensic trawling of the text to make the same points as everybody else in the examination room.

The bad news was – also - the breadth of the question. At the more advanced level you'd better be bringing something more to the party than the usual half-thought out sentence followed by a beefy quote to show you'd read the damn play.

I tried to play a straight bat, using scholarly language, common sense and some bullshit to give what I thought in the end were reasonable but low-grade answers. The only bit of high-risk strategy I deployed was quoting myself, using fictitious names. 'As Fischer-Brunnen says: "the avoidance of lust in the romantic scenes is almost a dereliction of renaissance duty"'. I figured that even if the marker realised I was making this up, it would at least be a bit different from 'Thus, as F R Leavis is at pains to remind us...' time and time and boring time again.

And so it was, on the most glorious of sunny Oxford summer afternoons, a June day of memorable brilliance, that the last bit of inked nib touched the last piece of examination paper. As we shuffled out of Schools into the real world, I felt in my jacket pocket, pulled out a miniature bottle of pre-mixed vodka and lime and started out on what would be a three-day bender. I was determined to have the first drink after exams.As expected, there was a small crowd of well-wishers. Some had already finished their finals, some still had that joy to come, but duty and pleasure required a convoy out to the 'Perch', to sit on the banks of the River Thames and to drink away the pains and struggles of the last three years. The champagne was icy and well up to tickling the nostrils, the girls were beautiful and played us like banjos and soon we were a nest of cheery, relieved, but slightly tired ex-students.

The next three days passed in a blur. The timescale was informally arranged so that by the time we sobered up we could see on the notice board how we had fared and what kind of degree (if any) each of us had been awarded. Meanwhile, I was utterly flouting the rules by doing my evening shifts at the Turf still wearing sub-fusc, which was a hanging offence if any of the university police – the Bulldogs – had been around. But my luck was in and I swayed and smiled through it all.

Finally, the big day arrived. The rumour was eleven o'clock, on the railings by the Sheldonian Theatre. One by one, my fellow students and I edged towards the pieces of A4 paper with their two neat rows of names and numbers. For some, this was vital. If you wanted to be a brain surgeon, top barrister or go back into academe you needed a First; if you wanted to do pretty well in the professions, a 2:1 was de rigueur, although you might get away with what became known as a 'Desmond' (in those days still just a '2:2'). Then there was the legendary Third. You had to be a sportsman, a boozer, or a just a bit thick to get a Third. It was known, euphemistically, as a 'Gentleman's Third'. There was also a non-Honours 'Pass' degree but that was reserved for students who couldn't quite spell their own names properly.

I found the English faculty's finals results and scanned the whole three sheets to see if my name appeared at all. As expected, I was not to be found in the heady heights of those who had been placed in the first class. Nor indeed the second – upper or lower. No – it was a 'Gentleman's' for

me. As much as I could have hoped for and, given my efforts, more than I deserved. I had the grace to realise that, even at the time.

I'd only gone and got me an Oxford degree. Insignificant me, the Cold War warrior who, until recently, had been raising morale in the divided city of Berlin, bringing news, entertainment and information to the English-speaking peoples. My cup was indeed runnething over. But not just at the moment. Time for a celebration drink. Me – a degree? I very nearly skipped to the Turf and another boozy shift.

*****

There is a footnote to my academic career, one of which I remain deeply ashamed to this very day. After JK finished his History finals, a few days later, we found ourselves back home, on the terrace at Parktown. A beautiful summer's evening again and, in a champagne-fuelled fuddle, we decided as ex-students, finished with studying, we'd make a little bonfire outside the Georgian terrace and set fire to our books.

Within a couple of minutes the deed was done and we had a bonfire going outside the houses. Suddenly the voice of an old man, heavily accented and in some apparent pain, could be heard behind us as we grinned at the fire.

'Boys! Boys! Vat do you sink you are doing?' said the voice, quietening down as he approached us, but filled with a horror we were already beginning to understand.

'You must never, never, burn books!' he said. 'This is what happens when people burn books!'

He clutched at his shirt with bony fingers and yanked up the sleeve. On the inside of his arm there was a crudely numbered fading tattoo. From Auschwitz. He was an Austrian Jew, a retired

schoolteacher. He had survived two years of inhuman imprisonment at the hands of people who burned books.

We were so, so ashamed. Almost more so when he gently forgave us, once we had promised we would never damage a book again. God knows, we meant it.

And that was end of Oxford. We went our separate ways, leaving Parktown, St. John's and the University until it was time to make the pilgrimage as an alumnus.

There was a sting in the tail with the Turf Tavern. Within days, Wally achieved daily bottle number three, went apeshit, locked up the pub and sacked the lot of us, including his wife, who went back to Brighton for ever. I heard through the grapevine that, after a very long sulk, he opened up again and elicited the services of the visiting professor of drama at St. Edmund Hall, one Richard Burton, as a temporary barman. There was a bit of a culture shock one night when the regulars were a bit surprised to find themselves being served ale by not only the Hollywood megastar, but also his equally famous missus, Elizabeth Taylor. I'm glad to know my replacement was up to scratch!

Chapter Six:

Let's Limbo Some More

Suddenly it was all over. Exams were no longer looming. Oxford had gone away and I was back in Berlin. The bad boy, who got a third. Others at Oxford with me, Chris 'Siggie' Romberg and Neil Mitchell, were warned by their parents: 'Beware the Third of Pete!' Luckily it became a joke, although my Dad was a little bit peeved.

As per usual, I made a beeline for BFBS and started again the usual round of doing interviews, reading out local announcements and practising being a 'yes indeedee' DJ. It took some time to get the chat right. First of all you learnt the mechanics, a bit like driving a car, then you 'forgot' them, as they had become second nature and you could now concentrate on the important bit, the chat between the tunes, and the extra bits and pieces you could bring to the party. By the time I left to go back to UK in the autumn, I was just about able to string a one-hour record programme together.

The crunch came one night in late August. Dad asked if I'd had a good summer.

'Yes, I've done quite a lot with BFBS.'

'That's not really a proper job, though, is it? They don't even pay you.'

I could see this ending in much shouting. I shrugged. The equivalent of 'wha'evvah''.

He came straight out with it. 'Your Mum and I think it'd be a good idea if you went back to England and started looking for a real job.'

I was annoyed, yet a bit relieved at the same time. At least we knew where we stood.

Within a fortnight, I was back in the UK, in Oxford, living in a cupboard with a Canadian hippie.

OK, that needs a bit of explanation. In real time, I went back to Oxford. Kate Williamson, my former landlady in Park Town, was very sorry but both rooms had been taken. Chris Romberg, in my old ground floor room, and a pair of gobby Yank returnees from Vietnam had collared the two rooms in the basement. But – and here was some good news – there was a four-foot by three-foot full-height airing cupboard at the foot of the stairs, right next to a huge electric storage heater. The bad news was that I would have to share it with a Canadian hippie, Dave Cardey, who had no job, no cash and lived off a few coppers made by busking in the city.

The good news for Dave was that we took a shine to each other from the first meeting. I had quite a few pounds on me (Dad was *very* keen to get rid of me) and I hated admin so instead of tooling round Oxford looking for a proper place to stay, I moved my cabin trunk into the airing cupboard, which acted as my bed, borrowed a few sheets, blankets and pillow from Kate and slept on the dizzy one-foot height of the trunk-top, which made it clear to the rest of the world I had nothing 'personal' to do with Dave, who slept on a mat on the floor.

Somehow, we muddled along, dodging into the bathroom when the pukka tenants were on downtime. We even snuck into the basement room and watched TV. But, come bedtime, we were consigned to our airing cupboard, where we slept with the door full open, because the room was too short and because we got the full benefit of the night storage heater.

After a few weeks in the airing cupboard, listening to the Vietnam returnees bragging about their exploits, Dave and I decided it was time to move. I found a huge cellar room in St. John's Street and Dave and I moved in, taking with us Frank and Rolf, two illegal white South African immigrants who had fled their country because they were a wee bit outspoken against apartheid. We also had two or three regular sleepover guests, which made life a bit difficult because the room had only one dilapidated double bed and a Victorian couch with very thin armrests. It was so short that if you tried to sleep across it, your knees and neck were on top of the arms and you would lose circulation very quickly, which was a great shame, as winter was approaching and there was no central heating.

Hippie Dave was alright, as he had a new-fangled 'space blanket' whose metallic surface redirected body heat. Whoever had the bed was OK. The others had to make do with the couch or the floor. I had read somewhere in a book that the human body gives off one kilowatt of heat every night, so, it was logical to fill the room up with half a dozen people – voilà: six kilowatts.

Of course, I should have calculated how much condensation comes with that heat and how it makes the room ultimately damp and smelly. But, 'everybody starts by knowing nothing' and for three pounds and ten shillings a week this was still good news.

We shared a Victorian kitchen upstairs, a cast iron tribute to black-leading, with the other denizens of the house. The front room on the ground floor with the lace curtains belonged to an émigré Austrian Baron student, who had little to do with us plebs. Upstairs, in two adjacent rooms, was the unfortunate pairing of a Nigerian and an Ibo. The countries were at war with each other at the time but in Oxford such protocols are forgotten. We all mucked in together, fuelled by Hippie Dave's daily cuisine of sackfuls of brown rice, remaindered bits of dead veg from places we never asked Dave about and crunchy Granola in the morning.

I was working for Oxfam in Summertown at the time. I'd got a job as a Christmas present packer, which involved being on my own all day in a low-slung warehouse, packing up Patagonian ceramic nose-flutes, Kenyan dolls made out of mud and flax and a variety of what could be honestly described as international tat, all of which were lovingly wrapped and addressed by me and left to the joys of the then GPO, who adored the *'fragile'* labels I stuck on the parcels, as it gave them clues as to which ones to choose as balls when they played Post Office rugby during their many tea breaks. This accounted for the other part of my job, which was replacing the broken goods that came flooding back.Still, it made a lot of people feel good. Including me. I was working for a charity that fed the hungry. I became more than a little disillusioned when I heard one of the Oxfam 'suits' banging on in the pub after a few as to how the point of Oxfam wasn't to feed the poor, but to shame the British Government into increasing foreign aid. I guess it was at that point I felt things weren't quite right, so I left. When the money ran out, I decided I'd give the dole a go.

I walked into what later became known as the Department of Stealth and Total Obscurity and filled in a three-hundred-page form. Now, remember, I'd just got me a degree from one of the greatest universities in the world. But could I understand this verbose and obfuscatory guff on the thick wodge of form in front of me? No. Luckily, I had Hippie Dave with me, who appeared to understand 'A' level Dolespeak, and after what seemed hours but was in fact hours, we pronounced ourselves satisfied that every 'i' had been dotted, and every 't' had been crossed. I walked to one of the down-at-heel pens, which contained a selection of sub-life straight out of Bosch's wildest imaginings.

I attempted eye contact. This proved impossible, as mine travelled inevitably to the trail of suppurating acne on the forehead of the Dickensian junior clerk now facing me, as well as the crests of blood from decapitated spots on the curled up collar of his once white shirt.

He examined me as though I'd offered him a plate with two steaming dog turds placed on it.

'Yes?' came the inevitable suburban whine through the long beaky nose. It wasn't a question. It was a challenge. A gauntlet, thrown down.

'I wonder if you could help me?' I said in grown-up English. 'I'm not working at present and I'm told that your department may be able to help in the short term with a little financial assistance.'

I felt proud of myself. Cool, calm and determined, but with a note of kindness. Surely a winning formula.

Our clerk screwed up his eyes to peer even more closely at me and then hit me with what turned out to be his ace.

'Were you a student here at Oxford?' he purred, almost kindly.

'Yes!' I agreed, falling smartly into his trap. 'I graduated last summer and I've been doing a few jobs, but the last one ended a few days ago.'

'Oh dear,' he lied. 'That's a shame. We don't give money to graduate students,' he smugged, with the satisfied smile of the sociopath who has yet again managed to diminish the totality of joy in a sometimes rotten world.

My need for politeness had disappeared with Spotty Muldoon's dismissal of my case. It was time to be pointlessly pompous, to make a meaningless gesture that might just liven up the proceedings. I stood back, assumed a posture and assembled my best ac-tor's voice. It carried around the sad building and I think for a moment brightened the day of the other benighted welfare seekers who sat in sad, serried rows of hopelessness.

'You don't give money to students?' I launched. 'You think students are all rich? Well they're not. But never mind. I just hope you never find yourself in my position. And before I go let me tell you something. In twenty years I'll be doing an interesting job, travelling the world, meeting interesting people and earning lots of money. *You* will still be stuck here, with your miserable outlook, your bloody rudeness, your cheap suit and your lack of human sympathy. You deserve this prison!'

I turned on my heel and left with Hippie Dave(and a flounce). There was a thin round of ironic applause as I made my exit. Now I *would* have to get a job. In the meantime, I did enough pub shifts to keep body and liver together.

A week or so later, an ad in the paper caught my eye. BBC Radio Humberside was about to open as one of the UK's new chain of local radio stations and they were looking for broadcasters. Well, I'd performed a good number of the skills they were looking for over the last two years, so without delay I filled in an application form and a not at all erroneous CV. Looking back, I should have gone for the more suitable post of station assistant than producer but, hey ho, enthusiasm makes up for a lot.

Not only did I get a reply back within the week, but an interview within the fortnight. And they would pay for travel, and a night's accommodation. Dave was very good at coaching me in job interviews – which was odd, as he'd never had a job in his life – but I spent all my spare time in the library, constructing a folder about Hull and its surroundings, basing my 'great leap forward' on my mentor, Dick Norton's, advice: 'If you want to get more interviews, organise it so press and PR information comes direct to your office and ask people to come to the studios to do interviews, rather than you going to them.'

I wrote a dossier of companies, names and press contacts, typed everything out, headed sections with Letraset and created a PR dossier of some substance. On the day itself, I took the earliest train I could to Hull and spent much of the mid-afternoon and evening familiarising myself with the city, its institutions and, in the evening, its pubs and people. It was fascinating and when I finally got back to the hotel, I wrote up my notes and then slept like a baby.

My interview was at 10 o'clock. John Cordeaux, the manager-designate, would be on the board, along with one or two BBC producers, civic figures and a very kindly white-haired gentleman. I thought the interview was going well. They appeared impressed by my homework, and my fluency in describing where and what I had visited in the run-up to the board. And then it happened. One of the BBC producers, as if trumping an ace, said, 'I see you're only 22 years old.'

I agreed that this was the case - yes, indeed, there it was on page one of my application form. Which they all had a copy of. Which they knew when they asked me for interview. Was this a problem?

'Well,' said the ace-trumper, looking a bit shifty, 'you are *very* young to be a producer.'

As this had come up long after I'd explained what I could bring to the party and I was hearing good things coming back, this sudden shuddering halt because of my age was clearly a problem.

'You need more experience,' said the producer. 'Try again in a couple of years.'

This was dismissal on an epic scale. The Irish blood started pumping. I think the kindly old chairman spotted this, as he leant forward and said, in pacifying tones, 'Is there anything you'd like to say to us?'

There was. I did. And although I believe the BBC to be the best broadcaster in the world, it deserved both barrels for this insolence.

I stood up. I scanned the long table in front of me. 'Yes,' I said, my voice a miracle of self control. Suddenly the end of any possible employment with the BBC appeared in sharp focus.

'Gentlemen, Humberside is the arsehole of the world. And Hull is ten miles up it. Good morning.'

After a pint or three, and a train journey back, I felt I had made the right decision not to work for them. At least Hippie Dave thought it was funny. And it did give me the idea to apply for a job with BFBS. What *had* I been thinking about? I could use Dick Norton and Sandi Jones as referees

and, with any luck, the dangerous John Russell was out of harm's way in Cyprus so I might get a clear run. I wrote to my spiritual home, asking simply if they had any vacancies.

*****

It was about two weeks later when two important letters flopped on to the doormat. One was the expected missive from BBC Radio Humberside, who were very sorry but I had not been successful in my search for employment with them, but they wished me all the best…

There was also a letter from CSM4(d) at the Ministry of Defence. What? It took me a second or two to remember that BFBS was a unit under the umbrella of the civilian management of the Ministry of Defence.

The letter was brief and to the point. They were offering me a voice test, in the bowels of BBC Broadcasting House. This in *no way* implied they would give me a job.

It was progress, though. On the appointed day, I appeared in the chamber of horrors – a dark green and mahogany basement, with that huge iconic biscuit box of a BBC microphone on a green baize table. A kindly producer explained that I would be given a short news bulletin to read (previous sight unseen) and then some continuity material to knock into shape in order to create announcements bridging two or three programme titles.

As was the case in Berlin, the voice and brain appeared to be working, but the rest was sweating and twitching – even more so, this being the proper grown up BBC. Somehow, I managed to steer myself round Gennady Nikolayevich Rozhdestvensky and the Conzertgebouw Orchestra of Amsterdam playing Mozart's 'Entführung Aus Dem Serail', as well as a host of other Pooh traps in a variety of languages. I left the bowels of the BBC, with my own in turmoil.

A week or so later, another letter flooded in from a Mr Brown, who was delighted to inform me that I had passed the voice test. As a result, there was to be, in three weeks' time, a selection board, to which I was invited. Time, details and location (an old ramshackle MOD building called Lacon House) were given, as was a rail warrant and an instruction to bring identity documents.

Again, I read up as much as possible about broadcasting, the BBC, radio, HM Forces, BFBS locations, plus my own notes in what I wanted to do with the service if ever I was in the position.

Thus suitably armed, up I went to my first civil service selection board. I learnt a new trick, by accident. When I was ushered up to the nth floor (the creaking lift took forever) I found myself in a homely anteroom, obviously the secretary's office. Unlike the real world, civil service secretaries are wiser than their masters, who, in turn, tend to be wiser than their ministers. A civil service secretary at that time knew several languages, every line of every MOD manual and exactly where each and every body was buried. When she spoke, her master listened, if he knew what was good for him. She was usually late middle-aged, simply but elegantly dressed and coiffed, with a pleasant half smile which, if crossed, could turn into the evil eye in a nanosecond. In a former incarnation she may well have been processing Wehrmacht codes in Bletchley Park. And here was the trick, which I only found out by accident: *she* would be part of the board, too.

The good lady in question gave me an initial look, to check if I was in good standing. Hair, hands, shoes, suit, shirt, tie... Checklist complete. Good manners? A couple of questions to establish that. And then, an invitation to take a seat and wait.

She was so like my Mum that I felt I could chat – so I did. I explained that this was my life's dream, that I was really very nervous and wasn't sure if I was good enough but I had to have a try for whatever vacancy this board might produce.

The good lady was very reassuring and within a couple of minutes was all but 'there, there'-ing, and finding me a cup of tea. Had I known the protocol, the addition of a custard cream might have given me the hint that I might do well in the forthcoming board, but I wasn't to know that yet.Finally, the call came. I entered a room that seemed to be the size of the average Olympic gymnasium. From ever so far away, a voice rang out. 'McDonagh?'

'Yes, sir?'

'Take a seat. Come on, man, we don't bite!'

I think they'd spotted my trembling legs.

Considering all of these were generalists, not professional broadcasters, looking back I think they were very well briefed and highly articulate. If there were any trick questions, I didn't spot them, and they were good enough to ask me in the main about what I'd done with BFBS, which by that stage was plenty. I had to explain the Berlin rock concert to them but I think they found my explanation as clumsily funny as I did and they had the grace to look interested.

Suddenly it was all over and I was told I could go. I spent a moment thanking them, making sure I caught the eye of each one in turn, and I stepped back into the secretary's office.

'There, it wasn't so bad, was it?' she said, as she handed me my coat. I made a point of shaking her hand and thanking her for having helped so much to steady my nerves.

I was quite surprised by her almost girlish giggle and slightly blushing smile. I joined in with the smile and we parted on excellent terms. I still believe to this day she was called into the presence and asked by the board what she thought of me.

And ever since then, I've always been nice to people apparently lower down in the pecking order. It's part of me anyway but it does seem to help advance your case.

*****

That Christmas warrants a flashback. (Shudder.) Vaseline on the lens and a foreboding chord in the background, flag up the impending tale of doom and misery…Christmas 1969 was to be my first and last Christmas away from home. Christmas Eve hadn't been so bad. A small crowd of us went off to the 'Royal Oak' in Oxford's Woodstock Road, trudging through the snow of what was going to be a magical white Christmas. The drinks flowed, there was peace and love to all men, Len let me do a bit of a stint and cabaret behind the bar and we had a licence till midnight, when we were all turfed out into the newly fallen blanket of pristine snow.

It was already Christmas day. I hiccupped in the sharp frosty air and started padding through the snow to Park Town. As I walked, I checked the inventory. Key, wallet, watch- check. Bottle of fifteen-shilling joke Hirondelle battery acid proper white wine from France – check. Packet of ten Bristol cigarettes with eight left in – check.

It was then I remembered, and my heart sank. Kate, JK and Boo Boo had all disappeared to the bosom of their families. The house would be empty. And unheated. It would be like Ebeneezer Scrooge's lodgings in 'A Christmas Carol'.

I was wrong. It was worse. The huge door creaked unnecessarily as I pushed it open. I turned on the hall light. I don't remember there only being a five-watt bulb. I swear the passage became darker when I switched the light on. I went across the landing to our room. It smelt of damp, old socks and the persistent dead mouse aroma of brown rice.

In honour of the occasion, I had bought a little plastic Woolworth Christmas tree, whose flimsy Chinese arms struggled manfully to hold aloft six cheap silver balls. Around it, only four Christmas cards (most had been sent to Berlin) were there to remind me that the world actually contained other people. The TV had closed down for the night. Not that it mattered: we didn't have one, only a tinny little portable radio. I soon found a station that was playing Christmas carols. I sat on the Victorian couch and pulled the cork on the bottle of Hirondelle. As long as I

remembered not to shake it, the bits of twig and dead rat would stay on the bottom. I poured a tooth-glass of wine, lit one of my eight ciggies and toasted the season.

About two hours later I realised that I had finished the bottle of wine and smoked the last cigarette. Now, the idea was that after a skinful at the Royal Oak, it would only need a top up from the bottle of wine and I'd be dog tired, fall asleep and wake up well into Christmas Day. Instead, I was wide awake. Even worse, I'd drunk myself sober. And I didn't even have any fags. And I was utterly, completely, appallingly alone. There was no other person I knew who was within contact distance. No phone, either.

The next half hour was spent in the ashtray and the carpet, trying to find strands of tobacco to knit a 'dog-end special', which I'd seen the tramps in Berlin do so many times. I managed to make up one, which all but disappeared in one puff of smoke, as most of it was carpet fluff. I even went out and walked for about a mile through the snow to the only cigarette machine I knew of in the area. It had been vandalised.

And that was it then. The worst Christmas of my life. A night in purgatory. I sat in front of my plastic tree and howled like a condemned man. Finally, I slept fitfully. When I woke and emerged, even more snow had fallen. Oxford had never looked more beautiful. The ancient yellowed Cotswold stone of the college buildings was radiant in the thin winter sunlight, the frost-rimed bare trees surrounded them with the finest filigree lacework and already the streets were filling up with humanity wearing its sparkliest Christmas face. Slowly but surely, morale improved. My step quickened and my pockets jangled. Fresh packet of fags, a Mars Bar for late breakfast and a co-ordinated arrival at the Royal Oak for Len's 'landlord's drinks'.

By one o'clock it was smiles all round. Great people, all together, having a festive laugh, while thousands of sacrificial turkeys were busy turning brown. There was a message from JK and Boo Boo: they'd be back later. And I discovered an extra fiver in the unstitched pocket of my coat.
There *was* a God and he lived in the spirit and festival called Christmas. I made a vow that I would never spend Christmas alone ever again. And I haven't.

Christmas the following year was spent in Berlin, comfortably cossetted by my folks, who seemed sympathetic to my plight and a bit impressed (not) with my attempts to hit the glitzy world of broadcasting. It was a lovely round of parties, prezzies and a much needed rest. And another one of those intermittent life-changers.

*****

Back in the real world, Mr. Brown at Lacon House sent me another MOD communique. It informed me that I had passed the CSM4(d) Selection Board – but in *no way* did this mean they were going to offer me a job. What I had in effect received was a two-year 'ticket of opportunity' in case a vacancy did arrive.

Well, hush mah mouf. I nearly had a nearly job. I took on a new job in London, delivering mail using the underground during the postal strike, until one day another MOD letter flipped onto the carpet. Ripping it open, I learnt that I was invited to meet both the outgoing and incoming Directors, BFBS, in their offices on the 5th floor at Kings Buildings in Dean Stanley Street, Westminster. This in *no way* meant they were going to offer me a job. I began to see a pattern and became more hopeful.

Came the great day and I took the train in good time to hit Westminster. I soon found the rather imposing building, just off the same square that housed the TUC's Transport House and the then Conservative party headquarters in Smith Square.

The situation, as it happened, was this. Ian Woolf was just about to take over from the improbably named Brian Cave-Brown-Cave as Director of BFBS and I had the privilege of being

interviewed for my first BFBS gig by both. (It was rumoured that the final part of Brian's doubly-hyphenated surname was added so that he might fulfil the conditions of a relative's will, which stipulated that the extra "Cave" be added in order to inherit Lake Windermere...)

Into a brown study, small and stuffy, I went, for a first grilling by C-B-C. There I was, with the sweat of the underground about me – the job delivering mail was tough going in the bleak midwinter– a young, impoverished ex-student (wages £12 a week – monthly rent in Bayswater £84 a month). C-B-C was a little old fashioned and, I suspect, not quite assured in the ways of the world.

'So, McDonagh, you wish to join the BFBS?'

'Yes, sir,' I confirmed. I felt my cause was doomed in advance, after the spoof interview I had recorded with the so-called President of the German Beer Drinking Federation, which, as you might recall, had accidentally been broadcast all over Germany. However, the story had clearly not percolated to the 5th Floor of Kings Buildings, Westminster. C-B-C eyed me in a rather patrician and benign manner and offered the following question.

'Tell me, McDonagh – do you collect antique silver?' This, with him holding aloft a Queen Anne silver teapot, and me, wearing a shiny suit and a cheap tie.

'Er, no.' I had clearly failed and, after some mutually unsatisfying polite conversation, I was shuffled three doors along to Ian Woolf's much grander office.

I knocked, as only a creature who did not collect antique silver teapots could.

"*YES.*" A voice I was to learn to love and fear summoned me to the presence.

He sat in a high chair, bay windows behind him, with an interrogator's sunlight beaming through directly onto the very low, overstuffed armchair placed strategically in front of the awesome desk. Through the filtered rays of the sun, I remarked a forbidding, steely-grey presence with eyes, hooded like a hawk, drilling into me. A French radio station was playing quietly from a giant elderly radio.

'Take a seat,' he directed, waving at the blowzy armchair. I did, and sank so deep into it that my chin was below the level of his Mussolini-sized desk.

There was a short (to me, 10 minutes; in reality about 5 seconds) silence. Then:

'What do you think about religious broadcasting?'

Gulp. I didn't. But in my 'Big Boys' Book of Interviews' I realised this was not a viable answer.

'Er – well, it's like sports broadcasting. Not everybody likes it, but it's got to be in the schedules.'

'*WRONG ANSWER!*' said Uncle Ian, triumphantly. He spoke in capital letters.

I knew then that I had failed. I can't remember a single word of what followed. But I do remember being summoned by Mr. Brown in the middle of my postal round a few days later.

'Mr. McDonagh,' I was told, 'you have passed the director's interview. Unfortunately (I died), there are not many vacancies in BFBS at the moment but a temporary position has arisen suddenly in Singapore. Would you consider it?'

Would I consider it? Does the Pope shit in the woods? Are bears catholic? A racing flood of emotions, followed by a determined 'Yes, please!' came from this pathetic, tube-stained, strike-breaking temporary postie.

They even gave me an advance of salary - £100. On my last night in the UK, en route to Lee Kwan Yu's paradise in the Far East, I tried, with a good Berlin friend, Chris Romberg (latterly HM Britannic Majesty's Military Attaché to Egypt), to emulate the then very popular Barry

McKenzie cartoon strip in 'Private Eye' - to achieve nirvana by eating a plate of prawns, knocking back some Fosters and then chundering in the old Pacific Sea.

Sadly, geography and antipodean supply considerations got in the way, so we had a killer of a night eating a prawn curry, drinking shed-loads of Swan lager and throwing up in the Serpentine instead.

I was going to be a broadcaster. In Singapore. And they were going to pay me.

Chapter Seven:

Far East, Baby!

My life changed overnight. I had been a happy-go-lucky, permanently drunk graduate doing a series of odd jobs in exchange for beer tokens, but now I was on the first step of the ladder that would end up with me as a household name, like Harpic. Armed only with a huge suitcase (nicknamed 'the leather donkey'), a copy of MOD Manual 13 extracts, a note of introduction to a Mr. Peter Buckle MBE (my boss-to-be), some travel permits and a passport, I made it to RAF Brize Norton to catch the Comet trooper to Singapore via Bahrain and Colombo.

RAF Brize Norton and Gateway House were an advanced exercise in RAF optimism. Not only did the main building look like a proper civilian 20th Century passenger airport, but a series of well-positioned bars, lounges and shops gave the impression of unalloyed luxury. WRAF personnel, clearly chosen for their looks and style, sashayed like air hostesses in the smartest of uniforms, and white-coated stewards looked after the officers in their own bar and mess. Cosy bedrooms were along the corridors, sound-proofed against the noise of military aircraft taking off day and night. Paradise.

I discovered for the first time that I had an 'EMR' – an equivalent military rank. As a raw broadcasting recruit, I was nonetheless an army department civil servant, in the grade of Executive Officer. This in turn gave me an EMR of Army captain, RAF flight lieutenant, or Royal Navy lieutenant. Gosh.

Later I discovered that EMR was to be used for travel and accommodation purposes only. Trying to pass yourself off as somehow equal to a member of the world's finest armed forces could lead to severe penalties, most of which were brutishly savage and efficient. Still, it meant I got to use the officers' bar and restaurant, which in those days still had meals on proper plates, and silver service.

I had a very pleasant evening people-watching and later on, following the noises of the greater number of people sounding happy, wangled myself an invitation to the senior NCOs' bar, where the real characters hang out. It was here that I learnt that we BFPS types – we were always being called BFPS – were in a unique position. Although we carried the EMR officer rank, we were one of the few organisations that had freedom of movement throughout the rank structure, so we could mix with junior, senior and officer ranks without too much let or hindrance.

I came away with a head full of knowledge and a belly full of rum, hoping my alarm clock would work and wake me at about 3am for an 0430 military flight to Bahrain.

Brize Norton is the only airport in the world that finds it necessary to operate a passenger service which only departs during the silent hours. Not only that, Brize Norton is the only airport that can wake the dead. They clearly become used to passengers taking to their beds in a drunken stupor and, had I been focusing when I hit my room, I might have spotted the vandal-proof speaker in the steel cage on the ceiling. On this occasion it decided to wake me with a 'bing- *bong!*', a banshee scream of feedback, followed by a stout yeoman voice advising me that our flight would be leaving in three hours and, once I had shaved, showered and breakfasted, I should report to the terminal office for boarding instructions.

I knew enough about the military that this would be a case of 'hurry up and wait'. It was one o' bloody clock in the sodding morning.

Eventually we were given breakfast, issued with more forms, had our papers checked and boarded the string of coaches for a drive through the February chill to where our big fat Comet was parked, about 100 miles from Gateway House. At least, it seemed that far.

We took off and luckily I fell asleep - a pointless exercise, as the RAF have a long standing tradition of WRAF load mistresses armed with Rosa Klebb scowls and trays full of paper cups full of over-diluted orange squash, waking you up what seems to be every hour to freeze your tonsils and have another peek out of the windows. Bahrain came and went. We formed a queue to disembark, traipsed through a transit lounge, had a chance for a ciggie and a nice jar or two from the NAAFI bar and then a quick leak before hitting the Comet for round two to Colombo.

I was by now well out of my comfort zone and beginning to wake up to the enormity of what I was doing: travelling 8000 miles away from home to do a job, most of which I'd never done before. I gulped, more than once. Then back to snooze, Rosa Klebb, peek and snooze until we landed at Colombo. We were advised that Colombo was a civilian facility and that we should be careful if approached by shifty locals. We landed and, for some reason connected with my need for a stiff drink, I raced across the runway to the terminal building, had my papers processed, climbed a huge spiral staircase and found myself in the biggest bar restaurant I'd ever seen. A huge circular open-air palm treed panoramic white-painted paradise and ...*Oh my God!*

Suddenly I was aware of an invasion of giant maggots coming at me from every side, in their dozens. They turned out to be a phalanx of white-coated swarthy Colombian waiters, obviously on commission or hoping for big tips, eager to serve the great white hunter and his bottomless throat and pockets. I chose one whose eyes seemed to be reasonably far enough apart and ordered up the usual large rum and coke. Twice. The others melted away as the rest of the passengers trooped upstairs.

I have a very happy memory of that hour spent looking at the tropical beauty of Sri Lanka and rather enjoying the idea of playing along with the locals' idea of this continuation of the Raj. There was no doubt in my mind that although the assumed mastery of the white races overseas had been an affront to the human race as a whole, nonetheless it had brought some stability and chances of employment where none had existed before. Sadly, it also brought colonial officials who were quite capable of destroying whole countries just by drawing official borders in the wrong places, bisecting tribes, families, cultures and civilisations with a green or red pencil in the name of tidiness. It was good just to take timeout to mull these things surrounded by the atmosphere of an imperial past.

Next leg: the Maldive Islands. The Maldives had yet to be developed as a holiday playground and the RAF had established a transit post on one of its many islands, Gan. This was the strangest of all RAF postings, as it was a strictly 'men only', unaccompanied nine-month detachment. The formula of 'men only' plus mixed transit flights made for some unholy and unwholesome images. As we landed at Gan, we noticed the perimeter fence was red and brown, with little flecks of white. As we landed and taxied, we could see that this fence was hanging with sunburnt RAF personnel, wearing white PE shorts and flip flops, burning up in the sun as they waited for the once-weekly treat of the air trooper to Singapore.

We came to a standstill, engines unwhined, steps pushed up, there was the usual punch of tropical air in the cabin, the DDT spray gun and then off we went for a two-hour transit. The noise from the RAF onlookers was amazing. A low throaty muttering, which slowly transmuted into a lusty lowing as dozens of mini-skirted mums and daughters stepped lightly from the big silver bird. All kinds of thought crime was committed by these sectioned Lotharios as the pussy pelmet parade swanned along the runway to the NAAFI lounge. The white caps of the 'Snowdrops' - the RAF police - made sure that lust remained only in the eye of the beholder.

Eventually, the last fair maid had clicked her way to the privacy of the transit lounge and the RAF types unpeeled themselves from the wire and went back to their duties.

After a drink or two, I thought I'd better send my folks a postcard. They didn't even know I'd left the country. God, it was hot. The only private place I could find was a toilet. I sat myself down, started to write and then suddenly it hit me.

A huge panic attack. What the hell was I doing? I'd never actually done a whole radio programme, I was a beginner and I was completely on my own. I started to shake and sweat all over. And then I burst into tears, drowning my sobs and gasps with the shirt I'd taken off because of the heat. This seemed to go on for a long time, but eventually I slow-breathed my way back to normal. I was still wonky, but the moment had passed. Another rum and coke, and all would be well…

The last leg wasn't a problem, as I was busy concentrating on what I was going to do when I landed at RAF Tengah. Would I have to go into town? Where was the BFBS station? Where was I staying?

*****

We landed safely at Tengah and within seconds I was scooped up by two very different gentlemen, one of whom was to be my new boss; the other would become a lifelong friend.

Peter Buckle, MBE, was a comparatively thin but elegant semi-intellectual with a razor sharp wit, which he deployed with malice and precision. He had the ability to make you feel about carpet-pile in height whilst administering the many and varied bollockings that come the way of a new BFBS announcer, but I was told he had a switch and could go from total hate to beneficent largesse in a nanosecond. The only grudge he ever carried was against life itself.

'Call me Peter,' he launched affably, 'and this is Stevie Withers. He'll be looking after you. Now, let's get your bags in the car, and we'll take you to your mess.'

I shook hands with Peter and then Stevie. I knew the latter was a character right from the start. His exaggerated sincerity and formal politeness didn't quite mask the man himself – one of nature's comedians, just planted in the wrong place at the wrong time. He belonged in a Restoration drama, or a novel by P.G. Wodehouse. Stevie Q. Withers could 'do' camp like it was

going out of fashion. He had a background in drama (both on set and off) and was as mad as a box of frogs, especially when drink, particularly Scotch, had been taken.

This was going to be a heady combination. We drove up a mountainous hill to the Kent Medical Officers' mess, overlooking Singapore's Keppel Harbour. The hill itself was lushly bearded by jacaranda, bougainvillea, rambutan trees and a general "ulu" or tropical jungle, which came alive at night with an orchestra of cicada and military drunks.

We reported in to reception, where what could only be described as a Major-Domo was enthroned behind a huge marble desk in the vast foyer of the main Mess building. Here Mr Singh could see absolutely every movement of entrance and exit, which occasionally earned him a few dollars for the privilege of a blind eye being turned. His huge beard and whiskers were surmounted by a giant turban usually not seen outside of a Walt Disney cartoon, but his presence commanded respect. I was given the key to a room in the annexe corridor, which proved to have great views over the South China Sea.

But first I needed to be briefed. We repaired to the bar. Here I learnt that I would be one of a three-person shift pattern. On day one, I would do early mornings plus late afternoons and evenings; on day two an 'office day' with a lunchtime on-air shift; on the third day I was free to do my own thing.

Having lived with BFBS Germany's schedule, which ran from 6am to 11:30pm, I was fascinated to find out that BFBS Far East, as the station in Singapore was known, was only on the air from 6am-8am, then off until 12:30pm-2pm, then off again until 4:45pm-10:45pm. And this with a broadcast staff of five (including Peter the boss, and programme organiser David Davis, who I had yet to meet). Everything was set fair, as I saw it that late afternoon in the bar of the Kent Officers' mess. Peter and Stevie were my new besht friensh. We were all quite hammered.

There was some loose talk of me turning up at the station tomorrow at some dumb hour to 'shadow' Steve, who was doing the 'A' shift (0545 -0900).

The rest is a bit of a fog. I made it to my new quarters – en-suite, balcony, shuttered - on on the first floor of the annexe, straight out of Kipling or Somerset Maughan. I could almost feel the solar topi and spinal brace keeping my lip all stiff and upper. Then I crashed and oblivion healed all scars.

The next morning, after a Mess breakfast of papaya, I was driven to the station and shown the ropes. The studios were custom built, with one wing for the English service and the other for the Gurkha service, which seemed to consist of massive piles of shellac 78rpm HMV India discs with fascinating pre-Bollywood titles. The only one I remember was 'Hello Darling', a novelty song with just those words as the lyrics. You had to be there. The Gurkhas were fascinating. The two main broadcasters – both characters – were late middle aged, a bit un-military and gifted with a huge sense of humour. Or put it another way, they smiled a lot, especially the senior man, Kishor Kumar Gurung, who steadfastly remained at the age of 55 from 1971 to his retirement in the late 90s. One day, when I'd got to know them better, I spoke to Jamyang Dorje Lama, a DJ very famous in the Gurkha community.

'Jamyang, you know when you take out your khukri, you're supposed to draw blood, even if you're only cleaning it. Is that true?'

'Yes, Mr. McD, sahib, that is the truth.' Jamyang was smiling. A bit worrying.

'And Jamyang, if your officer says,"Take out your Kukhri and kill Mr. McD", what would you do?'

'I would kill you, sahib.' The voice, and the smile, never altered. I looked at his eyes. He meant it.My training period with Stevie was great fun: we were there to buck the system. Stevie had a great Saturday Show, which ran late morning for two hours and was always crowded out by a huge selection of service brats trying to be cool. I acted as runner and hoped for my own show one day. In the meantime, he showed me how to store bottles of beer in the aircon to keep them icy, where to get decent satay and how to pre-fade listen to the BBC World Service in one ear, the output of the station in the other, and how to talk in between the two and connect them live on air.

In the meantime, I sat at the desk, played in the 'banded music green' tapes from London, which had to be interrupted every five minutes to give a time check – no matter what the music was doing at the time. Cue music: 'My Way' by Frank Sinatra. Coming up to the climax of the song: 'The record shows/I took the blows/ And did it... It's five minutes to seven, that's five to seven... My Way!' What a bugger's muddle. For the last half hour, we were allowed to play the latest discs sent to us from 'Head Office'.

I'd only been on station for a fortnight and was feeling a bit glum, because as we were going through the boss's office one evening after hours, Stevie and I had found a signal sent to the director, Ian Woolf, which stated starkly, 'Next time do NOT send a bloody recruit.' Buckle was notoriously direct to the point of rudeness and I knew then that I was going to be a failure.

The next morning I was sitting doing the Breakfast shift and in the last half hour I put on a track that had just arrived: 'Johnny Reggae' by (ostensibly)'The Piglets' but in fact another persona of the now-disgraced Jonathan King. It was a bit of sexual banter served up by a young lady of clearly easy morals, with an accent not before heard in the popular music genre - "Ere comes Johnny Reggae, Johnny Reggae Reggae, lay i' on me' -plus a middle-eight that was clearly a simulated orgasm. As the song played out, the phone rang. It was Peter Buckle.

Stevie had warned me about Buckle's infamous paint-stripper calls to the station. I held the receiver at arm's length. The sardonic voice hissed across the gap. It still sounded loud, and very, very, angry.

"*Brilliant* choice of music for breakfast time, Peter. I'm sure the garrison commander is *really* enjoying this obscene crap with his fucking cornflakes. What the fuck do you think you're doing, you stupid idiot, playing shit like this? Have you taken leave of your senses? She'll be giving him a fucking blow-job on air next.'

With that, he slammed down the phone, which saved me the problem of demonstrating that I was speechless. I'd never had a boss speak to me with so much venom before. God, that was personal. He must think I was a nothing - a nobody. My job was over and I would be sent back to UK in disgrace.

After the shift, I hung around the foyer, waiting for his little white Fiat to arrive. After a lifetime, he turned up and stepped into the foyer. 'Morning Peter,' he beamed. 'Beautiful day. Up for a drink later?'

I picked my jaw up from the deck and made a few agreeable noises. Was I in a parallel universe? Then I remembered Stevie telling me that Peter was heavy on the bollockings but also went in for instant forgiveness and never held a grudge.

I soon got to meet my other colleagues. David 'Dad' Davis was an ex-Marine commando (war issue) who had drifted into broadcasting and could make brilliant big band programmes, which would have been useful 20 years previously. During my ten months there he did the grand total of two specials. Otherwise, he produced the weekly programme schedule and spent lots of time researching the bottom of whisky bottles and generally carousing. The third announcer, with Stevie and me, was Rodney Burke, who had a voice to die for, was the laziest man on the planet and who could cat nap to perfection.Rodney's party piece was to shriek to a halt outside the station two minutes before his thirty minute slot live on-air, amble into the station library, pull a handful of random albums from the record library, bimble upstairs, open the studio door, get the first disc on the turntable, slide into his seat, open the fader and, in a dark brown voice, say, 'Good evening. This is Rodney Burke with "Announcer's Choice".' Yup, thanks to Dad Davis's fertile imagination, we had the snappiest programme titles in the world, as I was to find out a few weeks into my apprenticeship, when I was summoned to his office.

'Peter, I've been listening to you on air. You seem to have picked up the basics of what to say and how and when to say it.' He leant back in his executive's swivel chair, in the manner of a benign Lord about to donate a trifle. 'I want you to have your own half-hour programme, Saturday evenings at 5.45pm.'

I had died and was going to heaven. My own show. What could I call it and what would go into it? I already had dreamt up several winning formats that I knew would resonate with the lads in the trenches. Maybe a touch of comedy in short bursts, mixed in with… I was aware that Dad's lips were moving. I tuned in again. '…Saturday evening's a good spot: folk getting ready to go out. The show will be called "Pops With Peter" and the songs you will play will all be from the nineteen sixties. And I want it pre-recorded.'

'Thanks, David.' He waved me away. I went out into the corridor, shaking with anger. How cool was that – not. 'Pops With Peter.' The shame of it. Still, it was my own show.

I recorded the first programme. 'Jumping Jack Flash' was the opener, after the theme music, 'Red River Rock' by Johnny and the Hurricanes. It felt good and I felt like a real DJ, introducing myself properly by name – PMcD – and using all the clichés I remembered from my Radio Luxembourg and Radio One listening days. As it was pre-recorded, I listened to it on the highly compressed and filtered short wave frequencies of the mess radio. God, it sounded good. There was this low, butch voice, sounding every bit like a James Bond figure, booming out to millions all over South East Asia.

Dream on. A few weeks later, once my ego had gone platinum and stratospheric, I listened to a recording of the show on FM. The once butch voice suddenly became the infantile gaspings of a callow youth. You could hear the fear and trepidation in the shaky voice and also all the background sounds of the inept DJ wrestling with the equipment.

Brian Hart, officer commanding the local Hygiene and Malaria Control Unit, which consisted of Brian plus 600 Chinese coolies, had the job of keeping all open water outlets protected from the anopheles mosquito and thus malaria.

Bryan was a giant, rotund Scouser who took huge enjoyment in the pleasures of life. From the back door of his office was a stone path that led to what could only be described as a huge English country pub. Bryan had used his coolies well: they had built a three-bar pub, with a restaurant area, a dance-floor, an outside terrace and a well stocked series of fridges. In those days there was a lot of 'spare time' activity.

'The Anophalous Inn' even had its own UK style pub sign, which was basically a pissed mosquito. It was very popular and frequented by a variety of the units Bryan had met on his travels and, as he lived a couple of rooms away from Stevie and me at the Kent Mess, we were very much on his radar. His legendary cry of 'No drinking in the forenoon!', shouted ruddily at anybody of any rank at any time of the day or night, was always the precursor to another glass raised to the lips.

When the mess closed and Bryan came to be posted back to the UK, he turned up at the studio one day.

'Could you do us a tape with just the one song on it, all the versions you got?' he machine-gunned.

'Depends on the song. Let's go to the library.' Lance Daniels, the brilliant record librarian, raconteur and writer, held court there, over gallons of Anchor beer.

'What's the song, mate?' asked Lance.

'The Butch Cassidy thing.' Bryan knew what he meant. Luckily, so did Lance.

'Raindrops keep falling on my head,' pronounced Lance, with much authority. He flipped through the card index. 'We've got 46 versions of the bloody thing.'

'Pete, d'you reckon you could do me a tape with as many versions as'll fit?'

'Yeah – no bother.' In the end, we had two tapes with this song sung by the whole world and his brother.

But Bryan wasn't finished. Seeing in me a fellow toper and expert barfly, he consulted me as to a welcoming drink he could literally pass to each of the hundred or so guests he was going to invite to his farewell bash. I concluded that honour would best be served by serving refrigerated dry martinis, complete with frozen glasses, according to the legendary formula, 'eleventeen parts gin, one wave of the vermouth cork, olive on a stick'.

Came the day, came the party. The coolies had been industrious. Five catering-sized fridges, loaded to the gunwales with hundreds of glasses of pre-mixed and olive'd dry martinis, groaned loudly against the tropical heat. The music played loudly in the background. The drinks were strong. Very strong. We took casualties, some after only three or four glasses. The post mortem concluded it had been the best of bashes. Nobody noticed the bloody music.

*****

It would be fair to say that a feckless bachelor living in an Officers' Mess in Singapore will be more or less looked after - even one whose bar bill has more zeros than the Japanese Air Force at the height of WW2 and who had learnt how to dodge Mr Singh whilst spiriting out a young lady in a cocktail frock at dawn, after a night of celebration at the legendary 'Pink Pussycat' in Orchard Road.

With the closure of the Kent Mess, I lived in the Bukit Timah Road for a few weeks, at the house of our sound engineer 'Sani Poona' (as Stevie called him), until I ran out of rent as a result of spending most of my leisure hours, when I wasn't at the Tanglin HQ swimming pool, vogeuing as 'poolside DJ'. I spent most of my wages at the NAAFI Phoenix bar on camp, where I ended up mixing with the UK, Aussie and Kiwi squaddies who were based at the sprawling complex officially called HQ FARELF. For a time, I had a billet with the Aussies, otherwise I kipped in the cells in the guardroom, courtesy of the Welch Regiment, complete with all the tea and bacon rolls I could eat, in exchange for playing Tom Jones songs on BFBS. Or I slept in a spare studio on station, washing my laundry in the sink and hanging it up on the transmission mast. Buckle didn't like this a lot.

My drinking HQ, the NAAFI Phoenix Bar, was a tough environment. The Aussies and Kiwis were on R&R from frontline duties in Vietnam and were huge, very matey and not to be trifled with. It was some of the Brits who were a problem, as they couldn't handle the easy attitude of the battle-scarred Antipodeans. One night, I was at a table with some Aussies and a couple of Brits, one of whom seemed not too keen on me. One of the Aussies, Phil, spotted this, gave me a heads up on the wonky geezer over there and even sat me next to him for safety (the Aussies had adopted me almost as a pet.).

The next bit was vicious, and sudden. The Brit stood up, leant across the table and punched me straight in the face. My specs shattered and I went over backwards. The Aussies performed a battle ballet on him straight away and within a minute or so his dripping remains slunk off into the night. The Aussies took me to a very unsympathetic military quack. Ah yes, another Friday night drunk. He patched me up and sent me off to the Royal Military Police to report the incident.

While I was dealing with the redcaps, the germ of an idea came to me. 'What's my situation?'

'Well, it looks like you were the victim of an unprovoked physical assault. And you seem to have four sound witnesses to say so. So, it's up to you. Do you want him charged?'

'What will happen to him?'

"Well, shouldn't say this, but this one's got form for smacking people unprovoked. Reckon he'll get 112 in Colly this time.'

This was what I wanted to hear. 112 days in the Army Correctional Institute, Colchester, was known by Lucifer to be rather worse than hell. Psychopaths emerged, broken from their violent conduct and would spend their lives thereafter cooing at babies and stroking kittens. Colchester therapy was simply bullying bullies until they stopped being bullies.

And my cousin, George Pangbourne, was the RSM in charge of the 'shop floor' at Colchester.

'I think I *would* like to press charges.' There were no tears shed. I wrote a note to my cousin, giving a few details. Matey boy was a changed man when he left.

My final tales from Singapore must be about my time with 40 and 42 Commando, Royal Marines. Booties are odd drinking buddies. They eat live insects and write poetry. They hug each other, are fearsomely protective of women in their care and will bite their own legs off rather than leave a friend in trouble. And trouble is what we appeared to get up to every time we went out.

The Hyatt Hotel had a magnificent façade. On both sides of the central staircase there was a long sunken pond running across half of the very wide frontage. True, there were a lot of water-plantings, but through a beer haze the whole length, interrupted only by the central entrance stairs, looked a bit like a very narrow, but very long swimming pool. It was only a matter of a few displaced synapses for the marines to come up with the brilliant idea of an Aquatic Olympics at sundown. In the nude.

Of course, the gap in the middle meant that every so often during the booze-fuelled races, the central stairs were occupied by very hairy tattooed naked booties rushing from one pond to the next, while a crowd of about fifty marines, wearing only towels and grins, urged them on, to the astonishment and occasional delight of a very posh multi-racial clientele making their way in and out of the hotel. Marine radar meant that the fun and games were terminated and an escape effected before the blue-lit paddy waggons hove into view.

The other marine trick was 'upsetting the bellboy', which worked for a while until word got round the posh hotels in Orchard Road. A small crowd of booties would settle quietly in the cocktail bar of one of Singapore's huge American-style luxury hotels of the moment – Shangri-La, Hyatt, Malaysia and so on – and one of their number would go to reception and have a word. The story would be that the marine had arranged to meet a friend in the hotel but hadn't told him in which bar or restaurant he might be found. Could the hotel page the gentleman in question? Of course, this would be possible. And the gentleman's name…? This is where it got funny. Guests were paged, usually by a Chinese pageboy, holding a small blackboard on a stick, which also had a bicycle bell on it. On the blackboard would be written the guest's name, which would also be shouted out loud by the Chinese lad as he walked through all the bars and restaurants on the ground floor of the hotel, ringing his little bell to make sure everyone could hear. From the marine point of view, what made it so sweet was that in those days, the Chinese Singaporeans barely spoke or understood English.

Which made it all the more cruelly entertaining to see a very smart young Chinese lad, elegantly uniformed, wandering around the hotel shouting at the top of his voice. 'Mr Fuck! Fuck! Mr. Fuck!' with the same name scrawled in chalk on his mini-blackboard. It wasn't too long before this scam became impossible.

Very soon after this, we had news that BFBS Singapore was to close, as was HQ FARELF, and all of us would be sent to new stations. I seemed to have drawn first prize in the lottery – I was going to BFBS Cologne. We had a magic closing down party and I ended up kipping on the station sofa in the foyer. Next morning came the rude awakening by Peter Buckle, not in a good mood. 'Still gonking, I see, Peter,' he hissed.

'What's happening?'

'I've only been told by the British High Commissioner to put BFBS back on air again. Apparently Lee Kwan Yu [the charismatic Prime Minister] likes to listen to BBC World Service news on BFBS and now I've got to stay behind and run the station on my own.'

I sniggered. I couldn't help it. There *was* a God, after all. The speaker in the foyer was on and I heard our very pissed off and hungover Station Controller coin the legendary formula:

'Good morning. It's nearly six o'clock on the morning of Thursday 4th December, 1971. This is Peter Buckle, and I *am* the British Forces Broadcasting Service, Singapore.'

Chapter Eight:

World Record!

Leaving behind Singapore, and Peter Buckle in particular, was scarcely a wrench: he was not a bringer of joy and Singapore's permanently humid climate made me permanently wet and moody. Not a winning combination. I caught the RAF big silver bird back via Colombo, Bahrain and Brize. I was now a seasoned traveller and not even the Rosa Klebb orange squash routine upset me. After landing in Oxfordshire, we journeyed through welcome snow to Luton to catch the air trooper to RAF Wildrenrath, one of many bases in Germany, where more than half a million British Forces souls and their dependants kept our Russian friends from invading. Including, of course, me, armed with new skills honed to perfection in the Far East.

I'd street-fought against the Singaporean Armed Forces with the Aussie infantry, beasted the local population with 40 and 42 Commando Royal Marines and even held off over 500 members of the Singapore Army when they tried to rush the Tanglin Cinema which was showing 'Girl on a Motorcycle'. (I decided it would be a good idea to put my arm through the two pull handles on the large glass doors of the fleapit and nearly got it broken before a couple of mates wedged the doors shut with heavy furniture.) All of this made me the perfect bloke to hold off twenty-one Soviet armoured divisions.

We landed early evening at RAF Wildenrath. I must admit I was expecting someone from the station to meet me. I hovered around for a while until it was a bit obvious there was nobody much around - and certainly nobody who could be mistaken for a broadcaster.

And then I saw Walter. He looked like he could do with a drink. (He could.) He had scraggy hair down below his shoulders and an oversized Zapata moustache. He peered at me like a specimen in a jar.

'Herr Mek Dongah?' he tried. 'McDonagh,' I grinned with relief. "Sind Sie von BFBS?"

My German was rusty but Walter, who spoke little English apart from 'Beer', was delighted. Of all the people he'd ever had to pick up, I apparently was the first who'd addressed him in his own language – well, nearly! Walter was from Cologne, where they speak a local dialect called Kölsch (also the name of the local beer, which is worshipped). It sounds a bit like real German, except with a kind of softening "squish" sound about it, besht deschcribed like thish in translation. Walter later observed that I spoke to him as an equal - something lowly drivers weren't used to. My training with Tante Martha had paid off here.

So already I was being categorised as we sped through the kilometres to Cologne. Walter would be able to report to his German colleagues that the new guy was a German speaker who had time and respect for the local population. This, even as late at 1971, was still unusual. It had only been a year or so ago that the German workers at BFBS Cologne had been permitted to use the station bar and to address their UK colleagues without calling them 'Herr'. Otherwise, Germans were given the dismissive status of 'locally engaged' and were pretty much down on the pecking order.

Walter drove me to a pension in Cologne's rather expensive suburb of Marienburg, where bank chairmen and insurance CEOs lived in palatial mansions. On a leafy avenue I found myself in a very well appointed villa, Haus Marienburg, with a pristine and luxurious bedroom. The last thing Walter had told me was how to get to BFBS the next morning, when he and I assumed I ought to pitch up. It was five minutes down the same road, on the junction of Lindenallee and Parkstrasse. After a long haul from the tropics, I quickly fell asleep.

The next morning, a Saturday, the sun was shining. I was given the wonderful traditional German breakfast of cheese and ham slices with fresh-baked crispy rolls, accompanied with cup after cup of strong fresh-brewed coffee. I walked up the road, clutching my trusty old 'flying donkey' briefcase, heading to my new destiny. The signs were good. The sun was shining and dappling through the empty, frost-sparkling branches of the avenue's trees. (Every road in Marienburg is an avenue.)

Finally, I came to a sign on a gate at 61 Parkstrasse. It said 'BFN', which was what BFBS was called until 1963. This must be the station. There was a drive about 80 metres long. At the end of it, disproportionately small, there was a stout wooden door. This was it: my new place of work.

As I approached, I saw an unusual sight. The small wooden door opened and out stepped an elderly gentleman, patrician of feature, with what looked like a pink rinse in his mane of well-coiffed hair. He wore a pair of Dickensian spectacles on the end of his nose and seemed very occupied with dusting a toy with a soft brush, using the sunlight to examine his labours. What really singled him out was the blue towelling dressing gown he was wearing, along with a pair of bedroom slippers.

I approached this eccentric vision. I had a feeling I knew who he might be.

'You're the new boy, aren't you?' He peered at me as a lion his prey, or as a nobleman with a new serf. The voice was surprisingly 'common'.

'And you must be Uncle Bill!' I said, with much respect. He was 'Uncle' Bill Mitchell and he was famous. I had been listening to him for some years. His 'Kinder Club' programme was the stuff of legend, as were his 'Big Wood' stories, which he wrote and acted himself, using a variety of voices and spot sound effects.

He gave a rather wonky half-smile of acknowledgement. 'You'd better come in and have a cup of tea,' he said, and steered me in to the labyrinthine passages of 61 Parkstrasse. We came to a room not much bigger than a broom cupboard. In it was a massive model railway taking up ninety-five percent of the room; the other five percent was taken up by two rickety folding chairs. The walls and ceiling were dripping with flags, banners, mementoes of garrison visits, and the impedimenta that went with the honorary office of publicity officer for British Scouts in Western Europe.

Half a cup of Earl Grey later, I had learnt more about BFBS Cologne than a week of official briefings could provide. For a maker of children's programmes, Bill was uncharacteristically blunt. The station controller, John Parsons, was 'alright, but you never really see 'im.' His number two, the weasely John Russell, who had once banned me for life from appearing on BFBS, was simply a 'c***'. Apparently this was always Bill's nomenclature for the hapless senior programme organiser, but on this occasion the title dripped from Bill's mouth with extra venom, as Russell had just told him he would have to move his programme slot, modernise it and get rid of 'that bloody train set'.

'It's not a train set,' explained Bill, more than once, to those who made the error, 'it's a model railway'.

The other sketches of my new colleagues were then brought to life by Bill. I have to say that, apart from minor caricature, he was spot on. Although a loner and a confirmed bachelor (in the *old* sense of the word), Bill had a soft spot for those people who passed muster with him and I seemed over the years to own that ticket. It would be fair to say that he really made me feel at home – in the absence of any official reception, which still rankled a bit.

By the end of the day, Bill had found me a desk, showed me where everything was and introduced me to the few staff who were on Saturday duties – all of them German. I met two very formidable Network Control Room Engineers, Jürgen Bock and Dieter Gripp. Both were to figure hugely in my continuing struggle against the Russian hordes.

Once Monday had come around, I was officially greeted by the administration officer, Bill Moules, and his administrative assistant, Archie Hendry. I was advised that as a singleton I would be given accommodation in the 'chummery', along with three others, at No.1 Eckdorferstrasse in the English quarter, or 'Volkspark'. I was advised that the stationery cupboard was open from 1230-1300 on every alternate Thursday lunchtime. I was also advised that I was employed under civil service jurisdiction, which meant under the overall command of the military. Nothing about the job, I noticed.

I was finally advised by the administrative assistant that I was entitled to a ballpoint pen. Hendry removed a ballpoint pen case from one drawer of his desk, then took a ballpoint refill from another drawer and conjoined them in blessed union. Having done this, he rested the pen on his desk, passed me a ledger and asked me to sign for the acquisition of my new pen.

I made to pick up my new pen and was prevented by a less than kindly grip on my jacket sleeve. 'Nae, laddie, ye cannae sign with *that* pen. It's nae yours, yet.'

I looked at the florid face and its piggy eyes for the beginnings of a smile. Smile came there none. This horrid little Pict was serious. It didn't occur to me for a moment that I, as an HM civil service executive officer with the equivalent military rank of captain, actually outranked him and had parity with Moules. No, I was what I was, a novice broadcaster, trying to find his feet on a new station. I was going to have fun with these guys...

Over the next few weeks I was introduced to my colleagues and learnt another lesson. They were all professionals. I knew this, because for some reason they kept telling me they were. Something really niggled me that in almost any conversation I had, a moment would come when they would tell me a story, the point of which seemed to be that whatever had occurred had done so because they were professional.

I finally worked out that if all of them were telling me they were professional, it was because they thought I was a beginner, an amateur. Which I was. But I remembered my Dad's words: 'Everybody starts by not having done something.' I was going to have fun with these guys too.In the meantime, word came through, to everybody's surprise, that Dick Norton in Berlin had been taken ill again and that a temporary Berlin replacement was needed. The Cologne management knew whom they would have chosen but word came from Ian Woolf at the very top that McDonagh should be given a chance. To the annoyance of all, I was dispatched to my home town over the Christmas period. I had died and was going to heaven.

*****

A day or so later, I was ensconced in the bosom of the family, briefed by a horizontal Dick, holding court in the Officers' Club and feeling very much at home. Thank you, Uncle Ian.

Where it went wrong, Your Honour, was like this. I was invited to a New Year's Eve party. I was in a 'Girls – who needs them?' mood, after a series of man-made disasters with the distaff side, the man in question being me. My lifelong habit of severing connections from unwanted girlfriends by proposing marriage to them so they would panic and run away was working far too well. The word had appeared to have got around 'girls united' that McD was not a good thing. Anyway, it was one of those parties that finishes at about four in the morning with everybody wondering where all the hours had gone. There was drinking, dancing, snogging, prancing, voguing, posing – all the usual things that uncool people who are basically mates do when left to their own devices. Plus a 3am visit to the Olympic Stadium indoor swimming pool (one of us had the keys; don't ask) where we swam whilst eating bowls of cornflakes with milk. Most of the milk stayed in the bowls.

I remember staggering down Ahornallee, humming cheerfully in a boozy haze, climbing the two flights of stairs to our flat and trying to stick the Yale key in the lock.

It went in but the key wouldn't turn. Dad had locked the door from the other side. I tried and tried again. No, this was deliberate. I started to get angry, in the Irish kind of way, which is not to be confused with the logical kind of way. The logical kind of way would be to open the letterbox and sing through it, with increasing volume, until my Dad could not ignore the fact that his drunken son was making a scene. Or I could hammer on the door, with the same intention and possible outcome. But *no*, Irish logic was necessary. This goes in the following fashion.

'It's an icy cold Berlin night, with the wind blowing off the Siberian plain. Because I didn't wear an overcoat, I am already cold. I am livid at my Dad not letting me in after a party, especially as I was the oldest person there, twenty years old, nearly a proper man, with my own key, but here I am, being treated like a naughty school kid. Well, we'll see about that. I wonder what Mum will say to Dad when she finds out her only shivering son has died from frostbite in the snow? Hah.'

And with that, I retraced my steps downstairs and walked the short distance to Ragniter Allee, where there was a municipal park – a wide tree-lined pathway which went round a very large circular lawn, about 100 metres in diameter. The path was punctuated with wooden benches along the way but, as I trudged through the snow, there was no sign of the usual tramps occupying the benches. It was too cold.

My teeth chattered as the Berlin cold slowly infiltrated my jacket, shirt and vest. Although I carried on walking briskly for more than an hour, it was a one sided battle. My pride was exhausted. I would have to go back to the flat, and beat on the door until whatever would be, would be. I would take it on the chin. Anything was better than this bone-sapping cold.

I almost hobbled back up the road to our block. Already on the staircase I could feel some redeeming heat. Just in case, I got out my key, put it in the lock...

And turned it. Dad had unlocked the door from the inside. There was no time to hold a board of inquiry. I was inside once again. My room was first on the right. I didn't even bother with the late night fry up and glass of milk. I didn't want confrontation. I was frozen, tired and just about able to tear my clothes off, swing into bed, and that was very much that. Asleep in seconds. There are great traditions in the McDonagh family, one of which translates as 'silence in drunkenness', and means that if a period of time has elapsed after an incident to do with drink, it is forgotten. Hence nobody ever mentioned a previous New Year's Eve, when I was a kiddie and Dad had been pushed into my room by Mum so he could wish me a Happy New Year (they had both had a long night out in the mess). Father approached the bed with great dignity, tripped, measured his length across the bed, then slowly slid off until just his legs were pointing in the air. He then made the most of the opportunity by falling asleep.

On another occasion he came in to wish me 'Happy New Year', which he managed successfully before turning and attempting to leave the room via the very tall wardrobe next to the door of my room. It was a real giggle watching him steadily open the wardrobe door, climb inside, realise what he'd done and then crumple in a confused heap on its floor.

And then the one I held in reserve. One Saturday, Mum and I were going off to the NAAFI on Theodor-Heuss-Platz for some late morning shopping. As we waited at the pedestrian crossing, a hugely flamboyant American open-topped pink Cadillac shimmied past, driven by the most Marilyn Monroe-like of pneumatic blondes. This was remarkable but what made it more than interesting was that Dad, who'd gone 'up the road for a beer', was in the passenger seat. There was a second when my eyes locked with his and, for a millisecond, I saw fear. I glanced at Mum, but she hadn't seen anything. I stayed schtum. The rules are the rules. Once the event is done and dusted, you can't resurrect it. More Irish logic.

And that's why Dad didn't say a word about the previous night, once I'd surfaced. Mum was a bit martyrish, but that was normal. The atmosphere was a bit strained. It was after lunch when Dad finally broke the silence.

'Since you seem to like parties so much, you can come along with us tonight. There's an WRVS do on at No.6 Mess tonight.' The Women's Royal Voluntary Service. Oh yes. This was going to be a stonker. I'd spent some time in the NAAFI's WRVS lounge, where lonely soldiers used to go if they wanted a cup of tea and a kind word instead of the usual eleventeen pints and a shag.

The WRVS ladies were a fine body of women: all blue rinse hair and pale face powder, scarlet lipstick and the wonderful patrician yodelling of ladies who are doing good works. (Actually, that was the façade; they really helped young squaddies with a little tough TLC which kept morale up and incidents down.) But to me, aged 20, the idea of an evening in their company was right up there with watching paint dry on the side of a ship in a storm. I suppressed a shudder. Sadly, this was a penance and it had to be paid. Dad was capable of the most tremendous sulks if he didn't get his own way, the kind of sulks that grossly hamper everybody else's quality of life or even reasons for living.

I decided to go for broke and sought out my Singapore-tailored bright mustard suit, with the widest of Krushchev lapels and flares that flapped like performing seals at the bottom of my legs. Add to this a kipper tie whose design had clearly been inspired by a jackal throwing up a bad goat, a pair of over the top Cuban heeled cowboy boots and a hair-do clearly modelled on the Laurence Olivier version of Richard III (Irish hair curls up after a certain length to look like a superior pudding basin) and I was now ready to party.

We processed glumly down to the waiting transport. I sulked in the back with mum and all too soon we arrived at the spectacular No. 6 Mess, in prestigious Wallotstrasse in the Grünewald forest. We were greeted at the door by uniformed waitresses, who stole our outer clothing (snow on the ground, minus five, no escape, no public transport anyway) and shuffled up to the first floor reception room, where a dozen WRVS ladies were waiting in a greeting line to process their guests.

I remember walking along the line, being polite and charming. Each one appeared to be a parody of the next. Blue rinse, scarlet gash of lipstick on the mouth, OD on Max Factor's Crème Puff and always a dead animal, usually a winking fox, slung around the neck as a talisman against improper thoughts. Luckily, thought is free, and my mind was in the bar of the Officers' Club, enjoying a large one, instead of the gently warming coupe of Fabergold Sekt (NAAFI sparkling wine at 4/8d the bottle in old money – 24p in real life, and tasted like it). And then…

We seemed to have run out of WRVS ladies and, right at the end of the line, standing in front of me, was a goddess.

There was no doubt about it. This creature had wafted in from the planet Beautiful. There she was, just a few inches away from me, her intriguing half-smile, a cascade of auburn hair framing her blue-green Celtic eyes and brushing down in an elegant flow way past her shoulders. She was wearing a rich brown velvet dress, trimmed with gold braid, and the most simple but telling accessories in all the right places.

'I'm Tanya,' she volunteered, as I attempted a handshake that attempted to convey a message of undying love.

'Bahgla flaaht blim McD pruuhh shnit,' is what she thought I'd said, by way of response. (I'd actually said, 'Good to meet you, I'm McD', but I'd suddenly become tongue tied and it all went wrong.)

I mentally stepped back, thinking, 'Right, I've done my bit. What happens now?'

She watched me closely, clearly enjoying the way my mouth was flapping and my eyes darting around. I found out much later that she was also wondering if I was wearing the suit as a joke. The resulting smile provided greater impetus in the Lothario department. She leant forward, conspiratorially. 'Let's get a drink down at the bar.' Not only beautiful, but clearly pragmatic and intelligent. We made our way to the very snug all-comers' bar on the ground floor and proceeded to hoover down drinks as we found out more about each other. She was on Bacardi and Coke; I was on the usual Myers' and same.

It turned out her Dad, Jock, was my Dad's boss at BSSO, which meant she had officer status. Again, I was social climbing. What *would* my paterfamilias say? I suppressed another subversive smile and we got another round in.

We had met at around half-past seven. At about half-past eight, we were standing in the falling snow in the mess garden, in a little grove of fir trees, all of which had been crowned with a string of sparkling lights, which made for a twinkling pattern on the ice crystals of our snow carpet. We had known each other for an hour. I had to say something, as I was going back to Cologne in the next few days.

I don't know to this day where it came from, but out it blurted anyway.

'Will you come and live with me in Cologne?'

There was a silence – no, a pause – while the implications of this proposition were being processed. There was a smile and a gentle, but not dismissive, shake of the head and a quietly mouthed 'no.' Her eyes probed mine, looking for an explanation for this nutter in a mustard suit wanting to upend her life.

But there was no feeling of rejection, or annoyance. I had asked, it seemed, a reasonable question and had been given a proper answer. I wouldn't spoil things at this point by asking 'why not?' It was the most natural thing to go back to the bar and recharge both glasses and conversation.

By now, it was half past nine. I had known this eighteen-year-old for about two hours. We found ourselves back in the garden. My mind was racing, trying to form the words that might open the door to life-long happiness. And then, the Eureka moment. I could use the tried and tested phrase, but at the beginning, rather than the end, of a relationship.

'Will you marry me?' I asked. The words fell out of my mouth with unintended but practised ease. She smiled warmly. 'Yes, I will.'

It was as simple as that. We laughed, hugged, kissed, danced in the snow and raised our glasses. We were pirates on the high seas of the great love that we ourselves had invented. And on the first day of a brand new year, 1972, with me in the best job in the world. It turned out that Tanya worked for the very subterranean No. 3 Intelligence and Security Company and, much later on, I discovered that I'd been on their radar.

We decided not to tell our folks that night. We spent some more time behaving like young people in love and finally percolated upstairs to discover that widower Jock, too, had only proposed marriage to one of the WRVS ladies called Barbara, a rather 'Patience Strong' type of lady who, no doubt, would not only make him a very good wife, but also a bloody good husband. We stayed schtum and, at the end of the party, went our separate ways. I invited Tanya to come over to the BFBS studios the following day, as I thought a bit of showing off would add to the gaiety of nations. Mum and Dad seemed to have had a good time and clearly I was 'forgiven' for my late appearance the previous night. All was well with the world.

The following day dawned sunny and ice-cold. I woke up with the familiar haze in my head, which was slowly replaced by the most giant of internal smiles as I realised that I was going to marry the most enigmatically beautiful woman on the whole planet. Suddenly, life was different and amazing and wonderful, but I was still a bit cautious. I suspect Mum had picked something up, but nothing was said. The day plodded on until, after lunch, I told my folks I was going out for the rest of the day. They seemed content.

A ten-minute walk to Summit House NAAFI. There she was, waiting in a mini skirt, boots and an open winter coat. She looked even more exotic and wonderful than the night before. We made our way to the studios and I showed her all the kit we used for broadcasting. She was clearly interested and amused but not over-impressed. Which was OK.

At this point, I could give you a few lurid paragraphs of what my very modest northern Dad used to call 'The Sporting Page', featuring the various manoeuvrings that young love gives rise to when left alone but suffice it to say that once we had dressed and adjusted our clothing we left the BFBS studios three in number, rather than the two who had arrived. Our first child had been conceived. Not that we knew it then.

We carried on over the next two or three days and each encounter hardened our resolve to marry. Tanya had been acting as housekeeper to Jock since the death of his first wife but now WRVS Barbara would be on hand to fill the gap. As I saw it, the main difficulty would be with my folks' reaction.

I grabbed Dad after lunch one day. 'I'm going to get married, Dad.' I said it with emphasis, confidence, and directness, looking him foursquare in the eye, my chin a-jutting and my eyes ablaze.

Dad rose to the occasion. 'And who are you marrying?' he smiled sarcastically.

'Tanya Alexander,' I said. Suddenly I felt like someone trembling on the edge of a plank in the Spanish Main.

'Jock Alexander's daughter?' said Dad. I noted a look of suppressed panic and, bluntly, fear on his face. It was quickly replaced by a dismissive froideur as I nodded.

He gave his final opinion on the matter. 'Jock'll kill you,' he said, evenly.

He had reason for saying this. Jock had been used by the intelligence services pre-war, where he infiltrated future enemy dispositions on Bremen Harbour. Armed with a wartime commission, he was used widely for his knowledge of German and so it was not too far away from the work of the sub-MI5 BSSO in Berlin. He had a reputation as an interrogator in the old style. A line of sharpened pencils, each the same length, was his plaything on the wide desk from behind which he would question the more 'dodgy' of the refugees flooding in from East Berlin and East Germany. The only other thing on the desk that might have upset such 'customers' was the very much live pet alligator he used to play with. Also, any really dangerous potential agent worth his salt would have recognised the bulge in Jock's pocket, where he carried his favourite rubber cosh...

'Jock'll kill you.' Not the best of messages to hear, especially as later that day Tanya told me that Jock and Barbara had invited us to the fabulously exclusive lakeside 'Pavilion du Lac', the French Officers' Club, featuring six-course meals served on an airy terrace overlooking Berlin's magnificent Lake Havel. I found another suit (she'd given me her opinion of my mustard 'clown suit') and was picked up for the long drive to the 'pavilion'. My heart was in my mouth, and then my boots. Dad had pronounced. I was going to be killed.

*****

The lakeside restaurant, even inside the huge and airy conservatory, kept us warm without losing the view. The meal passed in a haze of unknown French cuisine, small talk and a mid-term hiatus when a course of turbot appeared. Turbot, I discovered, had been invented by somebody who hates PMcD and wants him to gag, shudder, feel generally ill and nearly vomit, when he clearly can't do any of those things. Somehow, we got through it.

The other problem was the nagging feeling that all was not well. I finally put this down to Tanya, who was sitting opposite me, kicking me on the shins to prompt me to ask Jock the all-important question. What I couldn't tell her was that I was judging the moment based on the amount of food and drink we were consuming and I was working on the theory that the more both of us knocked back, the likelihood of Jock felling me with one blow when I popped the question would be diminished.

The after-effects of the turbot and the kicking had not made for an easy lunch and, with business still unconcluded, Jock suggested we repaired to the bar for a little digestif and coffee. I was beginning to focus on the big moment. Tanya had given me up as spineless. Barbara was in her 'hello trees, hello sky' mode, as only an older widow who's been given a second bite might be, and Jock, who I suspect knew what was in the air, remained polite but impassive.

We sat. We ordered. An oil slick of a garcon appeared with some drinks. What in God's name had made me order a crème de menthe frappée? With Jock now sitting directly opposite me, his hooded interrogator eyes boring into my very soul, I might just as well have worn a pink shirt and painted my nails... It was the moment of truth. Those who are about to die. I cleared my throat. 'Jock,' I began.

At that very second, Tanya mouthed the words 'excuse me', peeled herself from the table and belted at lightning speed out of the bar and back to the terrace. We watched her go, Jock with some amusement. I knew then that he knew what I was going to say and I suddenly knew that he already knew the answer.

'Jock.' I repeated.

'Aye?' He was playing with me.

'I'd like to marry your daughter and I am officially asking your permission.'

There, it was out, and what a pity she couldn't have been there to hear my manly statement, even though its delivery was a bit shaky. Jock leant back in his chair, raised the glass of scotch to his lips, took a leisurely sip, put the glass back on the table and pronounced.'Aye. She's been meaning to get married for some time now.'

This was, I presumed, a Yes. At the same time, it was also bit of a put-down. The state of marriage was the prize. I was merely a passing participant who'd got lucky.

But it didn't matter. I was still alive because Jock hadn't killed me and I raised my glass of crème de bloody menthe to toast Jock and Barbara and the world and the trees and even the bloody turbot and - where was my future wife? Oh there she was, running up to me in slow motion for a big hug and then one for Jock and we all sat down and felt very happy and the world was just a lovely place and that was that.

Dad was surprised when I told him but he had the grace to offer congratulations. And the next day I was back in Cologne.

Chapter Nine:

The Golden Days

I am living in a millionaires' suburb in south Cologne. I have the best job in the world. My bosses are light years away from me. My life is in the hands of senior programme assistant, Robert Neil.

Robert is a kindly administrator who has learnt how to behave entirely from books. Everything he does is planned. It is he who gives me my 'pep' talk, which is not too many light years away from Baden-Powell's 'Scouting For Boys'. He is my moral tutor. I pay him back very badly.

My very first unaccompanied continuity shift came after only a couple of days on station. All I had to do was to turn up and voice announcements between programmes from 18:45 to23:30 hours military. My very first 'intro' would be to introduce 'The Archers' and the highlight of the evening would be my reading of the weather forecast, obtained by teleprinter from the met office, RAF Germany. Mum and Dad would be listening in Berlin.

Seems simple enough, doesn't it? But sadly fate, in its usual way, had contrived to upset my debut. The previous day I'd gone shopping in the NAAFI for the first time, bought a complete drinks tray full of all the main spirits and combos – scotch, gin, brandy, rum, vermouth, wines, beers, and mixers – and carried them back to take pride of place on the dresser in my little cell. I say 'cell' because the two windows in my room both had bars on them – a reminder that these houses were built directly after the war to house senior officers belonging to Control Commission Germany, the occupying power.

Documents from the immediate post-war days made it clear that CCG felt levels of rising hostility among the frustrated German population might lead to outbreaks of insurgency and, at the extreme end of the scale, of a mass uprising. That's why my little room had bars. Looking back, perhaps they were a bit dumb locating CCG Headquarters in Cologne, which the RAF had almost bombed into oblivion.Sadly, there was a more present and direct threat to me and it turned out to be the enemy within. I found myself on a rather gloomy Sunday, not having made any pals yet, sitting in my room with no company other than BFBS on the radio.

Maybe a drink or two in the afternoon might while away the time until I had to go to the station and speak to the nation. As long as I took it gently, no problem.

There's always a dilemma between what you think you can do and what you actually can do when it comes to the drink. In those days I thought I was immortal, and could drink my own bodyweight in booze before eventually succumbing to a smiling sleep. Eventually, I landed on a shibboleth that actually worked: if I drank up to three large Myers' and Cokes (standard bar doubles) I could still say the magic words, 'This is the British Forces Broadcasting Service, Germany'. If I had even a mouthful or two past the three-drink limit, it would start sounding like 'Thish ish the Britishsh Forshes Broadcashting Shervice', which, we were all agreed, was not fit for purpose.

Back in the room, a gentle Sunday afternoon music programme playing out on BFBS, a glass by my side, a racy novel, and plenty…of…time…

When I woke up, it was to the sound of the Archers theme. I was supposed to have introduced that programme. I had overslept. Not only that, I had overslept an *evening* shift. This must be a sacking offence. What to do? I've always hated waiting for the tumbrels. I literally ran the twenty minutes to the station and arrived panting to see the stern figure of Robert Neil, hands on hips, clearly wanting to have words.

Words I clearly deserved. He did not pull any punches. I was lower than the lowest thing on a scale of extremely low. I had let down myself, my family, my colleagues, my superiors and the whole service. I should be consigned to the fires of hell for having brought shame to this great organisation. I could expect no mercy. This was appalling. He certainly knew how to put his point across. I went into the persona of the martyred victim (if there was such a thing). I beat myself up in front of him. I was indeed lucky to bracket myself in the same line-up as pathetic scum.

My entrails should be removed via my nostrils and done up in a big scarlet bow around my throat. Rabid dogs should chew my legs at this foulest of transgressions. After all of this, I should feed myself into a giant mincing machine with my remains fed to a garden full of belching slugs.

This, anyway, was the general tone of the scenario being played out in front of the porter in the hallway of 61 Parkstrasse. Angry boss and apologetic recruit. Luckily, Robert could see the pain he had inflicted and suddenly his kindly side re-asserted itself. Of course, he had just happened to be on station in case I'd had any problems – so he was there anyway – but as he couldn't raise me (no phones in the 'Chummery', as our abode was known), he went ahead with the shift anyway.

He was sure I'd learnt my lesson and that I would never do it again. Luckily, his title was *Senior Presentation Assistant* so he had been given the official mandate to handle such matters at his level and therefore this would not be referred, on this occasion, to my nemesis, John Russell. However, he would call upon me to undertake extra continuity shifts as appropriate punishment.

Once Robert had checked that I was OK and had stopped gibbering, he took me upstairs to the studio, laid out the paperwork and left me to my own devices. Through the glass, Jürgen Bock and Dieter Gripp watched and smiled. They had seen young announcers demolished before. Pride comes before a fall. This one might be worth watching.

I started my first shift and somehow managed to get all the words out at the right time and in the right order. The big frisson of the evening was the longest announcement: the weather forecast. All through my life I'd listened to our radio at home and noted the form of words that I was now about to use: 'And now, here is the weather forecast for the remainder of tonight and tomorrow for North West Germany and Berlin.' The regional areas flew with practiced ease from my tongue: 'North Rhine Westphalia' and 'Schleswig Holstein'. I noticed a flicker of interest from the engineers in the Network Control Room (NCR). I hadn't paused at all at or during 'Schleswig Holstein' – now that *was* unusual for an Engländer!

At the end of the shift I went through to NCR to thank Juergen and Dieter for looking after me. I'd already said thanks to them on air and discovered that it was the first time ever that mere German staff had been mentioned by name on-air. They were more than friendly. They had to stay all night, monitoring the equipment, even though we were off-air. So they slept or, if they felt like it, 'broke bounds' and shimmied down the road to a late night bar or club. But tonight I had the unalloyed pleasure of their company. They appeared to warm to me as I spoke to them in German. They were a bit disconcerted by me using 'Du' instead of the more formal 'Sie' but they seemed to excuse this and it became something that was OK with them, as long as it was me saying it. (Just to give you some idea, there were one or two pairings of NCR engineers who had sat next to each other on shift for twenty years and still called each other 'Herr X' and 'Sie', instead of Christian name and 'Du'.)

Well, it was only a matter of moments before a bottle of schnapps was produced and some large measures poured. Before very long we were all in party mode and the laughter, fun, jokes and tall tales continued into the wee small hours. At the end, we vowed eternal friendship and I reeled my way back up to my little room on the Volkspark.

*****

That one encounter turned out to be my big break in Cologne. While my English colleagues were busy trying hard to get the German staff to co-operate with them, I found a lot of doors opening to my use of the

German language with an English attitude of informality and also to my mixing of the two languages into 'Jinglisch', which was to pay massive dividends later.

It wasn't too long after this incident that I was approached by Karl-Heinz Stieldorf, the station's German 'Mr Fixit'. In exchange for duty free fags and booze from the NAAFI, Herr Stieldorf would and could arrange most thing, including avoidance of parking tickets, overdrafts at the Commerzbank and very fair treatment by the local police. Karl, you see, also ran the BFBS Cologne bar and had caused it to be decreed that members of the Cologne police, by virtue of part of their job being to safeguard the lives and property of BFBS Germany, were entitled to associate membership of our duty free bar. This was so horribly against the rules that it was virtually a hanging offence but Herr Stieldorf and the rest of us thought, pragmatically, that as the nearest military unit who gave a damn were fifty miles away in Joint Headquarters Rheindahlen, then we could operate using local rules.

I immediately endeared myself to Herr Stieldorf by a). speaking to him in German, b). assuring him of my co-operation in the future for his hobby of collecting duty-free goods and c). nicknaming him – to his face – 'Graf' ('Count') in honour of his position as the local Capo die Capi: the Godfather, Count Stieldorf. Not only that, I added a 'von' to give the new full title of 'Graf Karl von Stieldorf'. This enjoyed popular currency and Karl did lots of things for me and the memsahib over the years as the result of this 'ennoblement'.

So, as part of my cold war warrior training I was now in the business of getting the entire German staff on my side. I took another lesson from Peter Buckle, my old boss in Singapore. He was always very nice to the very low paid staff and would take time out to ask the Chinese toilet cleaner about his family and how the children were doing at school, and at Chinese New Year would always give him a lucky red envelope containing a brand new banknote. I let it be known that Walter Schaaf, our driver, was a friend of mine, as well as Karl, most of the NCR engineers and a number of the porters, especially David Richie, and Gilbert Dennis, who doubled as BFBS's very own and very fine carpenter. Apart from continuity shifts, my first few months were spent filling in for colleagues when they went on leave. This was great fun; I loved limited runs, rather than doing shows forever. Simply put, I could use all my energy in a short-term push, rather than limping along at half cock for months at a time. Another reason I never became an actor. Our top DJ at the time was a real pocket firebomb named Richard Astbury, generally known as 'Asters' - or, in his parlance,'Aaaasters'. He had a pleasantly cheeky and semi-aristocratic Dimbleby accent, with a huge laugh in the voice itself, which made for very engaging listening, especially if you were a lonely 17-year-old Glaswegian child-bride with one up the spout living in an old block of flats in the wilds of a former Nazi garrison town on the North German plains while hubby was away doing an Op Banner tour of Northern

Ireland. Asters kept up morale with his cheeky banter, lots of it in the 'nudge nudge wink wink 'style, which even went down well with the husbands. Asters was a massive draw for garrison or station open days and BFBS outside broadcasts from wives' clubs and, with his actor's background, his style, slickness and professionalism, he was secretly admired by all of us younger broadcasters. I got to stand in for him once or twice and it always seemed to be both a delight and a huge responsibility.

Standing in for someone meant following very strict rules: you did not use the occasion to 'big yourself up' by introducing new ideas that you thought might work and you followed the main talent's schedule, fixed points and type of music (in the early 70s, before the days of strict play lists, music on the radio was still partly a personal choice, as long as it was generally top forty and golden oldies). Listeners expected continuity, not revolution. I did manage to slide in a bit of me but I think I got away with it, as nobody on station seemed to notice.

John Russell finally left to go to Cyprus and we were delighted when 32-year-old John Hedges, who had shoulder-length hair and wore a purple (!) velvet jacket, became Senior Programme Organiser. I was chuffed to buttons as, unlike the martinet Russell attitude, John was very much the creative brain, as well as the owner of a voice which was to become very known on BBC Radio Four until his recent untimely death. What I soon picked up on was that he hated being in charge of other people. He also hated 'admin' and therefore he was on my wavelength. Especially as he also didn't speak to colleagues according to their civil service grade. As a result, to me, and later to others on station, he was rechristened 'Smilin' John Hedges', as every time he had to do something official he put on what he thought was a 'serious' look.

John knew enough about human nature, and indeed broadcasting, to realise that young McD could do with a challenge. At this time, he had a bit of a gift to offer. He had been doing a 'Saturday Show', which was not at all like Stevie Withers' Saturday Show in Singapore, with its teenage crowd and spirit of fun, fluff, and flummery. No, John's Saturday Show was a showcase of progressive rock – those massive gobbets of impenetrable chord sequences and esoteric lyrics that had to be listened to in a dark room with an expression of sheer misery on the face. Nearly all of the music sounded the same and meandered through the airwaves with a shuddering lack of impetus that made us lesser mortals think of razor blades and wrists. Apparently, not to like this music was a sign of immaturity.

One day John Hedges handed me the Saturday Show. As boss, he couldn't be doing with presenting rock music on air. It would be bad for his image. I know he didn't actually believe that and that he was sending himself up, but I went along with it anyway because a). he *was* my boss and b). I really wanted my own show.

He gave me three weeks to prepare. I sat down and worked out a plan - one of my best ever, as it happened. What was needed was a fun show, with both Forces and civilian, English and German, invited audiences. It needed a really punchy delivery and little bursts of sound between tunes – jingles, stings, drop-ins – and surprises using spot effects and echo chambers. It needed customised and tailored fixed spot indicators – the audience needed to know every time and for all time what show they were listening to. Finally it did *not* need the turge and dirge of prog rock; it needed the contents of a squaddie bar's jukebox full of much-purchased tunes, which tended to be easy hummable bubblegum showcases of instant musical talent that gripped you straight away.

All this went into the melting pot, along with some other novelties. Out went 'Peter McDonagh, the announcer' and in came 'PMcD, the rapid-fire jock', at least as far as 'on-air' was concerned. My armoury was increased by a huge number of self-cueing broadcast cartridges, varied in length to accommodate all the jingles, stings and drop-ins we made. At the start of the first show, I had 150, and we made a further ten or so each week. Recording engineer Ralf Dickershoff felt some of the magic and, using my new fiancee's voice, we produced fifteen' I remember….1965/66/70 etc….I remember when' jingles using a little known track by a band called 'Trees'.

'Uncle' Ralf also helped me with an opening sequence. It needed to grab the audience firmly by the gonads and provide a great 'bed' for voicing over the menu. What we chose in the end was the opening of 'Under My Wheels' by Alice Cooper and an explosion FX into 'A Touch of Velvet, a Sting of Brass', all of which transferred on to one cartridge.

The time was nearly right. We were ready for lift off. But there was to be a problem. A clash of cultures. There was a complaint from my chums in NCR. *They* were responsible for monitoring levels during transmission. Already, with self-operational (self-op) studios, where the DJs played in their own records, the NCR role had been diminished. Now, the Plessey CT 80 broadcast cartridge player was the subject of their attack. Not only was it technically inferior (i.e. not of German manufacture, like the rest of the kit), but it was located with the DJ in the studio, not in NCR. This went to the Works Council, under the control of Graf von Stieldorf. The scene was set for a bloody battle. I sat on the sidelines, waiting to discover what the result would be. When it came, I think the whole station was surprised.

The case had been made that the placing and operation of the CT80 was a natural progression, and was required because lightning-fast button presses were needed to bring up the sound on cue – only the DJ could know which actual instant to press the button.

This turned out to be part of the reason for acceptance. I think some of it was also to do with the fact that it was me. I was slightly mad but I spoke German and treated the staff with friendly respect. I nearly blew it when Jürgen Bock told me, much later, that I was lucky the Works Council had agreed that this 'Schrottkasten' ('trash-box') could be placed in the studio. I said (in jest) that it had happened because I was an important 'programme officer'.

From that moment on, if Jürgen was ever annoyed with me, he would insult me by repeating the title in a really sarcastic way: 'You…you…programme officer, you!' As he was married to a Yorkshire lass, he had an incredible English and German accent that really suited his very bulky frame. It was much better having him inside the tent pissing out.

The day came for the big opening. I put a crate of Kölsch and a crate of coke in the studio. Uncle Bill had been briefed to make the appropriate continuity announcement. I had even written down the words he might use. After the station credit, he was to say: 'And now, a brand new exciting pop extravaganza – ' The Great North Rhine West Phailure.' Yes, that was the title, as it appeared in our weekly programme guide.

Bill looked at it before returning to the studio on the other side of the Network Control Room. He was clearly not impressed. He hated pop music of any kind. I remember one exchange I had with him.

'But it's *art*, Bill!' I nearly shouted at him.

'Yes,' he said. And paused. 'With a capital F.'

The moment came. The preceding programme finished and Bill intoned the closing credits in his 'patrician' voice, which made Brian Sewell sound common.

'You're in tune with programmes coming to you from BFBS Cologne,' the great man uttered. 'And it is with a heavy heart that I have to tell you that for the next two hours you are about to be subjected to a miscellany of allegedly popular music entitled 'The Great North Rhine West Phailure'. Normal service will resume in two hours' time.'

I couldn't have asked for any better introduction. I stabbed the cart machine button and the opening blasts defiled the airwaves. No time to be nervous – up went the microphone fader and out came McD welcoming the world and his brother to the hottest thing in town, yes indeedeee, and other DJ clichés, as we graunched into our opener, 'Run Run Run' by Jo Jo Gunne (still on demo acetate; it had yet to be released to the market).

People appeared in the studio, we all drank lots of beer and coke and, apart from one German teenager accidentally sitting on a turntable while the disc was playing, I thought we got away with it. Whatever 'it' was. I had acquired a toy dog, Hieronymous, at whom I chatted; I spoke to the kids in the studio and asked them what records they wanted; I then rushed down to the record library to see if I could find the track and ran back upstairs and got it on the deck before the previous one finished. It was a huge high and I felt it was working.

At the end, the small crowd of about twelve, nearly all German teenagers, drifted off and I looked through the NCR glass. Jürgen and Dieter were grinning – well, I'd given them name checks, and rather 'bigged up' their parts. This was working.

After a few weeks it seemed clear that we had a hit on our hands. The German staff in particular were pleased that the show was getting loads of coverage in the local press and all kinds of German and UK stars were being offered in the form of pre-release discs and interviews. I felt we needed a bit more comedy. Now, at the time BFBS used to run an extremely tired and tiresome German language series, as part of its mission to 'educate' as well as entertain and inform. It was called 'German for Beginners' and took the form of a series of robotic sterile non-conversations that were the really old fashioned way to ensure that Brits never learnt a foreign language. It was lobotomy on tape. All enunciations were painfully pedantic, prosaic and slow; animation, liveliness and expression appeared to be forbidden, and at the end of each episode you thought that 'Waiting for Godot' would be a barrel of laughs if played next to this turgid crap.

So Dieter Gripp provided the vehicle for our major spoof on this nonsense. We called it 'English for Beginners' and it lasted for about five episodes. The idea was that 'English Speaking Dieter Gripp' would be involved in a series of events that he would describe in English derived from the component parts of German words. So, 'Zuhörer' (listener) became literally 'to-listener'; 'fernseher' (television) became 'far-seer' and idioms such as 'im eimer' (broken down) now became 'in the bucket'. Our first episode started thus:

Anally retentive Pecksniffian English announcer (think OU, 1970s): 'We present episode one of 'English for Beginners'. Today, English Speaking Dieter Gripp has a problem. What is the matter, Dieter?'

'Oh, hello already Peter. I have a problem. My far-seeing picture umbrella is in the bucket already.'

'Dieter is telling us that his TV screen is on the blink. So what are you going to do about it, Dieter?'

And so on. Each week we constructed little scenarios that made the most of the German language and its little foibles. It seemed to be a talking point.

Until one day, Smilin' John Hedges asked to see me. He was all for the creative content of the GNRWP and, in an ideal world, he wouldn't dream of interfering, but...

'But what?' I asked him directly.

He shrugged and, for once, was a little embarrassed. 'It's out of my hands,' he said. 'The station controller wants to see you. There's been a complaint from the British Embassy.'

Rather like my first night on station, I appeared to have dropped myself right in it again. The station controller's office, a luxurious and large executive suite with its own cloakroom, was next to Smilin' John's poster-clad office. I presented myself to the controller's PA, Frau Vogt, who gave me the thinnest and iciest of smiles. She always enjoyed it when one of those gobby Brit show-offs got themselves into trouble. I gave her the withering look of a French nobleman meeting the gaze of one of the tricoteuses as he stepped in silken shoes from the steps of the tumbrel to keep his date with Madame Guillotine. Those who were about to die...

The station controller, John Parsons, was a sharply dressed senior civil servant, exuding gravitas and a no-nonsense attitude. He waved me to a seat and proceeded to screw a king-size cigarette into a cigarette holder. He reached for a hand-grenade sized Ronson lighter from the glass coffee table between us and lit up. He surveyed me calmly for several seconds, peering at me through tortoiseshell and gold 'executive' glasses, before exhaling and sitting back in his comfortable armchair.

'Now, Peter,' he began, in a very quiet and calm voice. I knew about quiet and calm voices. They tended to be a lot more frightening and wounding than loud bellows. 'This business with your Saturday Show. He looked at a note, and then at me. 'The Great North Rhine West Phailure'. He milked it so it sounded a bit common. 'I don't actually mind the idea of using the voices of our German staff on air. It would do us all a lot of good to be seen to be working together. The   days of non-fraternisation are long since gone. Or at least...' – he caught my faint look of surprise – '...they should be. So, that in itself is not a problem.'

'What *is* a problem...' - he inhaled, paused, and sent out a thin blue-grey column of disapproving smoke, almost like the Caterpillar in 'Alice in Wonderland' (stop grinning, McD) - '...is that the British Embassy has been listening to your send-up of the 'German for Beginners' series and they are not happy. Not happy at all.'

I could see he hadn't finished, so I contented myself with trying to make my face look solemn, instead of just falling about laughing.

'This could be very serious. If talks take place between the Embassy and the Joint Headquarters, this problem might even reach the Adjutant General's desk.' I didn't know this then, but the Adjutant General was really the Supreme Boss of BFBS – a combination of financier, editor in chief and hangman. Even Ian Woolf, the Director, was known to be wary of this colossus. 'I'm afraid you're going to have to stop these 'English for Beginners' snippets. Immediately. Do you understand?'

Oh, I did. Not for nothing was I a state registered coward as well as a Cold War warrior (self-appointed). I made to speak and, as I did so, Mr Parsons used an old interrogator's trick on me. As I made my first noise of reply, he carried on.

'You see, Peter, it might be possible to broadcast totally without restriction in the UK, but over here we have all kinds of responsibilities and...' He went on for the next few minutes. This was the lecture and he took me down the highways and byways of the legal, political and social dimensions of a peace-keeping power as guests of a sovereign country. He was very good but I was, bluntly, waiting for my P45, and orders to return to the UK.

He had reached the end. This time he *had* reached the end. I looked at him across the table. I didn't say a word. Finally, he sighed a tiny sigh of exasperation. 'Well, do you have anything to say?'

'I'm sorry Mr Parsons. I thought you hadn't quite finished. Like last time, when I nearly interrupted you.'

I think he understood that I had sussed his little power game and he wouldn't really be able to use it any more. But I was actually sorry, because now he was going to tell me to pack up and disappear.

'Well, Peter,' he smiled icily. I think we understand each other. No more 'English for Beginners'. I could do without the Embassy on my back.'

I almost panted with relief, like a spaniel spared the riding crop from the hands of the drunken squire. 'Are you going to let me carry on with the Saturday Show?'

'Of course,' he said. 'It seems to be going very well and my daughter seems to like it.'

I didn't know it then but he already had me earmarked for promotion, though it would take until 1974 for that to happen.

I gave Frau Vogt both barrels of the cheesiest grin I could muster as I left the execution chamber and scuttled in to Smilin' John's office to let him know the good news. Of course, I should have realised that John put up a hell of a case to let me and the Dieter Gripp material continue anyway but he couldn't tell me that then and I was happy enough that the show would go on.

Then, as the programme skies cleared, dark clouds began to form on the admin front...

Chapter Ten:

The Home Front

Life back at base had been interesting. Tanya had joined me in Cologne, where she was introduced to one and all by my pet name for her, 'Moo', which actually was a tongue-in-cheek version of 'Silly Moo', much used as a catchphrase by Alf Garnett in the TV show, 'Till Death Us Do Part'. We certainly got tongues wagging in the Volkspark: she already pregnant and we were still single. Even as late as the early seventies, this was not good. Added to which, I was only 22 and she was a mere slip of a girl at 18.

And then there was the business of how she arrived in Cologne. I went to meet her at the city's main railway station. She carried all her worldly goods in one suitcase. She was also wearing a dog collar around her neck. I had a dog lead. When we met, we hugged and then I clipped her on. This caused much eyebrow raising from the Cologne citizenry, but what the hell… We were young and laughter was pretty high on the agenda.

We set up home in the Volkspark in my one room at the chummery. (We did have access to a kitchen, a communal lounge and dining room.) There were three other residents of this strange arrangement. The first was Mavis, known as 'Socks' because she wore yellow ones all the time, which did nothing for her scrawny bird-like legs. Mavis worked for the NAAFI and was 'having a thing' with the portly late-middle-aged manager. Then there was Dawn, a junior civil servant, who was loosely connected to a wide boy by the name of Mick, who was the Volkspark's 'Mr Fixit'. He had served a spell in prison, which to us made him a bit exotic. Then there was Welsh Annie, a primary school teacher. She didn't know it at the time, but she was about to meet the love of her life.

What needs to be understood is that all three 'official' residents were in effect 'living in' with their partners, even though this was officially verboten. We figured sauce for the goose and

thought not very much about it. We got into an instant and pleasant routine, which in the early days had a lot to do with bacon sandwiches, as Moo wasn't heavily into cooking.

Then, one morning, early on, my little world came crashing down. I was summoned to see the BFBS admin officer, Bill Moules. (Remember, I was so wet behind the ears – I was actually this man's equal in rank.)

'Now then, Peter, what's this I hear about you living with a young lady in No.1 Eckdorferstrasse?'

He came right out with it. Across the way, the little piggy-eyed admin assistant, Archie Hendry, watched the unrolling theatre with a nasty little, 'Ooooh, he's for it,' expression on his florid Pictish face.

'My fiancée and I are certainly in No.1,' I confirmed.

"But you *can't* live together there. It's officially single accommodation.'

'Well, you try telling that to the other residents. They all have their other halves sleeping over on a regular basis.'

'That's as maybe. But BFBS will not tolerate this situation. She will have to move out.'

'But we're getting married very soon.'

'That's not going to be helpful. We have no entitled married quarters on the patch.'

'In that case, I'll pitch a tent on the banks of the Rhine and write to Ian Woolf, the Director, to tell him what's going on.' (This was breaking every rule in the MOD procedural handbook.)

I left, seething. Nobody was going to tell me whether or not I could get married. In great haste, we assembled what seemed to be our own weight in forms, translations, permits and consular letters, which would allow us to be married in the Cologne Registry Office. We rushed down to see the officials and to organise a date.

We sat in a long, airy corridor, opposite a pair of tall oak doors, smelt the lovely aroma of lavender wax floor polish and waited to be seen.

And waited. And waited. And I don't like waiting. A few excursions up and down the corridor. Moo was trying to keep me from losing it.

Finally, I did the only thing I could. Both of us stood up. I knocked politely (how can you tell?) on the giant door and swung it open. A less than pleasant sight met my eyes.

In the middle of the room, as if on a separate planet, was the largest desk I had seen in my life. Behind it sat what appeared to be a cockroach. On closer peering this turned out to be the facsimile of a woman. It was definitely Rosa Klebb. I peeked under the desk to see if she was wearing her knife-pointed black shoes. A pair of steel-grey eyes, framed by an Iron Cross black bun of stiff hair welded into place, glared at me with venom, contempt and implied superiority.

'There is a waiting room outside!' she barked.

Suddenly, we had changed our minds. If this was the office that opened the doors of wedded bliss, its guardian at the gate was no good advertisement or incentive. I had, so far, been calm but the Irish blood began to stir. Very quickly, I marched forward two paces, clicked my heels and raised my right arm – no, across the chest, in a *Roman* salute. Even a jobsworth is above that most obscene of gestures.

'Zum Befehl!' ('At your service!') I barked, as I clicked my heels again, spun around, and left before she could summon the secret police. We were soon outside, blending in with a crowd, and she didn't know who we were anyway.

The bad news was that obviously a quick registry office German wedding was now out of the question. Within minutes, my lightning brain, force-fed on adrenaline and rum, came up with a brilliant solution.

'Let's get married in Oxford!'

*****

This required some nifty organisation. I took some annual leave. We phoned our folks, told them we *were* married and that cash would do for a wedding present. Graf Stieldorf arranged with the Commerzbank for us to stretch the account for a few weeks to buy two BEA tickets from Cologne to Heathrow. After much juggling, we flew to the UK and found ourselves that same evening at the Cotswold Lodge hotel on the Banbury Road in Oxford, just down the way from where I used to live at Park Town.

The rules those days appeared to be that you had to spend a week in the UK and then, as long as you could produce two witnesses and turn up relatively sober on the day, you could get married.

On the second day, we popped in to the Radcliffe Infirmary and there it was confirmed that Moo was pregnant. This was on the cusp of being good news, as we tried to reassure the rather confused doctor.

We used the Turf Tavern as our campaign headquarters. Wally Else, the flamboyant and booze-filled landlord, had put a manager, Robert, and his wife, Bernie, in charge of the place.

Robert was a recovering alkie and drank gallon upon gallon of unfermented ginger beer. They agreed we could have our very short reception there after the ceremony. The reason it was going to be short was that we had to be at Heathrow later that same afternoon to catch our flight back to Cologne. We also trapped our two renegade and illegal immigrant South Africans, Frank and Rolf, to be our witnesses on the morning of 18th March 1972. The morning of the event saw us at breakfast in George's Café in Oxford's atmospheric covered market, after which we strolled up to the registry office. We were met by the twinkling Dickensian

figure of a gentleman whom we found out later resplended in the name of Islay Erskine Farquhar and, in a minimum of time and fuss, we received the magic ticket – we were married.

Straight back down to the Turf, where Robert and Bernie had put on a very nice spread. We had a very pleasant light lunch and, all too soon, it was time to climb into Bernie's car and hit the road for Heathrow. We had a breakdown along the way but a Good Samaritan fixed us up while I sat in the back and gibbered. Soon we were on the big silver bird, heading back to Cologne as man and wife. Whom Oxford had joined let no administrative officer put asunder.

When we got back to Cologne, we were dog-tired. So, on the first night of our honeymoon, Moo turned in for an early night and I slipped out for a nightcap or two at the 'Out on a Limb Club' behind the NAAFI.

There was only the barman there, and one of the BFBS engineers, Paddy Hegarty, who also quite enjoyed his pop. I ordered up my usual and sat next to Paddy.

'Good day?' he broke the ice.

'Yeah,' I said, in what could only be described as a bit of a flat and tired voice. 'Got married today, in Oxford. Just got back.'

Paddy swung round as the force of this news hit him four square. In the Volkspark world, this was Page One material. 'You got *married*?'

'Yeah. Nice reception, too.'

'But… but… where… Where's Moo? It *was* Moo, wasn't it?'

'Yeah, course it was Moo. She's back home, having a kip.' Paddy shook his head. This one was definitely barking mad. He bought me a drink, then I bought him one back, then we started again. Dear old pals. Eventually the barman threw us out and I went home to start our version of married bliss.

The next Monday I was back at work. I had a date with destiny. I walked into Bill Moules office. I gave him both barrels.

'I'm not supposed to live with Moo at Number 1. Because it's only for singlies, right?'

'That is correct.'

I played my ace. I took my brand new, very legal, signed by Islay Erskine Farquhar wedding certificate, out of my jacket pocket, carefully unfolded it and placed it on his desk.

'There,' I said, with a perhaps unnecessary flourish.

Bill peered at it. It was clearly bona fide. I could see his mind racing through the whole of MOD Manual 13 and its interminable regulations. Finally, his ability to find disaster in triumph came to the surface.

'Right,' he said, rather too dangerously. You're no longer single. You'll have to move out of Number 1. It's 'only for singles' (I joined in with the end of that one).

'And where am I going to live?'

'You should have thought of that before you went off and got married.'

Now I had him in check. "Where in MOD Manual 13 does it say that a civil servant may not marry during his appointment?'

'Well, it doesn't, of course. But there aren't any married quarters vacant in the Volkspark. We can't accommodate you.' 'There *are* some empty quarters on the Park. Why can't I live in one of them?'

'Because the two you're thinking of are above your grade. You're not entitled.'

'Either you fix me up with somewhere to live or I phone Ian Woolf directly and tell him I need to be posted out because the admin officer can't find me somewhere for me and my heavily pregnant wife to lay our heads.' A little bit of protective poetic licence was in order.

Checkmate. Even the plodding Moules could see the effect of him failing to find accommodation for a married and pregnant slip of a girl. He muttered darkly about getting in touch with the SSO (Station Staff Officer) in Düsseldorf and that I should come back that afternoon.

The SSO in Düsseldorf was always a choleric RO (Retired Officer), usually of Lieutenant Colonel status, whose job it was to be objectionable to as many people as possible for as long as possible. He in turn referred the matter to his henchman in Cologne, a terminally obtuse warrant officer, who was there that afternoon in Moules' office when I pitched up to hear my fate.

It would be fair to say that he shared Bill's belief that I was immoral in marrying 'for form's sake' and typically pushy, like all those radio weirdos who got in the way of them doing their peaceful admin. I was given a lecture about entitlement, breaking rules, pushing boundaries and sheer cheek in pre-empting the usual channels. The outcome was that I should meet WO Brewer outside the door of No 8 Pingsdorfer Strasse the following morning.

We duly met. It was a spring morning. I noticed the previous tenant's autumn leaves still covered the driveway of this magnificent colonel's married quarter, as we waited for Eddie to pitch up. He arrived in some level of dudgeon and gripe, clutching a clipboard and muttering darkly.

Before we went in, he gave an oration. 'You do understand that you are *not* occupying this quarter on a regular entitled basis,' he puffed. 'As this MQ is above your entitlement, you will be

occupying it on a *caretaker* basis.' There, that was putting me in my place. I would only be a caretaker. Wait one… What about…? I decided to go for it.

'Can we get this right? When we are living in this place, we'll be responsible for its upkeep, contents and good repair?'

'That's right.'

'And if we break or damage anything, we'll be liable to pay replacement costs?'

'Correct.'

'In that case, we'll be in exactly the same situation as anyone who IS entitled and occupying this house. OK, we accept, as long as you get the labourers round to clear last year's leaves. I refuse to take responsibility for them.'

The Warrant Officer was livid, but even though we could almost hear the whirrings in what passed for his brain, he had no comeback. The only sanction existed in his own interpretation of us living there. And I didn't mind him calling us 'caretakers' or 'unentitled', as long as we had the roof over our heads. We even got him to go down into the cellar to 'show' us how the big Teutonic beast of a boiler worked. Minutes after he'd left, in the highest of dudgeons, the boiler went out. For the two months we were there, it was never relit. We boiled water in saucepans. Baths were fun.

*****

Amidst a lot of laughter, we got on with the business of living together. We decided to hold a dinner party for another couple one evening, and what started out as a whole roast duck a l'orange became four demi-tasses of duck a l'orange soup. Bit by bit we learnt. Bit by bit the cuisine blossomed and soon it was time for baby number one – the baby conceived in the BFBS Berlin studio. The nearest military hospital was fifty miles of bad road away at RAF Wegberg, just outside JHQ Rheindahlen. Somehow all the right people got to the right places and little Tabitha was born. I had now been adopted in the role of utterly useless father. My first and sadly enduring reaction was, 'as soon as they can hold an intelligent conversation, I'll be able to do something useful'. I was bloody awful: no feeds, changing, or even anything north of grinning proudly, as if I'd put a lot of work in. Still, Moo was brilliant and it all seemed to work. Little Tabitha was doing the things that babies are supposed to do. Job done.

Until the day we went up country to open a Garden Fete at HQ 1 (Br) Corps. We were fêted as guests of honour and ended up sitting down for a lunch with no fewer than three brigadiers. Sadly, I could only understand 'junior officer' and wasn't used to these charmers being very nice about a radio station they thought was common, awful, below the salt, did nothing useful and then had the nerve to employ men who shouted during the gaps between pieces of jungle music played by long-haired morons. All in all, it was an educational day.

Back in Cologne, Asters and his then wife Jenny, who'd been looking after Tabitha while we were up country, gave us the bad news. Tabitha had been taken ill and she'd been rushed to RAF Wegberg. Hearts in mouth, we accepted a lift and a couple of hours later were camped out in the hospital, where we were to stay for the next three days.

Tabitha was in intensive care, in an incubator. Her chances were slim. During the remainder of her all too short life, the doctors couldn't pinpoint what was wrong. Given our youth, there were even doubts in the air about our competence as parents. Justified in my case, but Moo was a more than competent and caring mother. In the end I called for a priest. He was so good. We both said

goodbye, putting our hands through the side of the incubator in turn to touch the little hand. Soon, the breathing stopped. Tabitha had gone.

There is a silence that screams. There is a pit where time stands still. There is a feeling of nothingness. There is a hole in the soul. Then there are the blessings of tears, of memories, of the fabric of youth already beginning to repair the tapestry of tragedy. The death certificate stated baldly: 'absence of right pulmonary artery'. There was absolutely nothing to be done and nobody was to blame. Three of us had made a journey to Wegberg; two of us would return.

Luckily, Walter Schaaf, our pet driver, had come to pick us up. He hit the mood perfectly. He was less abrasive than usual, but kept up some light banter till we came to a friendly pub down the road. There, he sat us down and bought us beer till we felt a bit better. Then, he gave us what could only be called the pep talk from hell, very much along the lines of 'get back home and get started on the next one. It'll do you good. Life goes on.' Had it have been anybody else, I think I might have punched his lights out. But Walter was excused boots when it came to helping out in his own clumsy, rough and ready way.

A few days later came the ordeal of the funeral. I was surprised when the station controller's rather plush staff car, plus his driver, pulled up outside our quarter. John Parsons had quietly sent his car for our extra comfort. We drove to the chapel and cemetery at Rheindahlen, where I had the solemn and terrible duty of carrying my own daughter, in her tiny white coffin, to her far too premature grave. Many people were very kind that day and, all these years later, it is that which stands out the most in our memories.

*****

But, as the old record goes, life goes on, and so did we. Almost within weeks Mini Mac Part Two was on the production line. We kept our fingers crossed but the feeling was that the dark angel had tapped once, and that this time all would be well. Antenatal classes in those days consisted of Mum not drinking too much, so all was well. August 1973 was quite warm and I remember sleeping fitfully after a late party, with

Moo stirring uncomfortably next to me. At this time I swear she was at least fourteen months pregnant.

At about half-past four in the morning, I awoke to feel what must have been a major contraction. In my fuddled mind, I was having a baby. Not so. The Moo was hissing in my ears, 'Wake up. Come on, wake up, *now!*'

'Eeeuuurrghh – fahk ryin' owt loud – wha' wha' woz goin'on?' came noises from the mighty hunter, head buried under a pillow.

'I'm getting pains. I'm going to have the baby.'

I suggested Moo might like to go back to sleep, we could talk about it in the morning, and received a vicious kick. I was suddenly awake.

I put a few random clothes on, leapt out of the door, and ran down the road to where Asters lived. He'd said, after Tabitha's funeral, that if we ever needed any help, we could call on him.

And so, at about a quarter-to-five, just after dawn on a Cologne summer's day, I was hammering on his door, yelling noises about babies, cars, lifts and general urgency. A window upstairs opened and my benefactor-to-be surveyed the hungover fool below.

Eventually, he not only translated my jabberwocky, but dressed in record time, scooped up the Moo, and all three of us hurtled along the 'B' roads to Wegberg. Moo was contracting every nanosecond by the time we reached the hospital entrance. I rushed inside for help and in seconds a couple of RAF medical orderlies were on hand to turn the drama into a managed exercise. I stood with Asters on the entrance steps.

'Do you want me to stay?' asked Asters. I could have done with the company, but he had things to do and his own family to do them with. Anyway, now the panic was over, it could be hours before we reached the dropping zone.

'No, you go on back to Cologne.' I gave him a hug. 'And thanks for everything. Don't know what I would have done without you.' He drove off and I went inside. The receptionist pointed out the corridor to the maternity wing and off I trotted. This time I was going to be OK. Even the early morning hangover had disappeared.

One moment I was walking down the corridor. Next moment a starchy, white covered hand at the end of a sleeve pulled me in through an open doorway. It was a staff nurse and she was on a mission.

The mission was Moo, lying on her back on a narrow examination couch. There was no time for introductions. 'Hold her head!' ordered Starch and proceeded to make herself useful down around Moo's engine room. In the space of two minutes, there was a red streak, a 'wah', a well-fielded brand new baby and, within five minutes, a cleaned up package contained a guaranteed twelve cylinder female infant who actually didn't look like Winston Churchill.

Something of a record. A few minutes after that, the baby was in a cot, with a lovely yellow crocheted bed-spread catching the sunlight pouring through the tall side ward window, with one very happy and sleepy Mum and a Dad who was trying to put his finger on something we'd both forgotten to do in time.

We hadn't thought of a name. I guess it was because after what had happened we didn't want to tempt providence by thinking of names in advance. And so it came to pass that an ad hoc meeting of the naming baby committee was held and, that after some false starts, the name of 'Amanda' was chosen for the little angel.

Much celebration ensued. This included a wonderful cabaret when a mate of ours, Errol, a very imposing black serviceman and singer in a band, turned up solo to greet the new arrival with a bunch of flowers. This caused all kinds of frissons with the other squaddies' wives in the main maternity ward, where Moo was recuperating in the traditional Forces' way of old, with compulsory bottles of Guinness 'to keep up iron levels'. I wondered why I got funny looks next time I visited. Eventually, Moo's ticket to ride expired and we set off for Cologne and some more good times.

The next one could have been a complete disaster. Towards the end of the Cologne tour, Moo was pregnant again. This time around, we were old hands. We knew when the baby was due and, because of previous history, Moo was invited to the maternity ward in good time for a pre-flight rest and check-up.

At that time I was heavily into the folk scene and a good blues singer buddy by the name of John Kirkbride had become a pal, as well as a contributor to my then daily lunch show, 'McDonagh's Midday Mag', where, amongst other things, he delighted us with the persona of 'Deaf Orange Jefferson', a really bad bluesman who had released his only single forty years ago and preferred fishing to playing music. John also started appearing on the folk and blues circuit, both Forces and German, and was beginning to make a name for himself, including a single on EMI Electrola, the prestigious German record label.

Very luckily for us, John was staying at our place. (After the Pingsdorfer mansion, we'd finally been given a more suitable flat on the ground floor of Eckdorfer Strasse 7, a few doors round from our first illegal room.) One evening we were busy playing music, knocking back the beer and generally singing our hearts out, when our chum from over the road, Terry James, ran over to tell us that the hospital had been on and would I like to come over and have a word.

For some reason I was dressed in a bath towel and although it was January 8th and there was a heavy fall of snow on the ground, I dashed over barefoot to receive instructions. They were, very simply: 'Drag your sorry arse up to Wegberg. Baby is on its way.'

I went back and explained things to John. There was no public transport. I couldn't really knock anybody up (if you'll forgive the phrase) at this time of night. Road conditions were terrible. Nobody in their right mind would drive 50 miles of country roads in this.

And there, of course, was the answer. 'Nobody in their right mind.' John Kirkbride shtepped up to the plate. 'I'll take you,' he slurred gently. 'We'll take the microbush. It can't be that hard to find. Wegbird, you shed? Get shome clothesh on and we'll shet out.'

It didn't occur to me that Kirkbride was three sheets to the wind, that my map reading and navigational skills were nil, that we didn't have a map anyway or that the rusty old psychedelically-painted VW Camper Wagon was a sitting target for the local police. We set out and were soon bouncing down obscure country roads, stopping to peer at road signs.

We knew we were getting it vaguely right when we crossed the border into Holland. Luckily, it was hardly a formality – we were waved through – but we needed to get back out of the Netherlands and find out where our goal was. We stopped at a café and were given a hand-drawn 'map for idiots', which meant that, back in Germany, we soon found our target. We rushed inside. We were unkempt, still fairly ratted - John in particular, with his shoulder length ginger hair, full beard and hippie clothes, not looking like the kind of upright chap usually found in military hospitals.

We managed to blag it through reception and soon found ourselves in the maternity wing's waiting room. For some reason – relief perhaps, that we had survived the long drive in a blizzard, taking in two countries – we were giggling as only two drunk people who've escaped disaster can ever do.The laughter was interrupted by another starchy version of a staff nurse. She was obviously directly descended from Queen Boudicca and wore a very special frown and a single eyebrow drawn with a ruler on the upper part of her face, with a thin horizontal gash of a mouth built only to express disapproval.

She took in the scene of two naughty giggling drunks and barked out a question: 'Which one of you is the father?' The tone of voice implied she thought neither of us either capable or desirable of fulfilling this function. I actually raised my hand, just like in school.

'M…m…me, nurse,' I volunteered.

'*Staff* Nurse!' she sniffed. 'McDonaghue, isn't it?' It was close enough. After a couple of further exchanges, it turned out that one reason for her annoyance was that she had just been going off shift when Baby McD had come into the world.

Baby McD. 'Er, is it a boy or a girl?' I finally managed to get out with some clarity. I was a father again. It had an instant sobering effect. Even Kirkbride started focusing.

'It's a boy.' said Starch Mark Two, softening a bit as the joy, awe and magic of the moment sunk in. 'Go and stand by that window over there.' There was a window looking directly into a darkened room, where a number of little cots with little people in were just about visible. Starch disappeared round the back, turned on a low light and scooped up a little bundle of joy wearing just a loose nappy. She held the little angel up to the light so that I might inspect my son and heir. He looked so wonderfully ugly and really stood out against the pure white of Staff's freshly put on walking-out uniform.

It didn't stay pure white for long. A bit miffed from being moved around, the new McD decided it was time for his very first dump and the loose nappy wasn't quite able to contain the explosion of dark green liquid with which he greeted the onset of his toilet training. Starch mark two looked even angrier, but cleaned the pair of them up and then took me to where a very tired Moo was recovering. It had been a long night but she seemed happy to see the remains of me. The boy was to be called Oliver, which was my mother's maiden name. John and I left the hospital and managed to find Cologne again without mishap. It had been a long night and we had been very lucky.

Our upstairs neighbour, senior engineer Tom 'Moosh' Couzens, was the first to be told. He took us upstairs and we wetted the baby's head. Tom was a wide boy of the first water – he had 'liberated' the giant medium wave transmitter from the Nazis in 1945 for use by BFN without any other formality apart from his say so and when the Forces' broadcast operation moved from Hamburg to Cologne in 1954, Tom actually built and ran a mink farm at the bottom of the extensive grounds of 61 Parkstrasse. He knew each and every member of the German engineering staff and they feared and worshipped him in equal measure, as he always stood up for their rights. And he'd taken a shine to me, because he saw that I treated the German staff with respect and friendship.

One day we were sitting in the station bar. Just the two of us. 'What this place needs is a good rumour to stir things up,' he suggested.

I was interested. If Tom started a rumour, it would be taken seriously. I noted the mischievous twinkle in his expression. 'What kind of rumour?' I said, not without some trepidation.

'Oh... well...' he pretended to think. He would have planned this down to the last detail. 'Got it.' An expression of triumph appeared. 'You for Senior Programme Organiser.'

I snorted. The idea of little me, so new to the game, taking over the stratospheric role of SPO would mean promotion by two grades overnight, plus the acquisition of so much broadcasting practice and theory. 'You're joking,' I smiled. 'They'd never go for that one.'

Tom narrowed his eyes. There was a bit of score settling behind this one. He didn't really like the kind of programme staff who called themselves professionals and who treated his German staff like shit. 'Oh, they'll believe it alright,' he said confidently. 'They're all a load of big girls' blouses at heart. You just watch.'

Tom started his rumour and the result was instantaneous. Suddenly, all the programme staff stopped talking to me. It was as if I'd been sent to Coventry. This went on far beyond my comfort zone and was into the second week before I went to Tom and told him he'd won, the rumour had worked, and now could he please lift the curse. He did, and normal service was resumed, though I did get funny looks from time to time.

In the meantime, Moo and I were parents of a girl and a boy and learning how the rest of life was going to work out. I was still pretty much obsessed with the job and hating some of the old-fashioned thinking that underpinned our efforts. Things were going to have to change...

Chapter Eleven –

Folk In The Round

'The Great North Rhine West Phailure' carried on for more than eighteen months before the programme took a rest. During its run, there were two major incidents – one sad, one happy.

The sad one concerned the 'man in the astrakhan collared coat' and his two charges. One Saturday, before the crowd arrived, I ran into the studio with a pile of on-air material – we had about ten minutes to go until airtime – to discover the towering form of a man in a charcoal coat with an astrakhan collar, accompanying two rather scared and white faced children, who looked at me with wide eyes. It didn't require a genius to see at once that this man was a bodyguard and that he was in charge of this little boy and little girl, who were, unusually, wearing what could only be described as 'Sunday best'.

"Can I help?" I asked him in German.

He looked at me to assess my danger level. That was never going to be a problem. 'Is it in order for the boy and the girl to stay and watch your programme in the studio?'

I smiled warmly and made sure they could see I was smiling at them. 'But of course,' I said, and even arranged seats in what was going to be a very crowded studio.

They watched, silently and a bit stiffly, as I went through the on-air cabaret and record spinning that was my stock in trade, complete with talkback nonsense over the speakers to NCR. It was manic, as usual, and some visiting squaddies and German kids added to the atmosphere. At the end of the show, the guests departed, leaving only the bodyguard and the boy and girl. Neither of them had said a word.

'Thank you, Herr McDonagh,' said the bodyguard. 'The children enjoyed their visit very much. They liked your show. They would now like to invite you to their house to join them in a Coca-Cola. I do hope you will be able to say "yes"'.

Normally, I wouldn't have bothered, made an excuse, leapt off as usual. But something made me say yes. I was intrigued by these two little Midwich cuckoos. I put away my discs and notes and followed the three of them down the drive.

'It is just across the road.' Lindenallee, the same road as ours. The bodyguard pointed to a tall, thick hedge set behind a ten-foot close mesh fence. As we got nearer, I could see a small discreet gate and a keypad on one of the doorposts. The bodyguard pressed the combination, obscuring the pad with his large frame. There was a buzz, the gate opened and we walked a short way through the two-metre thickness of this thorny hedge.

As we approached daylight on the other side, it was like a different world. A giant villa, set in manicured lawns, and even a small lake. We entered the house through a side door, into this palace of a place. I followed the others by taking off my shoes and we padded into what must have been a main reception room. In Germany, you get used to parquetry when it comes to well-heeled and polished wooden floors, but I had never seen a floor that was a giant essay in *marquetry*, with the pictorial tale of a great medieval battle raging in a host of woods beneath my feet.

Everything spoke class, money, untold riches - an Aladdin's Cave. I was astonished. The children seemed a bit concerned but I told them I'd never been in a house like this and was just amazed and surprised.

And I was. Despite its riches, its style, its class and its expense, it was completely dead. The children were very nearly dead. The zombie behaviour was from years of being locked behind a giant hedge, not being allowed out into the street without a bodyguard and from a life spent without the care and attention of normal parents. The bodyguard told me that the father was the chairman of an international insurance company and was nearly always away on business. The very much younger wife had a very active social life and, Herr McDonagh, you know how it is... I did, and shrugged sadly. After about half an hour, having got the boy and girl to smile and say a few words, I gave them some BFBS stickers and a ballpoint pen each and said my goodbyes.

Their worried little eyes as I left that awful mausoleum remains with me to this day.

About a year later, two incidents happened in Millionaires' Row in Marienburg. The owner of a private bank, who lived directly next door to my Saturday Show studio, committed suicide.

The chairman of an international insurance company was murdered by intruders at his home in Lindenallee.

Something stopped me from checking the address on Lindenallee. I really couldn't bear knowing.

*****

But the highlight of my time on the 'Great North Rhine West Phailure' came on a rather quiet day, with only a few people in the studio. I had a buzz on talkback from Dieter. 'Rory Gallagher's been listening to the show. He wants to know if he can stop by.'

This was *the* Rory Gallagher, rock star supreme, who was doing a solo circuit in Westphalia. I'd announced three of his concerts that week, playing the big ticket halls in and around Cologne. This hero of mine wanted to 'stop by'.

'Where is he, Dieter?' I asked, trying to sound vaguely in control.

'He's with David, down in reception.' I was out of the seat and rushing downstairs in a moment.

'Hi,' I attempted, over the heavy panting. 'How's it going?' 'Foin,' he said. (I won't attempt more of the Norn Iron accent than that.) We looked at each other and clearly saw that booze and fags figured strongly in each other's lives.

'Would a beer be OK?' I hinted. It was gone eleven o'clock. A smile reassured me I'd hit the nail on the head. We went upstairs and I introduced him to Dieter, who did no more than blurt out, 'Well, you vill for us a song be playing then already?' Actually, it was more of a statement than a question, even with Dieter's deliberately garbled English.

'If you like. I've got my stuff in the boot. "Home Town" OK for you guys?'

Rory Gallagher was only going to play a live version of his massive hit, 'Going To My Home Town', on his battered old fighting mandolin, right here on my 'Great North Rhine West Phailure.' I watched like it was a dream as he and Dieter set up the kit in recording studio 'A' and jacked it through to NCR.

'I've got a bit of a surprise for you right now,' I smugged over the airwaves. 'And I can tell you he's live with us in the studio: Rory Gallagher.' He cued right in at eleven on the dial.

'Mama's in the kitchen baking up a pie, Daddy's in the backyard, "Get a job, son, You know you ought to try"...'

It was loud and proud, and the hairs on the back of my neck curled upwards. When he'd done, while we gave him as much applause and cheering as about a dozen people can do, he sauntered through to my studio and sat down in front of the guest mic. He was out of breath, which gave the perfect ring of authenticity to the performance. We had a chat, then he packed up and went on his way with a huge grin, a couple of 'prisoners' (two bottles of Gilden Kölsch beer) and a star struck audience, DJ and engineer. He really had been a diamond geezer and one of the nicest guys I shared oxygen with. He died far too young.

***** John Wheatland-Clinch worked for the Ministry of Public Building and Works in Germany and had played tea-chest bass with the Prague Symphony Orchestra; Squire Dave Gray ran the Gallows folk club in Herford; there was talk of an album of Forces' folk songs called 'Forces Folk' and some of the genre's great seventies stars flew out regularly to entertain a whole string of folk clubs which had become a new form of fun for the lads in the trenches.

It suited well: you didn't have to be sober – either in the audience or as a performer – and there was no British TV in Germany at that time. (It would be 1975 before a pilot Forces' TV service began.) It was something both singlies and 'Pads" (married people: 'Person Awaiting Divorce', in military parlance!) could take part in and you could get to see performers like the MacCalmans, Jeremy Taylor, Wally Whyton, Mike Harding, Harvey Andrews, Hamish Imlach, Isla St. Clair and the ever-lugubrious Jake Thackray. All of these felt a lot of goodwill towards HM Forces and this made for some brilliant evenings.

At BFBS we tapped into this strand of music and on a programme called 'Folk Folk', Jürgen Bock and I would take a driver and the BFBS outside broadcast van out in all weathers to remote garrison towns hundreds of 'klicks' (kilometres) away from remote Cologne. We would set up a microphone array; Jürgen would record the whole evening then we would pack up and drive off to the nearest Gaststätte for a few beers, a well-deserved kip and a brilliant German breakfast before shooting back to Cologne. Then Jürgen and I would choose which songs to play and we'd usually put a programme together of half local floor acts and half with the bill-topper. It was exhausting work but we loved it.

The van was a triumph of micro-engineering. Built by Mercedes, it had been customised in-house to provide a versatile piece of kit suitable for either live or recorded events. It could manage road shows with its own PA system - it just needed a Bundespost line from site to BFBS Cologne and anything was possible.Part of my training as Cold War warrior took place during the course of these folk nights. We'd learn how to approach a target zone at night in driving snow with black ice on the roads; how to negotiate entry into secure military barracks and areas when we'd left our identity cards behind; how to gain entry to one of the many messes for a pre-flight warmer and a snack and to find the right people with whom to liaise to make sure the rig and the recording went well.

My job was to do the smarming and charming, clearing permissions from the performers to play out their material on BFBS; helping set up the microphones; pointing the performers in the right direction and – the most important thing of all – to keep a list of the running order – names of songs and names of artistes, and ensuring it ended up with the right tape in the right box.

At the end of the evening came my chance to shine. After a long session of needle watching, Jürgen's priority was a cosy bar and a bellyful of beer. Before we left, this meant rolling up hundreds of metres of cables, mic stands, speakers and other stage kit. Other producers used to leave it to the engineer and driver to do this 'non-production' work. I did the opposite: I made sure I was out there humping and dumping. My reason was selfish – I wanted a cosy bar and a bellyful of beer too and the quickest way this was going to happen was if I chipped in.

I found out later that this had passed into locally employed staff legend: Herr McD may be barking but he gets down and dirty with the crew. A useful endorsement on top of me being able to speak 'auf Deutsch'.

One night, we were due up at BMH (British Military Hospital) Rinteln to record an evening with the legendary drinker and folk singer Hamish Imlach. He had become a star by having brought out a song that had been banned on BFBS Radio, until I started playing it after John Russell had left, called 'Cod Liver Oil and the Orange Juice' – a sort of harsh love song from the point of view of a 'Jack the lad' Glaswegian chancer. It contained the immortal lyrics:

'Hey noo Mary, aire ye doncin'?' 'Och no, Ah dinnae dance wi'children.' 'Aha-ha, didn't kna' ye wiz pregnant! Cod liver oil and the orange Juice.'

Sung lecherously by a spherical red-faced Imlach at the top of his whisky-sodden lungs, it was a masterpiece of vernacular culture. The squaddies loved it, knew all the words and always sang along.

We arrived very early at the home of the RSM, who was hosting Hamish for the night. We got there, had a beer or two and chatted about the night's floor singers and the kind of things we each needed from each other to make the evening a success. Jürgen then shot off to set up, leaving me to wait for Hamish (we usually did a pre-show interview with visiting stars).

An hour to go. No Hamish. And, as these were days before mobile phones, no clues as to where he might be. Had he landed at Hannover? Had they let him on the plane? We were all mid-panic when the great man hove into view, yawning horribly.

He was totally tanked. His eyes couldn't focus. What was infinitely more worrying, he couldn't talk, or make any other noise apart from a rasping, asthmatic wheeze. Two sturdy NCOs, one on each arm, hefted him through the front door of the RSM's married quarter.

Houston, we had a problem. This man-mountain was due to smile, chat and sing at a hall full of expectant squaddies in just under an hour.

Luckily, RSMs don't get to be RSMs because they can't handle the situation. This one peered at Hamish and delivered his verdict. 'Bottle of scotch and a glass!' he barked to his wife, who hauled forth same from the lounge cabinet.

Without further ado four fingers and a thumb of neat scotch were transferred to a glass and thence to the dry throat of the Imlach, who shuddered like a mighty whale might do if woken from an equally mighty sleep.After one glass (about three conventional doubles), Hamish could actually move most of himself and, more hopefully, his eyes and lips.

After a quarter of a bottle, he could croak in Scottish, and some simple words were discernible amongst the tirade of extreme swearing as he and his headache came to terms with each other.

After half a bottle his head was thrown back, he was laughing, he seemed alive, awake, compos mentis and glad to be wherever he was. Hamish had been restored to us. We poured him into the car and set off for a memorable concert. They cheered him to the rafters and he took many prisoners that night, drinking the RSM and many other gnarled veterans under the table.

Harvey Andrews was another controversial figure. Again, his song, 'The Soldier', a true song about a soldier who had saved many lives by throwing himself on an IRA bomb at a railway station, was huge among the troops in Germany - and banned on BFBS. I managed to get Smilin' John to let me play it on 'Folk Folk' as a special case and when Harvey came to do a show, I chatted with him and told him about my efforts to get the song airtime. We became chums and did several recordings together in Malta and Cyprus, as well as Germany.

But the Folk Folk highlight of all time was the extravaganza called, cheekily, 'Folk In The Round', which came from the Roundhouse in Hohne. This was an old SS Barracks, located in the shadow of the village of Belsen, high up on a hill. We all made the pilgrimage. We all came back very quiet for a time. There is little to see, but the symbols remain terrifying. As you walk through the demolished camp site, mound after mound of mass graves confront you. Each a long, low mound, at the front of which is a figure, a number. Just a clinical cipher.

Until you realise that this number refers to the number of bodies buried there. Here is one that reads '1000'; here, the next one:'2000'. You find yourself (we compared notes) hurrying to the next mound because you want to see if that number is bigger or smaller than the one you've just seen. You are compensating for not actually being able to imagine what the pile of a thousand emaciated, broken and diseased corpses must have looked like before disgusted British squaddies wearing face-masks ploughed them with bulldozers into the mass graves. Surely a sight to test humanity to the limit.

Back to the concert. The stage was huge; the cabling took a long time and, unusually, there were many rehearsals. As well as the MacCalmans and Wally Whyton, local star Little Mo Hart, an RAF daughter, was singing. She was a good chum and Jürgen and I had made quite a few recordings of her unique voice. We agreed she sounded a bit like Mary Hopkin, except better.

After a long rehearsal came the special finale. Little Mo would front a 'calling off' song in the shape of 'Amazing Grace'. Her voice, solo over a low humming chorus from the entire cast of singers, was a showstopper. Or at least it would have been, if one rather dumb soul, who had clearly taken on too much beer, hadn't been singing the word 'bollocks' at the end of each fairy-tale line. Eventually, it got too much for the compere, who came over and kicked the guilty bastard in the pants. I remember at the time how much that hurt. Anyway, sanity was restored and we ended up with a show which translated into two 'Folk Folk' specials.

*****

After a break, the 'Great North Rhine West Phailure' returned to the airwaves. There was to be one triumph and one disaster in this first tour of BFBS Cologne. The triumph was my first and only single, which achieved record (!) status in BFBS. Richard Astbury, working with Ray Schmidt-Walk from Polydor in Hamburg, had produced a couple of albums of comic and risqué songs, called 'Hang on with Asters' and 'Asters' Greatest Hits', which had enjoyed considerable success - so much so that Asters started to get pre-release record material sent to him directly from the label.

One evening, Ray invited Asters and me, together with English Speaking Dieter Gripp, to perform at an industry showcase in Neuss, near Duesseldorf. This was one of the first pre-video and pre-computer multimedia shows ever. It featured Asters, me and a West Deutscher Rundfunk American radio DJ called

Mal Sondock, all perched on a rickety wood and scaffold stage, playing discs, alongside a 16mm projector playing pre-video song films onto a giant screen on the end wall, and a stage for live performances.

It has to be said that the party atmosphere, the flashing psychedelic lighting and the suspicion of the presence of some Bolivian marching powder masked the reality of a gram deck needle jumping, as those decks were mounted on the same platform where 40 stone of assorted DJs and engineer were busy bopping. Eventually we learnt how to stand still and still look cool.

The highlight of the evening was a Swedish quartet who Uncle Ray said probably had a great future with the label. It was Asters who got to introduce this fresh-faced band with their debut song, 'Ring Ring'. Yes, *that* Swedish quartet, then known, pre-Eurovision, as Bjorn, Benny, Anna and Friede - later immortal, of course, as Abba. As a result of this particular evening, Asters' morning show received sub-master tapes and acetates of Abba's very latest hits well in advance of release. BFBS became the first station in the world to break new Abba material.

*****

At this stage we had an 'entitled' military audience of about 500,000, based in an area the size of England and Scotland, from Bonn in the south-west, Hamburg in the north and Berlin in the east. But our German audience was measured in millions – up to six million, in fact.

So there was Asters, doing brilliantly, and very well deserved, too. I felt I too needed to do something to upgrade my image. When it came, it came by accident. The management, in a rare intervention, had decided that the annual kiddies' party held on station each Christmas for German kids – mainly orphans – from the nearest home was going to be cancelled. This angered me so much that I got together with some colleagues and we decided to hold a private party for the thirty or so kiddies at our own rather large flat in the Volkspark. The management heard about it and even tried to stop it by withholding funds, but I was absolutely livid about this betrayal of Christmas and made up my mind to pay for half of it.

The other half was paid for by my excellent colleague and drinking buddy, Terry James, a Londoner who had a really gravelly voice assisted by much hard living and cheap brandy. Terry was a generous man who actually understood the audience he played music for. He and his then wife Linda were huge supporters of the party and a co-operative German staff ensured that we had all the kit we needed.

In the end, we had food, drink, party favours, decorations, a film projector, a box of up to date cartoons and even a man who could operate the kit. All we needed were some prezzies.

I will just mention that the Osmonds were huge in Germany that year. I say this because when EMI Electrola, Germany's premier international record label, phoned up and asked if I could do them a favour, I was keen to help them out. The Temptations were releasing a headline album in Germany on Tamla Motown and EMI Electrola wanted to attach a freebie EP, with forthcoming releases introduced in 'Jinglisch' by BFBS's PMcD. They sent me the tracks, I recorded some 'Jinglisch' nonsense 'top and tail' of each track sample - 'Also Leute standen sie by for ein really heisse piece of blastmusik comin' at ya von Stevie Vunder' - sent them back the tape and got the thumbs up. They loved it. What did I want as payment?

I was quite pleased with the haul: hundreds of albums and singles, a huge collection of Donny Osmond dolls easily worth £25 each, bright EMI Electrola kiddies' T shirts, bangles, yo-yos and a host of other toys and trinkets. Certainly enough to keep those German orphans happy. And, of course, when the 100,000 copies of the Temptations album were released in Germany, each one had a free copy of the 'PMcD Introduces' EP stuck to it.

The party was huge, a giant success, and Christmas was etched in the broad smiles and wide eyes of the German children as they were treated to a memorable afternoon with so much to eat and drink, with films and presents too. Bless.

Yeah, dude, I was big on Tamla Motown... Me and Asters. Not only Cold War warriors, but recording stars too.

*****

We got away with so much because our radio station, oddly, was many miles from our entitled audience and their army garrisons and RAF stations. In the early seventies this was not too much of a problem. Radio was still a mysterious and all-pervading magical medium with its own special ethos. You never got to see the plumbing and its stars would be invited to open garrison fairs, exhibitions and sporting events. As one of BFBS Germany's station managers, Charly Lowndes, so beautifully put it: 'BFBS Cologne is a handful of semi-pissed minor public schoolboys playing English commercial gramophone records for six million bemused Germans.' As a station we couldn't go wrong, as we had a captive and grateful audience, especially among German youths, who were starved of pop music on their own media.

But if the station continued to flourish, there were less successful times – certainly in this department. One of these was the re-launch of the 'Great North Rhine West Phailure'. After its first run I thought it was falling flat and I didn't seem to be able to get it back up to scratch. This turned out to be a self-fulfilling prophecy but the flywheel of previous success was still running. Still, I had to update it. I decided to increase the local German content, and, waiting in the wings and very keen to help me do just that, was an entrepreneur by the name of Rolf-Ulrich Kaiser. He ran the Ohr and Pilz record labels and had a stable of the most bizarre and avant-garde 'Cosmic Couriers'. Tangerine Dream were the headliners, alongside Klaus 'Quadro' Schulze, an electronics wizard who used banks of Revox recorders and synthesisers, vocoders and keyboards to put together loops of renewable and endless music. Then there was Janis Joplin-style throat-ripper Inge Rumpf and a host of new acts in the same image. We started to play their music on-air. It went down well with the audience who used to like Smilin' John's version of the 'Saturday Show'. My Brit and teenage audience weren't so keen. But hey, we were pushin' the boundaries, man.

Two events told me that I was being stupid. One Saturday morning we assembled a group of cosmic couriers to do live interviews and sing live over pre-recorded electronic music backing tracks in the studio. We'd even routed some echo and filter effects into the microphone channels. Came the show, and a bunch of trippy cosmic couriers shimmied into the studio, and crashed out in whatever chairs and beanbags I'd managed to put together.

I should have known better. Within minutes there was a smoky, sweet smell in the studio. The entire bunch had lit up joints and before long my eyes were watering. NCR could see what was going on but because I wasn't saying anything, they carried on monitoring levels and watching with some amusement as the GNRWP DJ started to go a bit red-eyed because he was also swigging beer, starting very much to go with the flow, man, and whee, before long, giggle, just a little bit under the hee hee influence of the pervasive tang of Mary Jane and her friends…

I somehow kept it together. We finished the show. The cosmic couriers were over the moon (and the stars, and the stairs, and themselves). I was waiting for the phone call, which never came. Luckily, the studio I was using wouldn't be in use again until the Monday. I used up some brownie points by swearing the porter and cleaning staff to silence and they did me proud. The studio smelt of furniture polish by office hours on Monday.

*****

But by now Rolf-Ulrich saw me as an honorary cosmic courier and told me one day that he had a plan for a global launch. We would assemble at Dieter Dierks' famous studio in Stommeln, on the outskirts of Cologne. Dieter was a legend – amongst others, he had recorded the legendary Tina Turner, who had a house in Cologne just opposite the BFBS studios. Here, we would stage a music and poetry event, headlined by Tangerine Dream, showcasing the other cosmic couriers and making it a huge press occasion. Top of the press invitees was the Germany correspondent of the legendary music magazine, Rolling Stone.

'Poetry?' I asked Rolf-Ulrich. 'And where's *that* coming from?'

I should have known better. Rolf-Ulrich was very kind, very flattering and very persuasive with the result that, after a drink or two to seal the deal, I was poet laureate for the occasion. I did ask for payment, for once. I said that in return for fronting Tangerine Dream and writing and reading a cosmic courier poem, I would require a full-length black velvet cloak, lined with lilac silk and closed with a giant silver hooped clasp. To give him his due, this was produced on the day itself.

I then completely forgot about the project until a call the night before, which led me – I must have lost my presence of mind, Your Honour – to put a roll of MOD shiny toilet paper into my typewriter and write reams of what I thought at the time was stream-of-consciousness new-thinking astral poetry. After nearly a whole roll of bog paper, I pronounced myself pleased with my labours and fell asleep.

Next day, when I read what I'd written, I knew it would require massive confidence to hypnotise people into thinking it was good, because it would only mean something if read fluently and with feeling. I couldn't understand a bloody word of it, which was not promising.

I was picked up and taken to Stommeln. Here, the biggest crowd of poseurs since the Baron Münchhausen Appreciation Society had gathered. These guys weren't like pop musicians. No, they took themselves very seriously, man. I found a spare sound booth and put on a silk shirt and my new cloak, and had my face painted with silver paint. I too was going to be a cosmic courier. A stage podium stood in the middle of the biggest studio. In front of a selected press audience, I began to declaim my poem. I felt a complete tit. I suspect the audience began to share similar feelings about the charlatan spouting random crap at them. I got away with it, as in I wasn't physically dragged from the stage, for about ten minutes, until the ever watchful Rolf-Ulrich finished me off on toilet roll sheet eighty-two with an MC-like, 'Thank you brother cosmic courier. And now – to take you from here on a journey to inner space – Tangerine Dream.' Now, Tangerine Dream are a class act and they are to be honoured for breaking new ground in the world of electronic music, but it has to be said that, after my performance, they could have played 'Baa Baa Black Sheep' on recorders and still sounded brilliant. My head hung low. My cloak still hangs in my wardrobe.

*****

The rest of my first posting to Cologne was a huge learning process, out of which came the following. First of all, I was never going to be a top line radio presenter; I didn't have a sustainable personality; I was too moody and liable to get bored and go off on a tangent. Secondly, rather like the job of being an actor, there was no joy in doing a daily sequence programme or show; this could soon become a treadmill. Thirdly, doing things as 'one offs' or 'short runs' put you very much more in the spotlight than if you were doing very well with a longer run of one or more broadcasting 'quarters'. You could put much more effort into shows that had impact.

And so it was that Smilin' John entrusted me in 1974 with 'Operation Travel Talk', in conjunction with BFES (British Families Education Service) and Lufthansa. There would be a competition, where secondary school over-16s would pair up and produce multi-media (well, audio-visual) 'exhibits'. The winning pair would accompany me to Hong Kong to make a radio documentary; the second-prize winner would go with a BFBS producer to Madrid and the third-prize winner would get a trip to Frankfurt. All expenses would be paid by Lufthansa.The competition was set up and administered by BFES. Secondary schools all over Germany entered, the not so good were filtered out and, eventually, about a dozen finalist pairs were assembled in Joint Headquarters, Rheindahlen, to be judged by an external panel. I went down to see fair play and to meet up with the winning pair. There were some intriguing and novel ideas – a photo album with sensor which added commentary to the next batch of photos when you turned the page; exhibits which started soundtracks when you pressed icons at fixed locations; slide shows with sound; dual-voiced recorded documentaries with visual aids – the standard was high, and the atmosphere was tense. Who would be going to Hong Kong?

When the prizes were announced, my enduring memory is of the first-prize-winner (her partner had dropped out), Sue Pursell, a leggy red-haired sixteen year old, author of the automatic photo album, falling in a dead faint, and luckily being scooped up by a couple of other competitors.

The rest of the judging went over my head, as the reality of the situation sank in. I was about to go to Hong Kong with a dangerously good-looking teenager. Admittedly, I was 26 and cheerfully married, but I could see dangers ahead. Luckily, Tanya was very understanding and even found it all a bit funny, and so one day a car picked up Sue and me and off we went to Hong Kong, where we spent a week embarking on a programme of visits and events put together for us by the Lufthansa PR team.

Any worries I may have had about Sue were replaced by other worries after we'd had our first evening meal in the penthouse (and revolving) restaurant of the Furama Hotel on Hong Kong Island. It was a very romantic setting, dammit, and I wasn't in any position to be romantic. I suggested we went to the cellar bar, where a Javanese rock band was playing.

Mistake. There was this bass player you see, Your Honour, and it wasn't too long before he and Sue made a connection, which I was not about either to break, or indeed to be in a position to break. I left her alone with him on the promise she'd be at breakfast at eight. As all good sixteen-year-olds can do, she bounced in the next morning looking very chirpy and full of the joys. I specifically didn't ask her about the night before, but she dropped enough clues for me to get the idea that our muso chum was a good sort who wasn't about to drag her off to a bed of shame or a den of vice. For some reason I trusted her and we suddenly became good mates.

The week was spent in a blur as we went from sight to sight, from breath-taking view to unique experience. Sue was confident, did excellent interviews and charmed everyone she met. The only intervention I had to make was when we went to the British Military HQ, where Major-General (later Field Marshal Lord) Edwin Brammall was Commander British Forces. Sue interviewed him on a portable tape recorder and was a bit surprised when, after she'd asked her question, he grabbed the microphone and shouted his answer into it so loudly that the needle on the sound meter jammed in the danger zone. I had to explain to him the principles of interviewing and being interviewed and, after an apologetic harrumph or two, he settled down like a good General and told the tale properly.

The week was over all too quickly and we flew back as if in a dream. The car dropped me off first in Cologne and before I said cheerio to Sue, she confided in me she was going to have to break off her engagement to the boy she'd left at home... We both laughed, both of us with some relief.

*****

I pottered through Christmas and the New Year. One morning, I walked into Parkstrasse 61. 'How do you feel about Malta?' asked Gilbert Dennis, in his capacity as porter/receptionist - the person who intercepted all phone calls coming into the station; the person who knew before anyone else who was being posted, where to, and when. Once Dennis had spoken, your number was up.

I thought about it. It was a smaller station, with a smaller staff and a smaller audience. But it was the Mediterranean, I could do with a change and I had done a full and largely successful Cologne posting. There would be others.

Three days later I was summoned to the presence. John Parsons handed me the brown manila envelope which contained my posting order to Malta. I would go on 25th March 1975. He wished me luck. I think he meant it.

I had one last task to undertake. The clearing out of the quarter. Mr Hudson, the Barrack Inventory Accountant, who hated civvies (and especially BFBS civvies), was waiting like a shrivelled praying mantis, to oversee my downfall. Number 7 Eckdorferstraße was about to be inspected with a fine toothcomb and a magnifying glass. We had the usual problems. 'March Out', the official handing over of the quarter, was undertaken with forensic precision. This included the embarrassment of identifying stains on the mattress, where differences were made between 'matrimonial' and 'maternal' stains, each of which had to be categorised, ringed in ballpoint pen and dated.

By the time walls had been checked for picture nails, the oven demolished in advance of the white glove treatment and the nastiest nook inspected for stray dust, the sense of intrusion was paramount, and hurting. This silly little man was exposing your every secret and any word could result in a march out being denied, and thus no possibility of onward travel to the next posting. Grin and bear it.

There was a final bit of light relief. By using deep reserves of politeness, charm and flattery, we had nearly 'turned' Mr Hudson – not quite to be on side, but at least not to be the vicious little prat he could be. I say 'nearly', because he had yet to emerge from the expansive cellar in which he was now ferreting with his torch, like some Goon guard in Colditz in another incarnation.

Suddenly a cry of anguish filled the welkin, amplified by the booming acoustics of the cellar. 'Mishter McDonagh!' came the voice of agony, propelled by its owner in a crab-like scuttle to the surface. 'Mishter McDonagh!' repeated the red-faced loon, as he stood in front of me, clipboard askew, panting as he tried to convey to me the gravity of the situation. 'There… it's a… you've got a… Mr McDonagh! There's carpet in-dye-*jean*-ous down there and it's set solid. I can't even unroll it!'

I looked at the poor man with some alarm, and not a little sympathy. His world had clearly been bouleversed; he was not a happy man, nor even the full ticket. I tried to get him to tell me the problem, this time in English.

It turned out that 'in-dye-*jean*-ous' was "indigenous", which in BIA-speak, meant 'locally made in Germany'. So, his beef was with that awful piece of rag masquerading as a hallway carpet that I'd hurled into the cellar a couple of years back when we'd moved in. I went below to survey the damage. The damp of the cellar had finished the work of the years of neglect. The carpet was actually sprouting mushrooms and moulds of various kinds.

After he'd calmed down, I managed to persuade him that it would have been a write-off anyway. With a reluctant hand (we'd agreed *some* minor damages and payments), he signed off my Married Quarter. We were now free agents, able to pass 'Go', collect our £200 and proceed to Malta.

Chapter Twelve:

Malteasers

'You are coming here with the right attitude and my guess is that you will enjoy your stay. The Island is small, true, but it is in very many respects a fascinating spot and if you are a man of sensibility you will find much to absorb you.'

So wrote my new boss, Brian Bass, from the Island of Malta, where I was due to pitch up for a new tour of duty in March 1975. Gosh, he sounded very clever. I was a bit worried about the 'sensibility' stuff but, as usual, put it into the background. We did the Air Trooper, this time from Luton. The only thing on my mind was the £600 in cash burning a hole in my jacket pocket. It was in the arrivals lounge at RAF Luqa that I began to formulate my policy about Malta. I could feel its influence about me from the first moments. Malta was an Ealing Comedy. It was as simple as that.

We were met at the military terminal by the tall and lugubrious figure of Brian Bass. He carried himself with all the dignity of a Jesuit priest. He was single, in his late forties and spoke in capital letters. In fact, he pronounced, rather than spoke. He was the least spontaneous person I had ever met. And, rather sadly, he took himself and the world far too seriously. It soon became clear that he was not over-fond of a boozy Oxford graduate who preferred playing pop songs to inspecting the entrails of old buildings and cultures. In those days I could never be accused of having the kind of 'sensibilities' that a man of Brian Bass's stamp could learn to love.

He was accompanied by one of BFBS's principal characters. She was known throughout the service as 'Auntie Kay' but the 'Auntie' was perhaps misplaced. She *was* BFBS Malta, just as she had imprinted herself on previous stations such as Palestine and Cyprus. She wore floral cretonne frocks, looked, sounded and behaved like a dowager duchess, and was also dangerously single.

Rather like the Black Widow, it was rumoured she had seen off one husband and several tottering fancy men along the way. Whatever the case, Brian and Kay appeared to represent the new and modern BFBS radio station I had chanced upon.

We spent a night or two in the British Hotel on Valletta Front, overlooking Grand Harbour. Watching sunset there on our first evening, with the evening rays warming even further the yellow ochre stone of the harbour fortifications, was a truly inspiring sight.

The hotel was typically Maltese: the word 'British' in the name, the Union Flag flapping on top of the building and the fact that English was murdered there as the regular business language all obscured the fact that a lot of the Maltese did not like their former British masters, a trait in which they were much encouraged by their Prime Minister. The incredibly anti-British Dom Mintoff, who had already sent the British Forces packing once, was gearing up to make Malta an independent sovereign country, with a lot of help from Red China and, a little more frighteningly and closer to home, Libya.

The inside of the hotel also spoke of its unique Maltese heritage. You got to the restaurant by going down a flight of stairs into the basement, where a white-tiled underground chamber looked like a nest of toilets in a London railway station. The lavatory in our room was encased in a 'room within a room', bang in the centre of a rather Spartan bedroom. The view was over Grand Harbour. We felt the history and, on balance, were glad to be there.

The next day was a whirlwind. We went up to the radio station, which was located in a compound that enjoyed the title of St. Francis' Ravelin, in Floriana. It sounded romantic but was, sadly, a bit down at heel. The station, it turned out, was run by no fewer than three people.

Brian Bass was Station Controller and was told what to do by Ian Woolf in London and Auntie Kay in Malta; Kay, in turn, was Programme Organiser and ran the UK side of the station.

Then there was Hector Frendo, an anglophile Chief Clerk. He loved all things British but was not always impressed by some modern Brits. Hector ran 'Listen In', the local programme guide, and was responsible for selling the advertising which kept the weekly paper in good condition. Hector was a member of the Marsa Club, which was 'the' venue on the island and the summit of any social-climbing Maltese gentleman's aspirations. As is usual, I made sure that I kept in with Hector, and with Connie, his panda-eyed secretary, who was not the sharpest knife in the drawer, but who, we all noticed, was certainly pneumatically-equipped.

I was given a desk opposite Hector's empire and we seemed to get on. The bad news was delivered early on. I was going to be doing the breakfast show. Ouch. I'd always had a horror of waking up in the morning, especially after a heavy night. But there was a carrot: it was expected that I was soon going to take over as Programme Organiser. Ian Woolf had told me so. With that in mind, I could put up with most things. Only a matter of time...

*****

Next on the agenda was finding somewhere to live. A house agent was found (by Hector) and we set off to look at a few places. It was assumed that all Brits would live in Sliema, which was the 'posh' area of Malta, second only to St. Julians, which was out of the range of most civil servants' pockets. Brian had warned in his letter not to live in places like Guardamangia, which was both hot and common, so of course we soon gravitated there to see how bad it was.

We found a town house there, three stories, convenience store and bakery a minute or two away, the Dick Palmer Bar and Mario's Pub just round the corner, plus the Ursuline Sisters' Nursery School just down the road for Mandy and Olly: it looked ideal. A Mr Azzopardi would be our Landlord. Along with a bank account, standing orders, official identity cards, NAAFI ration cards and other papers of entitlement for medical and family facilities, we were organised in the space of 48 hours. I unpacked the shiny brand new portable red typewriter I'd been given as a farewell present from Cologne and settled into life in the Mediterranean.

Life revolved around the radio station, Mario's pub in St Lukes' Road, home and the rather good 'Dear Friends' Chinese restaurant up the road. As was my custom, I made friends outside the workplace. 41 Commando Royal Marines had a few hirings on St. Luke's Road and they'd taken over Mario's as their favourite hostelry. It wasn't too long before I'd fallen in with a group of them, headed up by the formidable Yogi, a beast of a soldier who sounded not too bright, but actually was a sensitive soul who wrote pretty good poetry. Well, it was very good poetry if you were a fellow Booty who didn't fancy a good kicking…

It wasn't too long before Mario's had become my home from home. It was only a couple of minutes away. On summer evenings there was a pavement terrace and we often used to sit there after work and watch the world go past. Yogi would often supply the street entertainment. One evening, a couple of northern English teenage girls came tottering down the pavement on impossible heels, with far too much over-developed thigh exposed to the Maltese breezes. They noticed our table was talking English and decided to flirt a bit.

Yogi was not impressed and made it clear to the girls that their departure would be a joy to his soul. That, at least, was what he meant. The actual words would have stripped paint. The girls took umbrage and started whining about good manners and 'we ain't those kind of girls'.

Yogi had had enough. He bent down, scooped up a passing beetle – a big one – and, looking straight at the chief whinger, bit its head off and chewed the result.

The girls made a run for it, to the sound of much Marine laughter. Oh sure, it was very unsophisticated, but it was funny at the time. The only snag with booze and Booties is that occasionally confusion sets in, which can lead to aggression.

One afternoon, I was sitting with Yogi and one or two others in Mario's, when a stranger came in, a Marine who lived on camp and had just dropped in to see the gang. He was a very big and foursquare black Geordie, and I could see straight away that he was not the happiest of men. I then realised he was clocking my t-shirt, which said 'BFBS' in ten-inch letters across my puny chest.

It goes without saying that Geordie hated the radio, BFBS, civilians and mouthy long-haired gobshites sitting at table with God's finest. He also thought all DJs were raving poofters. This did not bode well. I found out later that Geordie had a very good track record when it came to close encounters of the hitting kind. I was a potential target.

Despite the best efforts of Yogi & Co. it seemed inevitable that Geordie and I would come to blows. Or rather, that Geordie would come to one blow and that my next address would be the middle of next week. I could see the train wreck heading my way. What to do?

Suddenly, my Cold War training kicked in. I would use my favourite weapon: drink.

Geordie stopped verbally trashing me for just long enough to make my play.

'Well, if that's the way you feel, I challenge you to a duel,' I got out.

It stopped Geordie for long enough for him to think about it. 'What kind of a duel?'

'Just me and you. Only one thing:' – I took my life in my hands – 'My choice of weapons.'

'Weapons?' said Geordie, and of course his pride kicked in. Knife, gun, rope, chains, razor, fist – what could go wrong? He grinned at the thought of an easy victory. 'Just you and me?'

'Of course. And whoever wins, it's a drink, a handshake, and no more aggro.'

'Fine by me. What weapon you going for?'

My turn to take the initiative. In a Cold War warrior voice, which had suddenly acquired confidence and purpose, I said the magic words.

'Double Fernet Brancas. One to one. Until one of us gives up.'

Geordie grinned a very ugly grin. All Marines can drink the enemy under the table. OK, he didn't know what this 'Fernet Branca' was, but if it came in a bottle he could drink it.

At this stage I'd better explain Fernet Branca. It is principally used after a very heavy night's drinking, where a swallowed measure will have one of two effects. It will either anaesthetise the oesophagus and upper gut, thus settling the stomach and its over-enthusiastic contents, or it will cause the drinker to throw up everything including his stomach lining. It sits on the shelves of bars as dire warning and last resort. And that's just a single. We were about to engage in doubles.

Oh, and I forgot something. It tastes bitter and vile. There is only one way to drink it: head back and aim the liquid straight at the back of the throat for an instant swallow. Any hesitation and the fiery, filthy, dark brown liquid starts to eat your mouth bit by bit, and you can't breathe, talk, or function.

Mario had seen me do the Fernet Branca trick before. He brought over two doubles of the unattractive liquid and plonked one down in front of each of us. We had the undivided attention of the other Marines. We raised our glasses at each other. Showdown. Yogi did the intro: 'One, Two Three!' Glasses to lips, and the contest started.

Mine went straight down the throat, in one. Job done. Geordie had a bit of a problem right from the start. As he'd never had it before, he tried a tentative sip, with the idea of necking the rest a nanosecond later. But he caught the taste and shuddered with his whole giant body. Then he took the rest in his mouth, where it burned and choked. Finally, he managed to swallow. Already his eyes had turned red and were beginning to water a bit.

'Same again, Mario!' I called out, with rising confidence. Not only is Fernet Branca a killer, it is also highly alcoholic and works instantly.

Two more glasses were delivered. The call was made and the pair of us necked our drinks. Well, I did. Geordie, having watched my technique, tried to knock it all back, but some of it must have touched the sides and again he found himself welling up, coughing and generally showing signs of distress.

It is a tribute to the staying power of Her Majesty's Royals that they will continue to try against impossible odds. A third round was delivered. Mine was successfully dispatched. Geordie's got as far as his mouth. He tried, but then slammed the still full glass down on the tabletop and staggered down the corridor to the Gents. An unholy gurgling racket from the bowels of hell was heard above the shrieks of unsympathetic laughter coming from the rest of the crew. Eventually, the only green-faced black man I had ever seen emerged, wiping his mouth. He stuck out his hand.

'You bastard!' he grinned. 'You had me there.' This was an amazing admission and we were forced to buy each other many better-tasting drinks to make up for it. Sometimes life could turn up trumps.

*****

Yogi went on to become a friend of the family, especially when he took on a Maltese fiancée, a thing unheard of in Bootydom. On the first Christmas we were there, we invited him and his good lady to share Christmas dinner with us. Yogi turned up suited and booted, with his demure bride-to-be on his arm. We sat down en famille to the Christmas spread.

Suddenly, there was a very loud knocking on our front door - sounds of English voices, raised in festive celebration. Clearly, whoever was at the door had imbibed. There was a body of celebrating Booties outside our door. Yogi listened for a second or two, then folded his napkin and, in the softest of voices, said, 'please excuse me for a moment.' He went out of the dining room, shutting the door behind him.

We heard him open the front door. We then heard a short conversation, which got quieter on one side and louder on the other. Then the sound of protest. Then a sickening thud, the sound of meat meeting metal, a sudden silence and the shutting of the front door.

Yogi came in, smiling through the pain of what turned out to be a slightly broken fist. 'A few of the lads. I told them we were having a quiet lunch.' Much later, we found out what had happened. The ringleader, Steve, had brought a posse round in the hope of a few free drinks. Steve was standing on the narrow pavement in front of the house, directly in front of a parked car. When conversation stopped working, Yogi had delivered an uppercut of such strength as to lift Steve over the car and down the other side, at which point the rest of the crew got the idea and hopped it.

*****

Just like Germany, a lot of my time was spent in the wonderful world of folk music. I soon had a Folk Show running on air and we recorded all kinds of acts from the forces and the local Maltese world. I got to know Flight Sergeant Billy Mack, a stalwart Jock performer and toper who spent his spare time in RAF Nimrods looking out for any Commies in the wrong places. An ideal companion for a Cold War warrior.

We enjoyed the odd joke and I reckon the best we ever pulled was the Polish Seaman. This was me, in heavy make-up, wearing a beret and a dressing gown, allegedly having been spotted in a failing vessel by an RAF Nimrod, hauled out of the Mediterranean by air-sea rescue, and currently staying with Billy until he could be repatriated. Billy was an ace bullshit merchant and soon had the folk club believing the tale. In the meantime, I wandered around the club (I hadn't been there before), smiling inanely and accepting many cordial drinks and good wishes from a typically friendly folk audience.

Much later on, at the bar, I made as if to whisper in Billy's ear. I had a little Russian, which helped sustain the illusion. Billy heard what I had to say, then turned away from the bar and hushed the whole building – a Nissan Hut with a few bits of home-made décor polluting its walls.

'Ladeez an Gennlemen – Geez your attention!' he began in broad Scots, which I won't go in to. 'This is Caryl Mrowicki who, as you know, was washed up on our shores and who wanted to come along and enjoy himself at Malta's top night spot!' (Billy could sell condoms to the Pope.)

'He'd like to thank you for all the drinks and kind wishes and, to entertain you, he'd like to toast you all and sing you a special song from his neck of the woods!'

A cheer went up and the barman, who was part of the scam, appeared with a round metal tray, on which sat twelve shot glasses that I'd bought earlier. Each was filled to the brim with a clear liquid.

I took a commanding position opposite the coal fire in the hut. Speaking in the finest imitation Polish (a few Russian words, plus Slavic sounds and a bit of German), I toasted the company, shouted 'adeen' (Russian for 'one'), drained the contents of the first glass and hurled it into the fire. A cheer went up. This was good cabaret. What they couldn't believe was that the next eleven glasses, each containing a generous double, also followed number one down the throat and into the fire. At the end I stood, swaying and smiling. I had a very, very attentive audience. They were waiting to see if I was going to drop dead.

Sadly, this was not going to happen. The glasses had contained nothing stronger than water.

However, it was now time for part two. Copying the stance of folk singers instantly recognisable the world over, I assumed a tragic posture, with my finger in my ear. I now looked like a very badly aligned Benny Hill. Billy hushed the expectant crowd and explained that Caryl was going to sing an old Bratislavian lament, which was all about a dying girl and her desire to be reunited with the lover she had once turned away.

I began, in a convincing baritone, to embark on a tear-jerking lament which consisted of many minor chords and much invented gibberish. Through my tears – go for broke – I watched the audience increasingly set their faces into polite interest as what must have been the most tuneless dirge ever heard in a folk club unfolded itself into this room of gloom. At the end it was a miracle that the reluctant audience hadn't slit its collective wrists. However, they remembered that I had been within inches of death and they had, after all, a duty of hospitality. So there were loud cheers and drinks all round.

Until Billy thought it would be a good idea to unmask the Polish seaman. When the club found out that, under the makeup, whitened hair, dressing gown and lack of specs was only BFBS pop-jockey PMcD, I can report that there was very nearly a lynching, and it cost me more than one round of drinks to keep the peace…

*****

On the serious side, I had to wait in the wings for the Programme Organiser's job, as Auntie Kay wasn't about to hand over before she was posted. I joined my fellow DJs at the time, Richard Gwynn and David Burrows, and we started planning the Great Broadcasting Revolution, as BFBS Malta was a part-time radio station. We invented a new evening sequence, 'The Five O'Clock Run', as a music & chat show to replace the very dire and dated 'Ask For Your Mother' (official title 'Ask For Another'), which featured the same songs every show. I can remember the bloody awful play list to this day:

1. We've Got To Get Out Of This Place   The Animals

2. I Love You Because   Jim Reeves

3. The Green Green Grass of Home   Tom Jones

4. Three Wheels On My Wagon	New Christy Minstrels
5. Stand By Your Man	Tammy Wynette
6. Little Old Wine Drinker Me	Dean Martin
7. The Anniversary Waltz	Anita Harris
8. Born Free	Matt Monro
9. My Brother	Terry Scott
10. Something	Shirley Bassey

You get the idea. All great songs – but not all together, three times a week, at peak drive time. We came up with the idea of more modern music geared to our younger audience.

As to the speech part of the show, we wanted to replace the tired old warhorse called 'Roundabout'. This was a half-hour speech show, which was compiled and presented by the same presenter who had murdered 'Ask For Your Mother'. It was described as a magazine programme with 'news, views, and topics of immediate interest'. In reality, it tended to consist of a locally-produced tape interview, with stock questions censored by the local Command PRO. Then there would be a sprinkling of COI recorded tapes, sent free of charge to overseas stations to promote UK ideas, inventions and trends. BBC Transcription sent little nuggets, about 3-5 minutes long, of reports and interviews and 'Head Office' could usually be relied on to send us speech material that they couldn't place anywhere else.

The result was a hotch-potch of 'boredom roulette' which, taken together with 'Mother', made for an hour of utterly wasted time. We wanted to replace this with a double-headed presentation, live studio guests and great tunes. We took the idea to Brian the Boss and he very bravely said

Yes. In the meantime David Burrows left, Chrissie Pollard arrived - and was on side - and we had us the beginnings of 20th Century radio.

We needed one more ace up our sleeve. What we didn't know at the time was that Ian Woolf, after his trip to the USA in 1970, had also seen the light and was keen to promote the 'entertainment' idea of our three-fold charter, like that of the BBC, to 'inform, educate and entertain'. Ian had seen the Yanks in action and their method of delivery was to use the music as an entertaining carrier wave, into which you could drop short, sharp nuggets of information. We'd arrived at the same idea and Brian was astute enough to see which way the wind was blowing.

The new format locked in, and turned out to be successful. In the meantime, Auntie Kay and Brian Bass were both shipped off, to be replaced by the old Berlin 'A' Team: Dick Norton as Station Controller and me as Programme Organiser. Dick hated having to leave the sophistication of Berlin for the dubious parochialism of Malta, especially as it was impossible to avoid the military. He found a spare nightclub, 'BJs', and became resident piano player there, while running the station in what could be called a relaxed way. Richard Gwynn, Chrissie Pollard and I were happy enough to get on with it, especially when we were joined by one of BFBS's greatest and most lovable characters, Pete 'My Cocker' Johnson.

I was busy doing my Morning Show one day when the studio door opened and an amazing sight in a salt-and-pepper heavy tweed suit was pushed in by Hector Frendo. 'The new announcer,' said Hector. I noticed a tremor in his voice.

'Good morning,' said the apparition, in perfectly rounded Received Pronunciation. 'I am Peter Johnson and I am the new Grade Five announcer. I'm very pleased to meet you.'

Something was wrong here. I couldn't quite put my finger on it. I indicated he should sit down alongside me. We would have a chat and I would introduce him to the audience. He agreed, nervously, and sat down, nervously. Again, this was worrying, as he had been with BBC Radio

Bristol for a while. Maybe it was jet lag? We conducted a very stilted interview and, at the end, I closed the mic as a song played out.

Suddenly, his shoulders seemed to go down and his whole frame relaxed. 'Shit, Oi'm glad thass over!' he burred at me in perfect Mummerset. His real voice sounded great. Warm, friendly, inviting smiles – just what we needed.

It took a couple of bottles of Malta's finest – Lachryma Vitis – to persuade him that 'PJ' from the West Country would go down better with our military audience than 'Pe-ter John-son' from the BBC. After that, he never looked back and became hugely popular for his eccentricities and driving habits. It is said he was originally posted to Cyprus because of Malta's driving standards and the resulting national industry of panel-beating...

*****

Staff seemed to come and go with amazing frequency. Dave Raven turned up at the station one day, asking to see Dick Norton. An unshaven hungover tousled idiot (me) asked him if he could help, as Dick wasn't in. Dave said no; it had to be Dick. Bit daft, really, but it did actually influence my thoughts when, a week or so later, Dick said he'd bumped into a club DJ, Dave Raven, who was looking for some radio work. 'Er, Pete, what would you say to...'

He recognised the expression on my face. He didn't even bother finishing the sentence. I wasn't about to take on a bloke who thought I wasn't important. Didn't he know who I was? I think that was one of the last times my stupid pride got in the way of common sense and, luckily, I was able to put the record straight almost immediately.

It was about two weeks later when I was invited up to the RAF Gladiator Club at Luqa for a huge Families' Disco Nite. It had been a while since I'd had a bop, so up we went to case the joint and get an idea of what music was popular on the dance floor.

The place was already throbbing when I got there. The DJ – more of an MC – was up on a scaffold stage, with a rainbow of strobes, flashing and static lights creating shapes and patterns around the giant clubhouse. He wasn't just churning out the tunes, he was masterminding the flow of the music and the responses of the audience. A series of shouts and answers indicated he was very much in charge of that floor.

Right at the end, he banged on Jeff Beck's 'Hi Ho Silver Lining' and the room erupted. Everybody was on the floor. I don't usually dance, but I was there too. We were shouting out the responses at the top of our lungs and the roof was about to come off. I peered through the beads of sweat. As I thought, it was Dave Raven. I walked up to him, apologised for my previous coolness and invited him up to the studio the following morning. He clocked my unabashed enthusiasm for what I'd just seen.

I still needed my "revenge". The next morning, a very charged up Dave (where *did* all that energy come from?) strolled into the studio, and started to cast a professional eye over our rather dated kit. (Pye mixer, rotary 'pots' – our main studio looked a bit like the radio shack on the Titanic.)

I chatted between discs until the moment arrived. We seemed to be getting on OK.

'Oh Dave,' I said, in a relaxed kind of way. 'Just got to pop to the office, pick up a local anno. Can you watch the levels?' This pleased Dave. He was trusted to be left in a live radio studio with a delegated function to watch the needle on the dial to make sure the level peaked at 6 on the ppm. So near and yet so far. Funny, McD seemed to be taking a long time. The disc was running out. Only one thing for it. Dave's BBC Newcastle radio training cut in. In seconds flat, another disc was on the next turntable and he was chatting to the audience, explaining McD had just popped out for a second and he, Dave Raven, was holding the fort.

I listened in my office for the next ten minutes, then went to the second studio, where we could see each other through the connecting window. He shook his fist. I grinned and went next door, to be greeted by a pretend-angry Dave, who hissed, 'You bastard!'

'Well, you've passed the audition,' I grinned. 'We pay peanuts, if I can get it past Dick. When can you start?' Dave was happy to be expanding his fan base, so a deal was quickly sorted. Dick was happy enough to go along with things and The Raven became a vital and popular part of the BFBS family.

In the middle of all of this, Roger Hudson, a former BBC World Service newsreader, arrived as Auntie Kay's replacement. He appeared in the studios one Friday just before lunchtime and, having had a few words with Dick Norton, oiled over to my desk and introduced himself. He was mature, urbane, totally relaxed and had the kind of voice a broadcaster would kill for. After a bit of shadow boxing (he was playing a psychological game I hadn't yet worked out), he invited me over to the legendary Phoenicia Hotel for a drink.

Once we were comfortably seated in their bar lounge, he opened the batting by telling me that BFBS Malta was a bit of a comedown but that he was sure he was going to enjoy his new job.

The 'new job', as I understood it, carried the title of Executive Producer and, although it was at the same level as my appointment as Programme Organiser, his job was more Senior Presenter than anything else. So I was interested to hear what he thought his new job was.

'Oh, Programme Organiser. Your old job. I take over on Monday morning.'

I scanned his face in panic, waiting for the laugh to appear to indicate the presence of a joke.

It didn't. The bugger was serious. My heart started pumping nineteen to the dozen. I'd effectively been winded in the solar plexus. My mouth just hung open, while Roger enjoyed the power of his words.

'But...er... Dick – um – Dick hasn't said anything about you taking over my job.' I'd give him one more chance to tell me this was all a cruel joke.

'Well, no. You know Dick doesn't like giving out bad news. He asked me to tell you,' said the dark brown voice, in coolly measured tones. In a daze, I finished my drink and we went our separate ways. Dick was away and wouldn't be back until Monday. I had the kind of lost weekend you wouldn't want to wish on your worst enemy. How could this have happened? Why had Dick just killed my career stone dead?

Monday morning saw me in Dick's office, white-faced and red-eyed. Dick seemed very relaxed – totally normal.

'Had a bit of a heavy weekend?' he nodded at my sorry state, all too evident.

'No,' I lied. 'Dick, do you have any problems with the work I'm doing?'

The pause was forever. Must have been all of two seconds.

'No – not as far as I know. You want to confess something, or did I miss the bit when you swore straight after the vicar's slot?'

How could he make a joke out of effectively demoting me? I began to get annoyed. 'Well, whatever you think it was, I don't think it warrants you taking my job away.'

'What *are* you talking about?' He seemed genuinely surprised. I began to become a little more rational.

'Taking away my job as programme organiser and giving it to Roger Hudson. And telling him before you told me. It's too much, Dick.'

'I would be if it was true. I think Hudson's been winding you up.'

'You mean...' The light began to dawn.

'I'm more than happy with what you're doing.   Your job is safe. Go and tell Hudson to fuck off.'

I danced out of Dick's office, found Hudson, and duly told him what Dick had said.

He merely shrugged his shoulders and grinned. 'It was worth a go. You know, you need to get a bit more confidence if you're going to last in this game.'

It was actually a good lesson, though I wasn't about to take instruction from this frog-like creature. I christened him 'Kermit' – and it stuck.

Chapter Thirteen:

Format 77 and Beyond

Chief Clerk Hector Frendo sat in his office and he was sore afraid. A slight smile played over his Mediterranean features as he remembered the golden days of BFBS Malta. A silent Peter Holwill, who kept himself to himself, used to enter his office using a back door, ensuring peace throughout the building. He never really left the office. It was almost a case of pushing notes under the door.

Then the rot had started. First, there was Brian Bass, bullied by Auntie Kay, who seemed to let his staff get away with all kinds of 'artistic' mayhem. The music had got worse too. Next, Dick Norton. Hector's advanced idea of what constituted 'Britishness' had been demolished by this playboy lounge lizard with the gobby Irish wife, who pitched up at odd hours and seemed to play the piano in louche nightclubs for a living.

If only he'd known. The worst was yet to come.

Dick had drummed his fingers throughout his year of exile in the Med's smaller posting. Luckily, he was going to miss Operation Drawdown, the final departure of British Forces from Malta. He was about to be sent to the bigger station of Cyprus, which at least was a step on the way back to Germany, which for him was the only station worth running.

There were many rumours flying around as to whom BFBS Malta would be getting as its next boss. It didn't look too good. Under the civil service rules of engagement, the policy of 'dead men's shoes' meant either one old-fashioned time-server or another, at least as far as we younger ones were concerned.

Then the rumour became fact. Ian Woolf had sent a letter to all station controllers. Dick was currently on leave, which left me as acting Station Controller. I opened the letter and saw, with mounting excitement, that Bob Pierson was coming to take over and that he was expected to instigate major changes during his time in Malta.

I was delighted. I had known Bob in Cologne, and he was the nearest thing I'd ever seen to Renaissance Man. He was well educated (the word 'Sorbonne' came into it). He was European, of Jewish descent, with a waspish sense of humour, a great sense of mission and a thoroughly transparent ambition to Be The Best. He was suave, debonair and had a wonderful voice, in tandem with a versatile and occasionally lateral thinking brain of giant proportions. He could be very sharp with those less well endowed with synapses who couldn't keep up, but was also in possession of a kind heart and a humane disposition.

In short, he was enigmatic, which made some people a bit frightened of him. As far as I was concerned we were going to move forward and Uncle Ian couldn't have chosen a better man to do it. I wrote a letter to Bob – he was at the time, BFBS Berlin Representative – pledging my support and loyalty. In the meantime, one or two 'copies' of letters from station controllers around the BFBS world landed on my desk. They were outraged at this amazing breach of protocol. How could Uncle Ian actually *promote* this upstart directly into a top job, when there were others ('Me, Sir! Me!') at the proper grade who could carry out the task with professional acumen, etc, blah, blah.

Sour grapes. I kept the letters to show Bob when he pitched up.

Bob arrived like a whirlwind. Never mind the first hundred days. He seemed committed to an agenda of change, change, change, in the first hundred hours. He moved Hector Frendo in an office shuffle and told him he was a Chief Clerk, not the local Capo dei Capi. He stamped on several versions of 'but we've always done it this way' and generally upset the staff in a thousand different ways. He even countermanded Dick's kindness in sending Paul, our junior clerk, to pick me up in the station van every morning, as I tended to get very sweaty and short-tempered during

the twenty minute walk from Guardamangia to Floriana. Bob called it 'the improper use of an MOD vehicle'. I sulked for a few days, but then that was that.

In the meantime, the upside was that Bob started bouncing ideas off me. I felt some honour and privilege in realising I was being included in something called 'the future'. The principal idea of what was to become 'Format 77' was the 70/30 concept. BFBS had traditionally ignored the fact that 70% of its audience was young, liked its information in bite sized chunks and enjoyed unashamedly listening to pop music. 30% of the audience were rather more 'Radio Four' types, usually found amongst the officer class, who thought 'the BFBS' ought to be playing more – and this is a real quotation – 'serious talks and uplifting music'. To them, pop music was 'jungle music' and all 'pop-jockeys' were 'inane' and 'common'.

It should be remembered that at the time, Leslie Thomas's 'Virgin Soldiers' was a popular book. In its pages it told of a Lieutenant Colonel's wife who had been ostracised by the rest of her Wives' Club on the grounds that she'd once had a request played for her on the BBC's 'Two Way Family Favourites'. That was the attitude of the senior military to possibly the greatest weapon for morale and community they had in their arsenal: their radio station.

But to the senior officer class, BFBS was 'Broadcasting (Army Welfare)' and was a minor irritant which, nevertheless, they wanted to control via advisory committees and even with direct attempts at intervention. Sadly, it has to be said that some station controllers opted for an easy life. As their staff grew older, they tended to play gentler music and not shout too loudly, which made them just about bearable to the officers, if still below the salt.

Bob soon cut the Gordian knot and explained to the Advisory Committee, who sat in the Royal Navy HQ in the wonderfully named Lascaris Ditch, that he had plans to change the output of BFBS Malta so that the majority of the audience would be happier listening to it.

One RAF Air Commodore (the RAF was always the most spiky opponent of all matters BFBS) listened to Bob's plans and harrumphed his disapproval, trotting out all the usual demeaning slogans about BFBS and its long-haired morons polluting the airwaves.

Bob had finally had enough.

'Could you let me borrow one of your Nimrods?' he snapped, in his 'taking no prisoners' mode.

It stopped the Air Commodore dead in his tracks. 'What do you mean, borrow a Nimrod?' he barked.

Bob repeated the request. 'I'd like to borrow one, so I can play with it. Could you get one up to the road by the radio station?'

'Is this some kind of joke? I've never heard such nonsense in all...'(And so on.) The Air Commodore was brick red, with little veins standing out on his forehead.

The chairman of the committee, the Commander British Forces, Rear Admiral Oswald Cecil, allowed himself a quiet smile. He could see what was coming.

Bob waited for the blustering RAF officer to pipe down. He left a small pause.

'I don't think it's an unreasonable request. You seem to think you know more about broadcasting than I do and you seem to be telling me what I can and can't do. Surely, by the same token, I get to play with one of your planes, even though I know nothing about flying.'

The bluster continued like bad short wave interference but the rest of the room laughed. Bob had made his point.

*****

The plan that became 'Format 77' was, at the time, breathtaking. Out went the gaps in the day when BFBS broadcast a 1 kHz tone instead of output. Out went Auntie Kay's legacy of 'Lunchtime Ladies', who yodelled announcements in voices far posher than HM Queen and played ancient album recordings of tedious classical music excerpts from discs clearly cleaned with sandpaper. Out went boring litanies of local announcements written in 'militarese', that galumphing art form designed to shout at the recipient, 'If it goes wrong it ain't my fault!' Out went the traditional 'I Love You Because…' requests. At least, they were severely rationed. Out went 'mixed' programmes during the period 0600-1900, to be replaced by sequence programming, which meant a live person doing a live radio show.

The spin-off from this was that BFBS could become a port of call for people who had something to say, an event to advertise, or a helpful tip that might benefit the audience. Instead of a BFBS reporter taking a portable tape recorder to an interviewee's place of work (after submitting a list of questions, of course), doing the interview, playing it back to the authorities for clearance and then finally getting it played out when it had become history, the Master At Arms could pitch up during the morning or afternoon show, be led into the studio and chat with the presenter about whatever issue it was.

Then there was the cherry on top: promotions. It was clear that commercial radio had gripped the imagination of the UK audiences and was knocking the competition, BBC local radio, into the middle of next week. Commercial Radio had big personalities and hit music and carried powerhouse thirty second ads in small bunches that contributed to the overall sound of stations. BFBS was not and is not a commercial broadcaster so could not carry paid advertising. Instead, 'promos' would promote the audience's events in a punchy format that complemented the style of the new generation of presenters and their music. Also, and perhaps most painfully for the greyhairs, Bob intended to drop the lengthy BBC World Service ten-minute news bulletins during the day and switch instead to a 'rip and read' telex service of BBC Radio 2-style three-minute news summaries, to be read locally. This raised eyebrows even further.

But with this master plan, Bob had steered the potential output from 'A Garden Fete is to be held at Taq Ali Primary School, commencing at 1430 and to be opened by the CBF's wife, Mrs. Cecil. Tickets, which are priced at £2.00, may be obtained by telephoning the Taq Ali school Secretary on 734 878' to a thirty second stab of music and voices doing sketches with sound effects and giving snappy details. These were pre-recorded items that could be played out, say, six times a day for five days, making sure everyone heard them.

It was clear from the admiral's reaction that Bob had sold the product well. He left the Advisory Committee with a stamp of approval, as long as the subsequent compulsory audience research exercise proved that his plan had worked.

Yes, Bob had sold the plan to the Advisory Committee and had only taken a few glancing swipes along the way. But now he had to fire up the staff. With most BFBS people, it was like pushing at an open door. I was very much onside and was joining in with some of the thinking and planning. Richard Gwynn, Pete Johnson, the newly arrived Richard Caperon, and executive producer John Crabtree were all in favour, as were the great body of volunteer broadcasters.

The schedule was drawn up and the new shows went on-air.

The new dynamic was unbelievable. Suddenly we were getting more cards, letters, competition entries, station visitors, phone calls and general interest in what we were doing. The BFBS output was ours, under our control and designed purely with the majority of the audience in mind.

Within a few weeks, London signalled its approval by interrupting our schedule with a two-hour daily radio show in the style of 'Format 77' – live guests, personality and pop in a free flowing magazine programme called 'BFBS UK', hosted by Tommy Vance. It would become one of the most successful BFBS shows, running for many years.

After a day of youthful, frenetic and stimulating programming, punctuated with UK news rather than the BBC World Service's occasionally mangled short-wave epic news bulletins - where, for days at a time, the lead story could be events in the Horn of Africa - we were getting a 'link with home' that was far more powerful for the local audience than the old staple, 'Family Favourites', had ever been. With the UK news feed, we were getting stories that were happening right now in your home town, with people and customs you knew. Knowing that your granny was listening to the same news as you brought you that little bit closer.

It was clear to us that the new schedule was turning into a runaway success. The 70% were now being well catered for. We had a spring in our step and a new confidence. Live guests trooped in and out of the studio building, which had become more of a meeting point since we started talking to, not at, our audience. The 30% at least had the sop of continued mixed programming from about 1900 until closedown. Comedy, drama, documentaries, longer news bulletins and other specialist programmes filled the airwaves. Weekends remained more traditional than weekdays. Later this would change too.

Brian Emmett, a retired Head of BBC Audience Research, was the accredited agent of every command's audience research exercise. He prepared the questions in consultation with BFBS Head Office, the local station and the local command. The questionnaires were sent out to representative audience samples and the results carefully interpreted for any bias. (On this occasion, one naval Lieutenant Commander's wife's responses were rejected as almost every one showed the same utter hatred of the new format - totally at odds with the rest of the sample.)

The results took a long time to appear. They had to be digested and promulgated by Head Office and the command. The last to hear would be Bob Pierson and, of course, the staff.

It was a triumph. Bob's brave move, 'Format 77', had been vindicated. It was even better than 70/30. Sure, there was still a significant minority, mainly among the officer class, who rejected the populist approach but 'Tabloid Radio' had found a loving home in the hearts and minds of the majority of the audience. I was especially proud that I had helped at the north face of this operation, that I had completely believed in what Bob was doing and that I had been there when there were worries to help sort them out. From that angle, 'Format 77' was an integral part of me. And it felt very, very good.

After a few weeks, it became clear that the format was working. When you're on a roll... One of the reasons for its success was the dropping of an old BFBS 'rule' by Ian Woolf. This rule stated that one hour of preparation was required to put one hour of music on air and four hours of preparation was required for one hour of speech programming. You didn't need an abacus to work out that if a presenter was on air from 0900-1200 each weekday, their hours under the old formula for a speech and music sequence would have been something in the region of fifty hours per week, even before they'd also done promotions, weekend work, outside broadcasts and other duties. And the civil service would say 'No'.

But with that formula gone, it was clear that if the record librarian prepared a sequence of tunes playable through the day with some kind of rotation, pre-recorded, packaged promos, live guests *in situ* and specific hourly 'clocks' signposting each event during the hour, then it took very much less than four hours, or even one hour, to 'prep' a show.

But the combination of thinking and events, beautifully choreographed and implemented by the Pierson Person, had effectively turned over years of BFBS's 'but we've always done it this way' thinking. The only problem was the rest of the BFBS world, full of controllers who thought like dinosaurs and staff who were a bit too long in the tooth to change into 'Format 77' players. At least they knew the writing was on the wall.

*****

Uncle Ian's sabbatical in the USA, before he transmuted from BFBS's Controller of Programmes into its new Director, had been spent keeping tabs on what the American radio industry was getting up to. Two things in particular had caught his eye and ear. One was the pacy format of US commercial radio and the other was automation.

How many days were wasted by announcers nursing one-hour tapes for hours at a time, pausing only to tell people,'... and you can hear the next episode of 'Hello Folk' with Wally Whyton at the same time next week. Now, to take us up to our next programme at nine o'clock, 'These You Have Loved' with David Gell, here's a little music from the Geoff Love Orchestra.' Then, 'It's nine o'clock: time for another helping of 'These You Have Loved'. Here's David Gell.' And so on, for a long shift – all of which ate up the working hours quota.

Now if you had a machine that could replace a speaking nursemaid, you'd be liberating a whole broadcaster to make programmes. You could record all the programme junctions on one tape, with appropriate pauses, then all you'd need would be a machine that could play out tapes, go to an announcement, then to music up to the next junction, then play an announcement, followed by the next programme. But then what would you do about joining the BBC World Service for the 9pm news bulletin? And then leaving it at 2109'15" (fifteen seconds after nine minutes past nine) precisely?

All of these problems were about to be magic wanded away by a beast of a machine called Schafer, constructed by the Gates Corporation, USA.

It was about seven-foot wide, six-foot high, and was in three vertical sections. Sections one and three comprised a bank of six reel-to-reel tape machines, vertically mounted; the centre section held clocks, the nerve centre, or brain, and a carousel that took a huge number of pre-recorded cartridges (for jingles, promos and other short items). There were also cartridge slots for 'filler' music.

The beast worked on two filing systems. One was a series of sequential folders, numbered 1-600. If you left the animal to its own devices, it would play, say, a musical track from Tape One, a spoken message from Tape Two and then the next track from Tape Three, Four or Five. All it needed to activate the next step was a 25 Hz tone (inaudible to humans) at the end of the audio on the tape concerned.

So far, this meant that you could pre-record a series of announcements that would 'pop up' at appropriate points during the Schafer playout.

But you also had time junctions to worry about, including joining the BBC World Service for news bulletins. So, overriding the 1-600 sequence file was a time file, where you could programme time-specific junctions. (Are you keeping up?) It was the devil's own business for us, as we tested the machine over and over again. Finally, we worked it out. The best way of describing it is to give you a whole junction as performed by Schafer:

2000-2057'30":   'Hello Folk' with Wally Whyton on Tape Machine 2

2055'25":   'Fill' music, duration 4'30", starts silently in Cart Machine 1

2057'30":   'Hello Folk' tape ends; 25 Hz pulse

2057'30":   Pulse triggers Tape Machine 1; announcer says 'more from Wally at the same time next week. And now, a little music to take us up to the BBC World Service News at nine o'clock.' 25 Hz pulse

2057'45"   Pulse triggers silent sense cancel at Cart Machine 1. Music fades up

2059'55"   Music ends

2059'55"   TIME CLOCK now overrides, and brings in BBC World Service GTS

2100'00"   TIME CLOCK brings in announcer on Tape Machine 1: 'This is BFBS'

2100'05"   TIME CLOCK brings in BBC World Service news

2109'14"	TIME CLOCK CUTS BBC World Service after 'and that is the end of the news from London.'

2109'14"	TIME CLOCK brings in Tape Machine 1: 'More news at one o'clock'

After many stops and starts, and use of words ending in -uck, -ugger and –unt, Bob and I had lift-off. We'd managed to get it to work.

The next bit was what to do with it. It was a few weeks after the launch of 'Format 77' and we were riding the crest of success. Morale and confidence were high. I sat with Bob in his office.

'Well, we seem to have cracked that. What's next?'

'I don't suppose…? No, it'd never work.'

'What are you thinking. Go on, go for it!'

'What if we were to go round the clock?'

'You mean – 24 hours a day?'

Out came the equivalent of the back of a fag packet.

'Look. During the day we broadcast live from six in the morning to seven in the evening. Then we task a broadcaster to nurse programmes through the rest of the evening till closedown at eleven thirty. Then silence till 6am.'

'What if we got Schafer to playout programmes, with pre-recorded annos, from seven to eleven-thirty, then use the banks of tape machines to play out music through the night?'

Enthusiasm is contagious. 'Hey, we could use extra tape annos to build an artificial show – call it the 'Sam Stone Show' - which would rely on the duty announcer recording, say, fifteen links, which would go in between random tracks. Sure, not quite the same thing as live broadcasting, because whoever was being Sam each evening wouldn't be able to credit the music tracks as he went along, but…'

'Yeah, but Sam would be a bit of a random figure – he never actually turns up for his own show. He's a kind of mystery star, so he's always referred to, but never heard in his own right.'

And so it was in January 1978 that a brand new 24-hour schedule hit the airwaves. The military was amazed and delighted. This would be the same military that operates twenty-four hours a day, seven days a week. It was very good that in guardrooms, on watch and off-duty, squaddies could still listen to their very much better radio station.

Ian Woolf received the reports back in London and dropped the bombshell.

All stations were to move towards the Malta model. This was going to be BFBS Tomorrow.

All over the BFBS world, superannuated senior staff were busy fulminating at what Malta had done to their lives. Life was going to be bumpy from now on. Bob's actions were ridiculed and some very personal words were exchanged but Uncle Ian was adamant. And, it has to be said, enjoying the flak.

*****

However, on the home front, things had been conspiring to change forever. Halfway through my tour of duty, Moo became pregnant again, and in October 1976 Alex, our next son, was born at the Royal Naval Hospital M'tarfa. This turned out to be a significant event, if only because the baby was very nearly born on the way to the hospital. We were driven there by the panel-beater's friend, middle-of-the-road (literally) driver and colleague Pete Johnson. Maltese roads weren't quite so easy going in those days and we bobbed along the rugged surface with both of us emitting little whimpers. In Moo's case it was pain; with me, cowardice.

Once the baby was born, the bad news began to emerge. The Malta drawdown was the news of the day. Military establishments were to close down. These included the Royal Navy Hospital, which was more than a bit worrying, especially when Moo announced the appearance of yet another mini-McD. The options looked stark. If RNH M'tarfa was closed, the only option was the Maltese St. Luke's Road Hospital, just down the road from where we lived. It was said St. Luke's patients cooked meals on camping gas fires by their bedsides and held Maltese 'conversations' (much yelling and gesturing) at all hours of the day and night. Not only that, but they used doctors from Libya and even, it was said, some from the Palestine Liberation Organisation.

It was clear that Moo was NOT going there. So we needed to be posted. Uncle Ian had mentioned that I would probably go back to Germany after Malta and so I began to formulate a plan for the winter of 1977.

If Uncle Ian didn't send a posting order, I would bloody well post myself to Cologne.

I used the civilian rip and read telex machine to send myself a purported posting order, quoting the usual civil service nonsense such as my civil service department and payroll number. I then took this to the travel office, where sea and overland passages for Peter, Tanya, Mandy, Olly and Alex were duly issued. We then used the tickets as authorisation to get hold of enough official military wooden crates to pack up the home and get everything shipped to Cologne.

Once everything was in place, I told Bob what I had done. This was going to hurt.

Luckily, he remained very calm. He asked all the right questions and seemed content with my reasons for wanting to go: at least it wasn't because I didn't enjoy working with him. There was a period of limbo while he spoke to Uncle Ian in London. Apparently the entrails were favourable:

There was a general 'Grrr!' at my behaviour but eventually the posting was rubber-stamped. Poor Bob received a sting in the tail, though. The Command Secretary, the civil servants' principal co-ordinator for MOD UK Based Civilians, dragged Bob into his office and tore him off a strip for 'Dickensian management' in sending a heavily pregnant woman and a brood of young kids on a long voyage in the bleak midwinter. Bob was at pains to point out that Moo was too pregnant to fly and that the McDs would have rather walked on their knees to Cologne through a hail of machine gun fire rather than have the next baby at St. Luke's.

We had a lovely farewell party at the Malta Hilton and the next morning we embarked on an Italian ferry that would take us to Naples, via the jolly and choppy winter waters of the Straits of Messina. But at least we were on our way and nobody had actually died.

*****

Time for a fond reminiscence.

My favourite person on station was the cleaner (sic) Angelo. A barrel of a cheerful man, with the florid face and stubble of an accomplished drunk, he bumbled around, creating mayhem. He crow-barred himself into a kind of hopsack shirt and trousers, with a wide and scruffy belly-binder holding him together. Amongst his tricks were regular attempts to vacuum clean the live on-air studio mid-programme and his imaginative use of inappropriate cleaning materials, such as trying to use Mansion floor wax to clean the connecting window between the two studios.

Angelo was also a great exponent of Maltese folk music. This is best accomplished (from the audience's point of view) with the singer in one village and the audience in the next. The rules of engagement were relatively simple. You assumed a fighting posture, threw back head and chest and roared at the top of your voice…anything you felt like. Volume was all. The louder you sang, the more you meant it. The words were secondary and brought up the rear to any tune which might have survived the ordeal. You got extra points for making it up as you went along.

I will never forget Dick Norton's farewell party in GP studio, a cavernous room that, sadly, wasn't big enough to contain Angelo's voice as he sang (at my request – tee hee) a farewell song to his outgoing boss. As a special treat, Angelo had elected to sing this valedictory anthem in his version of English. With a flask of the roughest red wine in one beefy fist, Angelo, accompanied by a vague thumping on the piano by me, launched into his tribute to Dick:

'YOU TAKE IT PLENTY YOU/DEEECK NOOORRRTON/HE STATION CONTROLLAIR/HE VERY GOOD MAN YOU TAKE IT/DEEEEECK NOOORRRTON/STATION CONTROLLAIR/HE TALKING/PLENTY BULLSHIT/OH DEEECK NOOORRRTON/PLENTY BULLSHITTTT!'

His little eyes surveyed an incredulous audience. Eventually, Dick laughed and the ice was broken. Angelo was roundly congratulated.

Angelo was also the subject and cause of two diplomatic incidents. The first was when Bob Pierson invited the whole BFBS staff to join him in hosting a party at the Royal Navy Lascaris Officers' Mess. Hector Frendo had warned him against inviting *all* staff, but Bob was adamant. So that evening we were treated to the horrifying sight of Angelo wearing his version of 'Sunday Best', a garish large-checked compost-coloured tweed abomination with a tie, on which could be seen many breakfasts. He had clearly tamed his spiky black hair with olive oil and it gleamed in the Mediterranean sunset. And dripped a little, too.

All was going well. Little dwinkies, dead things on sticks and the BFBS staff behaving as attentive and conversational hosts. A nice buzz. Then the scream cut through the evening air. A female naval officer, in her rather appealing uniform, which included a very smart skirt and black stockings, had just been goosed by Angelo. This was not just a breach of protocol but heading up for a board of inquiry. Only Bob's promise to saw off Angelo's straying hand with a rusty razor blade (or some such other dire in-house punishment) prevented the case from escalating. Luckily, the lady officer turned it into a joke, so all was well.

But Angelo's finest hour was the incident of the perplexed President. Richard Gwynn had pulled off a coup: he had invited no less a figure than the then President of Malta, Dr. Anton Buttigieg, to not only come to the station and give an interview, but also to read from his newly translated book of verse, 'The Lamplighter'.

Angelo was tasked to clean and polish everything in the cavernous GP studio, where the interview and reading would take place. A casual spectator would have noticed Angelo scrubbing and dusting very, very hard. This was *his* President and he felt a huge sense of obligation. While he was cleaning, one of the engineers came in and fixed up a number of sound screens, six-foot high by two-foot wide, on castors, around the interview table, with its two microphones. The attention then shifted to front of house, where the staff awaited the arrival of the President and his retinue.

The retinue turned out to be quite small – just His Excellency, his aide and a driver. He was politely oiled into the building, given coffee in the Station Controller's office, conducted on a quick tour of the building and finally taken to GP studio, where he met Richard Gwynn. The pair sat down and an interview was duly recorded.

It was now time for the good President to read from 'The Lamplighter'. An expectant hush preceded the warm tones of this most excellent of public speakers, reading sensitive and thoughtful verse with a wonderfully lilting baritone Mediterranean accent. It was a delight to listen to. How many presidents of countries were capable of demonstrating such a close affinity with the arts?

Suddenly, a frown appeared on the recording engineer's face. Something was wrong. It sounded as though a buzz saw was trying to cut through the studio wall. It became louder and louder. The

President stopped reading and, slightly disconcerted, was beginning to look like a man who would very soon be asking hard questions.

The engineer and two or three of us went into the studio. We stood listening, until the source of the sound, by now raucously loud, was identified. A sound screen was pulled back to reveal the remains of Angelo, lying snoring on his back, his face framed with crumbs from a half finished hobz biz-zejt (a local delicacy - a wedge of rough bread smeared with tomato paste, olive oil, pepper, olives and capers) and an accusatory empty bottle of red wine at his elbow.

It was very kind of the President to leave the room whilst Angelo was awoken, chastised and sent to hide in a broom cupboard until appropriate punishment might be meted out. It was even kinder of the President to take a gentle perspective on the incident. ('I expect you had the poor man cleaning and polishing all night for my visit,' he said.) And it was exceedingly kind of the President to continue the reading without the enthusiastic snoring of Angelo in the background.

After Dr. Buttegieg departed, Angelo was given the statutory bollocking, but nobody's heart was really in it. After all, it *was* Angelo.

Chapter Fourteen:

Odour Cologne

It was a choppy crossing, the sea journey from Malta to Naples. The ferry, packed with thousands of gesticulating and vomiting Italians, bounced its way through the Straits of Messina, with many an olive oil breakfast adding to the greasy slick on the otherwise blue waters of the Mediterranean. A very pregnant Moo, her brood of three on the outside adding to the burden of one on the inside, tried to make it from cabin to restaurant and back again, avoiding flailing arms and elbows. In short, it was a bugger of a voyage.

We finally made it to Naples, which we briefly saw in a suicidal taxi driven by a blind but gobby Neapolitan, who didn't seem to mind that we didn't speak Italian, as he didn't speak English. What worried us was that whenever he wanted to make a point, he would take both hands off the steering wheel to make a wide-armed shrug. When he REALLY wanted to make a point, he would not only do the shrug, but turn around in the driving seat so he could make eye contact to underline the seriousness of the point he was making.

Being good Brits, we put aside our biliousness and tiredness and fell into the old 'dealing with foreigners' routine. If he was smiling we grinned and nodded. If he looked angry we beetled our brows and shook our heads. If we really couldn't make out what he was saying we would raise our eyes to heaven and do one of his shrugs.

We obviously passed the Naples Examination. By the time we arrived at Naples Railway Station we had scored highly in his 'passenger of the month' competition. He carried our bags to the ticket office, complimented the beauty of our children and gave what I rather hope was a blessing for the happy event still to come.

It was the work of a moment to secure the appropriate tickets and climb aboard a train bound for Rome, where we would connect with a Trans European Express all the way to Cologne. As Head of Family, I thought I'd done rather well. Wife, bump, three kids all on board and a chance to beat the milling crowd down the heaving corridor to get a snack or two. I failed to notice the small black cloud over Moo's head. It wasn't going to be that easy.

By the time we got to Rome, even my nerves were taut as gazelle sinews. You could have played on me pizzicato. If a 'Which European country do you wish had never existed?' vote had been taken at that time, a huge cry would have gone up from McD & Co. with one voice: 'ITALY!'

We gathered our many children and many bags on an empty spot on the main concourse and I rushed off to get tickets, timetables and refreshments. I guess I was gone about ten minutes because when I came back I noticed the atmosphere had changed more than just a bit.

'Is everything OK?' I volunteered. As I spoke, I knew I had said the wrong thing at the wrong time and in the wrong place.

Moo gave me chapter and verse what she thought about Italy, boats, trains, postings, BFBS, me, and the awkwardness of having a child at the end of each arm, one on the hip, and one inside while I fannied about trying to play the great administrator. There was a special section devoted to my selfishness, thoughtlessness and general library of faults. I was painted up and down the platforms of Rome Station. Even seasoned Italians, not averse to semaphoring confrontation, gave us a wide berth. Eventually after the rage, and the tears, came the ultimatum.

'I am NOT getting mixed up with yet another noisy crowd. You take the kids, and go to Cologne. I'll stay here.'

There didn't seem to be much logic in this but I knew enough to know that Moo meant it and that I would have to pick my next words, which must NOT include the expression 'don't be silly!', very, very carefully.

Suddenly – inspiration. 'Tell you what – see that porter over there on Platform 9? I'll talk to him and see if we can arrange a whole compartment just for us, with maybe a 'Do Not Disturb' or 'Reserved' sign on the door. What do you think? Will you give it a go if I get us a private compartment?'

A pair of red eyes and a snuffy nose looked up at me (Moo was sitting on our 'Flying Donkey' suitcase) and I thought I saw the smallest of nods. Heartened by this, I strode manfully in the direction of the Italian Railway Official, who turned out to be rather more than a porter, but a kind of train guard, with extra braid and buttons on his uniform which marked him out as important, if only in his own world.

I decided that the 'bemused supplicant foreigner seeking help' approach would be suitable. In my best 'talking to foreigners' English, I offered the following:

'Hello. I am with my wife, who is going to have a baby, and we have three small children with us. We want to go to Cologne but my wife is delicate, yes? and needs quiet. Is it possible...'

At this point I gave up, as he made dismissive arm movements and said something that made it clear he didn't understand or speak English. As we already know, I didn't speak Italian. Impasse.

Then suddenly I remembered my old Latin Master, George Vale, telling us, 'Latin is not a dead language. You will all find yourself using it one day.' That's it! I would use Latin. Sadly, I was so rusty that only a few words had stayed in the memory bank. But any port in a storm. I very cleverly 'Italianised' some Latin and English words and threw this at him:

'Yo voglio una compartimento totalli solo por me famiglia a Colognia prego. Mi senora este grando estomac, e tutti tres bambini difficile mobile.'

He gave me the kind of look reserved for drug dealers and lunatics.

I repeated the gist of what I'd said. With many variations. I think he was enjoying the cabaret. He made no attempt to dismiss me, or to turn and go. He waited to see what I would do next.

Wait one. He was Italian. Mafia and all that. Money. I reached for my wallet and extracted some high-value lire bed sheets. I waved a collection of giant notes under his nose and repeated, with mounting frustration, my request.

He looked at me again. This time I had offered to sleep with his daughter. The red of anger began to rise on the barometer of his face. He had won. I had lost. I would have to leave my pregnant wife behind and complete the journey with three squirmy kids. And afterwards, everybody would think I was an utter shit.

It was then that the Good Lord tapped me on the shoulder. I remembered that Moo and the tribe were actually in sight of the good official, still sitting in the same place on the platform, only twenty yards away. I made a sweeping gesture in their direction.

'Mia famiglia,' I panted in sheer, tired frustration. This was my last card. After this, my ammo was out and I was a failure.

'Aaaah!' said the functionary, raising his arms in friendly approbation. 'Bambini!' He took in the vista of Moo, surrounded by three tired angels and clearly awaiting a fourth. He looked at me and grinned.

'Bambini!' he repeated. He and I walked over to where the Fallen Madonna, or at least McDonagh, was sitting, looking puzzled.

'I think this nice man is going to help us,' I said. The glimmering of hope began to stir. I reverted to hand gestures, to try to make it clear to the guard that we would really like our own compartment.

He led us to the train and found us an empty compartment. That involved a deal of gesticulating, as there were already some occupants there. He used his authority to send them on their way and installed us inside. He then produced an official looking sign and slid it into a little frame on the door. It declared (I think) that this cabin was out of order.

We had a very quiet and pleasant journey to Cologne. But I've always been a little wary of Italy since then.

*****

Pulling into Cologne's mighty central railway station, having shrieked over the Rhine bridge, we felt a great sense of homecoming. We'd already called this amazing city home for more than three years so everything was familiar, especially the brooding blackened giant of Cologne Cathedral, the remarkable edifice that the RAF missed when they virtually razed the centre of the city to the ground during the last unpleasantness. We managed to find a taxi that would take all of us and I resurrected my German to ask for 'Lindenallee 1, Englischer Siedlung, bitte.'

We pulled up outside the familiar façade of the BFBS mansion on Lindenallee. I paid the driver and decanted the tribe onto the pavement. I tried to open the front door. It was locked. As this was mid-afternoon on a working day, this was worrying. I stepped back and noticed that the low window of the admin office was open. It was the work of a moment to climb through it and stand once again in the office where I had fought off the demons of 'admin'. (In German, I still call it 'ettmin', because it sounds even more horrible like that.)

Suddenly the door to the next room opened and a former Second World War Luftwaffe pilot, Willy Grasens, strutted in. He looked me up and down, with some surprise and not a little annoyance. A stubbly stranger had pitched up in his domain and needed to be dealt with. He cut to the chase.

'How did you get in here?' 'I climbed through the window.'

'You should not have climbed through the window.' 'The front door was locked.'

By this time he could tell that, underneath the traveller's dirt, I was a well-spoken intruder and not likely to cause aggro or grief. However, *he* was the King of the Castle and he was a trained warrior with delegated powers. In Germany, that means dangerous.

I explained who I was, why I was there and why I had need of his services. Once the ice had been broken, the front door was unlocked and the McD tribe was duly documented and driven to our new abode, a massive old six-bedroom house complete with old servants' quarters, in Rösbergerstrasse, where the middle ranking BFBS staff lived. It was good to be home among the distempered walls, G-Plan furniture and every-need-catered-for items from the giant fridge down to the 'spoon, officers, salt, 1' on the vast inventory.

Mr Hudson, the Barrack Inventory Accountant, almost shuddered to see us again. It wasn't often he had to face a family for a second time. It was especially nasty for him, as he knew that we knew all his tricks and weren't about to be conned or fobbed off again in a hurry. He processed us, tight-lipped and workmanlike, then left us to our own devices. We were home.

*****

Cologne for the second time was very different, as the next few days would reveal. To start with, there was a new boss. John Parsons had swapped roles with outgoing Controller of Programmes, Pat Pachebat, who was now Station Controller BFBS Cologne, a position he had aspired to for many, many years. Pat was a personable, charming and urbane man. He disliked me utterly, and I him. Very early on he acquired from me the nickname of 'Fred Astaire'.

He might have thought it was a compliment, as he fancied himself as a ladies' man and a bit of a mover on the ballroom floor, but it had more to do with a story by Kurt Vonnegut in 'Breakfast of Champions' – the story of the alien from the planet Zog, whose only method of communication is by farting and tap dancing. He lands in suburban America, where he sees that the owner of the house in whose garden he has landed is unaware that his residence is ablaze. He rushes into the lounge, stands in front of the TV and tells the owner his house is on fire. Sadly, the man sees only a little green man farting and tap dancing and brains him with a handy golf club. Vonnegut's comment on this refers to 'man's tragic failure to communicate'. For us, Pat Pachebat was the man from Zog, pointlessly farting and tap-dancing his plans for the station.

And it must be said: Pat Pachebat and his staff had a great disconnect. Pat had a vision for his station derived only from his vision of How Things Ought To Be, whereas the rest of us worked on the premise of How Things Are. 'Format 77' had been part introduced in Cologne, but as most of the staff were over 50, it happened with little enthusiasm. BFBS Germany had always relayed BBC Radio Four's 'Woman's Hour' in the early afternoon. On Ian Woolf's command, the programme became a victim of the new format - until a petition of only 87 signatures, generated by a Brigadier's wife, hit Pat's desk. He immediately re-instated 'Woman's Hour', thereby driving a huge wedge of 'yesterday' into an already diluted and half-hearted version of 'today'.

As well as Pat, we had the added delights of Ken Doherty – once known as the only sane BFBS Station Controller – seething over only having the number two job of Senior Programme Organiser; Auntie Kay, who did the schedules, looked after her Mum and worked mainly down the road for the English service of Deutsche Welle; Keith Rawlings, in his late fifties, a charming and quite modern gentleman who quite liked some of the music he played and Uncle Bill, of Kinder Club fame, known for his hatred of pop music and soon to be known even more for his hatred of Pat Pachebat. Yes, it would be fair to say that the upper echelons of BFBS Cologne were embedded in their fifties and in THE fifties. The station sounded bad, tired and fragmented. After Malta, it was difficult to see how a station with five times the resources and three times the staff could make such a pig's ear of things.

Pat explained to me why 'Format 77' wasn't working in Cologne, why the Director and Bob Pierson were mad in thinking it was a worldwide solution, and that BFBS worked best when it served its local audience. (I had to wonder at this, given the lack of targeted listening coming out of the speakers.) Luckily, I was arriving at a special time. He, Pat Pachebat, was going to bring something special to BFBS Cologne that had been a runaway success in BFN Klagenfurt, Austria, during the late forties.

I made the mistake of looking interested and asking what this secret weapon might be.

'Radio Tombola,' said Pat, as if he'd just succeeded in splitting the atom.

'Oh shit,' I thought. 'He means it.'

'You mean,' I said, 'that you actually call out the numbers on air and people fill in the tickets at home, just like real tombola.'

He nodded, obviously glad that I was engaged with this revolutionary concept.

'But they can't shout 'House!' when they've got all the numbers.'

'No, but our porter, Paul Chapman, goes through the returned 'full house' tickets against the numbers called. That way we know who finished in the fewest numbers and they win the monthly jackpot.'

I made the mistake of laughing and told Pat it sounded so old fashioned that it might just work. Retro bad taste, if nothing else.

He glared at me. Whatever he'd thought of me before, I had now trodden on his dreams; I was an excrescence in his sight and must be cast out into the darkness of ill regard. I left the office, still sniggering.

But the worst was yet to come. Uncle Bill had been dragooned into being the 'Voice of the Balls' (it being 1978, we couldn't call it that on air). In the voice of Big Wood's 'Mr Badger', he snided out the winning numbers, sounding very much like a pervert sidling up to an unsuspecting victim with an improper request. To his eternal credit, Bill thought, like the rest of us, that this travesty had no place in the Forces' broadcasting of the seventies, but he stiff-upper-lipped his way through the whole charade.

If the senior part of the programme side was creaking at the joints, there was a flash of genius on the 'other side'. Senior Engineer Colin Rugg - 'Herr Rugg', or 'Hair Rug', as he used to call himself, to the amusement of the German staff) was a visionary, both on the technical side and as a great ally of the programme side. He had the revolutionary notion that if programme and technical staff worked together, then better broadcasting could be the result. Decades of 'us' and 'them' began to disappear as his influence grew stronger and stronger. His streamlined Heath Robinson inventions seemed to work: automated playout of announcements, machines acroynmed FARTS and ARRSE, and a desire to innovate and break some old taboos, such as the 'German equipment only' policy on station.

He brought in a Norwegian cartridge playout machine, which proceeded to eat any tape put into it. The NCR engineers smiled at each other knowingly as Colin retained his sense of optimism whilst pulling shredded tape from its entrails. But we were not ready for his ultimate triumph – the circular ergonomic presenters' desk.

Colin had started informal meetings of 'proggies' and 'techies' to see what each might do to help the other. After one session the idea of the circular broadcasting console was born. The idea was that you sat in the pod and had, thanks to a swivel chair, 360 degree access to kit, working surfaces and places to stack things so that everything was in easy reach. The headphones were suspended from the ceiling on a coiled flex from the ceiling in order to stop them from getting in the way: you just plucked them from mid-air (they hovered loosely at about head height) and never had to worry about the headphone cable knocking off your coffee or brushing your scripts to the floor.

Gilbert Dennis, porter and ace carpenter, built the desk to his own professional standards; covered in apple green plastic, it looked like Space City. It was kitted out with the latest turntables, cart machines and fader panel. We all wanted to use it – after all, *we* had had a hand in its design: clever us! (Good psychology, Colin...)

Mark Caldwell, a rather serious broadcaster, was chosen (perhaps as the most expendable if the kit blew up) to fire up the beast and submit her to a programme. It went brilliantly. The kit worked precisely as it should and the very nervous Mark rose to dizzy heights as his confidence grew with the ease of operation of the new mean green machine.

There was only one teething issue, which we all spotted. You couldn't miss it. There was a repetitive 'Scree! Scree!'noise coming from the output. Time to get the diagnostic kit out. Germany's finest audio engineers, armed with decades of knowledge, pulled the kit to pieces, checked every junction, connection and circuit and put it back together again.

Still, 'Scree! Scree!'Apparently the fault was not electrical.

So each bit of the kit was tested separately. Tape machine, gram, cart machine, fader board... All AOK. So it wasn't the kit at all. The engineers had drawn a blank. Could it be the worst of any engineer's nightmares – the intermittent fault? The kind of fault that only happens when it isn't being observed, a bit like Schrodinger's cat felling trees in a silent forest, or some such quantum leap? Only one thing to do. Another live show from the studio, and even closer monitoring.

A victim and a show were found, and the exercise repeated. Great show, happy DJ – and 'Scree! Scree!' heard sporadically throughout the show. What could it be? A very worried Colin Rugg considered the possibility of a damaged reputation. Suddenly, a light glimmered.

'I've got it,' said Colin. 'It's mechanical.'

We bowed in admiration to The Master. Of course. What else could it be?

He listened further to the 'Scree! Scree!' noise. Then he walked into the studio and started, literally, to bend his ear to various parts of the studio furniture. Then, with the look of a man who has Seen The Future And Found It Shiny, he emerged and told us with a flourish: 'It's the studio chair!'

Of course. The presenter jiggled around quite a lot in his chair and even the most confident of presenters tended to have little 'movement tics', where they kept rhythm with the music, or even with the flow of their own voices. The studio chair! What else?

A new studio chair was sent for and sat on. 'Scree! Scree!'... Well, it was the same model of chair. Time to try a different make of swivel chair. We had three more types. All of them appeared to emit exactly the same sound, in exactly the same way. Slowly, the truth dawned. It was *not* the studio chair. By now the entire engineering wing was looking drained and defeated. Anglo-German pride had reached a nadir.

There would be one more attempt to locate the fault during a live show, after which the new studio would have to be demolished in favour of an off-the-shelf standard package. Morale was rock bottom.

Mark Caldwell walked into the studio with iron in his soul. He knew it was his fault, whatever anybody said. He was doomed. The scapegoat. The person people point fingers and snigger at in corridors. Halfway through Mark's show ('Scree! Scree!'), Colin pressed the talkback button in NCR and asked Mark a question.

Mark had turned away from the microphone to set up a disc on the turntable furthest away from the front. He jerked his head around to answer. Suddenly Colin's eyes lit up. Realisation! He knew now what it was. A broad grin replaced the look of the hunted man. He took a conventional set of headphones, took them into the studio, plugged them into the front of the desk and pushed the ceiling-mounted 'cans' out of the way.

From that moment, the show was Scree-free. The guilty party had been the sky borne headphones (or rather, after some examination, the bearing that was there to let the cable turn with the presenter). A quick drop of the engineer's best friend, WD-40, and we entered the 21st Century of supersonic broadcasting. Colin was brilliant once again. Even the most grudging of our German engineers conceded that this was now a huge success.

*****

Colin was wonderfully subversive. He didn't actually confront Pat in his position of Station Controller; he quietly supported the good bits and helpfully undermined the rest. We both shared, with presenter Uncle Bill, an utter loathing of Pat's 'radio tombola', which polluted the airwaves for far too long once a month on a weekday evening.

On one occasion, Bill was on leave and Pat, who was really *so* very fond of me and knew of my great love of his crappy bingo show, gave me the poisoned chalice of presenting that month's edition of the wondrous programme. I shuffled morosely into 'A' Studio with my bag full of balls and my heart full of lead. Through the glass, I was delighted to see the cheery face of Colin Rugg, who had also been dragooned into participating in this nonsense.

I should explain that, this being the late seventies, BFBS had only just gone stereo. Colin told the wonderful tale of the activated stereo light. We sent a signal along the transmission path, which made the 'stereo' indicator on domestic radios go 'live'. Apparently, when the engineers had been setting up the stereo system, they activated the light a few weeks before they actually activated the stereo signal itself.

No sooner had their little stereo lights come on, than hundreds of listeners got it touch with BFBS to congratulate the station on being so up to date. This new stereo service was marvellous; you really could hear the difference; it was light years ahead of what it used to be – and so on. Colin didn't have the heart to tell them that the actual stereo signal hadn't started up yet, but calculated the savings that could have been made if we'd simply lied to the audience by just putting on the light without bothering with the rest of the package.

Anyway, back to the pantomime. 'Good evening,' I began. 'I'm PMcD, sitting in for Uncle Bill, and it's time once again for - dramatic pause, enthusiasm in voice –'Radio Tombola'! My engineer tonight is Colin Rugg (we all knew what Colin thought about being called '*my*' engineer!) and the Jackpot this month is DM1,500, so there's a lot to play for. I'll give you a minute or two to get your tickets and pens, so here's Boney M to get us there.'

The song was duly played. Colin was looking expectantly through the glass, trying not to laugh. I was returning the odd glimpse, also worried about 'corpsing' (going to pieces on-air).

'Right everybody, eyes down for a full house. On its own, number three. Four and seven, forty-seven.

Five and three, fifty-three. Kelly's eye, number one. Two...'

This made the shipping forecast, or even the German news, sound mildly interesting. God, it was tedious. A bit of me began to wander as I continued to read the seemingly endless list of numbers. This really was 'shit click radio' (as in, 'I wonder what's on BFBS right now? Oh, shit.' Click 'off' button...).

As I daydreamed and read more numbers, I was suddenly aware that the stereo 'picture' was shifting in my headphones. To give at least some atmosphere and excitement to proceedings, one microphone was pointed at the rolling drum that contained the plastic tombola balls. It took me a moment or two to realise that Colin had a hand on his mixing desk and was 'panning' the 'balls mic' from centre, to the left, and then slowly all the way through to the right. At home, the listener would have the impression of the noise of the balls moving from one side of the room to the other.

At the subsequent inquiry in Pat Pachebat's office, it was determined that even a saint might have fallen off the cross, given what happened next.

I couldn't help it. I just came out with it. 'In case you're wondering what's going on, Colin Rugg, my engineer, is actually moving my balls from left to right.'

Why did I say that? And why then did I look up to see Colin going deep purple and about to explode in hysterics? And how was it, with twenty numbers still to go, I spluttered and giggled my way through them, not daring to look up again? Luckily, Colin realised that if he 'moved my balls' again, there might be a diplomatic incident, so at least they stayed in the middle for the rest of the show.

The phone rang straight after my shift. The Station Controller was not amused and there would be an interview without coffee in his office. To Colin's eternal credit he took all of the blame and, being very much more senior than me, was given a mild chewing out. Pat contented himself with a 'next time' glare at me as Colin and I retreated.

The Radio Tombola nonsense had a fitting ending when it was noticed that there appeared to be a regular jackpot winner on the Dutch border. The laws of chance did not allow this to happen. The Army's SIB (Special Investigation Branch) were called in to investigate and they found a shifty man with the equivalent of a John Bull printing kit, who had been sending in 'winning' tickets printed after the event. At last, Radio Tombola died a well-deserved death.

*****

Sadly, the gradual process of taking the rip out of Pat Pachebat was not turning out to be a clever thing to do at all. Senior Programme Organiser Ken Doherty was delighted to announce that he was to be posted to warmer climes, to be replaced by the only man who could take the giant tanker of BFBS Germany and turn it around to face the future: Bob Pierson, my old boss from Malta. I felt a bit like John the Baptist sent ahead to prepare the ground for the Messiah. The signs, however, were not good.

Pat had already showed his hand by reinstating 'Woman's Hour', which blocked the through-the-day sequence programming of 'Format 77'. The usual reasons were given: Germany's a different case; we have real movers and shakers here; much as we'd like to, we can't go against our paymasters – there were more, but none of them appeared to concentrate on the needs of the majority of the listeners.

Then there was the average age and musical disposition of the BFBS staff. They, given their heads, would have played whatever they remembered from their own 'time of life', thus it was not unusual to hear big band forties music and middle of the road greats such as Ella Fitzgerald and Frank Sinatra. The one or two younger ones were playing top forty hits and real golden oldies but the rents in the music fabric sounded like a gearbox without synchromesh going from reverse to third. There was no attempt at music policy.

Then, in short order, two bombshells. Malta's old Schafer arrived in its packing cases and Bob Pierson appeared for his re-match with BFBS Cologne. He knew from the start that although he would have support from Ian Woolf at the top and from me, in whatever powers I could muster, the rest of the Cologne staff knew what was coming - and didn't like it one little bit.

Fairly soon after Schafer had been built and installed in NCR - to the absolute loathing of the control room engineers, for whom the word 'automation' was spelt 'redundancy' - it was test run. Despite some teething troubles, it wasn't too long before it could be partially commissioned. For a year or so, it dealt only with the evening 'mixed' programming, as Germany still closed down late at night with its famous Evening Hymn, Last Post and National Anthem sequence – one of the most memorable and popular parts of its output.

At about this time, Bob was on leave and, because I was doing the schedules and appearing to be the 'Senior Programme Assistant", I held the weekly programme meeting in one of the studios. It became very clear that there was a huge wave of sheer antipathy, both to Bob and to his proposed 'Format 77' changes. I tried to turn the tanker, but the tanker was having none of it. The crew's minds were set. But we had to move on. I would have to see my favourite person – Pat Pachebat, Station Controller.

I didn't bother with formalities, or the gateguard. I had run along the 300-yard covered walkway between the Parkstrasse studio building and the Lindenallee admin ('etmin') block, straight into Pat's office. Before he had the chance to remind me of correct protocol, I blurted out that the programme staff were in revolt against Bob's proposed changes, that everyone else knew that 'Format 77' worked and that if we ignored it we'd be a laughing stick and in any case Uncle Ian thought it was the way to go and the audience research backed it up and it was taking the service forward and…

I was coldly, sharply, but politely told to shut up. I was invited to sit down. I was than given a wonderfully calm and utterly patronising appraisal of Bob's – and mine – 'bull in a china shop' approach, especially with changes as fundamental as these, which he, Pat, was dubious about in any event, especially as Germany was a special case – and so on. As he spoke, I realised he had no intention of quashing the rebels or of helping Bob in his task to reset the output, the network and the station. Whatever respect I had for his authority disappeared completely. He was now part of the enemy.

It was to Bob's eternal credit that he understood entirely the provenance and nature of the criticism and between us we set out to do a little more in the way of explanation and some 'hearts and minds' bridge-building in order to begin the process of taking the others with us. Slowly, younger people were posted in and the old and bold given more 'out of mainstream hours' work to do. But it had all left a bit of a bad taste behind. Thank goodness for Radio Cream – it cures even the most rotten of ills.

Chapter Fifteen:

Bodies, Booze and Boo Boos

'Radio Cream' – Richard 'Asters'Astbury had coined the phrase. It was free and came out of your speakers. You rubbed it on your ears and it made you feel great. We happy few HM Civil Service disc jockeys enjoyed a privileged life in the ivory towers of our millionaires' suburb in southern and very leafy Cologne, and spent a lot of our time enjoying the many bars and speakeasies in the buildings.

There was always a piccolo of sekt to be had from mid-morning onwards in the recording channel near 'A' studio, run by the formidable Jürgen Bock, and from about noon until around half-past two it was possible to get a drink and a snack in the Lindenallee bar, where we rubbed shoulders with the German traffic & security police, who were unofficial 'honorary' members.

After bar time, I would occasionally invite the odd character up to my office, which was painted lilac and white (it cost me a couple of crates when the German painters had come round), fully carpeted (against civil service regulations) and scattered with armchairs which hadn't been discarded when the station changed to the less comfortable G-Plan furniture. Of course, it also sported a fridge, and many an afternoon was spent up there indulging in excellent company and not a lot of work.

Station driver, Walter Schaaf, introduced me to one of his buddies, a Deputy Kommissar of Police (Plain Clothes Division) from the nearby city of Düsseldorf. Friedo was a bit street-wise, actually chased gangsters and carried a real gun. What was important was that as long as we knew Friedo, we could enjoy the full protection of the law, even from the law. And that's how Friedo came to be invited to one of our parties.

He was greeted, as were the other guests, by our then butler (sic), the elephantine rock guitarist Mike Rogerson-Smith (more of whom in a moment), who used to greet potential guests at the front door bearing a carving knife and a black look. (All our *real* friends just let themselves in round the back and special friends were known to hop in our bedroom window from the garden.) Friedo enjoyed the strange company of Brits, who seemed very relaxed and easy going and, more importantly, enjoyed knocking them back and kicking off with a few songs and even sketches. As the night drew on, his normal policeman's guard began to drop.

Then suddenly, tragedy. Moo discovered that we had run out of Coke. How could the breadwinner subsist at the party without rum and coke? It was his favourite party fuel. Without it, the night would grind to a halt. She broke the news gently. My head jerked up, and I tried to focus through eyeballs that had already gone a bit fuzzy. I always prided myself on dynamic thinking. Now was an occasion calling for forensic and spirited solutions to a major problem. I focused on Friedo in front of me.

'Friedo, did you come by car?' I burbled, in German. Luckily or unluckily, Friedo burbled back, from a position of being mildly pissed himself, that thish indeed wash the case. His car was outside.

'Thass it then,' I pronounced, badly. 'I'll take Friedo's car - 's only jush down the road – an' I'll get shome more Coke from the kiosk.'(I should have mentioned – it was gone midnight.)

We bumbled out to the car. It looked a bit low slung and sporty to me. Never mind. I got inside and made myself comfortable. I was beginning to get a bit peeved with Friedo, who was peering at me through the driver's window, while swaying gently in the night air. He was a bit slow telling me where to put the key to start it and which pedals made the thing go faster and stop and where the gear lever was. Had he been a bit more sober, he would have noticed that the questions being asked were not those of a competent driver.

Eventually I started the car, waved him away and kangarooed slowly down the road, leaving the forlorn figure in the middle, wondering whether it had been a good idea to put his plain clothed, modified, go faster police car in the hands of a somewhat tiddled English disc jockey. The feeling of horror mounted when Moo came out and told him that the latest driver of his car was completely wrecked, on top of which he had never had a driving licence in his life. Not even a provisional one. Why? Because he always said his Irish temper would make him unsafe on the roads.

Friedo felt suddenly unwell and was steered towards the sofa in the lounge, where he could sit and contemplate the report he would be writing later that night regarding the complete write off of a Düsseldorf police car loaned out to a three-sheets-to-the-wind British partygoer.

Meanwhile, the driver was quite enjoying the experience. Once I'd mastered the gear stick thing and worked out which were the go faster and go slower pedals, it was a breeze, really. Being after midnight, all the law-abiding citizenry were long in their beds and the only cars out belonged to men of ill-will – thieves, murderers, rapists and hit men – who recognised a plain clothes police car straight away, and knew fine well to keep their distance.

Oh dear. The little kiosk in the suburbs was closed. Nothing else for it: I'd have to drive into the city of

Cologne itself. I ended up going through the three major ring roads, dozens of intersections and right into the Cathedral centre of the massive city of Cologne. I somehow parked, got a couple of cases of Coke, stowed them in the boot and drove off. Luckily, I had the river Rhine on my left, which was like a huge pointer going all the way up to a turning I knew, so I bumbled up Rheinuferstrasse with my precious cargo and was soon back at our house.

For some reason, Moo was there to greet me. 'You stupid…!' she began, hugging and cursing me at the same time. I thought I'd done well: mighty hunter routine and all that, bringing back the goodies. She seemed more concerned at the twitching wreck on the sofa inside who was burbling about the end of his police career. I walked up to Friedo and gave him back his keys. I read the expression in his eyes, reassured him I hadn't been stopped and that his car was in one piesh.

It took him a few minutes to do a quick inspection. Then we were, once again, the best of friends, with some hours on the drinking clock and plenty of Coke in the fridge.

It was a few days later that Friedo, having recovered, came to the station for a lower-key return match. He had a couple of hours spare whilst following a local villain and popped into the station bar at lunchtime, carrying a hardback book with him. I thought this was a bit strange – a copper with a book – but he left it upstairs in my office/clubroom and we went to enjoy a few at Graf Stieldorf's little bar. Good times, good times, plenty of craic – but eventually, at about two-ish, it was time for Friedo to put on his 'hunting villains' face and get back onto those there mean streets. I saw him off and popped up to the office for a quiet read and an afternoon delight. (I always kept some Krimsekt – Crimean bubbly white wine – in the fridge as it was light and refreshing.)

Suddenly the phone rang. It was Friedo. Had he, by any chance, left a fairly large hardback book in my office?

Yes, he had. I could see it by the door, on the top of my very tall and elegantly white-painted filing cabinet. Could I open the book and check inside?

I went over to the book, which was very heavy, and opened the cover. It was a false book. It contained a police pistol.

'Er, Friedo,' I gulped, 'there seems to be a gun in here.'

'Quiet!' came a low bark. 'Someone might be listening.'

I got the message, but thought it was time for a bit of cabaret.

'Hey, Friedo it's quite heavy,' I said, taking the gun out of the book cover. I checked it over. It was loaded. Luckily it was also equipped with a safety catch and I knew just about enough from my Army cadet days to realise it was safe as long as I didn't point and shoot.

So I pretended over the phone to do just that, to the background noise of a whimpering policeman who was about to lose a good friend and attend a very probing board of enquiry.

'Hey Friedo, this really is a good piece. I love the way the hammer goes back.' (I rattled the grip on the mouthpiece of the phone.) 'I wonder if I could hit the fridge door from here.'

I realised at this point that Friedo was beginning to have a seizure.

'Don't worry,' I said. 'It's back in the book and I've locked it behind some papers in the top drawer till you get here.'

Half an hour later, Friedo came back for his gun. It had been a wonderfully jolly lunchtime session but it took him a week or two to be able to laugh at it.

*****

One of the great delights of having a station bar was that whenever major record label companies were touting their latest stars, they would follow up an interview with a drink and some nibbles with us. On one occasion, we were about to be honoured by the presence of the huge (in more ways than one) star Demis Roussos, who had deigned to descend the Olympian heights to grant me a radio interview. He arrived with his retinue and behaved with the easy charm of the man who had made it to the top. He was effusively pleasant to everybody he met; he charmed the ladies, even the boss's frightening gate guard, Frau Vogt; he did his interview like a good star and said all the right things; he even recorded a couple of drop-ins for my show: 'Hello, I am Demis Roussos an' I always love eet when I leesten to the PMcD Show' - that sort of nonsense.

At the end of it all I wondered out loud to the record label rep if Demis fancied a quick jar at the bar and was cheerfully surprised when he said yes, he would be delighted, after such an easy and relaxed interview.

(My interview technique was scarcely Paxman-esque.) We made a progress down the long connecting corridor and up the two flights of stairs to the bar. If I'd been watching a little more closely, I would have noted that the good singer was a wee bit out of breath. But duty called and drinks needed to be sorted.

Also in the bar, by chance, were my kids. I'm not sure if they were all there but this tale only requires the notion that eldest son, Olly, still a toddler, was standing in the bar holding a bar of Cadbury's milk chocolate. However, there were some toys worth playing with in the annexe room of the bar, so Olly put his chocolate bar down on the sofa in a dark alcove of the bar room and went next door to play.

By now, Demis had a drink in his hand and expressed a wish to sit down. The bar stools were too much of a climbing expedition for the massive singer and thus it was that he was steered into the gloom of the alcove, where he sat on the sofa.

And of course, he was wearing his white full-length kaftan. And of course, his fundament went fatally to the very spot where son Olly had placed an open bar of Cadbury's milk chocolate.

And of course, none of us knew of this situation at the time. Demis continued to be charm itself and stayed that way for about twenty minutes. Then came the time for farewells. As Demis stood up, I glanced behind him to see if he'd left anything. Well, he had, in a kind of way. The chocolate wrapper, at least, was there on the sofa. The chocolate itself was on the back of his kaftan, in exactly the place where it was going to cause maximum embarrassment.

How to get out of this situation? We couldn't really tell him about my son and his choccy bar – makes a jolly tale now, but a Greek God with a king-sized skid mark on his kaftan is no laughing matter. I confessed to the record label lady what had happened. Luckily, she was a pragmatist and understood immediately the need to get Demis out without anyone spotting the outrage to his person, image and dignity.

She passed the message on to two of her acolytes, who formed a human screen around the nether regions of the humungous Hellenic. The whole party then negotiated the stairs, got into cars and made it back to base.

I was told later that Demis's dresser had also been told, was also pragmatic, and managed to remove the by now offensive garment without the superstar being any the wiser. It had been a close call.

*****

My colleagues also had fun with their studio guests from time to time. I need to explain that we had a wonderful love/hate relationship with the record companies. In simple terms, if we did a certain number of promotional interviews with up and coming German bands, they would bring us in the odd international star. The going rate was about five duff German bands for one decent, glow-in-the-dark, act.

Sadly, the 'local' interviews tended to consist of three questions, all of which seemed to elicit the same answer from every band:

'Could you tell us about your new single?'

'Er, it is...how says one...a new directions to us...and the record is...er...it is...very hot on the front side but also much warm on the backside...and it is a message from love...and with a strong beat...'

'And will you be touring in the next few months?'

'Ja, we make a whole of Westfalen tournee in two months and there we will playing be in the church halls and the communal centres of towns and willages...we make the first konzert at Obergürgelbergen Church Hall on Saturday...'

'What about travelling outside Germany?'

'Ach, ja, for us is very important that we shall go to Amerika und become a very international band. Klaus-Dietrich knows some people in der Okefenokee Swamp area, he has some family there.'

In other words, dire stuff. And that's before we played the song. Once. And then, blessed oblivion. One of my successors made the process even less painful by spooling the interview tape directly into the wastepaper bin, but I thought that a bit unfair.

We had done our five local interviews. High in the charts on this occasion was one-hit wonder Drupi, who was huge in the UK with his blinding hit 'Vado Via'. I did the negotiations and decided that Drupi should go on Stevie Withers' afternoon show. Stevie was over the moon – he loved that ballady kind of music and an interview from a real star was always a bonus.

Drupi, plus retinue, duly arrived while Stevie was already spinning discs in the studio. He gave Stevie a smile and a wave and sat down quietly so he could see the show through the glass. I noticed the record company rep fussing over him with a few hand gestures, which ended up with Drupi getting a cup of coffee, but he seemed quite happy just to listen, so I carried on pretending to be Stevie's producer. I went into the studio, set up a chair and a guest microphone and steered the great man in.

Stevie was coming to the end of a record so he looked up, waved to Drupi, said, 'We'll be on in a moment!' and brought the disc to an end.

'Manhattan Transfer and 'Chanson D'Amour'. This is BFBS, I'm Stevie Withers, and right now– a special guest. With 'Vado Via' riding high in the charts, young Drupi, the overnight sensation, is turning out to be very much in demand, so we're delighted that he's been able to take a few minutes out of his busy schedule to come and see us in the studio here in Cologne. Drupi – welcome! How do you feel about 'Vado Via' doing so well?'

There was a long pause. Drupi seemed to consider the question. His face displayed a variety of expressions. Sadly, none of them contained any noise at all, which is bad for radio. He took a breath and had another silent stab of thinking of something to say.

Nature abhors a vacuum; radio loathes a silence. Stevie had to step in. 'Well, Drupi, what I meant was, were you surprised at how quickly 'Vado Via' sold?'

Even Drupi realised that a noise had to be made at this point. Sadly, the only answer he could provide was 'que?'

Drupi did not speak a single word of English. I rescued him from the studio. Stevie made an excuse about his guest having a sore throat and played the record.

I gave the record rep the bollocking of a lifetime. Then I faced Stevie in the studio and he gave me the bollocking of a lifetime. Drupi made shed loads of money. Life is SO unfair.

*****

But it was my final recording session that nearly got me drummed out of the service. By this stage our most famous presenter on station was Rick Lunt (now Patrick Lunt, ex-BBC Radio 2 newsreader and presenter, voiceovers done while you wait). I'd already got into trouble with Pat Pachebat by mixing up his jingles, including one that spelt out his name with a music backing. 'R-I-C-K L-U-N-T – Rick Lunt!' became, with a bit of smart editing and a lot of mischief, 'L-I-C-K R-U-N-T – Lick Runt!' Pachebat was annoyed with that, and also with the 'Radio Moron' drop-ins which attempted to mirror Rick's very deep and slow voice.

For all my witty sabotage, which also included attempting to set fire to his stuffed parrot, Rick was a good chum and his programme was hugely popular, which made me wonder how that slogan came to be painted on the outside wall of Parkstrasse 61.

I'd better explain. Our former butler, Mike Rogerson-Smith, composer of a great guitar track called 'Day in the Life of a Carrot Pudding' (you had to be there), phoned me up one day to tell me he was now axeman for the Softies, a neo-Punk band. I was trying to sound neutral, as I had visions of safety pins, PVC jeans and people spitting at me. He began his spiel.

'We're touring cities from next month and we'd be grateful for maybe a recording or an interview – maybe a bit of contact with German radio stations?'

I was heading for the 'sorry, no time' approach when Mike reminded me how many meals he'd cooked for us and how many idiots he'd kept away from our door with his steely-eyed stare (and knife) and how he'd done all that for pocket money of only DM20 a week plus all the drink he wanted. I began to weaken and, just at the key moment, he played his ace.

'Oh, I forgot to mention. We've got a guest lead singer – Captain Sensible, of The Damned.'

Wow. This was solid gold. Not to be ignored. I arranged to meet the band at WDR Radio's home pub in Cologne's Wallrafplatz, just a few steps away from Cologne cathedral.

It turned out to be a long session. Captain Sensible was a quirkish, Harpo Marx lookalike and full-blown eccentric who turned out to be a prodigious beer drinker, as were we all that afternoon.

I had arranged for a local German music reporter, Winfried Trenkler, to pop along for a pop scoop and early on in the proceedings this earnest long-haired creature turned up wearing Lennon glasses and what looked like a pair of psychedelic paisley pyjamas – the sort you have to blink at in the vague hope they and their wearer might just go away. Winfried joined us at a scrubbed wooden table and was clearly keen to ingratiate himself. Sensible & Co sensed cabaret and we began to hatch a plot.

It was very childish but it would serve. Winfried asked early on if he might buy a round of drinks for the band in exchange for a short interview with Sensible. After lots of pretend negotiation, we agreed. He went off to get the round. We had a quick conflab. He was bound to want to say the equivalent of 'Prosit!'(Cheers!) when we raised our glasses in traditional salute to our benefactor. So what we were going to do was to respond with a unison chorus of 'Up Yours!' and swear blind that this was the normal Brit response for drinks. We were overheard by some rather hard-bitten WDR producers, who smiled sardonically in the background.

Finally Winfried appeared, followed by a waitress bearing a huge tray of beers. Once they'd been doled out, Winfried raised his glass. 'Prosit!' he started, then put his glass down and waved for silence, thereby ruining our plan at a stroke. But only for an instant. 'I'm sorry,' he continued 'What is it that you say for greeting in England when beer is bought?'

Hook, line and sinker. At rock stage projection level, the small bar was subjected to a 100 decibel yell from the Softies and friends: *'Up Yours!'*, followed by the draining of glasses. By the end of the afternoon session, the whole bar was toasting each other and passers by outside, with that most 'traditional' of English toasts. There wasn't a dry pair of trousers in the house.

After this, it was fairly easy to set up a recording session in our studios. Sadly, on the grounds that Pat Pachebat would have killed me if he knew his radio station was about to be occupied by a drunken mob of punk rockers, the session was scheduled for midnight, recording engineers and followers sworn to secrecy, and the porter duly bribed.

We all slunk up to Studio 'A' like a bunch of naughty schoolboys. There was a rehearsal of sorts, and a lot of swearing. I think somebody got hit. There was a bit of blood, but luckily we had plenty of painkillers, which came in cans mainly labelled 'Bier'. Luckily, Mike was in charge of the band and, because he was clearly the biggest and the loudest voice, what he said seemed to go.

Soon, the band declared itself ready to record. Sadly, we discovered at this crucial moment that Captain Sensible had gone AWOL. We finally found him astride a willing groupie at the bottom of a stairwell some distance away. It very nearly took three of us and a crowbar to separate them. What we didn't see was the scrawl he had done, involving a swastika and a moustache, on the portrait of Her Majesty The Queen hanging outside Auntie Kay Donnelly's office. Nor had we seen the slogan, in letters two feet high, drawn in black spray paint on the cream front-facing wall of the studio block wall, about fifteen feet up: 'Rick Lunt is a C....' No, we would discover these after the session, and spend three hours fixing the damage.

We finally assembled in the studio and a recording of sorts was done, followed by a very animated post mortem and a very long scrubbing session. Captain Sensible decamped to his hotel.

There was a sting in the tale. Pachebat did find out about the recording session but lips remained sealed regarding the horrors of the night. Sensible woke up feeling guilty about the drama and invited himself round to my house the next day to take afternoon tea and show his less excessive side. He was doing very well, until he discovered my moped. He took it for a very conspicuous ride along all the garden frontages in our street – including all the low hedges that separated each garden.

And that was my part in the Great Punk Revolution. Ouch.

*****

Back in the real world, antipathy to 'Format 77' was diminishing. With Ken Doherty gone and some of the old and bold replaced with younger and more dynamic presenters, the concept of popular sequence programme gradually became established. For Bob Pierson, it was perhaps the most difficult of times, but he never gave up hope and his determination got us through in the end.

The serious side of broadcasting always had to play second fiddle to our in-house cabaret. One of our principal boys was a wondrously camp presenter, Andrew Pastouna, whose voice dripped with Received Pronunciation. He made Brian Sewell sound common, even though he was of Greek lineage, with his parents running a fish parlour in Fazakerley (my version of the truth, which was that Pastouna Sr. was in the fish importing business on a grand scale).

Andrew had a serious side – he actually spent all his pennies on his collection of Royal Rolls Royces and Bentleys. Yes, cars that had once belonged to the Royal Family. His favourite was a brown, gold-flecked Roller, which he called 'Charlotte Russe'. It was fitted out with ceremonial brackets so that when Andrew went 'up country' to open a fete or make a personal appearance, he would drive close to the camp, then 'borrow' a prearranged army driver in Number One ceremonial dress to take him to the venue. On the right bumper, the Union Flag pennant; on the left bumper, the Pastouna coat of arms, and on the top bracket above the windshield, the plaque of the regiment or unit he was visiting. He knew how to make an entrance, our Andrew.

Oh, must I mention it again? He was as camp as a row of pink tents, in the days when it wasn't quite legal to be *that* camp. His friends included a number of grooms at Windsor Castle, where he stabled more than one of his cars. One BFBS padre used to dine out on a conversation he'd once had with Andrew:

'It was a bit cold last night, Andrew, wasn't it?'

'Cold? *Cold*? It was that cold, I had to slip on another soldier!'

We were very fond of Andrew. He may have been of the lavender persuasion but he was ours.

At one point he was presenting the Cologne end of 'Family Favourites', the most successful radio request show ever, which in its heyday boasted twenty million listeners on BBC Radios 1 and 2, as well as on BFBS overseas. At the London end in those days was Jean Challis, a lovely warm lady with the occasional inability to read the clock.

On this one occasion, our Andrew was sharing the programme with co-presenters from around the world – Canada, Cyprus, and Australia – as well as Cologne. Each country had done half an hour's worth of dedications with Jean and the time had come to say goodbye.

Sadly, this time Jean had miscalculated and she realised she had started on the 'cheerio' sequence about a minute early. So that time had to be filled. She decided to go round the world once more, asking each of her co-presenters for a farewell kiss on-air. The boys all got the message and airborne kisses were exchanged across the continents, until she reached Andrew in Cologne.

'Right – Andrew, my lovely Andrew,' she positively cooed with anticipation. 'Now, a lovely big smacker from you in Cologne.'

There was an awful silence. Then slowly, Andrew's voice came from far away until it sounded close and intimate, as though he'd been – well – bending over.

'I'm *so* sorry,' said Andrew, a bit flustered. 'What did you say, Jean? I was just bending down to tie my shoelace.'

To spell it out, it sounded like Jean had just puckered up to kiss Andrew's bum.

He pretended to be sorry, Jean pretended not to have heard the 'crack' about shoelaces, and the rising theme of 'With a Song in my Heart' brought the whole red-faced show to an end.

It didn't end there. Sitting in the BBC Radio 2 news studio in London was Don Durbridge, duty newsreader. He had heard everything and he knew Andrew of old.

Up came the pips of the Greenwich Time Signal. 'BBC Radio 2 news at two o'clock. This is Don Durbridge. Police in Manchester say...'

And that really was as far as he got. You could hear it coming from the first words. A tremor in the voice, the beginning of a snort by the time he got to 'Durbridge' and then a great rasping, leading to hysterical and animal-like laughing, with the occasionally gulped 'Sorry!' slowly being faded out with a rather more controlled voice telling us that our next programme would follow in a couple of minutes and here was some music...

*****

Andrew's Rolls Royce went on to earn its corn in two other areas. One Karneval – the famous festival celebrated with great fervour in Cologne, Dusseldorf and other western German cities - it was used for an unofficial cavalcade, which ended up with an impromptu German police outrider posse and a solo Rosenmontag – the Shrove Monday culmination of Karneval - tour by Charlotte Russe along the Cologne Carnival Processional Route. Andrew thought it might be a good idea to show the car off to the huge Karneval crowds in the city centre. In the back, he put Uncle Bill, wearing the full dress uniform of a Grand Admiral of the Oohbani Fleet (part of Uncle Bill's fictional world), complete with dress sword and ostrich-plumed hat. It was quite something to see the aloof figure of Andrew, in Edwardian chauffeur's uniform, with Uncle Bill lording it up, complete with white-gloved waving, from the back of this spectacular car. Tens of thousands of Germans, completely awestruck, waved back. Nobody had the remotest idea who this personage was but, by golly, he must be important.

The other example of Charlotte Russe earning her corn in Germany was when Andrew lent it to Mrs Thatcher during her 1977 Silver Jubilee progress to review the British Forces at Sennelager.

*****

I didn't know it at the time, but my Cologne posting was coming to an end, which was to be marked by the appearance of two brown envelopes. I had sat the next civil service board, which would mark my promotion to Senior Executive Officer equivalent, or Lieutenant Colonel in Equivalent Military Rank. The confirmation letter, contained in the first brown envelope, was delivered to me by Pat Pachebat himself one afternoon in 'A' studio, where I was recording, with the help of gallons of beer, a folk band from the 5th Royal Inniskilling Dragoon Guards. The boys were in the middle of a rousing version of 'Wild Rover', in a studio thick with cigarette smoke and beer fumes, with the producer (me) unusually beating time with a beer mug in one hand, a fag in the other, and bellowing along with the chorus.

Pat called for silence. He was clearly a boss, so the atmosphere went from full on to crematorium in a nano-second. He approached me with a wry smile on his face.

'I think you'll be pleased with what's in this envelope,' he said, glumly. 'Well done.'

It was ungracious and flat. He turned sharply and left the studio.

'Ha ha, boyo, you're for it, sure you are!' quipped one dragoon. 'Is dat yer P45?'

I ripped the letter open. It was from CSM4(d), my official Army Department at the MOD. This was it – I was promoted.

'I got my promotion!' I yelled. We carried on singing, minging, ring-dinging till we ran out of beer and throat. Nobody gave Pat and his miserable appearance a second thought.

It was the following morning, during the resulting the headache, that I noticed a little caveat in the MOD letter. I had passed the board, but not been given an appointment yet. The letter was valid for two years: if I hadn't been appointed to a BFBS Grade III position by then, I would have to re-sit the board.

This was terrible. How much more Pat Pachebat could one man take?

Luckily, I was to be put out of my misery. A second brown envelope arrived from BFBS Head Office in London. Ian Woolf had decided to post me in as second producer to Bryan Hamilton's Head of News and Information in London. My job would be senior producer of the hugely popular Tommy Vance daily music and chat show, 'BFBS UK'. I noticed Pat was looking more and more glum.

There were to be a couple of stings in the tail. The first was my farewell drinks party. It had always been the tradition that a whip round and a present was the order of the day, in exchange for a round or three at the bar. Sadly, Pat had declared that in order to prevent embarrassment to less popular members of departing staff, there would be a standard farewell gift of a glass-bottomed pewter mug, paid for directly out of bar profits.

I was livid, not just for me, but for others who would lose out as a result of this policy. Amongst our band of merry men and women, it was a long established tradition that you saw off the most popular staff members with a lavish gift because you were sorry to see them go. By the same token, you saw off the most unpopular with an equally lavish gift because you were delighted to see them go at last. A beer mug, indeed.

Luckily, at my farewell, the bar annexe was filled with a huge gang of my 'Auf Wiedersehen, Pet' brickie and chippie mates from a site just down the Bonnerstraße. They came laden with extra gifts and we had a good craic until it was time for the Station Controller to do my farewell oration and hand over my 'mug, glass-bottomed, departure, gift, official, one, for the use of'.

I have to say, he was actually quite pleasant, considering. I was still sulking a bit, so I had Graf Stieldorf fill the mug with a pint of rum and coke, which I held up.

'I'd like to thank the station for this gift of a glass-bottomed mug,' I enthused, as if I'd been given the Holy Grail. 'At least when I'm using it I'll be able to see who's watching me drink.' (In the past Pat had made lots of snide comments about the fact I was always drinking but rarely drunk.)

I don't think the message went home, but it made me feel better.

And the final gesture? I heard, months after I had left, that Pat had been walking with Colin Rugg down the Parkstraße drive, at the end of which were three massive black-painted wooden crates with my name and address marked out in white stencil.

'I'm glad to see McDonagh's got himself organised,' said Pat to Colin. 'At least he's got his boxes ready.'

'Oh, they're not for sending,' said Colin. 'Look – that's the Cologne address on the side. No, I think you'll find...' - and with that he lifted one of the lids - 'that those are his empties.'

That's what happens when you give McD a cheap tankard.

Next stop: London, Tommy Vance, stars in my eyes – and disaster.

Chapter Sixteen:

Guests And The Best

It didn't start well, that much was for sure. Sure, I had been promoted, had a new job title and an important position in Head Office. Oh, and my baseline salary had increased (marginally).

At the same time, we'd lost thousands in Living Overseas Allowance, now had to pay tax on booze and fags and instead of living in a posh married quarter in a leafy suburb of millionaires' Cologne, we were living in a tiny cramped maisonette in an Army block in Kingston-on-Thames, where we were being charged an 'economic rent' as 'unentitled' civilians. Plus it cost me a four-figure sum for the privilege of travelling to work.

I did the sums. We were getting less than half of what we'd had in Cologne. And this was an incentive to do what, precisely?

Life, in some cases, is what you get used to. The commute didn't turn out to be too bad or, in those days, too crowded. My office was nice: we had two vast rooms in Kings Buildings, Dean Stanley Street, in Westminster, a cough and a spit away from the Houses of Parliament and just around the corner from Transport House; out of our window you could see Smith Square and the Conservative Party Headquarters. In these rooms were Bryan Hamilton, department head, Julia and Sue, the secretariat, and occasional freelance producers such as Dominic Allan from IRN Sports and Carole Straker, who worked later on for Capital Radio.

More importantly, just round the corner, in Dean Bradley Street, was the BFBS pub – the Marquis of Granby'. It was our home from 1200-1445 and again from 1800-1900 ish, depending on the pressure of the day. It was friendly enough, except for those occasions when the union brothers from Transport House took it over during their conferences. Then the air would be thick with the wielders of the red flag, who literally couldn't hold their drink, as by the end of a session, the whole place would be sodden, the carpet squelchy with draught Bass and the atmosphere smokier than the devil's bum.

I got to meet the whole gang, plus a number of other BFBS personalities, during the first two days, and realised that I appeared to be the youngest one around. It felt like being in Cologne for the first time: I was surrounded by professionals, who kept telling me they were.

The awful truth was that many of the Head Office staff were people who had blotted their copybooks whilst serving out in the Raj and had been summoned back to the hub of the operation for re-training – and, it has to be said, drying out. This made for an interesting group, intent on disproving management's theory that if you made a drunk pay duty-paid prices it would lower his intake. This was generally not so.

Very soon on, I got to meet the star of our show, Tommy Vance - or, to give him his full name, Richard Anthony Crispian Francis Prew Hope-Weston. He was given the 'Tommy Vance' tag when he was touting his wares as a jobbing jock in the USA, hit on a radio station, displayed that dark gravelly voice for which he had since become famous, and was hired on the spot. (He was called 'Tommy Vance' because another jock, who was going to be hired but never turned up, was the real Tommy Vance. The station had all these expensive recorded name checks…)

Tommy was a lovely man when he was in a lovely mood and a bugger to please when he was being contrary. He moaned about the weather, the format, the briefs, the guests, his wife, himself and the world in general. And just when he had generated the big black cloud, he would grin sardonically, buy the whole world a drink and become lovable again. Producing him was a nightmare, as he seemed to ignore most of what you told him on talkback through the glass. He would stray from the brief and over-run the chat segments as he saw fit.

The worst thing was that he tended to bawl out his producer in public and praise him in private. This could hurt, so much so that on one occasion I told him that I didn't really like that kind of behaviour. He was genuinely surprised and apologised on the spot. He meant it, too. He bought me several drinks and we became 'beshfreindsh', for a while anyway.

Some months later my Number Two boss, the dreadful Brian Bass of Malta fame, asked Tommy during a session at the Marquis what he thought of me as a producer. I was standing in a separate crowd, but operating the broadcaster's trick of 'split cans' listening – tuned in to a conversation in one ear, but eavesdropping with the other. Tommy's answer bucked me up, especially as he didn't know I was behind him. 'Oh, McD?' came the familiar dark brown voice. 'He's the best producer I've ever had. Doesn't get in the way all the time.' I was made up. Unlike presentation, it's hard to tell when you're doing well as a producer.

'BFBS UK' was the title of Tommy's show. It ran Monday to Friday and was recorded three working days in advance so it could be posted out on tape to radio stations worldwide courtesy of the RAF. Any guest walking in would have felt he or she was entering an alien world. They would be greeted by the producer of the day (Bryan, Dominic or me), who would then be pushed out of the way by our very own engineer, Rockin' Ron Smith, who would then rudely say in a gruff, no-nonsense voice: 'Right, before you go on, two things to remember: don't say 'fuck' or 'good morning'. And today is Thursday, not Monday. Take a seat.'

The first point was obvious. We didn't have a delay system to prevent spare obscenities from polluting the airwaves. Secondly, each station played out BFBS UK at a different time of day, sometimes with a night repeat. To emphasise the day of the week, wooden block signs rested in full view of both presenter and guest.

Ron was a real comedian. He was the only person who was somehow able to tell Uncle Ian, any visiting dignitary, Tommy, or indeed the whole world, to Foxtrot Oscar and somehow never get into trouble. He was a personal friend of the TV star, Katie Boyle, and whenever she came on the show there was a welter of utterly over the top hugging and kissing, involving baskets of flowers, yappy dogs and Rockin' Ron doing his Lothario act, which was positively nauseous.

But he made for some good cabaret. One day our main guest was Roy Plomley, deviser and presenter for many years of the BBC's legendary programme, 'Desert Island Discs'. He was a shy, polite and very pleasant man, not a bit showbizzy, and sat down with the production team for a pre-show chat. Ron eventually steered him in the direction of Tommy, who was sitting looking at us in the cavernous studio. Roy looked at the semi-circular guests' side of the desk, sticking up from which were four microphones. Roy shifted his chair so that he was sitting exactly halfway between mics 2 & 3.

'Bloody hell,' said Ron, and rushed over to the talkback. He pressed the key.

'*How* long did you say you'd been doing Desert Island Thingies?'

'Thir...thirty years,' stammered the very off-mic voice of the legendary broadcaster, sounding a bit puzzled.

'And didn't anybody ever tell you you gotta sit *behind* the microphone, not next to it?'

'Oh, I'm *so* sorry,' said Roy, shifting his chair so he was in the right place.

On another occasion, our star guest of the day was none other than Glenda Jackson, who had recently clocked up a prize for one of her films. (Actually, it was an Oscar.) She slid into the control room one morning like a cheetah on the hunt. Although dressed down in black ski pants and a grey polo neck, she exuded charisma, and every single one of us was suddenly star struck as she bathed the room in a pleasant and easy smile.

'Hello, folks,' she purred. 'What do you want me to do?'

As producer of the day, my lips were moving, but nothing was coming out. It was – it had to be – Rockin' Ron.

'Wotcher, Glenda, darlin',' he started. 'S'pose you could always make the coffee.'

This was Ron's clunking imitation of a joke. Glenda wasn't about to be put out by this oik.

'Sure,' she smiled, and turned to our programme secretary. 'Julia,' (she'd been introduced and showed she remembered names), 'can you show me where the coffee machine is?'

Julia, not believing what was happening, steered Glenda out into the corridor, showed her the machine, cups and the makings. Glenda took our orders and made us our coffees. Then she sat cross-legged on the carpet and told us stories and jokes from the world of cinema until she went in to the studio and completely overwhelmed Tommy with a splendid and sensitive interview.

The format of the programme meant a lot of pressure. Two hours a day, five days a week, recorded in Westminster every weekday morning from 1000-1200, with four guests a day, the last one of which had to be a household name. Just some of the names over the years included: HRH The Prince of Wales (Tommy wore a suit for that one), Andy Williams, David Essex, Victoria Wood, Kenneth Williams, Clive James, Jilly Cooper and the then emerging talents of Elvis Costello, Ian Dury, Toyah Wilcox and Kirsty McColl.

I particularly remember Kirsty. She was very self-conscious about her image and just wonderfully shy as a result. She responded well, I noticed, during her interview with Tommy, to the softer, lower voice and as a result, opened up more than usual. Afterwards, she gave the impression that she'd really enjoyed the interview, so I invited her to the Green Room, where we had a pleasant chat. At the end, she asked me, 'What do you really think about my record?'

Given the title, its quirkiness and originality, it was very easy to look her in the eyes and say with every ounce of sincerity: 'It's a great song. It's going to be a hit.'

She leant forward and gave me a great big effusive, friendly kiss and a hug. I was utterly made up. I had just been snogged by the singer of a new release, 'There's a Guy Works Down the Chip Shop Swears He's Elvis'.

Without name-dropping too much, it entered my cabinet of magic moments, along with the time I'd been covering the German premiere of 'Diamonds are Forever' in Düsseldorf, where some of the lesser stars had come along to be interviewed. I found an American starlet with whom I did an interview in the style of a smooth-talking English gentleman interviewing a major Hollywood star, for which I received more than a peck on the cheek from film starlet Lana Wood, sister of Natalie. Yes, I had actually been kissed by Plenty O'Toole!

*****

It was about this time that changes were afoot. Bryan Hamilton was posted overseas and I found myself promoted to the awesome position of Head of News and Information. This is where I came to understand what 'over-promoted' really means. I knew from the start that trying to play it 'serious' would be an ordeal to a cheery pop jockey who was happy to play tunes to the lads in the trenches. More and more drink was taken, but somehow we kept going.

I brought in an old drinking chum, Johnny 'Boy' Walker (not the Radio 2 'Johnnie' one, although he too spent time as a BFBS freelance presenter), as my number two and we also hired Aj Webber, a charismatic recording star, who had done TV shows with Cliff Richard and was currently massive on the UK Folk Scene, as a combination of performer and producer.

We used Aj probably more often than we would have done because of Johnny's strange domestic situation. Most of us lived within at least commuting distance of Westminster. Johnny, due an inheritance from his much-decorated wartime RAF father, bought a railway station in Morpeth, Northumberland. He found a London pied-a-terre for Monday to Friday and took the Edinburgh flyer up for the weekends. Because he lived at a former railway station, he even managed to organise a personal stop for himself on more than one occasion!

Anyway, UK weather being what it was and bearing in mind the railway's insistence on listening to trade unions, we tended to use Aj quite a lot. On one occasion I had written to David Hill, editor of the now defunct 'Weekend' magazine, principally to ask him if I could invite his fiery columnist, Douglas Fairey, master of the rant, on to the show. David was intrigued. He said he'd like to show me around his empire before agreeing to my request. I asked if I could bring Aj and he okayed it. His car and chauffeur would be at our main entrance at 1215, after the day's recording. We were intrigued.

We walked out into the sun, to see a gleaming chocolate brown open-topped Cadillac with cream leather seats waiting for us. 'Peter McDonagh?' asked the chauffeur. I nodded. The door was held open and Aj and I slid into the luxury of this amazing beast.

We were then driven through central London. When you're in an open-topped, posh car, this is an experience. I felt like waving to the curious crowds. I did wave. Aj, who was as mad as me, waved too. We grinned like idiots. Soon, we were in the labyrinthine depths of darkest London, home of the press, the media, Soho, nightclubs, drinking dens and places you don't normally talk about. We were led up stairs and along corridors. We had no idea where we were. Suddenly, we were in front of a pair of giant polished doors. The chauffeur opened one side and waved us in.

From the gloom of the outside, we were immediately bathed in a cathedral of light in a multi-aspect room masquerading as an office. It was more like a lounge in Club land. Deep, wall to wall, Axminster; leather armchairs that needed lifebelts, so deeply did you sink into them; and the two focal fixes of the barn-sized palace: a Mussolini sized desk, dominating one side of the room, and a whole wall taken up by a hall of mirrors, providing a platform for what surely must have been the world's biggest cocktail cabinet.

A dapper and elegant figure with a twinkle in the eye emerged from behind a giant pot plant in one corner of this massive office. 'Peter. Aj. Good to see you! I was just in the middle of some putting practice.'

Sure enough, David Hill, all-powerful editor of one of the UK's top-selling magazines, was busy chasing little balls around the nucleus of his empire and trying to get them into overturned highball glasses set at intervals across the massive carpet. He poured us each what one of my previous bosses had called 'a big brown one', gave us each a putter and we joined him on the legendary David Hill course.

I knew while we were playing this game that he was assessing me in order to see if he wanted anything more to do with BFBS. I'd accidentally scored extra brownie points; I was wearing a fresh carnation buttonhole in my jacket, as was David. Pure co-incidence, but he noted it and said he was glad to see that even broadcasters knew what 'properly dressed' meant. This boded well.

After a few drinkies and a chat about an appearance on BFBS UK, David, as Editor-In-Chief, made the executive decision that we were going out to lunch. He took us to Wheelers, where we had oysters; he then took us to Ronnie Scott's, where we were whisked backstage to meet the great man; and then he aced the plot by taking us down the very seediest of back streets, through a side door, which led on to a gold, fur, leather and glass palace belonging to the 'King of Porn', Paul Raymond, at Raymond's Revue Bar. Paul met us, along with his tragic daughter Debbie (she killed herself some years later) and turned out to be far too pleasant for the rather seedy industry he represented. We had a laugh, anyway, before David had us driven back to base after an eye-opening day.

BFBS UK was no stranger to the slightly devious route of getting hold of people. 'PR guru', Max Clifford – recently on the receiving end of the media he spent so many years attempting to manipulate - used our show to test out some of his clients; if they stood up well in an interview with Tommy Vance, then the chances were that they'd be ready for national exposure in the UK. As the result, we had a steady stream of the mad, the bad and the glad.

And then we had our 'walk on the wild side' brigade. The most terrifying of these was the legendary armed robber, John McVicar. His handshake was soft and slightly moist and his eyes came up from nowhere to drill into yours with a powerful mixture of steel and power. There was almost an aura of evil transmitting from him but in prison he had studied for, and been awarded, a degree in law. He was clearly super-intelligent, if amoral.

'Well, he would say that, wouldn't he?' Mandy Rice-Davies was a key figure in the John Profumo/Stephen Ward scandal, which rocked the country to its foundations in the sixties. Parties, orgies, naked swimming sessions, espionage, duplicity – they were all centre stage, and here we had one of the central figures in the drama. Ms Rice-Davies sashayed in, complete with fur coat, jewels, a cheery smile and a really bubbly, infectious personality. She put her full address in the visitors' book:'8 Mittelstrasse, Zurich'. I commented on this lapse in security. She didn't bat an innocent eyelid.

'Publicity, dear boy,' she purred. 'It pays to advertise.'

She was witty and good fun and it was interesting to hear her side of the story. But the best was the day Linda Marchiano came to visit the show. I'd better explain that BFBS shared Kings Buildings with the Regimental Headquarters of a number of the Guards regiments and there were always a number of military types, usually in civvies, oiling in and out of the building past reception, where the security guard, Marie, kept and held ultimate power.

Picture the scene. Linda Marchiano is talking to Marie at reception, at precisely the moment two Army colonels in 'mufti' are passing by. I have come downstairs to collect Linda, once she's got her pass from

Marie. I arrive just as Linda says, 'Oh you don't have a pass in the name of Marchiano? Then it must be in my 'performer' name: *Linda Lovelace.*'

The voice carried to the two colonels, whose heads snapped round in unison as their jaws fell open. Yes, it was indeed the star of the notorious soft porn classic, 'Deep Throat'. I took her upstairs to the studio. Rocking Ron tried his best, but it has to be said that although Linda gave good interview, the light of natural intelligence did not figure highly in her list of talents...

I mentioned Marie, the 'Gate Guard' at the bottom of the steps leading up to the rattling lifts and dark staircases of Kings Buildings. She had a little booth, from which she conducted business. She had once been briefed with a single sentence, 'They Shall Not Pass', and her bulldog Norn Iron accent could cut a King to pieces.

On one occasion, former British Prime Minister Edward Heath had arrived for an interview. He had neglected to bring any ID.

Marie looked his minder straight in the eye. '*You* knows that he's Sir Edward Heath, I knows that he's Sir Edward Heath, but Oi'm sorry, Sor, without a pass that *says* he's Sir Edward Heath, he isn't coming in.'

It was only because of the IRA troubles and the patent giveaway of the Ulster accent that she wasn't carted off on the spot to the Tower by Heath's funny people.

However, her greatest moment was said to be when Olympic superstar Sebastian Coe turned up at Kings Buildings for an interview with the sports department. Marie clearly fell in love with him on the spot but still asked sweetly for his ID, which he gave her with his legendary modest smile. You could see the start of a deep relationship, had circumstances been different. She checked his ID, her eyes lingering on the chiselled features of this athletic Adonis. Then came the line that broke the spell and assured her place in posterity:

'You're very young to be a Sir,' she opined.

There was a long silence, while Sir Bastion Coe worked out what had just happened. He gave her an even more winning smile, said 'thank you' and went on up the stairs with the BFBS producer. The Knighthood would come.

It was a long time before we told Marie what she had done. She was mortified, but secretly quite enjoyed the perks of meeting the rich and famous, some of whom could be very friendly and chatty. When BFBS and the rest of the MOD left Kings Buildings, Marie was reassigned to another office. Tommy Vance put his hand in his pocket and bought Marie and her partner a package holiday to the Med. It was a nice thing to do.

*****

While doing BFBS UK as a producer was miles away from my first love of presenting live on air, it did have its upside. I was always nearly physically sick before going on-air and usually a nervous wreck until any show was well underway. At the end I would be like a limp rag. I figured only the loopy juice could keep me going and so there was a lot of that. Too much, as it happens, but that nemesis came later. However, the earlier training was to come in handy, in a very unexpected way.

Tommy Vance was going on leave and Dominic Allan had pulled off the major coup of getting sixties singing legend Kenny Lynch to front three BFBS UK shows. Kenny turned out to be one nice guy – he talked evenly and equally to everybody on the crew, put up with Rockin' Ron's awful jokes, took a huge interest in the guests we'd booked for him and the records chosen for the two-hour extravaganza. To his credit, he did keep reminding us that, 'Y'know, I've never done this kind of thing before. Are you sure?'

Of course we were sure. He was an international singing star, had his own series on TV, had sold millions of records, performed in front of tens of thousands – what could possibly go wrong? As the show's theme faded, we found out.

'Er... Hello there – I'm – er – this is... Kenny Lynch here and I'm...er - standing in for Tommy Vance and on today's show (loud rustling of paper and voice disappearing as he goes "off mic") we've got, er– a bloke called Jack, who does dialects from all over the county – er, country - and

he... can do all that – with actors who need to learn accents and many others but let's play a record and (voice disappears as he peers down to read tiny record label on turntable two feet away) here we have –er – 'Rivers of –er –Babylon' by the Boney M!!!' (The last few words shouted, with relief. The needle on the meter goes into the red. Rockin' Ron is wincing.)

Fortunately this was not live. We started again. Twice. But it was no good. By twelve o'clock (we'd been trying for two hours) we had nothing in the can. We were all dripping with sweat and disappointment, nobody more so than Kenny, who couldn't apologise enough. It was much, much tougher than he'd thought. The least he could do was to stand us a few drinks in the Green Room. We went downstairs and relaxed, along with a very upset Kenny. We spent the next hour telling him it wasn't his fault, as we all really rated him as a star and a diamond geezer. Eventually, when we poured him out of the building, he walked tall on a sea of goodwill.

We, on the other hand, had a problem. A missing recorded programme. Two hours of Head Office output, already scheduled for three working days ahead on BFBS stations around the world. We had to bridge that gap. But how? We had a look at the studio schedule and found out that if we started no later than two o'clock, thus finishing at four, we could do any quick edits, dubbing and then still get the tapes to the BFPO HQ at Mill Hill. The only problem was that we would have to record in segments, using three different studios in-between other bookings. Oh, and we lacked both a presenter and some guests.

And then I remembered I could present, and had done quite a lot of it over the last ten years. Why couldn't I do it? Then someone reminded me that it was forbidden in Head Office for production staff to present programmes. We sent a message to Ian Woolf on the fifth floor, explaining the problem and the urgency. He gave us clearance. Right, we had a presenter. Carol Straker, music producer, took care of the tunes and the various studio bookings. We managed to gather together three 'in house' guests and, just by chance, Dominic Allan was an old drinking buddy and colleague of rising star Jeremy Beadle, then billed as 'The Curator of Oddities' on his radio show, so we got him in as 'star' guest.

Somehow, the show was cobbled together, with the guest list changing even as we went. Eventually we ended up with three people with stories to tell. The only one who made it all the way through to the final cut was Jeremy Beadle, who really gave us a star performance once we'd told him the situation. I was particularly grateful to an ex-RAF freelance reporter, Ron Jones, who filled a slot about three nanoseconds after the suggestion had been made that he might like to appear to talk about his recent European trip.

The final product was shoehorned into one running sequence of 1hr 57min precisely and sent away to be dubbed and despatched overseas. We had sent warning telexes to all the BFBS stations, telling them that for the next three days PMcD would be presenting BFBS UK. There was a quiet acceptance; nobody actually complained but the general feeling was that this was the thin end of a wedge. Tommy, as a freelance, was on three to four times the salary of a staffer – quite normal in the business – and people were more interested to know whether I was getting megabucks for this change of role.

Strangely enough, I don't remember people saying my performance was either particularly good or bad. One or two, a bit later on, said I'd been 'awfully brave' but I've never really minded being patronised, on the grounds that patronisers generally turn out to be rather weak in themselves.

*****

Ron Jones had appointed himself my Guardian Angel and was forever warning me about drinking too much, and being a bit too outspoken with it. Somehow, I took it from him, as I could tell he was just being kind. He was about to play a part in one of the highlights of my career.

In my perennial search for guests to appear on BFBS UK, I had embarked on some long shots, the longest of which was trying to get an interview with my all-time hero, Peter Sellers. I looked for the great comic in all the telephone directories and little black books that I could find but drew a blank. He was above all that. The only thin suggestion I picked up was that I should write to him c/o his bank, Barclays. (It was a different age...)

I wrote him what I thought was a funny letter. It accused him of living off a military connection – Major Bloodnok in 'The Goons' – for years, without ever having appeared on Dear Old Army Wireless. The Lads in the Trenches overseas were very keen to find out how to fiddle the books and run away from the enemy and he seemed to have had years of experience...

Some weeks later, I received an answer, in verse, written by the flamboyant Yvonne de Valera, from his agency, Theo Cowan:

'Thank you for your grovelling note addressed to Peter Sellers

We know how much he'd like to help because you're smashing fellas.

Unfortunately, he's far away filming "Fu Manchu"

And may not chance upon these shores for at least a month or two

But rest assured we've written and told him of your plea

So keep the Army plonk on ice in case he's ever free.

Finally we'd like to say how much we liked your letter

So keep on taking all the pills - and we trust you'll soon be better!'

I was a bit surprised, only a few weeks later, to get a phone call from Theo Cowan's office: 'Peter says he's only doing two interviews this year.'

Oh bugger.

'And he's agreed to do one of them with you. Could you come to the Hotel George V in Paris in two weeks, Thursday, at about 4pm? It could happen any time after that.'

I was superlunary. Over the moon. This was the one. This would assure my place in broadcasting history. I tried to keep the schoolboy enthusiasm out of my voice as I agreed to the gig - and yes, I *was* aware of the rift with latest wife Lynn Frederick, but I wanted to talk to him about the Goons and the films, not the collateral damage. Yes, I would be on time. Oh, and Theo Cowan would cover the expenses. Thank you. Goodbye. I had died and gone to heaven.

Two days later, I died, hadn't gone to heaven, and felt real despair. It was on the news. Peter Sellers had suffered yet another major heart attack while filming 'Fu Manchu' and would be completely out of it for a long time.

Cancel Paris, hopes, dreams and the interview of a lifetime.

In the end, it was a few months later when the phone rang to reveal the honeyed tones of one of the nice ladies from Theo Cowan's office.

'Hello, Peter? We haven't forgotten you. Peter Sellers was asking about the radio interview that we had to leave up in the air when he was taken ill. He's back in London, he's pretty fit and he can do the interview tomorrow morning. Harlequin Suite, Dorchester Hotel, 11 o'clock. You'll be met in the lobby by his dresser, Michael Jefferies. OK?'

OK? OK? Paradise, with knobs on! Turning psychedelic cartwheels, I sent eternal thanks down the mouthpiece, gave the girl a telephonic kiss, assured her I would be there, put the phone down and sat there, grinning inanely and visibly shaking.

Ron Jones stopped by and spotted something was afoot. Close questioning gave away the story but I still only really half-believed that this was going to happen. After a bit of a chat, Ron suggested he should come with me to operate the big Nagra recorder, place the mics and keep an eye on the levels, leaving me with the sole job of listening and talking. I checked with Theo Cowan and got the go ahead.

The next morning we set out. To mark the occasion, a fresh pink carnation buttonhole and a crafty gin and tonic before departure. (Gosh, was I nervous.) We met the slightly camp but utterly charming Mike Jefferies in the Dorchester lobby. He looked concerned.

'I'm not sure what kind of Peter you're going to get today. Lynne's been giving him a hard time and last night he didn't get the Oscar for 'Being There'. He's very down. Anyway, he says he'll still do the interview. Let's go upstairs.'

We arrived in the Harlequin Suite, which overlooked Hyde Park through huge picture windows and over a sweeping balcony. We camped in the vast lounge and set up the kit in the dining room through an arch at the far end. Luckily, although the room was gigantic, there were enough drapes and soft furnishings to absorb echoes and bad acoustics. Ron set the two mics on the dining table, with two dining chairs facing them, turned in a few degrees to each other, rather than face to face. (Less confrontational for the English psyche.)

After a few minutes, we found ourselves waiting. Mike had disappeared to the far end of the lavish room. Suddenly there was some movement at the far end and Peter Sellers himself appeared, and started to walk towards us.

His face was almost a blank mask and seemed to have the consistency and fragility of rice paper. His shoulders were stooped and he carried himself as if in some physical pain. He scanned us through some spectacularly large shades and breathed out in an almost wispy voice as he extended his hand:

'Thank you very much for coming. I enjoyed your letter. I'll be happy to talk for the British Forces. I was in the RAF you knoeouw.'

The 'knoeouw' was pure Clouseau. Despite the pain, he was having a laugh. Maybe this would work, after all, but I must admit to being horrified by his wraith-like appearance.

We sat down and Ron kick-started the Nagra recorder. I asked my first question. There was a long pause. Then a miracle. It was as if a sleeping giant had just woken up. He stopped being a tired, bored, beaten, world-weary trainee ghost and launched on a Pandora's box of talents. Over the next half hour, we had machine gun bursts of his early career trying to compete with the dirty old men with raincoats in the Windmill Theatre, the days of the 'Goon Shows' ('the happiest days of my life'), the Pink Panther films and other big screen glories – with, at each stage, the voices and personalities that had made Peter Sellers a star with the English-speaking peoples of the world.

Here was 'Mate' from 'The Goons', who was based on an East London dodgy antique dealer; Bluebottle, who had started life as a real scoutmaster with a ginger beard ('Bentine kept sending me round people who he thought had genius. One night I open my door and there's this – this *idiot* wearing a scout uniform, with one of *them* baggy hats, baggy shorts, baggy knees; he only gives me a scout salute and says – in, I swear it, Bluebottle's voice – 'Michael Bentine said I should look you up. He thinks I am a genius, ha ha!''); then the tale of Clouseau and where *his* voice came from; the Indian, Mr Bakshi, from 'The Party' and, of course, Grytpype-Thynne and so many other voices that have become a part of popular culture.

He talked, with only the lightest of touches on the tiller from me, for just over half an hour. Every so often the fire went out, only to be revived for the next burst, the next batch of characters and stories. In the end I had to make ninety-four edits to the tape. But now, duty done, it was as if he was a young man again. His face was animated, his smile genuine. He spotted my Olympus camera – quite a good one. 'Good choice that!' he said. 'Fancy a few photos? Let's go out on the balcony. Mike, you want to take the camera? Get a few shots of us both? Bring your microphone!'

We positively bounced out into the noon sunshine. Twenty odd floors below, we could see a troop of Household Cavalry trotting along the road. Peter grabbed my microphone. 'Good morning, this is the BeebBeebCeeb, and this is Hugh Jambton ('Huge Hampton' – rhyming slang: 'Hampton Wick' – prick!) reporting on a beautifully sunny day, where a troop of Her Majesty's Household Cavalry are parading below. They are called the Household Cavalry as each of the Troopers has to own his own house...'

Thus we were treated to a free cabaret that would have cost millions. I was walking on air. Mike took some great shots. Ron and I were delighted. We took our leave on a fine April day in 1980.

Two months later, Peter Sellers died of a final heart attack. My interview was his last. The BBC contacted me. Could they transcribe part of the interview for their 'Listener' magazine?

Of course they could. They gave a précis of our conversation. Then, right at the end, our final interchange on tape.

'Where to now, Mr Sellers?'

'I don't know. I have no idea. I suppose that I shall continue, like my family, until I drop.'

He broke many hearts, as well as his own, when he did.

Chapter Seventeen:

Red Ken and a Sunset

Strawberries and cream on a suede shoe cemented my career path and my otherwise inexplicable rise to the top.

Among my duties in the rather exalted role of Head of News and Information was a brief to attend important external functions. The television service of BFBS, which sent out taped programmes and would soon enjoy a live link to Germany, was based in the London Weekend Television studios, where it shared some facilities, and some problems, with the resident broadcaster.

The advantages of house sharing with LWT were state of the art kit and the ability for an idea to become a programme much quicker than at the over-managed BBC. The disadvantages could all be drilled down to the arachnid-like union structure. Alan Sapper's powerful ACTT held sway and woe betide anyone who crossed the almost hourly demarcation disputes that dogged the unionised world.

A good example was the BFBS crew's desire to have an electric kettle in their office in order to make their own tea and coffee. A reasonable proposition? Not once the union got to hear about it. Which trade was going to purchase the kettle? Who was going to install it? Who was going to maintain it? And under whose administration would it be deployed? Needless to say, a separate union branch was involved for all of these activities. Man-hours were lost as various groups convened, with the blessing and support of the ACTT, to resolve this 'dispute'. In the meantime, the BFBS team had to traipse down corridors every time they wanted a brew.

Finally, the unions came to an agreement. They were prepared to allow a kettle to be located and installed in the BFBS office, as long as it formed part of 'a self-financing productivity agreement, without prejudice or infringement of existing trades or functions'. The BFBS people had no idea what this meant but eventually a member of the Electrician's Union arrived to inspect the kettle and plug it in. Honour was satisfied.

LWT were, for the most part, excellent hosts, and one lovely summer's day they held a party for BFBS Head Office to visit the LWT studios and mingle with some of the glitterati. In the end, there were more suits than lurex leotards, but LWT had pushed the boat out and amongst all the goodies there was champagne, strawberries and cream, and Frankie Howerd, on one of his many comebacks, as resident jester. He was just as nervously funny in real life as he was on camera and kept morale higher than usual at these 'staff dos'.

I found myself in conversation with a rather cuddly figure, who I just knew was different from the rest. He was charming about BFBS - animated, witty and downright funny. Also, early on, I noticed a very subversive streak and a complete candour. It turned out he was David Hatch, then Head of Light Entertainment at BBC Radio 2 and, of course, one of the stars of 'I'm Sorry I'll Read That Again' – one of my favourite shows. Here was a genuine case of hero worship. I found myself intrigued by his take on comedy and soon we fell into one of those exclusive conversations that you never want to end.

Sadly, this one couldn't have been terminated more dreadfully than if one of us had been shot. In the interests of circulating, one of our senior engineers, Paddy O'Gorman, and our Senior Executive Officer from the real civil service, Bob Hucker, suddenly pitched up in front of us and introduced themselves. Now, both were pleasant people but at that moment they were registering on the Richter Scale as Grade A Interference. After a few desultory and empty exchanges, I could see David was getting foot-tappingly annoyed. I know this to be true, as I was watching the foot in question, clad in an elegant tan suede shoe.

Suddenly, the scenario moved into slow motion. First, Paddy O'Gorman leant forward to be heard over the hubbub of a showbiz party to ask the star of 'ISIRTA' what he did for a living. He was then daft enough to speculate, given David's suit, that David might be a manager. It was kindly meant but the effect was rather spoiled. As Paddy leant forward, pressing for an answer, he tilted his bowl of strawberries and cream, and a large blob of the latter spilled out of the bowl, on to the toe of David's suede shoe.

Paddy looked down and up. David looked down and up. So did Bob and I, then we all looked at David. I very rarely, during our subsequent friendship, saw David look so dangerous as he did at that moment. He gave Paddy a searing, withering glance, and Bob and Paddy caught the danger signal, burbled an apology and retreated in seconds flat. David was still fuming, but realised that I was one of the good guys. He looked round the room. There was nothing for him there. I heard him use his favourite excuse for the first time.

'You don't really have to be here, do you?'

I picked it up. 'No, I'm pretty well down in the pecking order.'

David hissed. 'I feel a very important phone call coming on. Let's go.' And without further ado, off we trotted. He hailed a cab outside. We hit Westminster and St. Stephen's Tavern, the MPs pub that stood where Portcullis House is now. It was a delicious drinking den and the pair of us found window seats and carried on for much of the afternoon, talking about David's love of radio, BFBS, the BBC, and indulging in all kinds of broadcasting gossip. I felt truly privileged to be in the company of this great man, little thinking that he would be instrumental in helping me climb up the greasy pole.

By the end of the session, we were now clearly besh freindsh. I can't remember who decanted whom into a taxi, but we clearly both survived the experience. I remember burbling something about him appearing on Tommy's show soon as a guest, but it was up there in the vague cloud of alcohol and atmosphere.

A few weeks later we decided to hold the return match. David would come to Kings Buildings, fill the 'star guest' spot at the end of the recorded show, which would bring us nicely to opening time at the Green Room. David duly pitched up and gave a splendidly funny interview, full of stories about his more mainstream star chums such as John Cleese, Richard Briers, Barry Cryer, Graeme Garden, Jo Kendall, Tim Brooke-Taylor and Bill Oddie. At the end of the show we repaired to the Green Room, where I told David his performance in our 'star guest' spot on the show had generated the magnificent emolument and remuneration of £25.00 in Old Money. He wasn't too keen on accepting the princely payment, given the close relationship between the BBC and BFBS, and suggested it should be a case of 'Staff - No Fee'. I counter-suggested that we should both drink the fee and this we voted to do.

I think it would be fair to say that after that second bonding session, we had certainly now become bosom buddies. Although it was obviously fated, I didn't realise the implications for many years to come. David would one day become a Trustee of the board of management actually running BFBS and this would continue to work for the good of both of us.

*****

But right now, the situation in London was getting quite depressing. I hated living in the UK after most of a lifetime overseas and I was earning about half of what I'd been getting in Cologne. Then there was the drag of commuting, having to pay tax on everything and running out of money every month. Measures had to be taken, and often were. I was never sure whether or not this actually was an effective way of stalling payments, but it seemed to work: first, you got the blue bill through the post for, say, the electricity; then a brown one, with a minor threat; then a red one, implying castration if you didn't send them a cheque yesterday. At this point you had to keep your nerve. Next, a very nasty letter would arrive, threatening bailiffs, a plague of locusts and death of the first-born.

At this point, you sent them a cheque – but with a deliberate mistake on it, such as differing written and numerical cash entries or a missing signature. This worked with the pseudo-legal folk legend that 'intention to pay is indication of probity'. They couldn't remove your naughty bits if you'd actually tried to pay. Then, you would get your cheque returned, with a gentle reminder to get it right next time.

This is where the 'clever' bit came in. At this stage of banking progress, cheques could be cleared electronically, by being scanned for the contents of a metallic strip invisible to the human eye. A hugely powerful electromagnet could effectively 'wipe' the electronic data from the cheque, causing it to have to be processed by hand, which took an extra three days. (I told you it was folk legend!)

In the BFBS studios, we had a giant bulk eraser, into whose maw you posted large recorded tapes in order to 'wipe', or demagnetise, them. Now, whether or not this actually had an effect on bank cheques, it seemed to take longer for that very last correctly written cheque to clear the bank account, hopefully in time for the next payday, when the process would begin all over again.

Johnny 'Boy' Walker, my co-producer on BFBS UK, was also less than enchanted with London life, so a lot of our time was spent bemoaning our fate in the Green Room and the Marquis. We got to know our bank manager, who was an honorary member of the Green Room, and who seemed to enjoy the private company of the BFBS crowd, with its odd sprinkling of stars of stage, screen and music. He noticed gradually that both Johnny and I were getting poorer and poorer. Then he noticed that his branch of Lloyds was actually subsidising both our unofficial and perennial overdrafts. He decided to confront us. After a Green Room session one day, he invited us both over for an official visit. He hoped we wouldn't mind being seen together but might two birds with one stone be a good way to proceed?

We nodded, not knowing what was coming. We soon found out.

He painted us up and down his office. We were irresponsible spendthrifts. We couldn't keep this up or we'd soon be bankrupt. Could we not picture our huddled families standing on the pavement of despair, us having defaulted on our rentals? Shoeless, homeless, shivering in the workhouse because we couldn't be bothered to budget? What sort of men were we?

We knew what we were. We hung our heads. A two-barrel bollocking by an old-fashioned bank manager was painful and humiliating. It ended with the black cap:

"Give me your bank cards. *Now!*' Each of us put his bankcard in front of the All-Powerful.

He picked up a pair of scissors, snipped each one in two, scooped up the pieces and put them in the waste bin. Then he sat back in his huge executive swivel chair and grinned easily at us.

'OK, that's the hard bit done with. Relax. Here are your new cards - £50 limit, and only on a promise that you won't spend what you don't have. And here are cards for your new Cashflow accounts – a bit like a rolling overdraft. I'm giving you a credit limit of £300; you pay back a certain small amount each month. It's enough to keep you two in beer, with enough left over to buy me a couple, if you feel like it.'

We felt like it. At the edge of the trapdoor, the vision of the gallows was retreating. I ventured a remark. 'That's really good of you. I hope we haven't caused you too much grief.'

He almost sniggered. 'I don't think this branch is going to be troubled by the financial forgetfulness of Messrs Walker and McDonagh,' he said. 'Especially when you consider the main accounts I manage here are ICI and Imperial Tobacco.'

At last we felt we could smile again. But it was still heavy going, this budgeting lark.

The job began to take its toll, too. Finding four guests a day, twenty a week, over a thousand a year, two hundred and fifty of whom had to be household names, was a huge and nerve-racking undertaking. Not only did the guests have to be booked, but their books, plays, films or general

backgrounds had to be researched and translated into five lines of introduction and a list of ten questions for Tommy, who literally walked in off the street and into the opening signature tune of his two-hour show.

I can now 'fess up' to the invention of the BFBS UK book brief. Typically, a guest would be booked and a copy of his or her latest volume would be biked over, usually a day or two in advance. My job then, as producer, was to read the book and prepare a brief. So this is how it was done, when time was pressing (all of this pre-Google, of course):

a) Read front endpaper and introduction for a synopsis of the book.

b) Read back endpaper/cover for biographical clues.

c) Read a few pages from the beginning to get ideas on style, mood and content.

d) Skip to a page three-quarters of the way through the book, read it and then formulate a question specifically about what is happening at that point, thus suggesting to the author that the interviewer had read past the first few pages.

This system was born through a desire for self-preservation. If you got the brief wrong, there were two tongue-lashings in store, one from the author, the other from Tommy, who might have been made to look a prat, which he was not fond of. *No*-one had ever forgotten a phone call from the then BBC Radio London with reference to Bryan Forbes, the famous film star and director, who had just walked out of a live interview after the following exchange:

Hapless Interviewer: 'Bryan, tell us about your book.'

Furious Film Star and Director: 'No, *you* tell me about it. Have you read it?'

Hapless Interviewer: 'Well, no, but…'

FFS&D: 'Goodbye. I hate working with amateurs.'

And now he was on his way to us. Luckily, the 'Page 234 question' was asked at the top of the brief, complete with a quote. It saved the day.

*****

They say the devil makes work for idle hands to do. Thus it was that Kevin Stewart and I became friends. Kevin was a founder member of the then land-based pirate station, 'Radio Jackie'. (He is now Minister for Commercial Affairs for the States of Guernsey.) We both enjoyed radio so much that we decided to help each other out. We recorded output for Jackie in Kev's garden shed and played out the tapes from a swamp in East Molesey each Sunday. Kev let me guest as a DJ, where I became famous for breaking styluses, earning the title 'The Stylus King', and also being the only jock to use my real name on air – well, 'PMcD' anyway.

The return help came when Kev's shed burnt down and we needed somewhere to record the Sunday output of Jackie. I hatched a plot. I had access to some very fine studios in Kings Buildings, Westminster. Sure, they belonged to BFBS, but so did I. What if we were to go there after closing time on Friday night and record shows through the night in the three main studios? It was a plan.

The only objection would have been the Norn Iron gate guard, the notoriously strict Marie. Sadly, yet fortuitously, she was in hospital for an operation and her temporary replacement was a toothless old bloke called Jack, who was about as dangerous as an E-type canary. I discovered, befriending the ancient retainer, that he lived in very reduced circumstances and enjoyed brown ale. It was the work of a moment to buy him a few bottles, swear him to secrecy and bring in the entire Radio Jackie team late at night to record their output. I must have had a charmed life. We were never caught during the two or three months we used Kings' Buildings...

The other bit of devilment was the result of a session at the Marquis of Granby when we met up with a boozy old gentleman hack by the name of Lyndsay Shankland. He had fallen on hard times and was supplementing his drinking pension by writing very infrequent articles for the Daily Telegraph.

After getting to know him personally, we got to the stage where we clearly understood and trusted each other. Lyndsay seemed genuinely fond of BFBS and what it stood for, so it was simple enough to book him onto 'BFBS UK' to talk about his long life in journalism. This, of course, attracted an appearance fee (of £20.00), which we soon put behind the bar. He invited me back to his tiny Westminster council flat to meet his formidable gin-sipping wife, Joan Haythorne.

Yes, British film actress Joan Haythorne, who had appeared in 'Three Men in a Boat' and many other roles on stage and on screen. For some reason she hated what she called, with thespian venom, 'The Bay Bay Say' (BBC). Apparently they were withholding some disputed repeat fees and Joan couldn't abide their smug managerial front. She learnt to love BFBS though, as Lyndsay's appearance fee had bought a new bottle of Gordons and, while I was still in London, we made sure that the pair of them never went short of the milk of amnesia.

After a successful session at Lyndsay's little flat, I appeared to enjoy the status of honoured friend. So much so that one day Lyndsay came almost running into the Marquis and confronted me.

'My dear fellow! You won't believe what has happened!'

I would. This florid Edwardian figure had become a part of my life. I bought him a pint and raised an eyebrow.

'What is it, Lyndsay? Good news, I hope?'

'Oh yes, Peter, I think I may have done you some good. I am a friend of Lady Airey.'

I knew Lyndsay had connections but this was red hot. Lady Airey was the widow of Airey Neave, Colditz escapee, Second World War hero and Tory Cabinet Minister, who had been killed

by the IRA in a car bomb explosion within the grounds of Westminster Palace, the Houses of Parliament. Lady Airey had become the symbol of a dignified refusal of a widow to fall to pieces because of a cowardly bomber; her courage was the true inspiration of that now ubiquitous wartime poster, 'Keep Calm And Carry On'.

'Not only has Lady Airey agreed to come on the Tommy Show,' said Lyndsay, 'but if you're agreeable she'll give your name to Conservative Central Office to do some voice work for them.'

This was definitely going to be illegal but so was lending out the studios of BFBS to record pirate radio programmes. I was about say yes again...

Lady Airey gave an inspiring interview on BFBS UK. I was producing that day and there wasn't a dry eye in the house. The sheer determination of this proud widow was an inspiration to us all. The IRA had lost, would lose and right would triumph. It was the truth. No more, no less. Even hard-bitten old rogue Tommy was visibly moved.

After the interview, Lady Airey agreed to a glass of sherry in the Green Room, where she accepted the thanks and sympathies of all comers. She spoke about her idea of putting my name forward at Conservative Central office. 'I can't promise anything, but I think they might just listen to me,' she quietly understated.

Politically, Lady Airey glowed in the dark. Minutes after she had been to see them – that very afternoon – I was invited over. There I met one of the publicity officers – a chap called David Davies (as many publicity offers seem to be) – who found my voice familiar and actually pinned it down to Radio Jackie. I was impressed. These Tory boys were no chinless wonders.

The proposition was that I should act as a radio interviewer and speak to some of the Conservative Party Greats. These five-minute interviews would be broadcast as Party Political Broadcasts, even though they would be carried out as normal radio interviews. Please could I leave my bank details, as well as a pseudonym, as they didn't think 'Peter McDonagh', with its Irish connections, was a good idea under the present circumstances.

Like an old media tart, I decided to take on the name of my former Malta mentor and became Peter Pierson. This was going to be fun. Not only was I going to pretend to be an interviewer, but the sting in the tail was that I was going to ask my own questions, which, I was told, should be hard ones.

I have to say the first interview was the best, though not for the right reasons. Nervous as usual, I surveyed the large 'talks' studio in the Smith Square HQ. There was a round table and a couple of microphones. Along one wall was a huge, triple-glazed, window with the recording cubicle full in sight, full of Tory Party apparatchiks, technical people, and David Davies, supervising the show.

I heard a sound behind me, and turned to see the expansive figure of the then Party Chairman, Lord Thorneycroft, advancing, with an opulent smile and a general feeling of bonhomie.

'Peter, so good of you to come and interview me!' he began, and arranged himself slowly into a seat opposite mine. A lot of fussy little men were wafted away by one of the most powerful men in the country, a heavyweight with a fearsome reputation. Who was going to be interviewed – by me. I gulped. He noticed and smiled warmly. I was not going to trouble him. He could afford to be kind.

'Could we have a little bit for level, please?' came the almost reverential but tinny talkback voice of the producer. I nodded, took a deep breath and looking Lord Peter straight in the eye, said

'Tell me, Lord Thorneycroft, when did you decide to become Chairman of the Labour Party?'

Oh, what japes! I looked over his shoulder, to see absolute panic seeping out from behind the glass. Arms were waving, cut-throat gestures were being made, the producer was trying to say something on talkback but his finger kept slipping, then suddenly they spilled out into the room and all tried to apologise for my insulting behaviour.

As I thought would happen, the still very cheerful Lord Thorneycroft brushed all the little acolytes away, harrumphed and then said in his real Chairman's voice: 'You arses. That was a bloody joke. And a good one, too.' He waved at them. 'Now, enough. Back to your places. We've got an interview to record.'

We had. And we did. And the result went out on BBC Radio 4. I did a couple more with Cecil

Parkinson and Francis Maude but they didn't have the impact of the wonderful Thorneycroft interview. Who knows, had things continued to go smoothly, I could have been... No, let's not go there.

*****

Nemesis, you see, was drumming his fingers and waiting in the wings. It started quietly. Because more was expected from me as Head of News and Information, it was suggested at an annual review that I should 'up my game' and cover more serious topics. They wanted the comedian to play Hamlet. Ah well, I had five mouths to feed back home and a beer ration to sustain.

Through my contacts, I discovered a left-wing labour councillor, Tony Craig, who worked alongside and was quite a chum of 'Red' Ken Livingstone, the firebrand councillor who had taken over the Greater London Council as well as the Nuclear Free Peoples' Republic of Brent. Since we had editorial freedom, I thought it might be an idea to start a series on controversial figures. Sadly, my list of controversial figures only had the name of Mr. Livingstone on it. Looking back, I should have known better.

An interview was duly arranged and Tony arrived with the notorious left-winger in tow. He seemed mildly amused at being in an MOD building and about to be given the freedom of the airwaves to pass on his thoughts to the lads in the trenches. The interview started. It seemed to be going well. Both were talking in the right places, the needles were wobbling at the right level and the cassette to give to the producer was spooling in its little plastic recorder.

I should have listened more closely, but I didn't. And so it was, at the end of the interview, conducted in August 1981 on a sunny afternoon, that I gave Tony Craig a cassette copy of the interview and 'banked' the master tape. It needed to be edited at least to time, topped and tailed, and cue material written for transmission - oh, sometime soon, in the future.

I was at my local on Sunday when I first heard. Somebody in the know came up to me and said, 'Looks like your lot have shot themselves in the foot.'

I asked what he meant, and he pushed a copy of that day's Observer newspaper in front of me and my Guinness. What scared the bejasus out of me was that he was showing me the front page.

And the headline that barked out from the centre of page one:

'LIVINGSTONE STIRS 'TROOPS OUT' STORM'

This did not look promising. The article, written by Tony Craig, who had conducted the interview with Ken, quoted at length from the credited BFBS recording, including the bit I had missed.

'If I was to make an appeal, what I would say to everybody who's got arms and is carrying arms in Northern Ireland, whether they are in the British Army or the IRA, is to put those arms down and go back to your home.'

Tony had helpfully written in the Observer article: 'Mr. Livingstone's remarks could also be interpreted as coming close to offending the Incitement to Disaffection Act of 1934, which says that anybody who "maliciously and advisedly endeavours to seduce any member of Her Majesty's Forces from his duty of allegiance to Her Majesty shall be guilty of an offence."'

I started to shake. Shades of Lord Haw Haw, treason, a short trial and a firing squad all crossed what remained of my mind. As BFBS, we had published the original interview. As producer, I took full responsibility for the outrage. I was a dead man walking. The day wasn't helped by a trickle of sympathetic phone calls from colleagues wanting to know, essentially, how I'd let the story leech into the Sunday broadsheets.

There was almost a 'phoney war' atmosphere in Kings Buildings on the next day, Monday. The only thing I could actually put my finger on was that nobody really wanted to be in the same room as me. There was nothing to speak of in the newspapers. The day passed in limbo and I went home, a bit puzzled.

The next day, I found out why. Every single national newspaper had hit on the 'Red Ken' story and the headlines fell in front of me, one after the other. The Sun: 'Oh God He's At It Again!'; The Daily Telegraph: 'Livingstone In Ulster Army Row'; Daily Mirror: 'Row Over Ken's Call'; Daily Mail: 'Red Ken's Army Row: Why Won't He Shut Up?'.

The story even went international. The South China Morning Post shrieked: 'Put Down Guns Call Seditious'; The Sydney Herald: 'Now Red Ken Upsets The Army'; Hong Kong Standard: 'London's Leader In Row Over Ulster Call'.

I think it would be fair to say that BFBS had never received so much publicity over a single story in its then thirty-eight year life. Even the London Evening Standard got in on the act with a cartoon showing an illuminated 'British Forces Broadcasting Service' sign over a radio studio desk, at which a shirt-sleeved announcer was saying, 'And here's a request from a Mr Ken Livingstone of County Hall, London…' I was glad somebody was getting a laugh out of this, because I certainly wasn't.

The following day, there was a buzz in the building. Ian Woolf, the Director of BFBS, had been summoned back from his annual holiday by the MOD, who wanted to know, a) the answers to some exceedingly difficult questions; b) the proposed damage limitation scheme; and c) the name of the guilty bastard, so he could be sent to Room 101 for some serious remedial training by the funny people.

I was not surprised when the call came, mid-morning on the Thursday after the event, to attend Uncle Ian's bay-windowed office on the 5th floor. As usual, the sun shone through the window directly into my eyes.

'*COME!*' spoke the great man in capital letters. I walked in. He was facing the window, presenting his back to me. He suddenly spun round and hurled a small paper ball directly at me. It was a good shot. It bounced off my head.

'Pick it up and read it!' he commanded.

I unfurled the newsprint and found myself looking at the front page of that morning's Daily Telegraph. I read, with interest and blue funk, the following:

'Forces' Radio may ban pull out call… Mr Ian Woolf, Director of the service, which is broadcast worldwide, said consideration of whether the programme should go on-air would be his first priority when he returns to the office tomorrow after a three week holiday.'

I looked up from the paper to see the distinguished figure grinning broadly. 'At least they spelt my name right,' he said, in what could only be described as a friendly voice.

He then became quieter and more serious. 'First thing is, I want you out of the way of any reporters with vague ideas of follow-ups. So go home and stay there till I say it's safe for you to come back. I'll deal with the flak. Oh, just one other thing. You need to write me a letter saying you're unhappy in London and you'd like to go overseas again. That's true enough in any case, isn't it?'

I nodded, not believing my luck. I still had a job.

'You understand that there aren't any jobs at your present level on the overseas stations,' he continued, 'so I'm afraid you'll be asking voluntarily to take on a job at a junior grade.'

I nodded, still not believing my luck. I still had a job.

'Good. Well, since that's got your approval, I can offer you two consolation prizes. One, this thing will die down. In the meantime, it's given me a chance to fight the MOD - and I enjoy a good fight. Two, you choose which station you want to go to.'

I nodded, definitely not believing my luck. There was an afterlife.

I thought hurriedly. Cyprus would be the ticket. But it was so popular… Oh well, give it a go.

'What about Cyprus?' I said in a small voice.

'Excellent,' said Uncle Ian. 'I shall write to the Station Controller, Ken Doherty, later today to tell him you're coming. Now go home, stay at home and don't talk to anybody until I tell you it's OK.'

And so I went home to tell Moo that I had just been demoted and we were going to Cyprus for three sunny years in the Med. 'Back of envelope' calculations showed us that my income would effective double, even at the lower grade, and we knew from friends that Cyprus was (in those days) dirt cheap anyway.

After a few weeks, I went back in on the condition that I only worked for the music department and the Head of Light Music, veteran jazz sax player Eggy Ley, put me in charge of labels and paper clips till my posting order came through.

*****

There was only one more chore to undertake. For the last two-and-a-half years, our family of mainly young children had been stuffed into our tiny Army maisonette in Kingston. Amongst other drawbacks, it had a pale oyster-coloured fitted carpet, which covered the entire house. After a long battle with the kids, it was not in the best condition. Before 'march-out', while I was at work, Moo scrubbed that carpet until her hands bled. It would never be pristine again but at least it was clean and fresh.

Not good enough for the march-out, as it happened. The Barrack Inventory Accountant (BIA), who lived in the gatehouse of our housing project called 'The Keep', was even more of a sulking pig than our old friend, Mr. Hudson, in Cologne. He took one look at the carpet, and barked, 'March-out declined!' He refused to let us sign out of the married quarter. Under military rules, this meant we had to stay there until the house was fit for purpose – according to the BIA.

This also meant we couldn't go to Brize Norton to catch our flight for the sunshine posting to Cyprus the following day. We knew that he knew that. We also knew that the likelihood was that he was watching our upstairs window, to see if we were still up after it had got dark.

There was only one thing for it. We slunk out of the quarter and took the key to give to Johnny 'Boy' Walker, who'd driven up from London to give us a hand. We left all the lights blazing. Luckily, the exit was out of the eye line of the BIA and there was a back path to an open gate at the back of the compound, where we found Johnny waiting. He took the key to send on, then drove us to Brize Norton.

It was a very different way to end a posting. I added another strange statistic to my CV. We had done a moonlight flit! And now we were going to Cyprus. Life, once again, was sweet.

Chapter Eighteen:

Aphrodite's Isle

We arrived in Cyprus after the really hot part of summer and, thanks to some very slick organisation, found ourselves decanted straight from Larnaca Airport to Dhekelia Garrison, only a few miles down the road. There, we were 'marched in' to our new quarter in a compound called Minden Village, on a road leading down to the coast. An airy, four-bedroomed, high-ceilinged house designed for summer living, with cool marble floors, ceiling fans and wide balconies was a huge bonus. There was also a red-earthed garden, in which there was already evidence of exotic flowers. All this was going to be ours for the next three years.

My biggest problem was that I didn't drive. I'd always had a moped in Cologne, as it only required insurance plates, rather than a test, but this wasn't so in the Island Paradise. I did a few sums and worked out I could actually afford a taxi on regular hire, and so Sokratis and his cool Mercedes purred into my life. Sokratis would take me from Club to work, from work to Club or Mess and from there back home, plus any little trips Moo wanted to make, although she preferred her bike – the 'Tin Donkey'.

The Club turned out to be in effect my HQ. The Dhekelia Officers' Club, to give it its full name, was run for the benefit of military officers and 'entitled' civilians – UK Based Civilians, or UKBCs. It was on the rocky shores of the Med, next to the Sailing Club, behind the bosky 'Scout Wood', and was a one-storey, spread out building with a bar, restaurant, patio terrace, beach terrace 'bashas' – wicker bathing huts on the shoreline – and amazing sea views. There was even a diving platform, moored about 25 yards away from the steps, leading into deeper water. I did, during my time there, achieve instant fame by swimming out to the platform with one hand held on high, carrying a plastic bag containing a glass of gin and tonic, a packet of cigs and a lighter.

The bar was open through the day and provided a nerve centre for the various interest groups to come and catch up with the local gossip. Since working hours were from about seven in the

morning to about half-past one, the afternoons were principally designed for the local delights of brandy sours, Keo lager, the thick red fortified wine, Commandaria, and exotic liqueurs like Filfar, made from oranges. It was also possible, if you tipped the barman, to get hold of Zivania (pronounced 'souvenir'), a lethal distillate of nasty bits, which eventually would make you forget all your troubles on a permanent basis. Of course, there was also a full bill of NAAFI's finest duty-free spirits, beers and wines. Cyprus was never really designed to be a punishment posting.

It would be fair to say that the island was a boozer's paradise, and nearly all who came fell into the arms of Bacchus before too long. The medical profession even allowed for this by regarding a slightly higher 'liver count' as normal. However, this was marginal. To add to the difficulties, because everybody was in effect working part-time, there was plenty of time to do the rounds of all the clubs and societies on the island, all of which had bars.

My own fiefdom, at one point, gave me entry to the Officers' Club, the Garrison Officers' Mess, the Saddle Club, the Royal Engineers' 'Zulu Warrior' club, the Drama Society, the Victor Beach Club, the CESSAC Mission and beach bar, plus a host of local bars and mezze parlours.

It wasn't long before I got into a pleasant routine. I'd been assigned the teatime show – 1700 to 2000 – which gave me lots of spare time during the day. I would get up at about eleven, have a bit of breakfast, get on Moo's Tin Donkey and freewheel down the hill to Scout Wood and the Officers' Club. After a lunchtime sesh till about three, Sokratis would pick me up and drive me to the BFBS station, where I would prep the show, write scripts, phone for guests and assemble everything in the studio. A packet of fags and a glass or two of Othello red wine would fuel the operation and I'd be happy as a sand boy playing hits and chatting to a very receptive audience. At close of play, all I had to do was clear the studio, and hit the road with Sokratis to whichever venue was in my sights that evening, after which, home, chat, nightcap, pit. The simple life.

*****

The only fly in the ointment was Roger Hudson, who, after a little while, became my boss, as a then BFBS Grade IV Senior Programme Organiser. (I think I passed muster as a Grade IV – no longer Grade III! – Senior Producer.) I noticed, by the way, that I didn't feel any different being a humbled and demoted me. Mr. Kipling had got it right: success and failure were both impostors. I felt only like me, as I always had done. This was very heartening.

Because of this, and unlike the others, I used to take the mick out of our boss and Roger and I were soon locking horns with a kind of mutual respect. Calling him 'Kermit' used to peeve him mightily, so I tended to throw that around a bit in front of the others. It culminated in the studio starting the famous 'Not The Log Book'. And ended in tears.

The official BFBS Station Log Book was a leather-bound ledger, in which the occupant of the on-air studio would remark on operational events and problems during his shift. These entries were made on the left page and countersigned with action notes by the SPO on the right hand side. It was a hanging offence to write personal observations in the logbook and a similar capital offence to write something scurrilous, then try to excise it by scribbling over it or tearing out the offending page.

The 'Not The Station Log Book' was the subversive counterpart, the evil brother of the official tome. Here, on-air staff were encouraged to write any gripes, moans, opinions of the bosses, libels, calumnies, oaths, insults, or whatever came into their heads. Given that most of the staff liked a drink or two, this book gradually became a recognised way to go over the top and still get away with it. There was an unwritten law that the bosses didn't get to read it if they knew what was good for them, and this practice seemed to work.

The boss, Ken Doherty, had long since retreated to the golf course, where he spent all day ruining a good walk by smacking tiny balls over scrubby landscape into Cyprus's famous 'browns' (as opposed to 'greens'), which were in effect sand made to look dark by the infusion of motor oil. So Ken never got to see the book. The senior engineer would have agreed with everything in the book anyway and that only left Hudson, who, like all bullies (as we thought him then), deserved what we wrote, and we didn't care, so there.

But one night I remember someone writing a paragraph filled with such venom against Hudson and his works that I swear the page might easily have caught fire. It called him every name under the sun: his decisions were idiotic; his posturing asinine; his appearance and dress positively ridiculous (he favoured a nylon safari suit, with bits of him bulging out in the wrong places). All in all, it was the kind of pen-portrait that should never be visited by the subject of such bile. It was a great pity that, later on that night, Hudson broke the rule and read the book.

The next day, somebody spotted a new entry in the 'Not The Log Book'. As we turned up on station, each of us got to see an amazing development. On the right-hand page of the subversive tome, Roger Hudson had penned a reply. It was short, and made us feel even shorter. It struck home and changed a lot of our attitudes towards him. It read, simply:

'Frogs have feelings, too.' It was signed, simply, in his unmistakable handwriting, 'Kermit.'

*****

I was very happy on station. I chummed up with a very much younger jock, Simon 'Simbo' Guettier, and his then wife, the glamorous Debbie – formerly known as Debbie Ades, she acquired a t-shirt after becoming Simon's betrothed, which read 'Marital Ades'. Simbo was obsessive about four things in those days: Debbie, music radio, drinking and computers. They lived just across the way from us in Minden and we spent a lot of good times together.

The best was the week after Simbo had designed his own (green screen) computer game, which was in the form of a horse race with primitive spindly figures with legs, bearing, it must be said, little resemblance to horses, tooling round a racecourse. This required constant tweaking as one or more horses, after jumping a fence, would hit the ground and freeze. So each race might take an hour or two. But it didn't matter. Next to the computer was a drinks trolley...

A recipe for disaster. Our horseracing jag lasted from Monday to Friday of one memorable week, with time out only to go home, eat, freshen up and work. On the Monday we played on well into the night - and our drinks were on tap, complete with ice bucket topped up by Debbie, who was keeping well out of this 'boys' toys' nonsense. Gin and tonic, rum and coke, brandy and ginger – it was all going down well.

By the Wednesday we were running out of some provisions and too idle to get more from the NAAFI. We seemed to have formed a pact with the devil, that we would simply drink the entire contents of the drinks trolley. So, by the middle of the week we were already on scotch and tonic, rum and lemonade, gin and Lucozade, and other liquid horrors. In the meantime, we'd graduated to an early version of dungeons and dragons, continuing long into the night.

By the Friday night, both we and our drinks trolley were completely out of it. The pair of us were hollow-eyed and trembling from loss of sleep and far too much loopy juice and the drinks trolley was down to its last sentries. That night, I swear, we were drinking brand new cocktails, including parfait amour and ginger ale, banana liqueur and soda and, perhaps the worst of the lot, blue curacao and cold milk.

My lunchtime drinking companion was probably even more lethal than Simbo. Lieutenant Colonel 'Pip' Burrows had gravitated from India as an Imperial Indian Army British Officer. On retirement, he took up the position of Dhekelia's Housing Commandant as an RO (Retired Officer), and after that he was supposed to be a pukka chap and go back to the UK. However, he was allowed, against the rules, to remain as a member of the Dhekelia Mess and the Officers' Club.

Pip really did look the part. He had the whole Colonel Blimp thing off to a 't'. Apart from being rather thinner, the whole works were there. He 'harrumphed'. He was intolerant of anything modern. He had a less than 'appropriate' eye for the fillies. He drank, for Jesus, pink gins, which somehow went with his rheumy eyes and his red bottlenose. He hated women who shrieked or laughed too loudly and he would bite the heads off any children who dared to appear in the lounge area and stand on the strip of carpet near to the bar. (There was a serving hatch for minors outside and round the corner.)

For some reason, we got on well and every lunchtime for the time we were both there, we would meet up, buy each other drinks and put the world to rights. A lot of the then current military people saw him as nothing more than a washed up and sad old man but I found he had a great sense of humour and a youthful subversion in his extensive armoury. He even got to like our children. This was because at weekends we would walk down the hill to the Club en famille. Moo and I would bring up the rear and Mandy, Olly, Alex and Paddy would march, military style, in single file ahead of us. When they reached the Club, they would march inside, right up to where Pip was sitting, salute him, greet him with a 'Good Morning, Pip!' and then march out of the Club to the beach area. Pip loved this and allowed them leeway never before granted to Small Ones. He even referred to them as 'The Majors'. Tribute indeed.

*****

But storm clouds were gathering on the horizon. Maggie Thatcher was in power and wanted privatisations. It was decided that BFBS, with its eighty-nine civil servants, was ideal to use as a test case. If BFBS was to be merged with the more arms-length contractor, the Services Kinema Corporation, then the resulting union might – with a suitable dowry – be cast adrift from mother ship Civil Service, with its excellent terms, conditions, jobs for life and glow-in-the-dark pension scheme. A senior BBC man, John Grist, formerly Head of the BBC's New York Office, was seconded to see if such a merger would be possible and, if it was, to become the Managing Director of the new organisation.

It seemed to us that there was some kind of inevitability about this but we were convinced that Uncle Ian, who hated the idea, would see us alright and ward off the dreadful proposal. Nearly all of us signed a petition deploring the intention and many of us even joined Alan Sapper's powerful ACTT union, as we thought our own body, the IPCS, was a bit toothless.

But what we didn't know was that we were going to be privatised at any cost. This was a political move, there to establish a precedent. To take a bona fide civil service department and turn it into a private organisation would set a trend that would change the nature of state employment forever. We were taking on the government, the establishment and the inevitable. We were bound to lose.

On top of which, we disliked the SKC. They ran, as far as we were concerned, awful cinemas, playing out of date films; they rented out iffy tellies at huge cost and had a range of seedy shops selling inferior sound and vision goods. Merging with them would be like the Royal Shakespeare Company merging with Tesco. To be fair, they saw *us* as a bunch of posing nancy boys playing dreadful tunes while talking cock in posh voices to diminishing audiences. OK, we understood each other.

Uncle Ian flew out to see us. Peter Ginn, engineer and union rep, asked all the difficult questions with his arms folded and his feet up on a chair. A member of staff appeared, dressed as an usherette, holding a tray of melting ice creams, indicating the nonsense of SKC and BFBS merging. The atmosphere was harsh and unforgiving. Uncle Ian gave of his best but it was clear that there were darker forces at work.

And so it was that we were subjected to the most fearsome weapon in the government's arsenal. The plot was that a man from the Treasury would be sent out to review salaries, grades, terms and conditions of the BFBS staff, compared to similar posts in BBC Local Radio. A Mr Trevor Franklin would appear, take notes and write up 'The Franklin Report', which he would submit as material evidence. Because of the nature of the Treasury (the Bank which adores saying 'No!'), it was assumed that Franklin would take a cold-blooded appraisal and, as a result, provide evidence that could be used against the broadcasters if they chose to carry on arguing. If some of them left in frustration, then so much the better: new recruits could come in without bringing with them any outstanding civil service rights.

It looked like it was going to happen that way. Trev the Tresh went out to BFBS Cologne, where they stopped all normal activity to present a showcase of what they did. Then they had a cocktail party for the great and the good, with everybody in suits. Trev came and saw and took notes. He had seen similar showcases before and recognised them for what they were.

There was a repeat performance in Gibraltar. He was shown the things they felt he ought to see and at the end there was a cocktail party for the great and the good. By now you'll have got the picture.

Trev didn't know it yet but Cyprus was different, and it was all down to Roger Hudson. Yes, Kermit came good and saved the day. He had a meeting of all staff, where he told them that when Trev came, he was going to have to fit in with normal station activities. There wasn't going to be any showcasing. Trev could see exactly what went on for the rest of the year. Treat him nicely and if you see him hanging about, have a chat and take him to the bar.

'Oh – and just one other thing, ladies and gentleman. The Glosters up on the Green Line have asked if the BFBS crew can go up to their club for a bit of an 'anything goes' night. They're sending a bus to take us up there and bring us back and I thought we might use the opportunity to show how BFBS can party, as well as work.'

Well, we didn't exactly trust Kermit overmuch, but this seemed like a plan and so we agreed to an unspecified cabaret.

The Green Line? That was the heavily guarded border between Turkish North Cyprus, and the Republic of Cyprus, under Greek Cypriot control. It was a sensitive area and there were rigid protocols about movements close to and on the border. It was known that people had been shot.

The great day arrived. Trevor was taken from the airport to the BFBS station, where he met a lot of friendly people who seemed to be rushing about, very much doing their own thing. He guessed that was mainly for the audience. He wandered around wherever he wanted to go and occasionally he found he could sit down and think, without a man in a suit throwing facts at him. He began to like this. As the result of Kermit's plan, he was at last becoming able to pick up some independent information.

It was clear that the station was there for the audience; listeners seemed to be all around, both on station and on the end of 'phones on the live shows. The staff seemed happy and fulfilled. There was the odd bottle of beer around but everybody seemed on top of their jobs. Not only that, everybody he spoke to seemed to be saying that OK, sometimes the work was hard, but mainly it was a pleasure to be providing a service to an appreciative audience who deserved it.

By the time he got on the bus (yes, Kermit had persuaded him to come on the BFBS vs. Glosters Party Nite), Trev joined the others with a paper cup full of brandy sour in his hand, a Hawaiian shirt, and a beaming grin on his face. As well as the DJs and engineers, wives, girlfriends and boyfriends were also on board, adding quite a bit of exotic beauty and perfume to the proceedings. The old Army bus bounced remorselessly along the textured Cyprus road, heading north. A sing-song started. Then we approached the Green Line and Kermit stood up in the centre aisle and called for a bit of hush.

We didn't know quite what was coming but Roger Hudson, former BBC World Service newsreader, adopted the most serious of tones. His voice dripped dangerous authority and, far worse, the essence of complete and utter truth.

'Ladies and gentlemen, in a couple of minutes we will be entering the area patrolled and manned by soldiers of the occupying Turkish Army. As this bus carries large Union Flag symbols and is being driven by a uniformed British soldier, this should pass off without incident'.

Then the master stroke.

'But, ladies and gentlemen, if the Turkish Army for any reason should open fire, then please could you all lie down in the centre aisle, and could those of you who carry side-arms and personal weapons please secure them, deploy close to the front door of the bus, and await my signal. Thank you for listening.'

You could see Trev's eyes go very wide and his Adam's Apple do a big, big swallow. Turks with guns. Gallipoli part two. Oh dear, this wasn't in the plan. Still, the others seem unworried. Do they have to live like this all the time? Another mental note was made.

Soon the bus was out of the 'hard bit' (of course, there was no danger, but Kermit felt like stirring it) and bouncing cheerfully towards a lone Nissen hut in the scrubland. We all decanted ourselves out and went to meet the fighting end of the Resident Battalion, otherwise known as the 'Glorious Glosters'.

The Resident Battalion was split into two groups. For three months, half the battalion was assigned UN peacekeeping duties on the Green Line, effectively on full-time guard duty, while the other half of the 'Resbat', as it was called, was on general training duties and exercises, based at Alexander Barracks in Dhekelia. After three months, they simply swapped. But now the Glorious Glosters were waiting for us. They were *really* waiting for us, as their RSM said they weren't to start on the beer till BFBS arrived. And now the corks were popped and the bottles opened. And there was great joy in the land, because we'd brought the girls, who looked great to us in their glad rags and even better to the lads in the trenches, who had been stuck up in no man's land (and certainly no woman land) for a couple of months.

Trev was really relieved to be in the company of some roughie toughie soldiers with guns and started to relax again. People kept pushing glasses of scotch at him, which he was forced to drink so that he could be polite and grab the next one on offer. The BFBS girls waylaid him and took him on the dance floor. He even grinned during the most terrible spectacle of McD & Simbo celebrating the recent Falklands victory as they sang with the Glosters' house band a tribute to the recent smashing of Argentine Forces, 'Don't Piss On Me

Argentina' (freely and crudely adapted).

Very much later on, in consultations between the Glosters' RSM and our by now very own Kermit, it was established that the result of the night's encounter was a draw and that everyone might now honourably go home. We poured Trev onto the bus and were glad that he didn't give a stuff about the fierce Turkish Army any more. One by one, we were dropped off at home. It had been a splendid night, in more ways than one.

The remains of Mr Trevor Franklin, senior Treasury official, appeared bright and breezy on station the next day. He thanked every one he saw for a great and enlightening evening. A few hours later, he flew back to the UK, safe in the knowledge that he had been treated well and honourably.

Some weeks later, the Franklin Report was issued. It was not happy reading for the MOD suits. BFBS staff were operating at maximum efficiency, often in harsh and dangerous circumstances, which was not recognised in their official terms and conditions and certainly not in their emoluments and remunerations. All BFBS personnel should be solidly graded at the top of any existing pay spine and plans put in place to reward them further.

There were several other recommendations that could be traced back to Roger Hudson's vision and genius in the way the Man from the Treasury had been treated, including the finest accolade of all: Trev said it seemed strange that the Senior Programme Organiser in Germany should be a Grade III, whilst the same position in Cyprus, which had extra operational responsibilities, only merited a Grade IV. It was his recommendation that this anomaly be removed immediately. It was. Roger's phantom marauding Turks had given him a well-deserved leg up.

*****

Before nemesis struck our cosy little operation, we were subject to an invasion. No, not the Turks, but the Romanians. And somehow, BFBS became very much involved. I was sitting in my studio, doing my evening show and having a jolly time as usual, when the Programme Operations Assistant opened the outer studio door to a senior officer, looking very serious, holding a pistol and asking to speak to the senior officer on the radio station. This turned out to be me.

The Colonel who faced me in the studio put the gun away and then gave me the once-over. Well, apart from being a bit red eyed, smelling of wine and holding a fag, at least my voice sounded articulate and passably intelligent. Did I know about the Official Secrets Act? Of course I did. Because of my previous higher grade, I was cleared up to 'Secret' level. I told him this and it seemed to take his angst down a notch. Then, did we have a civilian telex machine on station - one that worked independently of the military? Yes, we did.

'Do you think one of us might use it?' asked the Colonel, now convinced he was talking to somebody responsible, despite that person breaking off to talk pop-jockey nonsense to the audience every three minutes.

I was a bit concerned. 'One of whom?' I asked.

'Oh, we have a civilian pilot here. He's made a landing with a passenger plane at the wrong airfield and he needs to report back to his masters in Romania.'

'If I'm going to let you use our machine, I'm afraid I'll need a little more than that, as I will have to make a full report as well,' I said, hoping I'd pressed the right buttons.

'Of course, you're right,' said the Chief of Staff. 'Here's what happened.'

He then told me the most incredible story. A Captain Martian, of Romanian Airways, had flown a small turbo-prop with thirty-eight passengers into Cyprus. Just outside the sovereign base area is Larnaca International Airport, where he should have landed. He missed it, completely. He aimed for another airstrip that he could see. Of course. That would be Kingsfield, the airstrip used for military purposes and by the gliding club. But, no – he'd missed that too. He actually put the plane down on the very short airstrip of 16 Army Air Corps, a helicopter unit. It was a spectacular landing and it would be a miracle if a plane could take off from there again.

As the story unfolded, I saw, outside in the control room, a very glum figure contemplating an assuredly grim future. Dressed in a shabby uniform, Captain Martian stood waiting to compose to his masters in Belgrade the words that would end his career.

Within a few minutes, the Colonel, myself, Captain Martian and a couple of Military Police were grouped round the telex machine, which I fired up and handed over to the beleaguered pilot. We even offered him a capitalist Coke, which he was happy to accept. Once the message had been sent and taped copies that I made given to the Colonel, with one kept for our records, they disappeared into the night and I went home, sworn to secrecy.

Of course they hadn't reckoned on a very large Romanian passenger plane in a British sovereign base area not being a talking point. Soon the whole island knew and was taking bets on whether the plane would get off the ground in a few days' time, or whether it would have to be dismantled and sent back to Romania by post.

The military hadn't reckoned with two things. Firstly, the forthcoming 16 Flight AAC Open Day was due to be held that Saturday. The main event at the fête was 'Sticker the Commie Plane' and huge numbers of permanent fluorescent orange stickers were zapped all over the stranded beast. Secondly, the lead story in the local forces newspaper, 'The Lion', was to be an editor's dream. He got out his biggest typeface to produce the headline, 'MARTIAN LANDS IN CYPRUS'.

On a successful footnote, calculations were made in Bucharest and, as a result, every fitting was removed from the plane, the barest minimum of fuel was left to make possible a short hop to Larnaca International, a skeleton crew got on board and it successfully took off, eventually finding its way back home. Captain Martian still owes BFBS a Coke to this very day but he did, in his own way, contribute to the gaiety of nations.

*****

We scored some good points during the rapid but inevitable retreat into privatisation. Our pensions were protected. Our terms and conditions remained, in effect the same. We were given the bonus of tax-free salaries overseas. We continued to be 'entitled' on military bases overseas. But we lost our independence and we lost Ian Woolf. There was a tangible sense of mourning as, in April 1982, we became 'BFBS, the Radio Division of the Services Sound and Vision Corporation.'

Chapter Nineteen:

Vultures to Penguins

One of the more delightful venues on the Dhekelia base in Cyprus was the Garrison Officers' Mess. It was unusual, in that most of its residents were 'in transit' – mainly young officers leading their men in annual exercises. One of our treats was watching the young subalterns come adrift and the bar, overseen by a part-time sheep farmer called George, was the place to go for the entertainment. If you got in early and grabbed a front row barstool, you could see the arrival of the Three Vultures. They were what the Army might unkindly call 'twin-baggers (you wear one on your head in case hers falls off) and they spent their long and languorous days teaching at the local primary school. It would be fair to say that they could drink most human beings under the table and also that they hated men with a passion. They didn't appear to be of the comfy shoe persuasion so we could only surmise that, coincidentally, all three had at one stage met up with men who had Done Them Wrong.

Watching them play suicide dating with the subbies was a joy. After several drinks, the young officers would try up their chat up lines, with petrifying after-effects. I have seen men who would cheerfully lead their platoon into a hail of bullets in order to take a machine gun post turn into ashen, gibbering wrecks from one of the Vultures' tongue-lashings. In the meantime George would pour them more and more drinks, until the Vultures had sulked at and insulted enough people for the evening, when they would lurch out to convene in one of their rooms and continue stirring the cauldron as they beefed up their curses. They hated Cyprus, men, themselves, the kiddies and life itself. It was nice once they'd left for the evening.

This now left the floor free for the second part of the cabaret. I would usually be in the bar with Simbo or the Great Midland Engineer, Peter 'Fook It' Ginn, whose attitude to authority was at the very least refreshing. This part of the evening was always fun.

'I say, George' one of the subbies would say, 'we're orf dine tine to Larnaca later on. Don't suppose you could give us a few phrases to jolly along the old Cypriots, what?'

George was his country's true ambassador. 'Of course, gentlemen. I would be happy to help you. Give me some words, and I tell you what to say for it in Greek.'

'Thank you!' one subby would volunteer. (Actually it would come out as 'Hengyop!' but George understood fluent Rupert, the unique language of   officers)

'Halfagaragedoor!' returned George. (Close, but Greek Cypriots would prefer 'efharisto'.)

'Where is...?'

'Subaru!'

'And what if you want to say to a girl that she looks very nice? What would you say then?'

'You should look gently into her eyes, then just say "polyfilla.' (The actual word is 'polygala', emphasis on the final 'a'.)

By this time we hardy few were stuffing table napkins into our faces to stop the hysteria. George would then give them a blistering list of utterly obscene words in place of the Greek Cypriot for 'beer', 'kebab', 'chips' and 'can I see you again?' which would ensure their night on the tiles would be unforgettable. We would stay behind to drink to their memories.

*****

However, the Curse of the Vultures was to afflict us all. I was at the Club one lunchtime. Pip Burrows and his lugubrious dog had tottered off to play 'hunt the traffic' on the Larnaca road, leaving Peter Ginn and me on bar stools watching Takis, the barman, wash glasses. It was a nothing day, which happened a lot in Cyprus. It was midsummer and too hot to do anything except drink and swim. And here we were, for the nth day, sitting on bar stools out of the afternoon sun.

'I wish something was happening,' said Peter.

'Me too. This gets boring after a while, doesn't it?'

'Um. What are we going to do?'

'I don't know. What is there to do?'

We looked nervously at each other. Having mocked the Vultures for the last few months, we were perched on bar stools, being miserable, and bemoaning our lot. We were turning into the them. Just like the three teachers – or indeed the creatures from the original source, the Scouse vultures in 'The Jungle

Book'.

I guess we mentally shook ourselves. We were, we decided, in a rut, and needed to do something different. It was early spring, 1983. Our colleagues in BFBS had finally been allowed to go to the Falklands to provide a morale-boosting radio service to the brand new garrison of 1800 souls. We were livid that they wouldn't let us go to the South Atlantic during the conflict of 1982, but we were refused point blank. All this would change in time.

A call had gone out from Head Office for volunteers to do four-month unaccompanied detachments to Stanley, to share facilities with the then Falkland Islands Broadcasting Station (the wonderfully acronymed FIBS) and to spend as much time as possible on-air and doing PR. To my slightly brandy-soured brain, the Falklands in their inhospitable midwinter sounded better than a leisurely long hot summer in Cyprus…

So, why not?

'Tell you what, Peter: let's volunteer to do a Falklands gig,' I said.

Peter Ginn thought I was joking at first but he too got excited by the idea and by the end of the session we both agreed stoutly that we *would* volunteer.

We told the boss, Ken Doherty, who gave a wry grin, but said nothing. As a former military officer, he might have told us that Rule One was always never to volunteer for anything. Our requests landed on desks in Head Office. Peter's fell on comparatively stony ground. There were a few volunteers ahead of him so his impetuous offer would not be accepted, for some months, at least.

My request, however, landed on the desk of the Controller Programmes, Brian Bass - the man who wrote, on one of my annual reports, 'This man will never amount to anything in the service'; the man who thought I was a sensitive polymath, when in fact I was a boozy pop-jockey specialising in inane chat. Oh yes, he would enjoy sending me into exile with the penguins, where the winds howled and conditions were primitive. As he approved my request with almost immediate effect, he almost felt a twinge of sympathy. It soon passed.

*****

Back in Cyprus, the message came through via Ken that my presence would be required in the South Atlantic from April to August. I gulped. This was now real. Moo was not too happy about me visiting a recent war zone but I began to recall the attitude of my youth, where there was no real danger and we were all immortal. There was a last supper and I trickled off to Larnaca International to catch the flight back to the UK.

Once there, I was briefed on how to behave down south. More importantly, I was given a military purchase order to buy 'foul weather gear' from a specialist shop in Victoria. I came out with parkas, over-trousers, thick gloves and some serious boots. After a day or so meeting up with old faces from Head Office, I shot over to Brize Norton for the longest journey in the world.

It was for me. Jock, the owner of the Fairwinds Taverna on the Larnaca Road, had given me an emergency kit of two Underberg mini-bottles and, on the advice of Roy ffoulkes (yes, that is the correct spelling), who had preceded me down to the penguins, a bottle of Night Nurse. ('Never mind the instructions, just down the lot. It'll knock you out.')

We landed in West Africa after a few hours on the RAF plane. As usual, muscular load mistresses forced hourly orange squashes down our throats, so a sleep was out of the question. It was searing hot outside and we still had the misery of the last announcement ringing in our ears. The local authorities would not allow us to use the air-conditioned terminal building because a flight full of returning Royal Marines had trashed the bar the previous week.

And that's how I came to be standing underneath the shadow of the big jet's wing, with the temperature cracking the thermometer, nursing a parched throat and the beginnings of withdrawal symptoms, including the shakes. I was not in a good way. I remembered the emergency kit and knocked back the two Underbergs. That brought some temporary relief.   As soon as we got on board for the next tedious leg to Ascension Island, I necked the Night Nurse. I was soon out of it, though I do have vague memories of being shaken by the load mistress to pass on my orange squash.

I woke up with a splitting headache and noticed with some horror that the effects of both Underberg and the Night Nurse had passed. I was beginning to get the shakes again, added to which, I was beginning to get very nervous about this whole detachment idea. What if I collapsed and had to be 'casevaced'? What if I had a breakdown or a series of panic attacks on air? I began to fall into a 'spiral of doom', which was only interrupted by a hairy evening touchdown between the volcanic ash-covered peaks of the entrance to a landing strip at Ascension Island.

They had briefed me that I should report to the BBC World Service HQ on the island, where somebody would know what to do with me, but I was so out of it, standing in the middle of the arrivals shed, with no idea of what was going on. I remember having to fill in an immigration form with both hands because I was shaking so much. Then I heard the booming voice of a very large, but smiling, US serviceman say the word 'bar'. In the recesses of a foggy mind, this was a word I very much understood, so I followed him.

The bar we fell into was a Hollywood set from an over-the-top remake of 'Carmen'. Pneumatic ladies in outrageously coloured micro-frocks danced, buttock to expanding buttock, with snake-hipped moustachioed Lotharios in boiling temperatures, a heaving mass of people who knew how to have a good time, especially when drink seemed to be plentiful and at duty free prices.

I kangarooed to the bar and made my first mistake. It had taken me so long to avoid the human traffic that I decided to order two gin and tonics instead of one, to cut down the waiting time. Then I made my second mistake, in ordering doubles. As this bar offered doubles as standard, I had just ordered a total of eight shots – American sized and therefore more generous than the British ones. This was followed by my third mistake. I was shaking so much that I would never have been able to raise the glass to my mouth, so I asked for drinking straws. The popular myth is that if you suck your drink up through a straw, it gets you loopy quicker.

It is not a myth. Standing at the bar, I ploughed through both drinks. A miracle. I had the full use of my hands again. I was going to live! I joined in the party atmosphere, had a few dances, told a few Puerto Rican servicemen they were my besh friendsh and eventually staggered out into the tropical night.

But the Good Lord had not finished with me just yet. A detachment of Rock Apes (beg their pardon, Royal Air Force Regiment) was on its way south and one of them recognised me as a BFBS-type from Cyprus. I must have played him a request at some stage, because suddenly I was included in their party. They could even offer me a bed for the night, after which we would have a last breakfast before embarking on the final, nastiest leg of the flight – way too long in the belly of a Hercules, not quite designed with passenger comfort in mind.

Some wag discovered a guitar and the Rock Apes learned that I had a talent for singing rugby songs in a fashion deemed 'not too bad for a civvie pisshead'. The result took us all the way through to 0500 military, which is the ideal time to have a quick wash and slide off to the breakfast tent. Here, we enjoyed the daily miracle carried out by members of HM Forces everywhere: after a serious night on the beer, they are able to face a full English afloat in a sea of lard, with the slimy fried egg somehow remaining intact for far too long despite many attempts to skewer it. With tinned tomatoes curdling the yolk and the blackish smear of mushroom trails against the grey-green greasy backwash of the frying fluid, the whole plate, in the dawn light of Ascension Island, took on the satanic vista of a Caravaggio murder feast.

Eventually, a kindly sergeant with a clipboard called us to order and explained that it was now our unique chance for today's pleasure trip on the big Hercy Bird down to Port Stanley. We would please arrange ourselves in an orderly way and try to keep still, as the seating comprised two lengths of canvas running down the inside of the fuselage. There would be no drinking or smoking on board and the flight would take thirteen hours, if we got there.

I had heard the story of a Combined Services' Entertainment comedian who had made it, against his better judgement, as far as Ascension, then had boarded the Hercules for Stanley, only to discover that the flight turned back just before the Falklands as the weather was too harsh for landing. This meant more than twenty hours of discomfort and two doses of in-flight refuelling, which is a bit bracing, even for the passengers. At that point, back on Ascension, he gave up and was flown back to the UK. Not the kind of story you wanted to hear when setting out.

I was bricking it. Luckily, there was enough beer still in the system to get through the worst. We found ourselves in a metal tube, with only a couple of tiny round portholes, a view of the flight deck up forward and eventually some daylight when they lowered the rear ramp.

The central part of the fuselage was crammed to about eight-foot high with kit and some of the cleverer lads had nested up top. The rest of us sat on the canvas strip running down each side of the payload. Conversation was impossible over the racket; even the loadmaster could scarcely get his instructions out.

'Gennlemen, in a minute or two we'll be takin' off for Port Stanley. Lunchboxes will be handed out later. Drink or smoke and you're on a charge. If you want a piss, there's a bucket behind the curtain here or if you're feelin' brave you can always 'ave a dump off the tail ramp when we're underway. Don't forget to 'ang on to the rope.'

With that, we were off. We'd got used to the noise of the aircraft on the ground. The take-off and climb to cruising height reminded us of our imminent hangovers and our mortality. I peered around in the gloom of the badly lit khaki cocoon. God, this was miserable. And I didn't have a book! Remembering 'Papillon', I decided to embark on a series of intellectual and physical exercises to keep myself alert. I started counting the rivets in the fuselage, the number of ropes holding the kit down, the holes in the netting and the number of times the loadmaster walked up and down, checking that his little charges weren't breaking the house rules. I also flexed muscles without actually shifting position, as each squirm would bring a wee swearie from immediate neighbours: if I moved, they moved, and if they had achieved the nirvana of a nap, they could be well upset.

What appeared to be about three weeks passed before the calm, confident voice of the pilot came on the speakers to tell us that we would now be joined by a nice plane that had come to refuel us. Unfortunately, we were flying too slowly on level flight for the fuelling aircraft to keep speed with us without stalling so we would be executing a shallow dive to tart up our progress and allow its fragile refuelling hose to connect with our nose cone and pump lots of kero into our tanks.

So, let's get this right. We were going to go into a screaming nose dive while a couple of young RAF Johnnies were going to play an aerial version of 'pin the tail on the donkey' and then squirt thousands of gallons of aviation fuel in our general direction while we cowered on our canvas strip. I looked around me. There appeared to be others of the same mind as me. 'We're all going to die.'

Such is the understated brilliance of the RAF that, apart from one metallic 'clunk' early on in the proceedings as the nozzle connected, we neither saw nor felt anything untoward until those of us who had a view onto the flight deck saw the fuelling plane disconnect and disappear, job done. At this stage all of us Doubting Thomases became battle hardened veterans. 'Oh, mid-air re-fuelling? Nothing to worry about.'

*****

That was Cabaret Part One. Part Two was the feeding of the many. The MOD had laid down the precise dietary requirements for a roughie toughie squaddie on a long haul flight. To say the Officer Commanding Culinary Delights lacked imagination or generosity would be an understatement. The loadmaster, in his role of Jesus Christ, moved amongst us, and yea verily, to each of us in turn was given a white cardboard container, lunch, HM Forces, for the relief of. It would have been a kindness to have printed the slogan 'not for human consumption' on the box.

Once the lid had been prised open, the contents instantly lowered morale. One bag of crisps, clearly stored under a box of lead weights. Very crumbly. Even powdery. And is there a 'mutton and mustard' variety in the real world? Next, a sandwich. The good Earl would surely have sued at the notion of his name being used to describe two flagging, moist pieces of remaindered Mothers Pride, hiding a wafer-thin slice of transparent reconstituted ham and a smear of Army high-octane mustard, with the scab of a deliquescing tomato ring adding moisture to the sparse comestible.

Two more items completed this failed feast: a Golden Delicious cardboard apple and a small waxed carton of Ribena. It was the ultimate fifties picnic, written badly. Of course, we ate and drank very slowly, not just because of the taste, but because we knew we still had hours to go and this, at least, was activity. A man mountain sitting next to me, who I had seen eat half a cow at breakfast, spent about 40 minutes delicately disassembling the contents of his white box before succumbing, as we all then did, into a sporadic bovine coma that saw us through the next few hours.

At last there appeared to be news. Luckily, my head was still operational, although my bum had frozen numb some hours ago. We would attend to that later. The good news was that there was so much fear of the unknown – we were, after all, entering an operational area where less than a year ago, people were seriously going 'bang' at each other – that my body had forgotten to shake or panic; there was just curiosity and the will to survive. The loadmaster put us out of our misery. The weather in Stanley was good – a few crosswinds, but not a problem. We would be landing in an hour.

You could feel about eighty sets of shoulders fall an inch or two into 'relax' mode. Soon the engine note changed and before we knew what was really happening we made a clean and safe landing at Stanley International Aerodrome, recently repaired after being bombed by the same RAF to deny Argentine landings. We taxied erratically and de-planed into the obligatory hut. Here, civvie passports were stamped by Falkland Islands immigration officials and we looked forward to our various billets. I was to stay in a B&B called, at the time, 'Harrier House'.

But, no. Life with the Forces is never that simple. A duty jobsworth corporal duly appeared and gave us a prepared lecture on minefields, Argentine munitions, actions to be taken, areas to avoid, what an anti-personnel mine could do to you and how to report a suspicious device. Someone should have told them that they might as well have recited the Koran at us after thirteen hours in the belly of a Herc. Anyway, it was finally all over and I walked to freedom, and towards one of the strangest people I ever met.

*****

There to meet me on the other side of the barrier was Terry Nicholas, detached from the BBC Caversham Monitoring Service to become a pop jockey and reporter with a brief to entertain and inform the lads in the trenches for four months. I was putatively his boss, but as I have never really got to grips with bossing people, I followed his example, which, looking back, might not have been the wisest thing. Even at that stage of my career, I tended to believe everything I was told, and Brian Bass in London had told me that I would be working with a BBC man who was also a priest. And indeed, the bearded, bespectacled, ruddy-faced smiling chubby guiding me onward *was* wearing a dog collar.

As our regulation Land Rover bounced along the pot-holed and bomb-damaged road leading to Stanley, Terry intimated to me that he was not just here to broadcast to the lads in the trenches. Once we'd got to our room, he would give me a full briefing, as I was an MOD civil servant, and had therefore signed the Official Secrets Act. I began to wonder where all of this was going. The driver dropped us off and we lugged my kitbag up to our shared room on the first floor of Harrier House, a pleasant and well-fitted building on Ross Road, overlooking the inner harbour of Port Stanley. Sitting squat in the middle was the SS Rangatira, otherwise known as 'Rangatraz', which was an RASC supply and accommodation ship. She was an ugly sight. (The 'Coastels' – floating accommodation blocks, had yet to arrive.)

Terry watched me for a few minutes as I unpacked. I saw him watching me and felt suitably uncomfortable. Then I realised he was monitoring my every move. He had a very serious expression on his face. He was about to tell me something very serious, and very important.

I finished a basic unpacking and sat down on one of the two beds. Terry looked at me. He had a conspiratorial glint in his eye. We lit up. He made to speak.

'Always knock three times - two fast, one slow – when you come into the room. You may see me do this...' He rolled off the side of his bed, facing the door, and made the shape of a gun with his fingers as he knelt. 'I was trained to do this by Mossad, when I was working for them in Saudi Arabia.'

Oh boy. This was going to be fun. I might have as much as three months with this guy.

'The BBC job is really just a cover. Like this dog collar. I'm actually a Muslim but sometimes you have to make sacrifices. Look, I won't bullshit you, but I may ask you from time to time to drop some phrases into what you're saying on-air.

'Bit of advice. Don't let this place get to you. If you ever need a quick fix, I've got something here in the wardrobe that helps. But be careful - it's very strong and quite addictive.'

With that, he rummaged through his socks and knickers drawer and produced a tobacco tin, from which he extracted what looked dangerously like a highly addictive snuff box. He took a pinch and passed it over to me as he fell into a paroxysm of 'Too much, man! Oh, wow!' and other such hippie, druggie utterances.

I took a pinch. When in Rome. I was used to snuff. It was snuff. As on the label, 'Birmingham No.1 SP'. I was beginning to learn stuff about our Terry. The good news was that he was eccentric but essentially harmless. Walter Mitty could have taken lessons from him but, in the world of broadcasting, this was not unusual. The bad news was that I would have to play along with his fantasies if I wanted a peaceful life. He enjoyed a drink, he smoked fags – he couldn't be all bad. I decided to rub along but I would try to find a 'get out of jail free' card as soon as possible.

*****

The Government Broadcasting Officer of FIBS (Patrick Watts, the DJ who was on-air when Argentine forces landed in April 1982; he received an MBE for his role in broadcasting news of the invasion to the islanders) was away, so Terry and I had more or less carte blanche to get on with things. The outgoing BFBS Representative, Charly Lowndes, had shouted a clue to me as he boarded the home-going Hercy Bird: 'Close the gap in the afternoon.' There was a period of silence between the lunchtime transmissions and the late afternoon. I took my first executive decision. We would have an 'Afternoon Delight' music show, with a few local military and civvy announcements to show that BFBS and FIBS were working together.

Without too much fuss, we went ahead. To be honest, I was expecting a wave of gratitude for us filling the empty airwaves. Wrong. The Falkland Islanders, like the military, will always delay judgement until they have worked out the consequences of what's happening. And so it was with our 'Afternoon Delight'. One morning, after my usual routine of Breakfast Show, admin, editing interviews, morning scotch break and station banter, I was on my way up for a lunchtime drink at the Rose Inn, where we were very welcome in the public bar. This was squaddie-proof, and was constructed from a single pouring of concrete – walls, floor, ceiling, bar top. It sold red, blue and green tins (McEwans, Tennants and Kestrel). Enjoyment was discouraged by Velma Malcolm, a formidable landlady with a baseball bat at the ready, who scowled at the licentious soldiery, with the house notice framed behind her perilous frame:

'NO SINGING. NO DANCING. NO SPITTING. NO FIGHTING' it advised, helpfully. It would be fair to say we were tolerated. As I made my way to the Rose, I was stopped by one Cully, an ancient Falklander who was definitely one of the old breed.

'Hey, boy, I wanna word with you,' he said in the wonderful Islands accent, a kind of amalgam of New Zealand and West Country, with a delightful drawl. He introduced himself, swept me in through his garden gate, plonked me down in a chair and fetched me a tin of blue.

'Now then,' he warned. 'What you been doin' messin' around with the baaarx?'

I was a bit stuck here. 'Baaarx' is what I heard. Then I followed his finger to a small shelf in his lounge, on which was sitting an old Rediffusion box. Suddenly it became clear. I might have made a huge mistake.

Before FIBS was broadcast through the air, it had been a piped Rediffusion service, which meant that the speaker was always left on. The service was not continuous – breakfast music with BBC World Service News, a transmission at lunchtime and another in the evening. But sometimes, say if there was going to be a fire alarm in Stanley during 'silent hours', someone would phone Patrick Watts at home and he would cycle to the station, switch on the kit, take an old Jimmy Shand LP off a nail in the studio wall, play a track to warn listeners of an announcement, tell them about the fire drill and then switch off and disappear.

All of this was fine. It had always been done this way. Cully, and his friends, had enjoyed the afternoon silence. It was when he had his nap, after a couple of tins. And now here I was, filling the silence with pop music, jungle music, all that 'bloody bang bang bang' getting in the way of a man's sleep.

I was mortified. Part of my brief was to help the two communities talk to each other. This sounded like a diplomatic incident in my first few days. Cully played me like a flounder. Eventually he gave up, stuck his head back and roared with evil laughter.

'Got you there, Chay, dinni?' he bellowed. 'Got you good an' proper!'

I was both relieved and honoured. He had called me 'Chay', which is Falklands for 'mate'. More tins were consumed. As I weaved off to the Rose, he chuckled and kept repeating his choice of request for the new Afternoon Show. ('Might as well have a tune I like as well as that muck you people play!')

'Yellow Bird!' he yelled, louder and louder, at my departing figure. 'Up high in banana tree!' I too was giggling by now.

Claudette Prior was the Station Administrator and she made sure FIBS protocols were kept up by Terry and me. Claudy had a tremendous personality, really liked the military and worked very well with the BFBS people. She was classic Falklands: direct, straight talking, honest to the point of pain and a very loyal and splendid friend. Or, if you read her wrongly and upset her, the very worst enemy you'd ever find. Luckily, our paths met harmoniously, and we seemed to get along without drama. Very soon she invited me to take up residence for a very much smaller rent at her house, and I soon found myself in a comfortable billet in a cosy part of Stanley, with all mod cons and no more mad Terry pointing gun-like fingers at me every time I walked into the room.

It was going to be a good detachment, after all.

Chapter Twenty

The Governor's Taxi

After a while, I settled into the strangest of routines, with plenty of accidents along the way. The first was caused by my complete inability to respond to an alarm clock – a bit of a problem for a breakfast show jock. The FIBS studio in John Street was only five minutes' walk from Claudy's house but many a time I had to use the old 'transmitter failure' excuse to cover the fact that I was still giving it zeds in my maggot (sleeping bag, on the couch in the living room, where the fire was).

'Transmitter failure' was a trick of last resort. You sneaked into the studio, made sure everything was on, then opened the microphone to catch you in mid-sentence, as if the transmitter had suddenly kicked in. Then after a few minutes you apologised for the silence. It didn't really work in the tiny community of Stanley, as there were usually enough people up early to notice that the lights weren't on and the door was locked.

Eventually the Headquarters got fed up with this and assigned the routine RMP patrol to call at Claudy's house, pull me out of my maggot, watch me put my foul weather jacket and boots on, drive me to the station, literally prop me up by the door as they fished in my pocket for the keys, then march me in, sit me down in the studio chair and pour me a glass of scotch. Only when they heard the first grunt would they leave me to my own devices. The adrenalin did the rest.

The main FIBS/BFBS studio was an unholy shade of pink. It was unique in the world of broadcasting in that the studio was also the engineering workshop, which made for some interesting broadcasting when the engineer was repairing kit at the same time I was trying to do the funky chicken like a sex machine. There was often less than a meeting of minds until Head Office, in its wisdom, withdrew the engineer and we were left to our own devices.

In the meantime, I had been left alone with what effectively was my own radio station. It was really just a corrugated iron shed on a muddy, pot-holed, back street of a wintry Stanley, with its high winds, snow, blizzards, and a grey gloom that seemed to wrap us up in its miserable grip. Thanks to the magic of radio, this soon became 'The mink-lined studios on the 87th floor of Broadcasting Towers in the heart of downtown Stanley', where there was a continuous supply of nubile maidens, free-flowing champagne and all the comforts of home.

This concept held dangers, as I was to find out. Unlike the larger BFBS stations, there was no distance or security of access, so anyone could just walk off the street and into the studio. This was great – instant audience response. Until one day, a gorilla of a marine marched purposefully into my studio in mid-programme, put his face about a millimetre from mine and suggested gently, 'If you fuckin' play "Moonlight Shadow" one more fuckin' time you'll be wearin' it where the sun don't fuckin' shine!' Always good to have audience feedback. Well, nearly always.

It could be a bit embarrassing. The structure of HM Forces means that officers are all chinless Ruperts and aren't to be trusted and padres are pretty OK but completely loopy with all that God chat, so if you're a squaddie with a 'sad on', you're a bit stuck. Luckily, a place that offered both beer and sanctuary existed – and we were it. Many a time I listened to the lads' problems. Advice tended not to be needed – all they needed was a non-military environment with some good tunes, a sympathetic ear and the bonus of a beer. But it could still be dangerous.

One Sunday I was doing an afternoon show and I had a couple of visitors. The first was an older military type, wearing running kit, who popped in to say hello and take a breather from his run and the weather. He took a seat and we chatted between the records.

Soon after, a Royal Navy matelot poked his head round the door.

'OK to come in?' I was about to do a link so I nodded, gave him a wave, pointed at the beer crate and did my bit. Once I'd surfaced, we said hello properly and, without further ado, he launched on a huge diatribe on what he thought about the Falklands, the government, his officers, this stupid bloody posting and how much of a waste of time it was, and how he wished he could get his hands on the twats up at HQ BFFI (British Forces Falkland Islands) so he could give them a piece of his mind.

All the time, my other visitor sat and nodded sympathetically, without giving anything away. Our naval friend carried on talking, now giving it large about rations, working conditions and the unfairness of it all. My older companion listened carefully for about another five minutes, then got up and said, 'Well thanks, PMcD, I'd better get on with my run.'

Matelot was interested. There was something in the older person's voice.

'Who was that?' he asked, perhaps a bit nervously. This was going to be fun.

'Oh, that's Keith,' I said, low-key. 'He sometimes drops in to see what's going on.'

'Right. Seemed OK. Didn't say much. What does he do?'

'He's Major General Keith Spacie, Commander British Forces Falkland Islands.'

'Oh fuck'.

I was now faced with a matelot, recognisable in uniform, who had just bad-mouthed all of the Commander's works, plans, dreams, ideas and infrastructure. I could see him wondering which way he could best do himself in, as what he had said spooled back through his head. No, he was now a trainee corpse.

Over the next hour I managed to convince the hapless sailor that the Commander had heard far worse than this. I also pointed out that Keith was in a civvy workplace, not in uniform and was not wearing any signs saying 'Important'. Finally, I suggested that the General had probably found the conversation quite funny. After a few more tins, I sent the poor matelot on his way, still not entirely convinced that he was not going to be keelhauled.

*****

To be fair, I had two run-ins (or should that be runs-in?) with General Keith. The first was over the three-number code messages we used to send over the airwaves. All of this originated with the Chief Clerk at HQ BFFI, who arranged for duplicated sheets of the code to be sent to all units. The code, typically, might be '131', which, if you looked in the index, might mean 'total wanker'. So someone would give me a call or send me a card with 'Signalman Joe Turner is a 131'. There was a code to cover every obscenity in the book, and, for a while, the foulest of insults passed across the airwaves with impunity. General Keith heard about it and had a gentle word with me. It was gentle enough to let me know what intense horrors I could face if I didn't stop it NOW. So we went back to the occasional requests for 'Four Golf' and 'Mike Hunt'. (Say them quickly...) Every new BFBS detachee went through that particular baptism of fire and subsequent sniggering.

The other one, looking back, was really stupid, but I admit I got carried away. It was said that even beyond the Booties and Paras, the Argies were really scared of the Gurkhas, because they had heard that the Nepalese warriors not only slaughtered their enemies with Kukri knives, but also hacked them into pieces and ate them. Now, at the time, we were broadcasting on short wave, which meant we were clearly capable of being monitored in Buenos Aires. Given the situation, the Argies were almost 100% likely to be listening to us intently every second we were on-air.

So I invented three battalions of Gurkhas and each day reported on their movements around the islands. In what passed for my rational mind, I figured we'd be a lot safer if the Argies thought we had 1,800 extra troops, armed to the teeth, adding to the already existing 1,800 strong garrison.

After a few days I had a quiet visit from General Keith. He was very pleasant, asked good questions and told me it would be a good idea if there could be a military round-up 'magazine' once a week. Strangely, I agreed with him. Not just because he was a General and therefore, because it was an operational area, effectively my boss, but because I had long believed that programming ideas were best when they came from the audience. So we sang from the same hymn sheet. As he left, he worked a 'Columbo' on me.

'Oh yes, PMcD – just one other thing. Can we lose the Gurkhas, please? It isn't helping.'

The Gurkhas suddenly went quiet. I'm sure the Intelligence Units were happier.

*****

After I'd done the Breakfast Show and tackled the day's admin, I would go up the hill to Claudy's house for my daily 'sad on'. Part of the price of being the daily party animal on- and off-air was the need to have a little space to sit down and unwind, to get rid of the kind of negative thoughts you have when you're thousands of miles from wife and family. I would go to my room, pour a glass of scotch and have a little cry. After about an hour, batteries recharged, it would be back to base and on with the motley to continue having a few laughs.

25th June approached and I began to pick up on a vibe that indicated that the military were arranging a 'Fixmas' in the bleak Falklands midwinter. I was invited to a Christmas lunch at the FILOG HQ, a Fixmas cocktail party at the EOD (Bomb Disposal) HQ in Stanley and there was even an invitation to a 'Mahogany' (Hogmanay) party arranged by one of the Scottish units.

Patrick Watts, the FIBS Station Manager, had returned from foreign parts by now and was rather upset at what Terry and I had done to his radio station. Terry and Patrick didn't really get on and I felt at times that I was playing piggy in the middle, being the state registered coward that I am. Patrick was about to be very displeased indeed as the BFBS side of the station decided to embrace Fixmas. We bought out all the Christmas cards from the Pink Store across the way, put up some decorations and played Christmas songs all day on 25th June. My insurance policy of only playing songs and not religious carols paid off, when one or two traditionalists accused us of taking the name of Our Lord in vain. I spent a little time drawing up a play list and invited the harrumphers to criticise our playing of songs such as 'A Winter's Tale' by David Essex and other such harmless seasonal tunes. But our card was marked.

The highlight of Fixmas Day was a special invitation to EOD HQ, under the patronage of its Commanding Office, Major 'The Mighty' Quin, a huger than life character straight out of Commando Comics. He laughed a lot and there was a twinkle in his eye as he greeted Terry and me in the shadow of a reclaimed (and still live) Tiger Cat missile, at the base of which was a festive saucer of milk. I invited the Quin up to the studio for an interview and got more than I bargained for.

It started off quite innocuously. EOD was very popular with the Islanders. A year after the conflict the locals had reached the point where they really wanted the military to leave them to it, but there was a special place in their hearts for this small, dedicated unit which was deactivating and removing mines from the many fields and beaches on the islands. The Mighty Quin played our interview straight but protocol went out of the window when I asked him what his most dangerous moment had been. He told me about the huge WW2 bomb he had taken on a barge up the Thames through central London to be exploded at sea, how they had passed County Hall, the then Headquarters of Ken Livingstone's Greater London Council, and how, for a moment, he realised that he had the power to blow up Red Ken and his rabid followers with just one tap of his little bomb disposal hammer.

'Were you tempted?' I asked cheekily. He tried not to look too serious.

'No', he sighed, eventually. 'I like life too much - and anyway, he'll do it himself one day.'

You wouldn't have heard *that* on the BBC.

But there was worse to come. At the end of the interview, we made all the usual goodbye and thank you noises at each other, then...

'Oh, McD - just one thing.'

'What's that, John?'

'How would you like to join us tomorrow? We're having a day on the beach, clearing a new field. Like to tag along? We'll look after you.'

The Mighty Quin was inviting me to join him and his crew on a mine clearing operation in unknown territory. I guess it was rude to say no, so I swallowed hard and committed myself on-air to a big boys' day out. Oh dear.

*****

I didn't sleep too well that night. To be honest, if it hadn't been for the extra scotch, I might not have slept at all. Early next morning an EOD jeep pulled up outside Claudy's place and a cheery corporal invited me to hop in. We drove to a cabin by the beach, where the rest of EOD was getting dressed into various Michelin Man outfits - not the full Ned Kelly regalia, but some protection. I was given some anti-magnetic boots with very thick soles, and a kind of undercarriage sling (which I gathered later was a complete joke). We all enjoyed a huge mug of tea laced with white rum and then took off in the general direction of the nearest minefield.

John explained that the Argies had almost adhered to the Geneva Convention by handing over minefield maps, giving the locations of where the mines had actually been laid. Unfortunately, as he said, they couldn't count, or were a little 'devious'. The first field we walked into had been comprehensively cleared. According to the map, it was supposed to contain ninety-six mines. EOD had discovered one hundred and twelve. Quin thought that was a bit unfair. I tended to agree with him.

At the end of the first minefield, Quin turned and gave me a serious talk.

'We're now going into a minefield that we've visited and made a pathway through, but haven't cleared completely. Now it's up to you. If you walk the length of this field, walk precisely in my footsteps, unless I detonate a mine, in which case freeze and one of the other guys will take over. OK?'

He looked carefully at my face, decided that the panic was only temporary and that I would say OK.

Gulp. 'OK.'

A small group of very brave and determined men, and one jellyfish, started out on the route. The senior man, a sergeant, found an anti-personnel mine with a booby trap a couple of yards from the path. This was a trip wire, with the APM hidden behind a small rock. If you didn't see the wire it would go off, taking your lower leg with it. Not fatal of course – but that was the point. A dead man was one unit; a badly wounded man required two others to stop fighting to rescue him. As we walked along, I found myself singing, over and over again, that line from 'Good King Wenceslas': 'In his master's steps he trod, where the snow lay dinted.'

It was, in fact, snowy mud, which, coupled with the piercing wind, presented a totally forbidding and dark landscape, even at the height of the day. After an hour, we found ourselves at the beach perimeter. Quin pointed out the huge discs of the anti-tank mines, which you could see rocking in the swell on the silver sands of the beach. In the distance were the remains of a freshly exploded cow that had wandered too far.

'The anti-tank ones are the worst. We can't actually defuse them, as they're quite unstable. They're also housed in non-biodegradable plastic, so we're just going to have to let nature and corrosion do the best they can.'

'You say they're unstable. Does that mean they're likely to go off on their own?'

'It hasn't happened yet. But the boffins think it might at some future date.'

I was very, very scared.

'So what are we going to do?' I asked.

'Up to you,' said Quin. 'If you want your EOD Flash [a red badge in the shape of a bomb], then I'd take one step over the fence and just stand on the beach after Ginger's prodded the actual area. You will then have been solo in an uncleared minefield. You'll even be able to brag about it in the Rose, although I'll deny it ever happened.'

He grinned. I nodded. Ginger prodded. I raised one tentative leg, then the other, over the lowered barbed wire. For a whole nanosecond, which lasted a week, I stood in an uncleared minefield. Then I hopped back smartish and tried to keep my legs from shaking.

In the Land Rover on the way back, the Mighty Quin asked Ginger to give me my EOD Flash and my 'stick'. I was given a small black tube, like a squat ballpoint pen. Unscrewing the cap, I noticed it contained a needle.

'What's this?' I asked rather naively.

Quin chuckled. 'That's your morphine,' he said. The others were all smiling. 'Just in case your leg fell off.'

I was done for. Totally exhausted. Out of it. They drove me back to EOD HQ in Stanley, where I was presented with two more tokens of the day's achievements: a pint of double strength Wray & Nephew's finest white rum tea and a box containing one gross of NATO multi-coloured condoms.

I felt a right prick. When I wrote home and told the Moo what I had done, the intensity of the growling from Cyprus was about as terrifying as the minefield encounter. But I was glad I did it – once.

*****

The social life while I was in the Falklands was quite fantastic. There was always an excuse for a celebration and even in misery there could be the solace of buddies and beer. On more than one occasion down the Rose, we'd be witness to a bunch of the lads coming in and forming a 'doughnut' round one of their number, who would usually look like he'd just had some bad news. This would be a 'Dear John' outing. The sad one would have got a letter from his wife or girlfriend telling him it was all over. It was then the bounden duty of his mates to exorcise the wrong by getting him thoroughly legless and feeding him all the propaganda he would need to get over it. As you might imagine, a lot of the chat was generic, sexist and typically 'hurt male' but at the end of it, the hung-over squaddie would remember his mates rallying round in his hour of need, taking his mind off the pain for a while.

I had a small part in this. Terry Nicholas, who by now had gone back to the BBC, had donated me his dog collar and I used to wear it down the Rose on Sundays, claiming to be a Minister of the little-known sect, 'The Sons of MacLeish'. There was the obligatory back story of how the original MacLeish had broken away from the Kirk because it was too miserable and had founded his own more cheerful religion, the principal tenet of which was, 'enjoy yourself as long as you don't upset too many people'. After a few tins, I would pass among the groups, offering unwanted advice and revelling in the way most of the lads would get all tongue-tied when faced with a pissed vicar. Hey, it was good for morale and I even made a few converts.

But of all the parties I went to during my four months, I guess the best had to be at 'Cardboard Cottage', the home of the RAF Supplies mob. It was called Cardboard Cottage because the Argies had improved ventilation by blowing out the windows, which in the main had been repaired with... There were about sixty of us there, mainly young men, with a sprinkling of Falklanders, a few 'lumpy jumpers' (female soldiers and airwomen) and a closet Rupert or two.

The highlight of the evening was the arrival of the then Civil Commissioner, Rex Hunt, and his wife Mavis. They were accompanied by their chauffeur, Don Bonner, and two very elegant young ladies from Government Shed (Government House actually, but it was a bit clapboard at the time). All were wearing elegant evening attire, cocktail frocks and the like, but being the Falklands, these were teamed with the obligatory welly boots.

Rex presented a jovial figure. No stuffed shirt, he launched himself into the party with vigour, talking to anyone and everyone, listening to what they had to say, then dropping in a positive word or two before taking another deep swallow and moving on to the next person. A mate of mine, Smudge, decided in his cups to unburden himself to this smiling figure in a navy sweater and pinstripe trousers. He banged on for five minutes about how the place was a complete shit-hole, why we shouldn't have taken on the Argies, what a waste of money all this muscle flexing was, blah blah. I tuned in about halfway and decided I'd better rescue him before he ended up being transported or clapped in irons. Rex, somehow, was sounding sympathetic without agreeing. I made some excuse and dragged Smudge away, still hissing about the locals and their ugly women. We had another Keith Spacie moment when I told him who he had been poking in the chest, and thus another gibbering acquaintance of mine thought he was going to be shot.

But Rex wasn't that kind of man. He knew that the young'uns, eight thousand miles away from home, needed to let off steam, and he was happy to let that happen. The party continued and Rex and Mavis were really enjoying themselves. We were enjoying their company too. Mavis drank her gin and tonic as though she'd just invented it, but we learned later that over breakfast the following morning, and after any morning after the night before, it was Mavis who would give a blow-by-blow intelligence report of everything – yes, everything – that had happened the night before. Even when she appeared to be giggling tipsily, she had total control of the most powerful radar in the South Atlantic. Their style was determined by their treatment of Don, the chauffeur of the only London taxi ever to be used as the Governor's official car, complete with the royal cipher and Union flag on each door, alongside the flag of the Falklands. Don occasionally had the odd pint at such parties (he always came in with the Governor's party, and was always part of it) and it was rumoured that, on more than one occasion, Rex had driven Don home. It was part of the great Falklands experience.

*****

As the detachment went on, I became busier and busier. On a really hectic day I might start with the

Breakfast Show, walk into town to do an interview with one of the units for the weekly programme, 'Forces Roundup', have my 'sad on' hour at Claudette's, then back to the station for admin – reports to London, calls, etc. – then a quick pint in the Rose. In the afternoon I would pick up the recording equipment and walk it down to the Town Hall, where I would set up for an outside broadcast recording of the Folk Club, which was huge in Stanley. Then, back to the station to read out some items on air, have a quick nibble, then back to the Town Hall to achieve the impossible – to engineer the recording, of which I was also MC for the evening, and sometimes one of the acts. This in front of a crowd of 300-400 people, heaving with the locally brewed Penguin Ale.

This was concocted by gentleman DJ and brewer Phil Middleton, who rejoiced in the stage name of Firkin Phil, especially after you drank his Penguin Ale, which had two unique properties. It was the fastest-working milk of amnesia ever and, if you were constipated, it acted as a lightning cure. Sadly, the bogs in the Town Hall were limited in number, which led to some unpleasant sights around the perimeter of the building.

My time in the Falklands was coming to an end. In August 1983 I would be returning to Cyprus after four fascinating months. We were now in the 'Andes' stage. I'd better explain.

When I first got there, the situation was black and white. The locals called us 'Wenneyes' ('when I was in Cyprus, Germany, Singapore,' etc.) and we called them 'Bennies', after the simple chap in the woolly hat in one of the big TV programmes of the time, 'Crossroads'. As Falklanders wore the same kind of hats, it seemed apposite, if not appropriate, which is why General Keith put a stop to it.

There was a public proclamation that no longer was the indigenous population to be referred to as 'Bennies'. So the military, with its usual black humour and speed of wit, came up with the new word: 'Stills' – as in 'still a Benny'. It took the Command a few weeks to crack this code and, once again, a notice of proscription was issued from HQ BFFI. The military responded with 'Andes' – 'and 'e's still a Benny' - at which point the Command either gave up or realised that no Falklander could really object to being compared to a large South American mountain range.

*****

Claudette was mainly responsible for my farewell party. I remember some of it - certainly that Rex popped in, as did some of the Ruperts at HQ, who I thought really didn't like me very much. I seem to remember that we had a splendid time and somehow they contrived to get me pointed in the direction of, and then aboard, the Hercy Bird that would take me home. They even managed to smuggle a few miniatures into my foul weather jacket. Also, Moo had been sending me a supply of Valium from Cyprus, where you could buy the stuff over the counter without prescription. I had easily enough to get me to Brize Norton and beyond, and that's precisely how I managed the entire journey, Ascension Island stop-off included, without any pain, or indeed memory, of any part of the many take-offs, long flights or landings.

This, I know was very dangerous, but I had been dreading the long journey home and now I was back. The end had justified the means. But I was exhausted, horribly unfit and now damaged by both drink and drugs. They tell me I pitched up at BFBS HQ in Dean Stanley Street with a bottle of cognac in one hand and a ciggie in the other, making my way to the fourth floor where I sat in on BFBS UK with Tommy Vance. Apparently I'd brought a posse of friends with me but I can't remember to this day who they were. A day or so later, I found myself on a civvie flight on Cyprus Airways to Dhekelia. Although a lot more sober, I was in a total daze.

Arriving at Larnaca, I poured myself off the plane and more or less fell into Moo's arms. Apparently I was largely incoherent, shouting at Cypriot grannies and making an arse of myself. We made it through immigration and customs. Moo seemed very keen to get me home but I was determined to see Bill, the landlord of the Fairwinds Taverna on the Larnaca Road, so I could thank him for the Underberg salvation kit he had given me a lifetime ago to help speed me on my way down to the penguins. Moo was against it but we stopped there anyway, had one or two, and I thanked Bill properly.

Duty done, I was now able to concentrate on the rest of the journey back to Minden Village in Dhekelia – home. As we pulled up, I realised why Moo had wanted to get me back as quickly as possible. She had arranged a homecoming party for me and all the good ole boys, the usual suspects, were there, ready to ply me with brandy sours and hear my tales of derring-do from the Land That Time Forgot. Which was a pity, as I was verging on incoherent.

Luckily, now that I'd stopped moving and was safe at home, recovery was pretty rapid. Once I'd got a plate of party food down me, I gave a reasonable impression of a chin-jutting hero who had conquered minefields and terrifying landscapes to bring musical civilisation to a primitive people. (This was totally unfair, as most Falklanders are experts in engineering, building, plumbing, farming, finance, philosophy, politics – you name it - and precisely the kind of people you'd want with you on a desert island.) Baron

Munchausen was alive and well that night.

*****

I dined out on my Falkland stories for the next few months. It was back to the old routine, except that I began to feel sluggish and shaky. I couldn't hold my drink like before. One day, the RAMC colonel in charge of the medical centre in Dhekelia bought me a large G&T, took me aside and gently told me that I was drinking too much and needed to go for a blood test. I rather missed the point, thinking that if he was buying me a strong drink, then I couldn't be that bad, so I put it down to gossip and spite, and carried on regardless. But a seed had been sown, and it wasn't too long before things came to a head.

I was on my way back to the station from the club one day, when suddenly I had a panic attack. This wasn't totally unusual. I had always had panic attacks to do with reading the news after an incident in Cologne some years earlier where I grabbed the news late from the telex, bolted up a huge flight of stairs and started reading while still out of breath. The resulting wave of panic nearly made me faint but I gulped my way through it and from that day avoided being on news duty as much as possible.

So here I was, in the taxi, with a panic attack on the way. I got to the station and picked up the news summary. I gave it a quick scan and walked into the presentation studio, where Penny Vine was doing an afternoon show. I looked at her. Then I looked at the news. Then I asked her to read it, as I couldn't. Then I rushed out of the studio to my office. I phoned the medical centre and just grindingly, breathlessly, pleadingly said, against a flood of tears, 'Send an ambulance to BFBS. I am very sick.'

Some minutes later I was lying on my back in the medical centre and a nurse was trying to take blood. I fought her off. Eventually a medical orderly came in and physically held me down. I was given some tranquillisers and sent home to rest. I really was in a haze – no idea what was going on, only that something was horribly wrong. A few days later I was summoned to see the Senior Medical Officer – the Colonel.

He looked very serious and told me about LFTs – liver function tests. Apparently, the normal reading was 28 whatevers. In Cyprus, they allowed for the extra pressures of short days and too many brandy sours and gave a Cyprus 'norm' of 36. Unfortunately, my reading was over 600, which put me in immediate danger. I would be taken to the Princess Mary's Hospital at Akrotiri, on the other side of the island, for further tests and actions as necessary.

'When will I be going?'

'As soon as your wife arrives with your overnight bag.'

It was a tearful and short reunion. Within minutes of Moo's arrival, I was packed into an ambulance and bounced along the wonderful Cyprus textured roads all the way to Akrotiri, on the other Sovereign Base. Strangely enough, I felt as if a weight had been lifted from my chest. The panic attacks disappeared. I didn't know it then, but I would never ever be afraid of shadows again. This was a new adventure.

Chapter 21

The Alkie Ward

I was lying in a hospital bed, in a side ward. Every so often nurses popped in to feed me, shift my bedding or take my temperature. The occasional doctor came in, poked, prodded, wrote things down and left. Nobody was telling me what was going on. They were all very professional and friendly in a Forces kind of way but I was at a loss to work out what might be wrong with me.

I've always thought of myself as possessing the curiosity of a journalist. And the persona. Maybe it's a kind of mild schizophrenia but I do find myself able to stand aside and observe me with some degree of objectivity. I realised the creature inhabiting my body was damaged in some way, that observation was taking place and that there was nothing further I could do.

So I relaxed into the routine. The only problem was going to sleep at night without my usual alcoholic cosh. Already my brain was racing, as it started to escape from my poison of choice. Luckily, there was a small common room just down the corridor and I was given permission to retire there with a handful of videos. My first night was a long watch. They'd given me enough drugs not to get the horrors of instant detox but it still felt scratchy and uncomfortable. Eventually I fell into a fitful sleep. Queen Alexandra appeared in my room, surrounded by a golden glow, but for some reason she was upside down. I remember clearly sitting up in bed and composing a short speech which I delivered to Her Majesty the Late Queen, imploring her to present herself the right way up and thanking her for her visitation, which was much appreciated. My door opened, a nurse looked in, saw I was talking to Her Majesty, curtsied and withdrew. This dream was so real, I even asked the nurse the following morning if she'd seen Queen Alexandra. It would be fair to say she gave me an old fashioned look.

My first full day at The Princess Mary's Hospital (TPMH), Akrotiri, was beautifully sunny and the lunchtime rays scythed across the crisp sheets on the bed. I had a light lunch, then thought of cleaning my teeth. I approached the sink. Suddenly my body stiffened and the upper half started to grip itself in a choking, half-drowning rictus. Something dreadful was happening and I had no control at all. I started to scream in pain and a long jet of blood shot out of my mouth and began to pump out. I managed to press the emergency button for attention. A few moments later I was out of it and the doctors became very busy indeed.

I woke up some hours later. It was daylight. In fact, it was tomorrow. I was drugged, exhausted and could barely see the small group of white-coated doctors standing at the end of my bed. I eventually managed to wheeze painfully, 'What happened?'

They quietly explained that had I not managed to find that button, had I not been in the hospital at precisely that time, had the doctors not got to me in record time, I would surely be dead. What had happened was that years of drinking had ruined the blood vessels in my oesophagus – the correct name was 'oesophageal varices' – and they had finally overloaded and effectively erupted, which accounted for the bloodbath.

They told me further that I must now understand that I was an alcoholic and that further tests would have to be done. Meanwhile, BFBS London was being advised. I did not know it at the time but the Director of Radio, John Bussell, had already decided that I was worth saving and had agreed I should attend the Alcohol Training Unit at the Queen Elizabeth Military Hospital in Woolwich as soon as possible for drying out and rehab.

Strangely enough, none of this was frightening. I was still in observer mode. I went for an ultrasound scan of the liver. This confirmed the other major worry: I had cirrhosis, which sounded like a death sentence.

Still, I had enjoyed a good life and had managed to pack quite a lot into my thirty-six years on the planet. I was told that giving up booze at that stage was vital and I was really worried about how I'd cope. That night I slept another dream filled non-sleep: I was in my hospital bed, right up against the bar of the Dhekelia Officers' Club, talking to Colonel Pip, who was sitting in his usual place. Various people came and went, all of whom bought me a drink and totally ignored the fact that I was wearing pyjamas in a hospital bed, surrounded by drips, charts and trays of medical instruments.

The next day brought further news. In consultation with the MOD, HQ BFBS, Moo and the hospital authorities, I would be casevaced (casualty evacuation) to the Queen Elizabeth Military Hospital in London the next day. They were unable to say what my treatment would be, nor how long it would be, but I paid close attention to the seriousness of the words, 'your best chance'. In the absence of my having comprehensive medical knowledge, I decided to countersign the form. I didn't know how this would affect my posting, my career, my family or myself. I just knew it had to be done.

*****

They sedated me for the flight and I was clipped into a special bed space on the plane. The flight was uneventful. I was picked up by an ambulance at Brize and delivered to QEMH Woolwich, a splendid low-level modern complex in rolling green hilly lawns. I was parked in a side room while the usual bevy of consultants and nurses came and went. They didn't tell me at the time but I was too ill and weak to join the Alcohol Training Unit. Years of drinking without eating had taken its toll. I had a huge vitamin deficiency. The highlights of the next few days were massive and painful vitamin injections. I guess I grinned and bore it, as the Catholic in me told me that I had sown the wind, therefore I must reap the whirlwind. All of this was my fault and nobody else's. What I was suffering from was the result of sin, not disease. I don't know if this helped or hindered but it got me through that particularly nasty time.

Eventually, I was deemed fit enough to move to the ATU (known throughout the hospital as the 'Alkies' Ward'), where I was asked to sit down in a communal lounge while they found me the right bed and set it up for me. I didn't realise at the time that this was a psychological test, to see how I would react to my surroundings and the other patients. Remember, I hadn't really spoken to anyone on a purely social basis for a good few days. Somewhere in the background, the nurses and the white coated corporal orderlies were observing my actions and reporting back to the charismatic and robust Dr. Sylvia Blunden, a psychiatrist by profession, who headed the unit.

Luckily, because of my BFBS background, I found it very easy to chat to all ranks - and indeed all ranks were represented on the ward, from general to private. Before too long several of us were in a huddle, comparing notes, telling tales and jokes and secretly rather relieved to find out that there were others in the same boat.

The ATU worked on simple procedures. A military referral to the unit was deemed to be a course. A course that you passed, by not drinking and showing positive signs of recovery, or failed, by any evidence indicating that you'd had a drink, however small. If you passed the course, you were marked fit for duty and went back to your regiment or formation. If you failed, you were 'RTU'd' (returned to unit) for the ultimate sanction: discharge from HM Forces.

The unit's routine was simple. Wake at six, wash, take medication, go for a cross country run, breakfast, education (films and lectures), lunch and uplifting recreational activities – anything from basket weaving to printing, model making, dancing and even reading. Then further education, supper, TV, chat and games, bed at 2200 military.

My whole body shuddered at this awful routine but as the days went on I began to taste and enjoy the food for the first time (even though we were all still very heavy smokers) and even looked forward to the best of cuisine from the very accomplished Army Catering Corps chefs. We had good choices and the diet was designed to help our bodies return to some semblance of normality. My weight when I was admitted was 89kg. After a few weeks of the Woolwich routine, when I was eating three meals a day, I was clocking in at a steady 67kg and feeling a lot healthier.

After about three weeks I was invited to have a personal interview with Dr. Sylvia. I use the word 'invited' in a military kind of way. One of the reasons that the ATU's success level was 87%, more than five times higher than expensive civvy rehab units, was the underlying military discipline - the fact that the staff could actually order you to do things.

Dr Sylvia was firm, kind, and candid. 'Alcoholics are usually affected in one of two ways,' she began. 'The drink either goes to your body or your brain. I'm here to deal with the brain part. The good news is: your brain is OK. From the moment you walked in, it was noted that you held rational conversations with your fellow patients and were very quick to use wit and humour to fit in, even though you were still in some pain. So, I really only have one question for you. The 'short' course is six weeks; the longer course is twelve. I recommend the full twelve, but this is your choice. Which is it to be?'

I looked carefully at her face, and made my decision. Even if I didn't have a job after this, I was much better off taking the long way round. I agreed to the full twelve. Sylvia appeared almost relieved. She could now recommend that I was likely to succeed and this would have some bearing on John Bussell's decision as to whether or not I should be kept on.

Now that I'd agreed to the Full Monty, I threw myself into the course with some determination and gusto. I helped the less literate squaddies with their paperwork – even their letters home – and soon I was given some respect as a specky-four-eyes brainy civvie gobshite – high praise indeed. We were allowed wider and wider access. I used the hospital chapel more than a few times. I would go for long, sunny walks listening to Gordon Lightfoot, Cyndi Lauper and the Flying Pickets on my little Walkman. Life was stress-free, and very pleasant. It was improved further after a kind visit by my director, John Bussell, who gave me the good news and the bad news: my job was safe but I would be posted back to the new BFBS London (no longer 'Head Office') in Paddington Basin.

*****

I had a job. This was magic. I felt that it was some kind of reward for following the rules. From that moment, I was known for my Pollyanna approach to life. It was good to have a constant stream of visitors, including my parents, who were rather bemused by what had happened to me, but I managed to put a reasonable gloss on everything. The summer continued, long, hot, pleasant and balmy, and the only grit in life's Vaseline was the attitude of the white coats, the rather cynical corporal orderlies, who had not tasted the milk of human kindness for many years. One of them told me that I'd be dead before I was sixty. So powerful was that statement that I remember breathing a sigh of relief once I'd passed that particular marker. Also, in our open discussions, one of them admitted that he felt nothing but contempt for soldiers who drank themselves stupid and ill. All a bit sad. But on one occasion I remember their attitude causing the biggest laugh of my entire stay.

It was decided there should be an inter-ward football shield and three wards were selected to take part: the Cardiac Ward, the Psychiatric Ward and the ATU ward. Teams were selected by the orderlies, which was how I came to be playing, and one particular afternoon, we traipsed down to the main footy pitch. The event had been advertised and in the captive market that was the QEMH, we had quite the little crowd of spectators as the first match - ATU versus Psychiatric - kicked off.

It should be noted that hard drinkers and wayward thinkers seem to be able to kick a ball with some degree of intelligence, venom, and accuracy. The match soon developed into a real game of football and somehow this got to the white coats who were monitoring the crowd to see that nobody pulled any tricks. The cause of political correctness was undermined to the nth degree by the shouts, mainly from the white coats, as they became excited and upheld their team's cause. Had a casual outsider been passing, all he would have heard would have been the repeated cries:

'Come on the Alkies! Come on the Loonies!'

The ex-boozers won – and again, against Cardiac Corner. We picked up the shield and celebrated with Coke.

There were occasional sadnesses as the course went on. We lost a few of our number to the breathalyser. After a few weeks we were given permission to go into Woolwich, about a mile down the road, on our own or in small groups. One or two groups found themselves in far too familiar territory and went on the lash. They were breathalysed on their way back in to QEMH and immediately RTU'd. In one or two cases, this was the desired effect, but in the main you could see the regret and pain as the crystals made their accusation. There was even talk of one of our course committing suicide after he'd left, but that tale was never confirmed.

The reinforcement from the 'education' could not be understated and, after a time, we were given the freedom and encouragement to feel good about ourselves once again. We were taken to a pub for the evening ('you're going to have to get used to it') and given strategies to manage to be sociable without alcohol. Above all, the message gradually became 'Set yourself free and enjoy life.' I was now slimmer, sun-tanned and getting good food and sleep. But as well as my body, my brain was screaming to do something. I really needed to get back to the workface. I had plans.

One day we had a 'state visit' from a major from the Kenyan Army, who was investigating the workings of the ATU with a view to setting up a similar operation back home. I was invited again to Dr. Sylvia's office, where I was introduced, with a smile, to the good major.

'This is Peter McDonagh,' said Sylvia, kindly. 'He is a *famous* drinker.'

I guess she thought I could give a reasonably light-hearted but sincere appraisal of my experience in the Unit. The three of us had an enjoyable chat, with plenty of laughter on all sides. It was nearly time to go back to the real world.

There was one last official visit. My invisible Station Controller from Cyprus, Ken Doherty, had been ordered by John Bussell to visit me in hospital. I don't think it was for my benefit; it was to confront Ken with the fact that he'd had a member of staff in his care who had very nearly killed himself drinking over a two-year period. I actually felt sorry for Ken and tried to make the visit as painless as possible for him. This was quite hard, as he was a very proud man, an ex-Physical Training Instructor Officer, who clearly was against abuse of the temple of the body. Still, all things pass and so did Ken.

*****

Soon it was time to pack up and convalesce... er...somewhere in the UK. Luckily, I'd picked up a four figure Falklands bonus, plus I hadn't spent much of my wages over the previous three months, so renting a place was not going to be an issue. It was at this point that Robert Neil, my old mini-boss from Cologne and current Cyprus colleague, stepped in. He had a 'spare' three-bedroomed semi in a leafy part of Shooter's Hill and he simply 'gave' it to me until solid plans could be made. All I had to do was pay the rates and utilities. This was a huge burden lifted and the house and garden were a bright symbol for the future. I almost felt guilty for lampooning him as 'Norbert Reil, the famous German newsreader' who mangled the

English language with devastating regularity: 'And now here are the news, and this am Norbert Reil rearranging it.' Yes, I felt a bit guilty. But it was good to have a sense of humour back.

Moo arrived with the kids from Cyprus. This was another huge bonus – the biggest of them all. I owed them so much. The children had all been properly briefed and managed to remain being kids without walking on eggshells. We went for walks, we played in the garden, I bought and watched videos and I just couldn't wait to get back to work, though the idea of walking into the new BFBS London, at Bridge House in Paddington, did get the adrenalin pumping.

Came the day and I set out for Woolwich station to catch the Commuters' Special to the Big Smoke. I soon learned that British Rail was not the cleanest way of travelling. I maintain to this day that before the train set out from the depot, a squadron of 'cleaners' hurled buckets of dog-ends, fag ash, old chewing gum and burger wrappers onto the floor and seats of each carriage and then sprayed the air with a special 'yesterday's curry' perfume. It was still August and hot as hell. Plus it was packed with a surly crowd who patently didn't want to be there but who had accepted their fate and were swaying with the lurching progress of the train like a cattle truck full of zombies.

After a similar hell on the sweltering Underground, I finally made it to North Wharf Road, People's Republic of Paddington, and took the lift to the first floor HQ of BFBS London. Unlike the austere Dean Stanley Street HQ, this was a fully functioning radio station with seven studios and plenty of open-plan space and glass-fronted offices. Outside ran the Paddington Canal (just round the corner it became the Regent's Canal) and there was a dual aspect view: on the one side, Paddington Station, and on the other, Paddington Green Police Station. Always good for a bit of cabaret.

I reported to the Station Manager (no longer Station 'Controller'), Mike Robertson. Mike was a very kind man who had rarely visited the darker side of life and wasn't quite sure how to handle an apparently keen and disingenuous 36-year-old broadcaster who was bursting with energy and enthusiasm, looked tanned and fit, but who was in fact very nearly a terminal alcoholic. We soon established a protocol that made it comfortable to talk to each other in the same room and I hinted that I would be obeying orders. He introduced me to my two 'line managers', Chris Russell, Head of 'Speech' Programmes, and Charles Foster, Head of Music.

Here was my first hurdle. Both were younger than me. Chris had been a raw trainee when I was *his* boss in Malta. Charles was about 12 (or so it seemed!) but, like Chris, carried a good degree of authority. I think it took me about five minutes to realise that them being younger than me wasn't going to be a problem;

they had not been handed these jobs on a plate and they were both on top of their briefs. They treated me with a respect I felt I had yet to earn and a kindness that I still felt I didn't deserve.

When a drunk stops drinking, he needs something to replace the alcohol, but also something extra. Alcohol dulls and debilitates. Life goes into slow motion and most things can be put off. When this handbrake is removed, the word 'career' comes into play, not as a steady climb up the greasy pole, but as a continuous burst of energy that drives you on relentlessly. There is a need to work three times as hard as before, and for longer. It becomes an obsession. In fact, it becomes a drug, like alcohol.

The way I saw it, I had taken three months off on sick leave to treat my self-inflicted condition. Therefore, I needed to replace those lost hours and add them to my working week until they had all been absorbed. By this time, a few months in, we'd left Robert's house, as he had found a paying tenant. Fortunately, we'd been 'rescued' again by Station Engineer Joe Medhurst, whose Dad was a builder and who had an empty, renovated, house near Woolwich. We moved in, rent-free, and bought furniture, planning that one day soon we would buy a flat in London because commuting was doing my head in. I was working on some music programmes and the odd BFBS UK show with Tommy Vance, Adrian Love and Richard Vaughan. On the odd occasion, I'd even present the show myself.

I was a bit disappointed to be back on BFBS UK, especially as 'the management' ordained that I would have one Chris Boulton-Fleet as my senior producer. I did balk at this, because Chris was a freelance and therefore not family. Not only that, he had the annoying habit of telling the world exactly what he was doing on a blow-by-blow basis. He would dictate his briefs to a secretary, instead of doing them himself, he lorded it around the fairly compact office and he never, ever, stopped talking. He was on 'transmit' the whole time and, as any broadcaster knows, you need to be on 'receive' more than 'transmit' if you're going to have anything meaningful to say. He had to go. But I was in no position for this to happen and Charles, who had commissioned him as producer in the first place, thought he was a Good Thing.

In my life fate has often supplied the appropriate deus ex machina at the right time, and the fate of the gobby Chris was no exception. For some reason, which still might generate legal nonsense if I try to describe it, Charles fell out with Chris. When Charles falls out with you, it is the equivalent of the judge's black cap. Suddenly there was no more Chris, and Roberta Symes arrived on the scene.

Roberta had worked the Guildford-based commercial station, County Sound. Broadcaster, actress, university graduate and general great personality, we became good chums as well as colleagues. Life was now one hundred percent better. I was working with her on BFBS UK, as by this time Tommy Vance and

Richard Vaughan had left and, sadly, Adrian Love had joined the Choir Invisibule.

This was distressing on two counts. The first was that Adrian was the most gentle of gentlemen and the first big star I knew who behaved with any degree of humility. The second was that he too was an alcoholic.

Our new presenter was the very personable and accomplished Richard Allinson, owner of the driest and most intelligent wit in Christendom, who joined us in a semi-detached way and cheerfully went along with most of our ideas. When he disagreed, I think it would be fair to say he managed to swing the situation so that we had thought of the idea he actually wanted us to think. Sounds a bit Irish, but such was the sophistication of the Allinson brain – like the bread, there was 'nowt tekken out'. We settled down for a good run, and once again I found myself enjoying going to work.

I'd arrive about 7am, have an early breakfast with Roberta at the Dudley Arms pub across the road – the 'Deadly Dudley' as it was known - then get down to the show, after which I would sit at my little open-plan work station, plotting ideas for the future.

Sometime during this period, the Director of Radio, John Bussell, had determined that life up at the Services Sound and Vision Corporation's headquarters in Chalfont Grove, leafy Bucks, was too far away for a Streatham boy to feel comfortable, so, to the chagrin of the quiet but effective station manager, Mike Robertson, he moved into Bridge House on a more or less permanent basis. We now had both the Admiral and the Captain on the Bridge. It was going to be messy.

It also gave me the opportunity to plead my case for an overseas posting, which is what the whole family wanted. John was adamant that QEMH had recommended a period of five years quarantine before I could be trusted 'out of area'. I was convinced that Dr. Sylvia had recommended a period of two years, and I was now about twenty months into this posting. I duly formed the one-man 'Bridge House Escape Committee' and made frequent visits to John's office to plead my case. It took ages for him to agree to talk to Doctor Sylvia and when he finally did, he wouldn't tell me what she had recommended. I called her and was pleased that she told me what I wanted to hear: that for a person in my position her recommendation would always be a period of two years purdah, but then most foreign postings would be permitted. Armed with this information, and the knowledge that my working ten hours a day, seven days a week, was achieving results, I was confident of a posting in the not too distant future.

Then something really spooky happened. Red Ken Livingstone, who had inadvertently supplied me with a two-and-a-half year summer holiday in Cyprus after the 'sedition' incident of 1981, was ousted as Leader of the GLC, its demise engineered by Maggie. Ken responded by holding a massive free fair on the South Bank and Moo and I took the kids down there for a day out. There was a fortune-teller holding court in a jazzy tent and I decided, for a laugh, to have my fortune told. There was the usual mumbo jumbo about the future (at least there *was* one) but the line that stuck in my mind was: 'You need to look out for seven blue stars; they will open a new direction for you to travel.' This went into a pigeonhole in the back of my memory bank but it wasn't too long before it would be resurrected.

*****

I was called into John Bussell's office one day. My hopes were high. I was firing on all twelve cylinders. I'd even put myself forward for a few promotion boards and had interviewed well. But what was this all about? Surely not success for the Chairman of the Escape Committee?

No. John Turtle and Bennett Maxwell of BBC Radio Training wanted to run a course and this time, instead of prescribing the content of the course themselves, they wanted genuine BFBS input in drawing up a schedule. John Bussell suggested that we might go to BBC Radio Training in Portland Place to have a preliminary chat.

A few days later we went to see John and Bennett in their rather fine offices, where we chatted about which parts of the BBC and BFBS operations and cultures we should focus on. I noticed that our Director was quite subdued in the presence of John Turtle, who had a natural authority about him, as well as unlimited access to all levels of the BBC. He had the power to ask the Director General to make an appearance, for example, or to ask Tony Blackburn to deliver a lecture. Radio Training was a key department of the BBC.

By the end of the meeting, it had been agreed that Bennett and I would co-write a course training document. As Bennett was clearly a busy man and as I was available seven days a week, it was clear who was going to do the bulk of the work. The resulting draft document had plenty of input from me and was fine-tuned and sculpted by Bennett to look like an E-Type schedule. I think we were both quite proud of the result.

I was particularly chuffed with the 'White Network' exercise. This was where, on the last day, all the lessons of the course would be tested as the eight or so course participants operated a phantom radio station in real time, with directing staff in the background throwing problems at them throughout the day as they tried to simply continue broadcasting without the plumbing showing.

I decided that instead of 'Radio Penge' or something similarly dull, we would set the BFBS station in the fictitious post-colonial island republic of Angora, located between the Nicobar and Andaman Islands - quite exotic, but far enough away to present every kind of logistics problem – and famous for its military base and its government's hatred of the Brits.

As part of the course background material – and, for the first time, using a computer – a dirty, great, squatting IBM thing – I produced an entire background for Angora (which was a composite of all the BFBS locations I knew). I gave it a President, a fractious Prime Minister, a national flag, an anthem, a capital city, infrastructure, social gradings, political parties, customs and a news service. I engineered Soviet infiltration and even cast John Turtle himself to play the part of Sir Gregory Tweed OBE, Her Britannic Majesty's High Commissioner for the island republic.

The course document was approved by Director John and BBC John, and was sent to the printers, with the encouraging insert that the course directors were to be Bennett Maxwell and Peter McDonagh. This surely had to bode well.

A couple of days later a large brown envelope landed on my desk. I opened it and frowned a little. All previous BBC course documents had featured the full heraldic BBC logo on the front page, with a headline title in bright red ink.

This document was printed in royal blue. I felt a strange frisson and peered a little closer. Then I saw them. Then I counted them. Part of the full BBC logo comprises a bar with seven stars printed across it. Yes, it had happened, as predicted by the GLC fortune-teller. Seven blue stars: 'A new direction for you to travel.'

For the second time, thank you, Red Ken.

Chapter 22

The Power of Nefertiti

I was enjoying my time in Bridge House. The job was fun and I had at last managed to dream up something a bit new: 'Topifax'. The idea was that, on smaller stations, where there was a dearth of interesting chat to put between discs and nothing in a format that could be 'inserted' into the overnight music tapes, it would be a good idea to have broadcast cartridges containing totally self-contained gobbets of speech/news/magazine/feature material.

As I was still working seven days a week, and as I was no longer producing BFBS UK, I was given a small budget and set out a schedule of producing seven speech items a day, seven days a week, which could be recorded, edited, dubbed and despatched to the various BFPO addresses around the world. We managed to persuade some top reporters to take just £20 per item ('for the lads in the trenches') and although fulfilling the quota could be a bit hairy, and quite a few times I had to add an instant monologue, Topifax seemed to go down well, especially when I gave overseas staff the chance to syndicate local items using the system.

I was hacking away one day, when the phone rang. It was British Airways. With a big surprise. We had always supported them as an airline and it was time for them to say 'thank you'. There was going to be a special flight to Berlin in a few days' time. Would a BFBS member of staff like to go? I asked them to hold, rushed to station manager Mike Robertson's office, and asked him for permission. I was surprised at how quickly he said yes. Back to the phone and I told BA that I would be delighted to go. I was given joining instructions for the following Friday and told it would be a return flight, coming back on the Sunday. Ideal.

On the day, I arrived at Heathrow and immediately got a bit confused. The number of the desk existed, but it was clearly marked 'Concorde'. I looked more closely. No doubt about it: Concorde – London to Berlin. I booked in, just not believing my luck. I continued not to believe my luck as I sat in the oyster grey leather seat, directly behind Colin Marshall, then CEO of British Airways, and Sir Roger Traill, Lord Mayor of London. They even spoke to me. In a continuing dream, we took off, and very soon we were on the east coast of Britain.

I heard Sir Roger lean over to Colin and ask, 'Any chance of breaking the sound barrier on this hop?'

'I'll have a word,' said the great man, and disappeared into the cockpit.

When he came back, he said to Sir Roger (and even had room for a bit of eye contact with me), 'Pilot's filed a flight plan. We go north, past Newcastle, then shoot down the coast at Mach 1 before turning east for Berlin where we left off.'

And we did just that. Up the coast, 180 degree turn, then we watched the big display in front of Colin and Sir Roger as it climbed up to, and beyond, Mach 1. There wasn't much in the way of a bang – but there was a real frisson and the plane seemed to change attitude. We were in the brave new world of supersonic flight. It was a good moment to be British. Within a few minutes we turned and resumed our short flight to Berlin at conventional speed.

There were two more surprises to come. Since 1949, aerial access for the Allies to West Berlin had been via three narrow air 'corridors', limited not only by width, but also height – all planes had to fly at around 10,000 feet inside the corridor. If they didn't, Soviet MIGs would appear and it was known that unless instructions were instantly obeyed, the delinquent plane could be shot down.

However, for some reason never quite explained, Concorde was given permission by the Soviets to enter West Berlin above the height of the usual corridor, which it required in order to give safe flight over a longer period. So, for the first time in about fifty flights, my entry to West Berlin would be a one-off. We landed and I noticed the huge crowds out on the observation platforms.

After an accelerated immigration and customs procedure, we were assembled in a cavernous lounge and bar, where free champagne and canapés had been laid on by the Stadt. A high functionary of the airport made a speech in English, remarking on our unique flight, and ending with the immortal line, 'End I am sure zat this special flight vill be making an entrance in ze Book of Guinness!' He was rather pleased by our delighted response.

For the next two days we went to function after function, party after party, from a huge classical concert at the Olympia-Stadion's huge Waldbühne amphitheatre (last time I'd been there was to see The Kinks), featuring a properly pyro'ed 1812 Overture, all the way through to a special dinner with the General Officer Commanding, Major General Bernard Gordon-Lennox, at the Dorset House mess. Add to that a visit to a beer garden – thank you Schultheiss – several craft fairs and a boat trip, and it would be fair to say our feet didn't touch.

On Sunday morning came the greatest of great surprises, which turned out to be life-changing. It said on the itinerary: 'Visit to Schloß Charlottenburg, followed by visit to museum.'

The Schloß was beautiful, a really ornate palace constructed for Frederick the Great, and we were given the VIP tour, which involved wearing chamois over-socks to protect the delicate parquet floors, still in pristine condition. Afterwards, we were told it was only a short stroll to the museum. We walked along in bright sunshine, chatting amongst ourselves. We climbed the steps to the museum and adjusted our eyes to the darkness of the décor: everything was black, with only spotlight stabs and enough dim lighting to see where we were going. We turned a corner and my heart stopped. I remember gasping in astonishment.

There, in a special glass case, on a central plinth in its own area, was the immortal bust of Queen Nefertiti. I felt her influence straight away. I knew I had come home, in more ways than one.

I should explain. The first time I had seen the Egyptian queen was at the Berlin-Dahlem museum when I was a kid. I'd got a bit scared of the glass cases full of mummies and had raced ahead to where a blue velvet curtain enclosed what was obviously a special place. I sneaked in behind the curtain, looked up and was transfixed. It was the haughty, beautiful, remote Queen Nefertiti and she gazed at me across the centuries. Even at my age, I knew she was special and I continued to gaze at her until Dad found me and took me reluctantly away. He later told Mum I'd been unusually quiet after being spooked by this odd statue.

It was only much later, in Malta, that I started to piece together what Nefertiti actually meant to me and how she would continue to affect my life. I was offered a British Airways inaugural flight from Malta to Egypt back in 1976 and was soon installed in the Oberoi in Giza, overlooking the pyramids. One of our jaunts was to the National Museum in Cairo, which housed the best and most famous of all the antiquities. Principal amongst them was the golden sarcophagus of King T. Yes, King T. I still firmly believe that if I articulate his name, then bad things will happen to me. Even if I read his name anywhere, I will always repeat the name of Nefertiti as an 'antidote'. And this is why.

During the course of our visit to the museum, groups of twenty-five people were allowed into the inner sanctum, where the golden sarcophagus had pride of place, presented behind a rail, at about bed height, so you could look down on it. I joined the last of these parties for the day and very soon I was staring at the golden face of King T. I felt a powerful force wrapping itself around me. Slowly, the buzz of the crowd disappeared and I was held entirely enthralled by this life form – it *was* alive – from thousands of years long gone. Slowly my head cleared and I realised that I was the only visitor in the room. The rest of the party had disappeared and only the guard on the door remained. He was looking at me in an anxious way and indicating with his watch that it was time to go. I walked out of that museum in a daze, conscious that I was carrying something extra about me.

Hindsight and events forced me, much later, to try to make some kind of sense of these events. After I'd first seen Nefertiti in Dahlem, I enjoyed a charmed life. I had a great upbringing, plenty of fun, enjoyed school and did well. I got to Oxford, became a broadcaster and joined BFBS – another ambition fulfilled. After I saw King T., the bad luck cut in: particularly the demotion after the Red Ken incident and the booze-fuelled breakdown and near-death in Cyprus in 1984.

And now here I was, seeing the most beautiful woman in the world once again. I knew, beyond any doubt, that my luck was about to change again. Nefertiti had made it happen. Topifax, the BBC training course authorship, my seven-day working weeks – all of this was about to pay off. I returned to the UK from West Berlin in triumph, bursting with joy and delighted to face the world.

*****

Within a few weeks, I noticed that John Bussell, our doughty Director of Radio, was beginning to treat me slightly differently. He had genuinely taken on board what Dr. Sylvia had told him: that in her opinion I would be fit for overseas service come April 1986.

John was a proud man and didn't want to be seen giving in to a member of staff. But he was also generous of spirit and humane. So, one day, in the early summer of 1986, I was summoned to the presence. Through the glass wall of his office, we looked like boss and employee having a quiet chat. There were one or two onlookers but they couldn't see anything.

'I suppose you're here as Chairman of the Escape Committee?' started John, not unkindly.

I didn't quite fathom the twinkle and so started a bit down. 'Not much point, John. I've tried everything. Not only that, it seems I can't get a promotion, thanks to this mobility ban.'

'Look at me,' said John, changing gear, 'and don't start leaping up and down. I went to see Dr. Sylvia last week at Woolwich and she finally put me straight about your case.'

I knew about this but I was staying schtum. I began to feel something rise inside me. Morale?

John continued. 'It's now June, but I thought you ought to know. I intend to post you to Cologne in

September, as Deputy Editor News and Information. This is to be kept a complete secret between you and me. If you tell anyone – including your line managers – I will withdraw the offer. So try not to look like the cat that got the cream. Off you go - and don't grin!'

I gave him what I hoped was a curt nod and mouthed a quiet 'thank you' before rejoining Planet Earth. Inside I was dancing, and hugging Nefertiti, who was entirely responsible for this change of heart. I was going back to Cologne. I'd be back on all twelve cylinders again.

One of my sharper colleagues, Chris Russell, stopped me in the corridor. Chris could see right into your soul.

'What was that all about?' he asked.

I dismissed the visit with some reference to a BBC course, which seemed to satisfy him. I then went home and told Moo. There was much delight. Living with four children in a one-bedroom flat in Kilburn had not been easy for her, especially on little money, given our mortgage interest rate of 15%. But these days were coming to an end and, thanks again to Nefertiti, we even found us a tenant via the MOD: a colonel would take over our sweet little flat in Victoria Road as a pied a terre and actually pay the mortgage. And in Cologne we'd be getting living overseas allowance. This would be life changing.

*****

Just one more thing to do: a decent farewell party.

I decided to incorporate my BBC training course and chums into proceedings. As well as John Turtle and Bennett Maxwell, I was delighted to be working again with my old Falklands sparring partner, Terry Nicholas. He was still as mad as a box of frogs, and therefore a shoo-in in my Angora radio training scenarios to play the part of the Angoran Prime Minister, His Excellency The Right Honourable Rabee Quimquatt Protha, BA (Dunelm), Prime Minister for Life of the Island Republic of Angora. To see Terry's ruddy, bearded face, encased in full Arab head dress, complete with flowing robes, spitting anti-British slogans in a sneering Middle Eastern accent was actually quite terrifying. Whenever he made an appearance at BFBS Angora, he would inevitably cause a diplomatic incident. He always insisted the welcoming committee should sit on the floor while the Angoran national anthem was being played (as a mark of respect). He would insist on BFBS having his country's appalling news service telex in the studio so that we could use the 'superior' ANA (Angoran News Agency) service, rather than 'that rubbish from the

BBC.'

Terry worked with me on three BBC/BFBS courses and at the end of each course we debriefed the students in the cellar bar of the Portland Arms, next door to the BBC Radio Training building. Terry would generally begin the proceedings with a pint of wine, before starting drinking. His capacity for alcohol was bigger than mine had ever been. I, of course, in my new capacity of ex-boozer, was on pints of tonic. Terry and I organised the party, which brought together a lot of old chums and contributors, as well as the inadvertent cabaret for the evening, the new BFBS Head of Radio, Bill Bebb, an ex-BBC man who had taken over from John Bussell.

Bill, it would be fair to say, was a muso's muso. He lived, breathed and loved live music, and his warm and engaging personality made him many instant friends among the sometimes suspicious BFBS crew. He never boasted but it was known that if you dropped a name from the music world, then Bill had probably produced that name for a BBC show. I was dead chuffed that he agreed to come and say 'hi' to his troops at my farewell bash. He arrived quite late but instantly merged into the scene. Years of practice.

At one stage we were having a quiet chat in a nook of this rather large and dimly lit cellar bar, when my old Cyprus sparring partner, Simon Guettier, decided it would be a good time to petition his new boss.

Simon had a problem. He was at last settled in London, with a great flat and a steady job. His loves of curry and angling were happily served and his love life was fine. He was a settled man. However, John Bussell had decreed that Simbo should do a six-month detachment to Belize. This was not a good idea. Simbo had fair skin and was almost allergic to the sun. He'd suffered in Cyprus and certainly didn't want to go to Belize. Much beer had been taken. And Simbo was about to state his case to his new boss.

It was quite an entrance. It started with a lurch, a grunt and a fairly large Simbo leaning forward in the general direction of Bill, finger stabbing the air.

'Wovvi gotta do to get ouda thish Belize crap?'

He expatiated on this theme, and variations thereof, for about five minutes. He shouted, he pleaded, he cajoled, he wailed, he sought pity, then ruined it by calling all bosses bashtards and, a moment later, besht frens. In short, had he been pleading a case at the Old Bailey, the beak would have had him for contempt within the first thirty seconds.

I watched Bill carefully, as there were enough people gathered by now to restrain Simbo if he went totally gaga. Bill sat back in his chair throughout, with a look of mild interest, an occasional 'oh dear' look of sympathy, and even an occasional 'yes, I know' comment in the gentlest of voices. Eventually, Simon realised that what he was saying was bollocks and duly shut up and ambled away. He said much later that getting it off his chest was probably all that was really needed.

Sadly, it wasn't quite the end. Simbo had huge powers of recovery and it wasn't too long before his tall figure was looming over us again, his face almost whiter than white and his expression that of one who has farted loudly at the Coronation in front of millions. His mouth appeared to be working but nothing seemed to be coming out of it. Bill invited him to sit down.

There then followed an apology of such rococo style and labyrinthine density that the red flock wallpaper nearly crawled off the Portland's walls in embarrassment. How could he have been so crass - at a private party - on Bill's first day? No knowledge of the background – I ought to resign – I feel so bad – of course I know it's not your fault I've got to go to Belize – really am so terribly sorry.

A quiet arm went up for silence. Bill smiled with genuine understanding.

'No, that's fine, Simon. Quite understand. Been there myself. Don't worry about it. No harm done. Sometimes good to get it out of the system. Have a drink.'

It might have worked at the BBC, but Simbo was up for wearing the hairiest of hair shirts and nothing was going to get in the way of him humbling himself after being a total twat. He banged on with another fifty variations on the apology theme. Finally, with genuine but quiet annoyance, Bill stood up.

'Listen, Simon,' he said. 'I am in the business of forgetting everything you said back there. But if you carry on apologising, I'm going to be well upset. Stop it.'

Sadly, this did not compute. Luckily, it gave us all a breathing space while an extremely confused Simon tried to work out how he could possibly be in more trouble for apologising than for calling the BFBS senior management a bunch of c...s

It was a great party.

*****

Normal service was resumed the morning after - our last day in the UK. Roberta helped us with the cat, Giles. We flew BA to Cologne direct and went straight to our new home in Immendorfer Weg, where someone had 'marched in' for us. Not one of the really big houses, but four bedrooms and a study, with a decent patch of garden. We had died and gone to heaven.

We unpacked and took Giles out of his crate. He immediately took himself off to the top of the tallest wardrobe for two days. I pitched up to the studios, which hadn't changed that much since I'd left. Nearly all the old familiar German faces were there. This gave me a huge advantage. I was shown round my old stomping ground, pleased to see that not a lot had changed. After meeting several new faces on the UK staff, I was shown to my new office. It had one complete glass wall overlooking the long, luxuriant lawn and woodland glade. There was also a giant unused fireplace six feet high, which gave the room a character and presence. One wall – about fifteen feet long – was occupied by a giant white pin-board. This would be great for plotting events, series and charts.

But the highlight of the room was the praying mantis. At least, that's what I thought it was when I first went in. It turned out to be Uschi, my PA/secretary. The 'praying mantis' came from the way she kept her hands keenly poised over her electric typewriter. After the introduction I asked her why she was sitting like that.

'I was waiting for you to dictate to me this evening's script,' she smiled.

The smile disappeared when I produced my brand new Amstrad word processor and printer, which I put four square in the centre of my very large desk. I sat in my executive swivel chair. Uschi was watching me. She looked upset.

'Is there a problem?' I asked lightly.

'If you are doing your own scripts and I don't have to type, then I haven't a job any more.'

'Wrong. I don't want two of us to be working on the same thing. It's quicker for me to write my own scripts, as I can change things very easily with this machine. What I want you to do' – I stood up and walked over to the rack of portable tape machines – 'is to take one of these and learn how to use it to do reports and edit interviews.'

'But I haven't been trained.'

'My last job involved a lot of radio training. Now, would you like to be a reporter, or just sit there watching me?' I smiled, expecting a positive answer…

…which finally came. 'Oh, Mr. McDonagh, this is so exciting. I'll get started right away.'

'You do that. Play with it till you get used to it. And in future, it's 'McD', and I prefer 'du' to 'Sie'.'

I may not have changed the world that first day but at least I'd changed Uschi's world. It felt good. I was home again. And this time, without booze. I had a new job. The sad thing was, nobody was actually telling me what that job was.

*****

I seemed to have taken over the editorial control, staff and output of the 'German news'. This was a service supplied via telex by the Deutsche Presse Agentur, who produced it for a domestic German audience - an audience that understood the hinterland and the fabric of German political and social life, not an audience of HM Forces who needed a lot of background information before they could pick up the nuances of, 'Earlier today, one hundred red-green asylum seekers in a concerted effort tried a bank to break into.'(This was an actual 'translation'. Red-green referred to the politically left SPD party and the Green party acting in concert over the granting of political asylum to a particular group of refugees.)

As you may have noticed, the verb in the sentence tended to get pushed towards the end. This was because the news 'writers' (translators) we used were generally Brits who'd spent so long in Germany that German had their first language become and they in the habit of German sentence construction using getting to were.

In short, the German news was a twice-daily disgrace. It was obtuse, labyrinthine, unspeakably tedious and totally garbled in its English format. A listener phoned one day to complain about a headline from that morning:

'This morning in Frankfurt an unmasked man entered a bank and a hold up ensued. He escaped with considerable amounts of Deutschmarks.'

That would be the entire 'story'. It was my mission to get rid of it. Sadly, my line manager and former BFBS UK production colleague, Johnny 'Boy' Walker, who operated out of Bielefeld, and my Station Controller and patron, Dick Norton, had both become messianistic speech freaks, which resulted in a daily half-hour 'Evening Report', as well as live guests in sequence shows and the bloody German news.

The 'Evening Report' came from either Cologne or Bielefeld, with either Johnny or me presenting. The raw materials were much of the usual: the odd live guest, but mainly tape after tape after tape of anodyne three-minute interviews about anything with a pulse. Our job was to shoehorn a few gobbets of this tedium into some kind of order and make sure the programme ran to time. It was very disheartening. All over Germany you could hear squaddies and their families switching off their radios and turning on their TVs.

What finally got me very motivated to slash and burn was the evening that the 'show' was being presented by Tom Scanlan, a senior producer, because Johnny had spent the whole day interviewing Ralph Dahrendorff, the then Head of the London School of Economics. Given that Johnny and intellectual endeavour had only been occasional partners, he'd conducted a pretty rigorous interview on the future of Europe and the place of the United Kingdom within the European Community (as it then was). The following sequence, to its eternal shame, was heard on air.

Dahrendorff: '...and from this we can deduce that as long as the will of the United Kingdom remains positive, then an enhancement of the present European situation is not only possible, but almost certainly achievable.'

Scanlan: 'Professor Ralph Dahrendorff of the London School of Economics, talking to John Walker in Hamburg today. The Rheindahlen Flower Club had its annual Summer Display today and Monica Dutton, our Rheindahlen reporter, was curious to know about the range of blooms on show this year...'

There are non sequiturs and non sequiturs. And then there was something like the above. From the sublime to the ridiculous. Steak and custard. I was chewing the carpet when this was broadcast. Luckily, the fates were playing new games. Dick Norton retired at the age of sixty and, to the surprise and delight of many, engineer Colin Rugg took over as Regional Director, Broadcasting. Colin had always been a programme person and had always had the greatest of democratic insights into how BFBS could best work. We sensed revolution in the air.

After a few months, I found myself being called back to London, to the extreme annoyance of the Cologne management. My BBC/BFBS course-writing skills seemed to be required, along with my presence at a few more actual 'BFBS Angora' white network days, where the plots became even more complex, including the best one of all, where we 'changed' the BBC news.

It happened like this. Our news service was now broadcast from BFBS London to most overseas stations via satellite, which cut down on the number of local newsreading operations. This meant we could afford to use proper newsreaders, which helped stamp authority on the BBC's General News Service 'rip and read' summaries. We used this service for BFBS Angora. On this particular day, Don Durbridge, a well-known BBC Radio 2 newsreader, was on shift at BFBS.

Meanwhile, the Angora network was being held in two locations – BFBS Bridge House (which also contained the BFBS news operation) and BBC Portland Place. Bridge House acted as a satellite studio to the main Angora studio at the BBC.

During the morning, the unreliable local Angoran news service, ANA, had been reporting the appearance of a Soviet 'trawler' to the south of the island, but there had been no confirmation (of course) on the BBC news, so the BFBS staff were not transmitting the trawler story. OK so far. Meanwhile, in John Turtle (Sir Gregory Tweed)'s office, a lunchtime drinks party was being held for all the available staff of BFBS Angora – the entire course group, with the exception of a duty continuity DJ, who was in the middle of a lunchtime show. All was well and nothing could possibly go wrong.

The Prime Minister of Angora, HE The Rt Hon Rabee Quimquatt Protha, BA (Dunelm) (the BBC's Terry Nicholas) made an impassioned speech about the Brits leaving Angora forever ('Anglis Bilanka') and curiously mentioned the Soviet 'trawler' that was making a special friendly visit to the Island. Willis Thoroughgood, MBE, President of the British Residents' Association (BFBS's Richard Astbury), gave a warm-hearted reply in his usual meandering and toothless way and a toast was made 'to Angora'. Some serious swallowing then began. All those in the know kept an eye on the clock. It was one minute to one. A speaker was already playing the output of BFBS Angora.

You must remember that, at this point, all the course members were relaxed because every member of the potentially dangerous directing staff was at the party and therefore nothing could go wrong. It didn't seem odd when Sir Gregory Tweed asked if we could be quiet for a moment, as he always liked to listen to the lunchtime news. Still nobody smelled a rat. The volume was turned up and the BFBS Angora DJ pressed the news jingle. Up came the reassuring tones of Don Durbridge. The lead story was duly read, followed by three or four more short items.

Then the room went mad. Bodies crashing around everywhere, as everybody heard Don Durbridge read the following, ostensibly to the entire BFBS world, live from BFBS London:

'Earlier today, a Soviet so-called 'trawler' was sighted off the south-west coast of the Island of Angora, close to the Nicobar Islands. It was observed by independent observers in the area to release a number of flares, after which it became clear that the ship's back had been broken on the coastal rocks. It now appears that the trawler was a nuclear warship, and that the seas around Angora are likely to be contaminated by nuclear waste.'

The directing staff smirked quietly. We'd got them. Hook, line and sinker. So, how did we do it? It was actually quite simple. Don had recorded a separate BBC one o'clock news summary, inserting the special (fake, obviously) Angora story. This tape had then been routed via land-line from BFBS London to the Angora studio at the BBC and played out at one o'clock, so the news the course delegates thought was coming via satellite was in fact a total spoof. The BFBS network, of course, received the proper bulletin read live.

*****

Back in Cologne, my campaign to get rid of the German news was falling on deaf ears, even after a visit by John Turtle in his capacity of radio training supremo. He made a point of there being witnesses in my office when he kindly picked up one of the translated news bulletins from earlier in the day, read through it with obvious distaste and said, with genuine surprise in his voice, 'You don't actually *broadcast* this nonsense, do you?' It was a major nail in the coffin.'

But the deus ex machina was one of the newsreaders. Even today, I cannot mention his name, as he is one step short of a vexatious litigant. He was Anglo-German and his convolutions included such delights as 'the cream on the jam'. He was unlikable, as he was the kind of person who is never wrong and who calls himself a professional. (I learned early on in my career never to trust anyone who tells you they are a professional. If they are, it should be obvious.) Anyway, our hero distinguished himself by mixing up actions taken by the mayor of one major German city with those of the mayor of another major German city. Given that the alleged actions included the smoking of marijuana and consorting with round-heeled ladies, blaming the wrong person was a dangerous, actionable and unforgivable thing to do. What compounded the felony was that our hero did the same thing on two separate occasions. Colin Rugg had a very long conversation with the mayor who we had publicly accused of drug taking and fornication. To our relief and delight, the wrongly accused mayor found it all very funny and said he would dine out on that story for months!

So we weren't about to be taken off the air for the grossest of all libels, but our 'professional' newsreader didn't know that. We struck while the iron was hot. I dragged the errant scribe over to Colin's office, where we did dual outrage at him until he actually admitted a mistake had been made. We then added some more outrage until he actually admitted that he had made the mistake. We had him for gross misconduct, as he'd done it twice. Colin put on the black cap and sentenced him gone. It took a tribunal or two and some taxpayers' money to get rid of him, but finally his spirit, like the German News, was laid to rest. For me, that was 'the cream on the jam'.

Chapter 23

The Greasy Pole

One thing you notice when you stop drinking yourself stupid every day: you stop being stupid. This means lots of thoughts whizzing round the synapses. This, in turn, means loads of energetic thought patterns all looking for a home to go to, a project to work on, a plot to carry out. It was about now that I seriously thought of reversing my demotion after the Red Ken incident of 1981.

First up was the vacancy for the highly regarded job of Berlin Station Manager. Berlin was, of course, my home town. The job involved a lot of PR but also the opportunity to interview top world figures from the worlds of politics and show business. Everybody went to Berlin at some stage. It was impossible to fail.

I discovered I was one of three candidates for the gig. Each of us had to be interviewed by the regional director, Colin Rugg. I went for my interview. It was going swimmingly until he asked a 'set' question.

'Do you know much about Berlin?'

He knew I'd lived there for my first 20 years and that I knew Berlin intimately. He also knew that I was quite attached to the place. I once became very upset in the Berlin Officers' Club when a transient major informed me loftily, 'Peter, there is *so* much to do in Berlin. I'm sure you'll enjoy it.' Even the nonchalant and elegant barman, Günther, froze in his tracks when he heard that piece of accidental crassness.

'Do you know much about Berlin?'

I think as soon as Colin asked the question, he wished he hadn't. Mild-mannered PMcD suddenly became a snarling, frothing-at-the-mouth animal, gripping the arms of the interviewee's chair with white-knuckle strength.

'Do I know much about Berlin? God, what do I have to do to escape from this bloody nonsense? Of course I know Berlin and you know that I know it well. What kind of a question is that? Is this another way of saying, 'Oh you're just a failed drunk so we'll ask you the token questions and give the job to somebody else?' Eh? Eh?'

It was childish, pathetic, unwarranted and, as soon as I'd done ranting, I immediately felt sorry for the good natured and well-respected Colin. I waited, rabbit in the headlights, for the death sentence. Instead,

Colin mildly apologised, saying he thought it was only fair to ask all three candidates the same questions. I realised that this did make good sense and that I had been a twat. I apologised to Colin and left the room. Ah well, there'd be other jobs...

Such was the down to earth nature of our regional director that as soon as he'd seen all three candidates, he came to an immediate decision and called me over to tell me that I was the new BFBS Berlin Station Manager, before posting a notice telling the rest of the staff.

I rushed home to tell Moo the good news: we were going to Berlin, and I was going to be the boss. It wasn't exactly a promotion in terms of grade, but it was a promotion in status and perception: they were trusting me to do an important job. I danced the light fandango, had an early dinner and was preening in an armchair, when the doorbell rang.

This was unusual. We didn't get visitors. It was one of those things. I went to answer the door. It was a colleague, Jon Shilling. He was also a St. John's College, Oxford, man. His discipline had been Chemistry. His chemistry with me was not good. He was very good at his job and was quite popular with most people on station. He was kind and helpful but for some reason he didn't like the way I worked and I, being a little bit reactionary, didn't like the way he worked. My way was a bit erratic, a bit Jackson Pollock, and then only sporadically, when I was in the mood. Otherwise I'd shut myself in the recording studio and play the piano in full view of the passing trade. His way was methodical and, to my way of thinking, obsessed with filigree detail in one small area of the broad canvas to be covered, while I wielded a six-inch brush and a massive tub of paint.

Jon was clearly upset.

'Come on in'. I volunteered. Sit down – have a drink.' I was magnanimous in victory.

Jon wasn't. 'I prefer to stand.'

The cliché fell out of his mouth and started a puddle of gloom in the room. However, I wasn't about to join him.

'So, what can I do for you?' It was a genuine question. Maybe I could be helpful.

'I think you know why I'm here. It's about the Berlin job. I think it's grossly unfair that Colin gave it to you.'

I froze. He was serious. He was having a pop. This was no longer a border dispute. This was going to be war. My voice went cold and quieter.

'And why do you think that?'

'To start with, everybody knows you spent most of your life in Berlin.' I snorted in disbelief. 'And you speak German'.

'And that makes my appointment unfair?'

'What with that and the fact you keep being sent for to go back to the UK, it's clear you're somebody's favourite.'

A dig too far. I explained that another reason might have been that I was the best candidate – maybe not in my eyes but, given the outcome, most certainly in Colin's. If he had a complaint, it was Colin who needed to hear it, not me.

'Thank you for coming, Jon. Now, if there isn't anything else – goodnight.'

It took a bit of the gloss out of the day – but not much.

I managed to get my revenge on this outrage a few months later, when Jon was going on leave. At the time, he was doing the drive time show from 4-7pm - a music magazine programme that had replaced the bloody awful 'Evening Report'. Jon was doing a good job with the show. He had a monthly competition which attracted about 600 entries - quite something for 1987, when the volume of mail had decreased significantly thanks to phone-in competitions.

What ruined it was my 'briefing' from Jon before he left. It was as if he was handing me the keys to a beloved Ferrari. He took time to explain every detail of the show and its workings, including (I swear) how to start discs and write cue material. It was a primary school lesson delivered in what I took to be a very patronising way. Eventually, his mouth stopped moving and we waved him goodbye for the month.

I got to work. I replaced his competition backing music with 'Crockett's Theme' from 'Miami Vice', a haunting backing track with a low burn factor – i.e. you could play it loads of times without it getting on your nerves. I doubled the frequency of competition announcements in each show and made a bigger showcase for the spot. This went against the usual rules that you should never alter a show's format while guest presenting, but Jon had really annoyed me with his briefing. Soon, the change in competition placing brought about a flood of mail. Part One, done and dusted.

Next, just by happenstance and serendipity, a German rock promoter approached me to publicise a huge concert at the Westfalenhalle in Dortmund, one of the biggest venues in the country, where superstar Lionel Richie was to do a special one-man show. This was on the scale of the second coming, as far as Germany was concerned, and the promoter kindly offered, and gave me on the spot, no fewer than ten pairs of tickets to hear the great man say 'Hello' to tens of thousands of fans. This was huge.

I ran a parallel competition for the month and invited entries of an imaginative or unusual nature. Very soon the huge white board in my office was covered with correspondence including flowers, knickers, revealing photos, hand-coloured cards, 3D models, dolls, bottles – all with competition answers whittled, drilled, embroidered, painted, pasted, nailed, sellotaped or glued onto them. Within a few days, Uschi and I had nearly covered the white board with the most colourful profusion of colours and shapes ever seen in Cologne. Meanwhile, the other monthly competition entries needed extra cardboard boxes to keep them together. We were getting sixty to one hundred entries a day and the momentum was actually building. On top of that, I was having a ball and my head was exploding. Hey, I could still do this DJ lark at the age of 39.

Jon came back off leave and we bumped into each other outside my office, where he had his desk.

'So, how did it go?' he asked. He was cool, man, cool. What he'd really meant was 'So, how much of a struggle was it to walk in my shoes?'

'Oh, not bad,' I lied fluently. 'I'll bring the competition entries in. I told them you'd draw the winner when you came back.'

I walked next door and picked up the first box of entries.

'How many did you get?' Jon was very, very eager to know.

I suppressed a huge victorious grin.

'Oh, this box has about four hundred,' I said. I put the cardboard box on his desk, then went through and, one by one, brought in the next five boxes. It was interesting watching Jon's blood pressure visibly climb as each fresh box made an appearance. I'd arranged the boxes so that each held visibly more than the previous one. Jon was not liking this at all.

Finally, I stopped bringing boxes in. Six of them covered the entire surface of his ever-tidy desk.

'How many entries did you get?' he finally asked, by now convinced this wasn't just a bad dream.

'One thousand, six hundred,' I said, very slowly and very clearly. (The subtext was 'four times as many as you get a month.')

He muttered softly to himself and shook his head. 'I don't know how you did that, but that's quite a result.'

'Thanks. Oh, by the way, I ran another little competition alongside it. I know I shouldn't have, but I couldn't turn my nose up at ten pairs of tickets to see Lionel Richie at the Westfalenhalle! Come and have a look – I asked for off the wall entries.'

He walked through to my office. Uschi was grinning, too. The off the wall entries were in fact *on* the wall - a Cinerama vista of amazing fabrics, objects, colours and textures; hundreds of multi-coloured entries all wanting a piece of the action. There was a silence, a low key, 'Well done', and Jon wandered back to his own office.

Yes, I know, I shouldn't have done it. But there are times when someone who really gets on your tits needs sorting. Not the actions of a saint but he never questioned my abilities again – at least, not to my face.

*****

In the meantime, our umbrella organisation, the Services Sound and Vision Corporation (known to most employees as the Sid Sausage Video Club) had said goodbye to its Managing Director, the rather mystical former BBC New York bureau chief, John Grist, and had appointed the fiery and eccentric Alan Protheroe, who had been Deputy Director-General of the BBC under the disgraced Alastair Milne, as the new MD.

Alan had literally climbed over fallen trees in central London to attend his final interview for the job, thanks to the great hurricane of 1987. He was in a hurry to change things. He would be responsible for bringing Colin Rugg back to the UK and arranging for Charly Lowndes to become Station Manager of BFBS Germany in Rheindahlen, which was a small radio unit, but was also the HQ of the SSVC TV operation.

Charly had been the Senior Programme Director in Cologne and this position now became vacant. There was much speculation as to who might get it. I was due to become the Berlin manager so I was out of the running. Or was I?

I approached Colin, who gave me the pragmatic advice that there wouldn't be any harm in me going for it. So I did. In something of a dream (I really wasn't expecting to be given the job), I cruised through the promotion board in a very relaxed manner and thought no more about it.

A few weeks later, I was back in the UK doing some BBC radio training work, when Bill Bebb, Head of Radio, took a few of us out to lunch. There was a lot of speculation. Roger Hudson asked the question, 'So who's going to be SPD Cologne, then Bill?'

Bit of a cheeky question, but Bill wasn't the man to stand on protocol. He nodded in my direction.

'You're looking at him,' said Bill.

It was said in such a low key and light-hearted way that nobody really believed him and there was a bit of a nervous laugh around the table, including from me. Bill spotted the disbelief and smiled the smile of a man who really knew.

A few days later Colin told me I would be taking over from Charly Lowndes as Senior Programme Director, BFBS Germany, on promotion. I was back where I'd been before my demotion in 1981. Not only that, but because of my heightened status, I was able to move into Charly's vacated mansion – seven bedrooms and servants' quarters over the garage, right next door to the Cologne NAAFI. Oh, I had made it, alright. I was disappointed not to be going back to Berlin but this role was something I had aspired to ever since my days as a jobbing jock back in the early seventies. Luckily, the staff, especially the Germans, seemed very happy for me and life continued cheerfully as I planned and implemented various programme ideas that had been waiting for times such as these.

I swapped secretaries. The SPD's secretary, Lynda Koch, was a lovely lady, filled with charm - and with the most extensive parade of reasons why she couldn't come to work. She also had her finger on the pulse of the station. Sadly, her office was across the corridor from mine. I brought her in and made her effectively my own admin officer. Her role included organising events, at which she was particularly good. If we needed presents, special catering, flowers or special stationery I would ask Lynda to do a town run, which she loved, and I could always rely on her taste and judgement when it came to returning with the right stuff.

While all of this had been going on, a secret plan was being formulated to move the headquarters of BFBS Germany from the media city of Cologne to a northern Army HQ at Herford. At the same time, a series of satellite radio stations, based on Bielefeld and Rheindahlen, would be built in Paderborn, Hohne and Gütersloh, with contribution studios in other forces locations such as Dortmund and Brunnsum in Holland. A huge amount of the groundwork was done by Charly and Colin and I was invited to contribute.

As I had lots of time and energy (I was still effectively working seven days a week), I started to collate pages of input and editorialised them with my own contributions, including charts, graphs, maps, and diagrams, which I translated into Apple Macintosh pages (in those days a 258kbit B&W computer) and hand-coloured with felt-tip pens. It was a labour of love.

I gave it a title, 'Team 90', a timescale for the projected move to Herford and bound all one hundred pages of it in a heavy leather binder. (To make sure it didn't get lost, I made an identical duplicate copy. This turned out to be the cleverest thing I'd done.) My idea in doing it was to suggest, with the help of Colin and Charly's work, what we might be capable of doing. My main thrust was improving our dealings with our core audience – the military. My experience on small stations in Malta and the Falklands had shown me that we were at our best when we were part of the military community, not living sixty miles away in Cologne's delightful but irrelevant La-La Land.

Somehow, this weighty tome ended up on the desk of Alan Protheroe and, with hindsight, I felt that somehow there had been a connection. Alan tended to lead from the front and took no prisoners. He was a wolf who walked by himself and selected people to talk at and to when it suited him. But I didn't know this at the time. I was merely living through a period of immense change.

*****

We heard that Colin Rugg was about to leave us, to become Director of Engineering back at the SSVC HQ in Chalfont Grove. This was, on the face of it, a significant promotion but Colin was hacked off as it rather closed down his ambition to become the next Director of BFBS, after my old sparring partner, Pat Pachebat, who was soon to retire. This led to a lot of speculation as to whom the next Director of BFBS was going to be. It was generally assumed that it might well go to a BBC figure.

Colin Rugg's farewell party was a good ole BFBS thrash, with loads of booze, eats and even a Russian balalaika quartet snatched from a busking session in Cologne's Hohestrasse shopping district. It was held in our house and was an evening of great fun, tinged with sadness, as we said goodbye to Colin, who had been an enlightened and modern boss who really looked after his gang of somewhat egomaniacal broadcasters. He gave us the benefit of a wondrous farewell speech that had most of us finding the room very dusty and requiring the immediate application of Kleenex to the face.

The following morning I was climbing the spiral staircase to my wonderful, balconied office on the first floor. I passed the chief engineer, Peter Attrill, who I'd known, liked and respected since we'd first worked together at BFBS Singapore in 1971. I did the usual 'Morning, Peter' to be rewarded by the curtest of nods. Hmm. He must have something on his mind.

As usual, secretary Lynda Koch was late. (After months she had still not got used to the tone of my voice whenever I greeted her late arrival with 'Morning, Lynda! Doctor, council or solicitor?') Her absence meant that I would have to wait for an explanation as to why my in-tray was piled a foot high with the staff records for all the locally employed (mainly German) personnel. When she did come in, her explanation was given like a nanny talking to her charge.

'Those? They're the monthly work sheets. You're supposed to sign them and return them to me.'

'OK,' I said, still a bit confused. 'But why have I got them? Surely the Station Manager gets to sign these?'

'Well, Charly Lowndes is in Rheindahlen. Didn't Colin tell you last night? *You* are in charge.'

Oh, bloody hell. What a way to find out. I was now the senior person in Cologne – the de facto station manager. Top cat. Follower in the footsteps of John Parsons, Pat Pachebat, Dick Norton and Colin Rugg. One of a very few. I made a few phone calls. Yes, everybody seemed to think I was in charge of BFBS Cologne. No wonder Peter Attrill had seemed a bit peeved. Then several other things occurred to me. As de facto station manager, I now also had the use of the really big office, connected to mine by a side door. This office had a desk even larger than mine, three telephones, a plush carpet and a suite of expensive lounge furniture, instead of scuzzy ex-MOD filing cabinets.

I decided I would 'hold court' in the really big office but actually work from my SPD office, with its Mussolini desk, French windows and the balcony looking over our manicured lawn. One quiet afternoon, I was rummaging through my new domain, when I discovered a particularly well-hidden file.

It turned out to be the bosses' very confidential and 'ooh naughty' file and it held a lot of information and comments about staff, past and present. Most of it was more or less true but there were some bits that deviated from the truth. The bits about me were very interesting. I had been seen as potential promotion material quite early on by John Parsons, but that seemed to stop once Pat Pachebat came along. My fortunes revived again when Dick Norton was in the seat. Colin hadn't added anything.

*****

It was time to try out my wings. We made a good fist of the biennial International 'Photokina' trade fair down at the Cologne Messegelände. Baz Reilly was our principal presenter, interviewer, reporter, coffee maker, greeter, showman, entrepreneur, producer, engineer and star. We broadcast a number of three-hour sequences from a huge, glass-walled studio that opened onto the main concourse. We caused quite a stir with the mainly German public, many of whom were BFBS fans and were amazed that Baz would spot them outside the glass, wave them in and give them a quick tour, while his current disc was spinning. German broadcasting was very much more formal than this and, to this end, the regional radio broadcaster, West Deutscher Rundfunk, were in much bigger premises, with scores of staff, all working out of sight to produce rather prosaic speech reports and lengthy interviews with Herr Doktors and Herr Professor Doktors.

The two cultures eventually clashed. On Day One, a man in a suit came to view our operation. He was given a coffee and a tour by Baz, who had a disc playing while he was also dubbing a taped interview that he'd done at a stand down the corridor. Even for BFBS, this was mulit-tasking, but for WDR, this was anarchy. The visitor left, shaking his head and muttering, under his breath, 'Es kann nicht wahr sein!' ('It can't be true!')

The next day, two WDR-types turned up – yesterday's man and a chap in a sharper suit, who was shown the BFBS operation, and was also full of incredulity as to how we operated. By the fifth day, the numbers had grown to include WDR engineers, administrators and system analysts, who all left, saying to each other that this couldn't possibly be done – all this output, and just a presenter in the studio? And yet, here it was, patently working.

We had clearly captured the hearts and minds – not, unfortunately, of our primary audience, the military, but of our very much larger secondary audience, the German public. This love affair was not destined to be permanent, as a revolution in German commercial broadcasting would force the country's huge public broadcasting service into a massive rethink. BFBS would lose a large part of its German audience, which was right and proper, as younger and more dynamic forces hit German radio like a tsunami.

We ended up doing the full week at Photokina and it was a howling success. The only fly in the ointment was the presence of the SSVC Public Relations Officer, former Army Major Roger Edwards-Jones, who managed to upset one of our star guests by greeting him expansively at the entrance to the glass studio and asking him if he was there for an interview. The guest concerned was a bit surprised by Roger's question but confirmed that he was indeed there for that reason, and so was rewarded with more daft questions: 'And who are you? What do you do?'

At this point a rather better-dressed record company official took the hapless Roger aside and explained in joined-up talking that this was Eric Burdon, formerly of The Animals, who had enjoyed a little success with some songs and was considered one of the finest white blues singers on the planet. Now, could we please stop this silly nonsense and let Mr Burdon do his appointed thing with Baz Reilly. Even Roger finally knew when to shut up and melt away…

*****

Alan Protheroe, the new MD, called for a Programme Directors' conference at BFBS London. This was highly unusual and caused ructions in the upper management layer. Surely it should be a Station Managers' conference? There was one of those every year, when important decisions were made by senior people. How could you have a group of number twos arguing network policy when it probably wouldn't be ratified by the top management? There was muttering in the ranks of the former barons. Alan gently reminded them that *he* was the top management and that he wanted to hear ideas, schemes, dreams and plans from the people who, in his opinion, had probably been silenced by their superiors. It goes without saying that I thought this was utterly brilliant. By now I knew Alan had seen my leather-bound volume, showing how we could squeeze so much more out of our people and systems. We would have, at the very least, an exciting time.

On the afternoon of the second day of the conference, we were sitting round a huge circular table, waiting nervously for the arrival of the great man. When he arrived, it was clear that he had been enjoying a rather jolly lunch at the BBC. He was in sparkling form, with just the slightest hint of drink having been taken. Some of our number were offended by this. I was all for it. As an ex-drinker, I still preferred the company of those who enjoyed the hop and the grape and the grain, and thought them far better company that some of the tight-lipped pecksniffs who coped on coffee and sparkling water.

Alan terrified the proceedings by launching into a vicious attack on BFBS. We were plodders; we were stuck in a rut; the organisation was creaking with admin overload; we'd 'always done it this way'; we were cowards; we lacked both backbone and vision. He damned us utterly with an eloquent flow of Welsh rhetoric, which contained far too many home truths for its recipients. At the end, he sighed deeply and sat back, looking into the middle distance, his eyes hooded, still poised to strike. I finally found the courage to ask:

'Alan, if BFBS is as bad as you say it is, why did you take on the job?'

'I'm soooo glad you asked,' he almost whispered, his eyes now burning. Then, taking everyone by surprise, we were bathed in the glow of an unexpected eulogy.

It was the difference between Milton's 'Il Penseroso' and 'L'Allegro' - two opposing interpretations of the same human situation which used to be a requirement of a classical education, leading to the art of debate, of deploying your best skills to make arguments for causes you might in reality oppose.

Alan painted a picture of BFBS's glorious past, its victories, successes, triumphs and its hugely capable staff, all prepared to go the extra mile to squeeze the maximum from an ever-reducing pot of available resources. He told us how proud he was to be our boss and how he hoped that we would join him in this new great crusade to make sure that BFBS was known and loved by each of its present and potential audience around the world.

After this second part of Alan's exposition, we were all quite pleased at the compliments that had been flying around the room, if still a bit confused. There were still one or two pockets of resistance. Having been told at the outset that we were to say anything and everything we liked, my old sparring partner Jon Shilling was moved to ask: 'Alan, can I ask you – how long is your contract with BFBS?'

Alan's voice always dropped half an octave and about twenty decibels when he wanted to make a point.

His head went down like the cobra he was, and he answered Jon with one chilling sentence:

'Surely, Jon, your question to me should be, 'How long is MY contract?'

The subject was not pursued any further. Instead, for the first time, BFBS programme chiefs, as opposed to the top bosses, argued and fought and agreed and raged and laughed in a completely free-flowing discussion about what we should do in the future. There were some brilliant ideas flying about and even I felt I'd added my tuppence worth to the brainfest. I was alive, adrenalin was pumping and I was flying at thirty thousand feet.

All too soon the afternoon came to an end. Alan appeared to take his leave and we stepped out into the corridor, still chatting in disbelief about the marvellous opportunity we'd all been given. Suddenly someone gave me a nudge. From the glass-walled office at the top end of the corridor where we were still all standing, Alan was beckoning, with a bony and crooked finger, and pointing specifically – at me?

I looked for confirmation – he was behind the glass, about fifteen feet away. He caught my eye and, yes, my presence was required. In front of my colleagues, I walked the longest walk of my life, along the corridor and into the glass-walled office.

Alan pointedly closed the door. He did not ask me to sit. He stood a couple of feet away from me and launched into a tirade. From the outside, it was impossible to hear what was going on, but one thing was certain: Alan's face, contorted with anger, was right in mine; he was emphasising point after point with arms pumping out the beat of every nuance of thought he was imparting. It was a frenzy. To the spectator, what must have added to the frisson was that I too had adapted my style to respond to what Alan was saying. My face was red, I was clearly shouting, my arms were flailing and I was definitely answering back.

Everyone could see that this was the end for McD. No-one could upstage Alan – he was an unstoppable force. I was history.

Inside the room, it was surprisingly cordial. Alan's rage was against the old stodgy BFBS. He wanted it changed. Did I want to help him change it? Yes, of course I bloody well did. Well, what was I going to do about it? Well, if I were to be handed a bigger part, I could help change it.

Alan then told me that after Pat Pachebat retired, he would be taking over as Director of Broadcasting. He needed someone to run BFBS Radio as Assistant Director. I was to apply for the job. Yes, he knew I had history and issues. That shouldn't stop me. Would I bloody well apply?

It took me about two nanoseconds to realise he actually meant what he said. A deep breath, then, 'Of course I'll bloody well apply.'

'Off you go then, after me, and don't say a word.'

He turned his back on me, pushed the door opened, his face still in an apparent rage, and marched purposefully down the corridor, with my colleagues flattening themselves against the walls as the Welsh wizard made his dramatic exit.

Once he'd left, I walked quietly back towards my compatriots, apparently white and shaking. They were curious, and full of both sympathy and schadenfreude – the natural mindset of broadcasters. I managed to make sad victim noises at them until we'd gone downstairs for a post-mortem in the Deadly Dudley over the road, where we continued to scheme and dream. BFBS had just become really interesting again.

Chapter 24

Jackpot

So. The stage was set. I was going to apply for the new position of Assistant Director (Radio). Despite the word 'assistant', it was clear from the job description that the appointee would have day-to-day control of the worldwide BFBS operation, answerable only to the MD himself. I completed the application form, and waited.

A few days – not weeks – later, I was told that I would be one of three people to be boarded for the position. The other two were formidable competitors.

Charly Lowndes was my old boss in Germany – younger than me, but with vast intelligence, and an incredibly skilled broadcaster. His application of logic was second to none and in argument he tended to be able to knock 'em all dead. He looked a bit 'academic' – beard, sandals and very informal clothes – but this didn't get in the way of a committed, personable, articulate and fun personality.

My other fellow potential greasy pole-climber was the legendary Richard Astbury, at that time station manager of BFBS London. Richard was a wonderful combination of radio star, brilliant producer and presenter; he was charismatic, the life and soul of every party and had an instinct for who and what made good radio. He had even taken a sabbatical to run Riviera Radio in the South of France. Urbane, cosmopolitan and very well spoken, 'Asters' had to be a shoo-in for the role.

Then there was me. Damaged by drink, unmanageable, contrary, spiky, devious, Walter Mitty-ish, self-centred, scared of most social situations, a virtual sociopath – but with the ability to make plans and get my own way. Not too pretty, but you fight with what you've got.

As an 'entrance exam', Alan had asked each of the three candidates to prepare a paper that should examine the BFBS operation and suggest how it might develop over the coming years. He devoted a lot of rubric to this part of his exposition. It was a tall order, as he had not given any clues until now as to how *his* thoughts for BFBS were formulating.

Right at the end, almost as a footnote, he had added a paragraph about a new service. BFBS 2 would be based in the UK and would replace all the local attempts at providing an alternative service overseas. (It had long been a tradition to dump programmes that didn't fit the 'Format 77' mainstream BFBS 1 operation into the dustbin of the local BFBS 2, which meant a lot of disjointed and second rate programming.)

Alan was asking for a no extra cost, twelve hours a day, five days a week service that would complement BFBS 1 and be available by satellite in real time to the European stations, Germany, Cyprus and Gibraltar.

Armed with our briefs, we set out to prepare our submissions. We agreed that once we had handed in our papers, we would show each other what we had done. The due date arrived and papers were finished. Charly and Richard gave me their submissions and I gave them mine.

For the most part, in our different styles, we had addressed the case of the future BFBS with three very workable proposals.

Charly's was weighted towards mathematics and logic, and Richard's to showbiz, personality and better trained people on air. Mine took into account automation, more international interchanges of programming and the use of ISDN to carry items from further and further afield.

The real surprise came with each candidate's treatment of the proposal for a no cost BFBS 2 operation. Because Alan had treated it as a final, almost throwaway paragraph, both of my colleagues had more or less drawn up a quickie schedule, almost in sketch form – very much the afterthought they imagined Alan had intended.

For some instinctive reason, I felt that Alan was more than a little interested in a future, centralised BFBS 2 operation. So I drew up no fewer than three options.

One was for what had been demanded: a five day a week, twelve hour a day operation, using BBC Radio 4 and BBC Transcription discs (plays, documentaries and features). It included a new home for 'The Archers' and a lunchtime music magazine for the duty announcer, who would be extracted, at no extra cost, from the worldwide BFBS 1 pool.

I then developed my BFBS 2 into an eighteen hours a day, seven days a week service, and, finally, a 24/7 all-singing, all-dancing operation. All of this had been prepared with appropriate charts drawn up on the Apple Macintosh, with block transparent coloured Letrafilm turning a rather boring set of charts into a multi-coloured vision of the future. I was very pleased with the result, which looked good. I just hoped that the picture inside did justice to the frame.

All three of us now knew we were to be boarded for the job. What we didn't know was the composition of the board. As usual, I was nervous beyond all measure as I paced outside the room, realising that the next hour was likely to be the most important in my professional life. Suddenly the spirits of Charly and Richard loomed over me. They cast a long shadow. They were both brilliant broadcasters and, goodness me, did I respect them. Finally, I was ushered into the execution chamber. Abandon hope all ye who enter here. I was bricking it.

I scanned the very neutral, but serious faces in front of me. Diane Trigg, Personnel Manager, who had written to me following my alcoholic collapse saying that if I ever did it again, I would be out on my ear, no questions asked. Next to her, the very kindly Deputy Managing Director, Air Vice-Marshal Bill Bailey – a small man with a powerful engine inside him. He had made it from airman to AVM in a distinguished career. Then, Alan Protheroe, clearly in command and in control, and glaring at me as though I'd left my flies undone.

And there, right at the end, was the outgoing Director of Broadcasting, my nemesis, Pat Pachebat. I might as well have gone home straight away. No need for an interview. Pat would surely veto any appointment. He was very cold and professional. He even gave me a thin smile and a curt nod.

The batting opened and a series of bouncers, googlies, yorkers and underarms were delivered from every direction. Somehow, I seemed to be keeping my head above water. After a little while, I even felt in control, and my answers became somehow brighter and delivered with more impact. I was cruising along quite happily. So far Pat hadn't asked me anything, but seemed to be occupied writing notes. Alan noticed Pat's comparative reticence and invited him to ask me a few questions.

The first couple were harmless, reasonable, operational questions, which I fielded without too many problems. Then, suddenly, Pat changed gear. He asked me about my inconsistent behaviour in the past, my history of drinking in Cologne, the effects of my anti-social behaviour. Each question got me a little more annoyed, but even if this little patrol boat was sinking under the superior fire of Pat's battle cruiser, it wasn't about to lose dignity and break the line. I steamed onwards, answering his damning questions as best I could. I was being pummelled, but somewhere in the back of my mind I knew I dare not lose my presence of mind, or, far worse, my temper. Each question received a polite reply, and sought to distance the old me from the present incarnation. Eventually, Alan appeared to have heard enough from Pat. He raised an arm to call for silence.

'Peter,' he said, and I detected a note of compassion in his voice, 'I think we've heard enough. What I'd like to know now – is there anything you'd like to ask us?'

Suddenly, from above, the angel of l'esprit d'escalier hovered over me and perched smartly on my shoulder.

'Yes, Alan,' I said gently. 'There is one question I would like to ask.'

'Go ahead,' said Alan, with a flourish in my direction.

'I realise that the chances of this happening again are very small indeed. But if it does, can I please have your assurance that next time the interview will not be a history lesson?'

The board members looked at each other, and then at me. What kind of a question was that supposed to be?

Alan knew. He realised what I meant and he knew what he had to do.

He leant forward, his arms resting on the desk, until his chin was only a couple of inches from its surface. His eyes hooded over and seemed to gleam with predatory pleasure. He waited for what seemed like a lifetime. Then he spoke in a very, very quiet voice. We all strained to hear.

'Peter, you have my promise. These matters will never be spoken of again.'

It was clear that he meant it. He had in effect closed down Pat completely. He was telling me that he was ignoring the poison that Pat had tried to put into my submission. Whatever the outcome, I felt completely vindicated. I walked out of the boardroom on a cushion of air, light, and happiness.

Once all three of us had endured our board, we all met up in an Italian café on the Edgware Road and compared notes. I was still in a bit of a daze but I managed to keep up as we told our tales of how well or badly we'd done at various stages. What I found mildly amusing, but quite reasonable under the circumstances, was that towards the end of our chat, both my colleagues were drawing up future scenarios for the BFBS each of them would be planning if they got the job. I was a brand new BFBS Grade 3, having only just been returned to the nobility after the disgrace of Red Ken and the unspoken drink disaster, and on top of that had never actually been appointed as a station manager. But I didn't mind. Pat Pachebat had been ordered to wind his neck in and that to me was a huge result. So, with a song in my heart, I returned to Cologne.

A couple of days later, two of our DJs happened to be in my office. Jonathan Miles and Glen Mansell were two of the cheekiest and funniest characters in BFBS. Jonathan, who was both gay and camp, had come out on his first evening in Cologne, and was amazed that all of us said, 'So what?'

Glen's avowed aim in life was to 'beat the boss'. On one occasion he'd asked me for permission to buy twenty-five promotional T-shirts for an on-air competition, which I approved. When the bill for seventy-five T-shirts hit my desk, I called him over, with mayhem in my mind. I showed him the bill.

'"Well? Twenty-five T-shirts? This is for seventy-five.'

'Oh yes, right. Should have said. Twenty-five small, twenty-five medium, twenty-five large…'

'Get out. Now. That's the last time…' (Etcetera, etcetera.)

Jonathan, Glen and I were having a fairly cheery natter, when the phone rang. It was Pat Pachebat at SSVC HQ in the UK.

'Hello Peter. Pat Pachebat here. Are you alone?'

The voice sounded dispirited, tired, defeated and very, very sombre. I looked up at the two grinning twerps in my office. Oh, sod it!

'Yes, Pat. I'm on my own,' I lied.

'Alan has asked me to phone you…to phone you with his congratulations. We're just about to release the information worldwide. You have been appointed the new Assistant Director Radio.'

There was a tiny pause, enough for a clenching of teeth. Then, in a voice usually reserved for the death of the Monarch, the one, hollow word. 'Congratulations.'

I was trying not to betray anything to the lads in the office. I replied in exactly the same tone of voice that he had used with me.

'Thank you very much, Pat. It was very kind of you to let me know.' For all my colleagues would have surmised, there had been a minor setback oop at t'mill.

I sat back in my big boss's swivel chair and tried so very hard not to smirk. Glen picked up that something was going on but I refused to be drawn. I sent them packing, closed the door and did a victory dance which completely eradicated any shred of residual dignity I might have shown up till then. Fifteen months before I had been a demoted, demoralised recovering alcoholic producer. Now I owned the shop.

*****

Within the hour, telex machines around the BFBS world were passing on the information that I was the new Assistant Director (Radio) and that I would be taking up my duties in the New Year, 1990.

I was amazed and delighted to receive lots of cards, letters and messages of congratulation and support. The most unexpected of all was from *the* Director of BFBS - there had really only ever been one who counted – Ian Woolf, now some eight years into his retirement. He congratulated me on being the youngest man to take on the mantle of BFBS's leadership and offered both good wishes and advice for the years ahead. We went on to have many a fruitful lunch at Church House in Westminster. Listening back then to an interview that Ian Woolf did for the BBC World Service, I had remembered, and always will remember, my favourite Woolfism: 'The system is that we will fight the system.' This seemed to be an excellent mantra and I did my best to follow it.

We'd now been in Cologne for just over three years – a full posting. The sadness was that soon after I started my new job at Chalfont Grove in the UK, BFBS Cologne would close down.

The two mansions in Parkstrasse and Lindenallee were crammed full of memories that had taken me from being a young man to middle age. It began to occur to me that, in many ways, I could no longer go back. I could never be posted overseas again; I couldn't really misbehave, join in with some of the daft things that broadcasters get up to; I would have to make myself unpopular by throwing out the waste; and, worst of all, every year, via an annual report, I would have to sit in judgement on my former contemporaries. 'Poacher turned gamekeeper.' I began to feel the weight of future responsibility.

On top of this, Moo was not best pleased that we were now effectively out of circulation. Also, she was doubly annoyed that we would have to find somewhere to live in the UK. We would have to sell the Kilburn flat and move a lot closer to Chalfont Grove, one of the most expensive parts of the UK. There was going to be wall-to-wall admin for the first few months. All the kids were at boarding school but would require space at home during the holidays. And all of this had to be carried out on UK pay, without allowances. Not only that, I'd forgotten that we had to pay extra tax on previous boarding school allowances. I did the sums and discovered that, once everything had been paid and accounted for, I was getting £70 a month for groceries.

Ouch.

The next piece of news was delivered after midnight from Liphook, Hampshire, where Mum and Dad lived in retirement. It was a very shaken and disjointed call from Dad, to tell me that Mum had just died of heart failure. I flew over and arranged the funeral. I was in a daze but Dad was away with the fairies. I didn't know it then but it was the beginnings of dementia. He quietly agreed with everything I said, as we arranged matters from the burial to the power of attorney that

I would need to manage affairs, once the doctor had told me that Dad was no longer capable of rational thought.

We buried Mum in Bramshott Cemetery, after a quiet but very English service in the church where they had married back in 1941. It was as we were grouped around the already lowered coffin that I suddenly remembered something that had been niggling me all day. Mum had wanted to be cremated. I could almost hear her scolding me for not paying attention. I was forced to smile.

I decided that Dad should come back with me to Cologne. I shunted him up the Portsmouth line till we found a photo booth for a passport photo. We obtained a visitors' passport, then still available, and flew to Cologne. Dad looked totally withdrawn from the world but smiled if anyone spoke to him, was generally affable, and quite content if a beer was imminent.

By Day Two, the situation appeared untenable. Dad was wandering around the house, removing cups, glasses and any other utensils he could find, pouring beer into them, taking a swig, and then putting down one container to go and find another. The kids were worried and a bit frightened. I made plans to move him out in two days' time, on New Year's Day. Somehow, we managed to steer him away from harm. From Liphook came the news that Auntie Mirrie, his sister, would come down from Middlesbrough to look after him for a while.

With some kind of Relief of Mafeking just round the corner, I thought we'd give Dad a treat and take him to the BFBS Cologne New Year's Eve party, in aid of the network's official charity, 'Wireless For The Blind'. The party took place in the massive foyer of the Parkstrasse building, while at the top of the stairs, in the studio, requests and dedications were being pledged for charitable donations. I walked with Dad to the radio station. Usually, this took half an hour, but Dad had absorbed only the one word, 'party', and kept going through every garden gate and house entrance along the way with a curious 'Is this it?', as if he were asking the question for the first time.

By the time we got there, the party was in full swing. I asked my good friend, Alan Clough, to keep an eye on Dad, and pour beer into him if he was empty, whenever I was called away to sort anything out. Cluffie was happy to oblige and even listen to Dad's rather esoteric burblings from another life and, at times, another dimension.

I was running around the building, making sure everybody was doing the right thing at the right time. Every so often I'd cast an eye on Dad, who still seemed to be relaxed, at ease and enjoying himself. In fact, a lot of the old party-animal sparkle had resurfaced, helped by eleventeen pints of Cologne beer.

The Wireless For The Blind party tradition was that, just before midnight, all the staff, volunteers and family members would crowd into the on-air studio to do the New Year countdown and sing 'Auld Lang Syne'. Once we'd all crammed in, it was almost impossible to move for a load of swaying bodies with celebration on their minds. We watched the clock expectantly and were all well aware of the extra drama of being in a live radio studio.

It was time for the countdown: 'Ten...nine...' The voices seemed to get louder and more raucous as the clock ticked away to mark the end of 1989 and the beginning of a brand new year and decade.

'Three...two...one...*Happy New Year!*' A huge cheer and a round of applause.

And then it happened. From the middle of the crowd, his rich baritone totally drowning out Glen Mansell at the microphone, a voice well in its cups really set the studio on fire, belting out the old classic song, '*You're Gonna Miss Your Big Black Momma Some Of These Days!*'

At that point, someone had the presence of mind to lead Dad out of the studio, his warbling instantly replaced with the more legitimate 'Auld Lang Syne'. He knew what he'd done, the old bugger. I didn't have the heart. We were taking him back to UK and an empty house the next day.

I took him home and left him in the tender care of his long-suffering sister, herself no chicken, and slave to a host of ailments. Feeling suitably guilty, I slunk back to Cologne straight away to pack up and push off from abroad for the last time.

*****

Within a few days I was installed in a tiny office in the SSVC Headquarters at Chalfont Grove, an old estate halfway between the stockbroker belt villages of Chalfont St. Giles and Chalfont St. Peter in South Buckinghamshire.

Chief Broadcasting Assistant (Radio), Mike Robertson, my former boss, but now my de facto admin officer, organised some new quality office furniture. Diane Trigg from Personnel provided me with the most smashing secretary, Becky Merrett, who soon learned how to operate me to our mutual benefit. It was all very funny as, by nature, I didn't do the power thing and I had a rather relaxed idea about how people should behave around me.

I discovered that, to some degree, Alan Protheroe, who I'd been totally scared of, was, in fact a pussycat in private. Often, after 'morning prayers' with my fellow chiefs and directors, he would bend the bony finger and invite me to sit down for a private chat, where no holds were barred and we could discuss what we should be doing.

Our first strike was to begin the BFBS 2 European satellite-delivered service from Chalfont by February – five weeks away. A storeroom at the end of the broadcasting corridor in Chalfont was turned into an operational radio studio. I drew up the first ten-hour, five-day schedule. It was a hotch-potch of BBC Radio 4 relays, BBC Transcription Service discs and a few in-house programmes, including a live hour between 1200-1300.

On a Monday morning in early February, a very nervous freelance, Phil Jay, opened the microphone to announce to the world that they were listening to the new service of BFBS 2, broadcasting to Germany, Cyprus and Gibraltar. To highlight the 'international but local' nature of the new service, Phil then read out the weather forecasts for each location after the first BBC news bulletin.

Alan Protheroe was there, alongside Colin Rugg and me. Honour was satisfied: we had launched the very first BFBS satellite-delivered service to a good part of the military world. I was off to a good start.

*****

We all gathered in Alan's office to congratulate each other. Hadn't we done well? In the background, the speaker was on and in my mind's eye I could see beads of sweat on announcer Phil Jay's brow, as a very, very old and well-used 33 1/3 rpm BBC transcription disc recording of Episode One of 'David Copperfield' played out to that part of the BFBS audience who disliked pop music.

'The BBC presents David *click* Copperfield, an adaptation of Charles Dickens' *click* novel in thirteen episodes *click*.'

Unfortunately, many of the older transcription discs had obviously been cleaned with sandpaper, given the number of surface scratches. If you were lucky, you got a click. If you were unlucky, the needle would kangaroo all the way through the episode, leaving a lot of room for 'And now, to take us up to our next programme, here's Geoff Love and his orchestra with Wagner's Ring Cycle.'

Remember that wonderful line from Monty Python – 'Nobody expects the Spanish Inquisition?' It was as early as Day Two that I heard it. It taught me a huge lesson when it came to dealing with our mercurial Managing Director.

I wanted to keep my presentation hand in so decided to present the Lunchtime Show whenever I could. I decided to lead by example and presented the show on the second day of the service, playing, among other middle-of-the-road tunes, Glen Campbell's 'Wichita Lineman' – for me a rather poignant and pleasant classic. Little did I know this would result in – the Spanish inquisition.

I'd no sooner finished the show and introduced a lengthy BBC relay starting with 'The World At One', than the phone in the studio rang. It was Alan Protheroe. The voice was clipped and cold.

'You will come and see me at once,' he almost purred, before hanging up.

I realised that something was terribly wrong. I walked across the courtyard to the mansion house, which contained the tall-windowed MD's office. I knocked, received a curt 'Come', and, for the first time, was *not* invited to sit down. Also, I noted with some horror that Alan, who preferred to sit in one of the reproduction antique leather chairs, was sitting upright behind his desk.

Without preamble, he launched into a character assassination of his newly appointed Assistant Director (Radio), which covered my parentage, my education, my judgment, my sensibilities, my sense of occasion and my overall intelligence. He didn't repeat himself once, even in his choice of swear words.

A précis of what he said was: 'I don't like country music. It's only for morons. Who wants to listen to the caterwaulings of redneck drunks and incontinent shaggers? What did you think you were doing playing that utter tosh on my lovely BFBS 2?I thought you had half a brain…'

Well, you get the drift. I was an evil loser who had no right to exist. Lower than an amoeba, I should immediately hand in my dinner pail and retire to a side room with a silver salver, a glass of whisky and a loaded revolver, and do the right thing. How could I now possibly walk alongside men of innate breeding, after inflicting such torture on our deserving audience?

I surmised that, as this question, like all the others, was spoken in High Welsh rhetorical mode, it might be best not to answer. I just stood there and took it all on the chin, with a suitably piaculative expression on my rather strained face.

Eventually, even Alan ran out of steam. The temperature and quantity of his bile and venom slowly cooled and lessened. After about ten minutes, we were back in the realm of 'You see, Peter, I really don't like country music – so let's just have no more of it.'

No revolver. No expulsion. No enduring shame. He fetched me a glass of tonic from the cupboard and poured himself a large scotch.

'Now,' he said. 'When are we going to extend the schedule? I really want us to go seven days instead of five. It's the only way.'

I swear I heard a snigger outside his office door. Rosemary, his wonderful PA, was used to his foibles and always enjoyed her boss's cabarets. I found out later that 'It's the only way' was one of his greatest mantras, as well as being his copper-bottomed seal of approval.

I soon discovered what a marvellous actor Alan actually contrived to be. We were sitting in his office one morning, having a chat, both in 'high-flying' mode – schemes, dreams, plans and lots of 'the only way.'

Rosemary stuck her head round the door. She hissed at Alan (she was allowed to), 'Alan. It's half past eleven – Mr Smith is here to see you!'

It sounded important, even though I have spared the gentleman's blushing by calling him 'Smith'.

Alan was incensed. He muttered to me, 'What right does Smith think he has, trying to burst in when we're talking shop? Doesn't he know there's a time and place?'

I nodded sympathetically. Ten minutes later Rosemary's head appeared round the door.

'*Alan!*' she stage-whispered. 'Mr Smith has been waiting for ten minutes. You said you wanted to see him. Remember? He's retiring from SSVC after forty years' service.'

Alan seemed even more angry. 'Well if he's hung about for forty years he can manage a few more minutes,' he snapped. 'Tell him I'll see him when I'm ready.'

We went back to our chat. Alan was beginning to twitch. I was seriously concerned when Rosemary appeared for the third time. This time she marched into the office and closed the door behind her. She squared up to Alan and called him a graceless, ungrateful animal. Mr Smith had to go to his own farewell drinks with his staff and here Alan was, pretending to be a 1930s mill-owner, kicking his staff in the teeth. He would see Mr. Smith *now*.

Alan knew he was beaten. He asked me to leave by the side door of his huge office. As I walked through the door, I heard the Welsh wizard, his voice oozing charm and comradeship, greet the unfortunate Mr. Smith.

'My dear Smith – may I call you Robert? *Do* come in and sit down. A quick drink? The very least you deserve at the end of your long and distinguished career. No doubt you could tell us one or two tales of your life and times with the Corporation?'

I closed the door quietly. I had discovered that sometimes, there is more than one 'only way'.

*****

Meanwhile, a dark shadow was about to cross our path. The Foreign Office had examined the latest prognostications and there appeared to be no doubt about it: Iraq had invaded Kuwait. It was our bounden duty, along with forces from the land of the brave and free, to go to war against the regime of Saddam Hussein.

The situation suddenly came close to home as BFBS was given every encouragement to 'borrow' spare short wave frequencies from the BBC in order to broadcast morale-boosting request programmes to the troops deploying to the 'Op Granby' theatre in Al Jubayl, Saudi Arabia. Our programmes were also being heard, as we discovered from a smuggled request, by the captured British Army Kuwait Training Team, imprisoned by the Iraqis at an oil refinery and totally cut off from civilisation, apart from a borrowed Russian short wave receiver.

It was decided that, in the run up to what looked like an inevitable war, we would build and run a radio station in Al Jubayl. We had the clout of direct approval from the UK Force Commander, General Sir Peter de la Billière. We were also seeking, for the first time, approval from the MOD for BFBS Radio to embed with the troops in a war zone. This was heady stuff.

It then occurred to me that as the man in charge of BFBS, I would be expected at the very least to fly over to Saudi and open the new radio station. Gulp.

Chapter 25

We Go To War

It was now definite. Coalition forces would assemble in Saudi Arabia and begin an assault on Kuwait to drive out the Iraqi invaders. George Bush Senior and John Major were the principal players and, for the first time, BFBS was invited to deploy to what the military, with characteristic deadpan understatement, call a 'hostile environment'.

After some rubber stamping fun at the MOD, we were eventually given permission to open a radio station in Al Jubayl in order to play 'The Abba' to several million bemused Arabs, as well as our very own 7th Armoured Division, led by the charismatic Boys' Own figure of the then Brigadier Patrick Cordingley.

But first of all, other things had to happen. I had asked Charly Lowndes to act as our chief negotiator with a British Liaison Group and the Saudi Government. His job was to persuade everyone that a BFBS station on the ground would improve morale and provide a valuable tool for the Commander in order for him to talk directly to his troops. Charly would also attempt to allay any fears that the Saudis might have regarding pop tunes with evil slogans, inappropriate verbal images or blasphemies of any kind.

Luckily, Lieutenant Colonel Glyn Jones, Head of Force INFO, and his deputy, Squadron Leader Pat McKinlay, were intelligence operators of the highest order and they reported directly to the Commander British Forces.

General Sir Peter de la Billière was not only a committed BFBS fan, but a senior officer who had actually experienced BFBS and its capabilities when serving as Commander British Forces Falkland Islands. So, as far as the military side was concerned, Charly had the fairest of fair winds at his back.

Sadly, there were two major obstacles in the way: the Saudi government and our own MOD. Before too long, extensive meetings were taking place between the Saudi hierarchy and Charly, who had the backing and clout of the FINFO team. Gallons of cardamom tea were slurped as the group sat cross-legged in voluminous but airy tents in the middle of the desert, going over the pros and cons of freely-radiating foreign broadcasts from a different culture being broadcast to impressionable Saudis, as well as to roughy-toughy soldiers.

As the negotiations continued, our makeshift radio station kit was being assembled in the sands of the British Forces garrison at Al Jubayl, on the west coast of Saudi Arabia. The town itself was some way up the road – a ghost town built for occupation once the oil ran out, with huge water desalination plants and an almost 'plug and play' infrastructure costing billions. Troops were arriving and we were getting a bit embarrassed that the American Forces Network (AFN) was already broadcasting a live and local radio service to Al Jubayl REMFs (Rear Echelon Mother Fuckers!) while we were trying to build a radio shack out of an old sea container and whatever kit we could smuggle out of Chalfont Grove.

I decided to take a gamble. Many of our team of stars had already volunteered for Gulf War service, should the balloon go up. One such was Alton Andrews, who had a very direct attitude to broadcasting, a simple professional mindset and a refreshing candour. This readily made up for the fact that he knew more about music than virtually anything else. I didn't even have to call for him. He appeared in my office, not for the first time, and asked for permission to go to the Gulf. It was a case, that day, of nth time lucky. I grinned at him, and said, 'Alton, you've got it. I want you to go to Al Jubayl and broadcast BFBS to the lads in the trenches.'

'I'm on the case,' said Alton, and I knew he meant it.

He was about to leave in order to sort out his ticket, clearances, visas, ID discs, jabs and gas training – yes, this was serious: the Iraqis had form, remember -when I dropped the bombshell.

'There is a problem. Our own radio studio doesn't exist yet and we don't have any transmitters, either. So you're going to have to ask the Yanks for some AFN airtime. If we do it through their HQ in California, it'll take forever. So it'll be up to you.'

Alton assured me he was *still* on the case. If the Yanks said no, the best we could hope for was a string of pre-recorded voice track dedications to play into our main BFBS output. Not the same thing. I waited for the phone to ring. While the war situation was imminent, and later live, I insisted each of our broadcasters carried my home number and said that they could call me, day or night.

After a few days, I got a message back from the front line. Alton had knocked on the door of the AFN operation, explained himself and sat in the foyer of their radio station with a coffee while Colonel Robert Gaylord, the AFN Saudi Arabia chief, phoned Washington. He must have put a good case, as very soon Alton was established as a BFBS representative, sharing airtime with AFN and building himself something of a reputation as a crazy Brit – nicknamed 'Jeeves' - who had a really fresh way of broadcasting.

Meanwhile, in the sands of the desert, permission to open our own studio was very slow in arriving.

Awash with sweet tea, our heroes went back and forth with the intricate and extensive politenesses, courtesies and alien protocols demanded by Saudi law and customs. Finally, although they didn't quite realise it at the time, they arrived at a meeting where it was clear from the chief Saudi negotiator's smile that there was to be positive news.

After the obligatory first gallon or so of sweet tea, the smile seemed to spread wider and wider among the Saudi contingent. It seemed right and proper for Charly and the liaison team to join in. Some minutes later, a verbal agreement was issued. Well, it seemed, on the surface, to be an agreement. It was certainly less than clear.

'We are giving you permission to make in our country test transmissions on a non-interference basis,' said the Saudi chief.

Once they had said goodbye to their Saudi hosts, the FINFO group analysed the results. It seemed clear. In case anything went wrong, the permission (for that is what it was) could not be put in writing. This was not the Saudi way. Their word was much more important. They would only break their word if we broke ours first. Also, 'test transmissions' gave them the option to shut us down without diplomatic comeback or loss of face. The 'non-interference' simply meant 'We'll let you get on with it, subject to you following all the rules we've talked about and the stipulation that your service will not physically interfere with our own broadcasts.' In other words, the Saudis had said 'Yes'.

This only left the MOD. Eventually, Colin Rugg discovered a very quiet Royal Navy Commodore, who appeared to have no connection either with broadcasting or the imminent war, but who took control of the situation and managed to put the final piece in the jigsaw. This was the last time that BFBS was not automatically included in the ORBAT – the Order of Battle – as an automatic, 'must consider', component of any operational deployment.

*****

So, the stage was now set and the real hardware needed to make ready the operation could be procured and shipped, by the book. We would be given a priority for military airfreight to transport our generators, transmitters and towers to Al Jubayl. We could also now send our staff out there, openly and in numbers. By early December, we had a small echelon of broadcast engineers building a chain of transmitters up and down the huge hinterland of Saudi Arabia, using a satellite delivery service as well as landlines, in order to get the signal up country. (This was unlike AFN, who had a series of local mobile stations.)

All appeared to be going well and we had decided that 15th December 1990 would see the official opening of BFBS Middle East. (We decided on that name as the fortunes of war might just force the station to change location.)

I travelled with Combined Services Entertainments Manager Les Austin to RAF Innsworth, where we were given some very eye-watering gas mask training, which involved being locked in a shed, waiting for the command, 'Gas! Gas! Gas!', putting on our gas masks very quickly and filing out of the shed, coughing a lot. Les had a beard which, miraculously, didn't break the airtight seal of his gas mask.

We were then led into a huge gymnasium, where an RAF clerk was stamping out ID discs ('dog tags') for Gulf personnel. I gave my name, stalled at my blood group, which I didn't know, was in the middle of saying, 'Oh, I can't remember', when I heard the hammer go down. The clerk had heard 'Oh' as 'O', and so that was my blood group. I reminded myself not to get shot.

Les asked for and got his disc, then caused quite a stir as he asked for a second disc for his charge.

'Name?' the clerk asked, in his 'I've got hundreds of these to do before lunch' voice.

'Sir Harry Secombe,' said Les.

Yes, the greatest Goon of all had agreed to make a 'grip and grin' visit to Al Jubayl at the same time we'd be opening the radio station. Suddenly the clerk woke up and nothing was too much trouble.

On our way out with all the kit – including a nuclear, biological and chemical oversuit and boots, jabs, papers and discs - I discovered there was one more hurdle. I was stopped, rather curtly, I thought, by an RAF Wing Commander. Still, my hair was just a tad long to be mistaken for military.

'Have you got your AIDS certificate?' he asked, sharply.

'No,' I replied.

'Name and host unit?' he continued. He wrote down my name and 'BFBS', signed the piece of paper and handed it to me.

I think he meant me to move on but I'm a bit suspicious about senior military officers handing out random bits of paper. This one carried out a simple, one sentence, slogan.

'I have examined this individual and have discovered that he is free from AIDS.'

It was pre-stamped, pre-signed and rather prescient, given that no examination at all had taken place. I then told him that BFBS stood for the British Forces *Broadcasting* Service. He went a bit pale and asked for the paper back. I told him that I was quite happy to accept it and that he shouldn't worry about me leaking this information to the BBC, as we were both batting for the same side - a revelation that didn't exactly ease his discomfiture. I compounded the felony with a big wink and left the building with our hefty kit bags, ready for the off.

The next day, I presented myself at RAF Brize Norton, home of 'Fly By Night Airways' – or the big Hercy bird to Riyadh. Les and Sir Harry were due to come out on the next day's flight, so I was travelling alone. There was the usual nonsense of 'hurry up and wait', but finally we were on board and we set our minds to neutral for the next few hours. The flight was not only uneventful, but shortened by the fact that I had some ear defenders, which managed to subdue the impression that a food mixer was inside my head, scrambling my tired brain.

We arrived at the military section of Riyadh International Airport at about 10pm local time. I was rather hoping to see our Station Controller elect, Chris Russell and to find out how to cross the country to Al Jubayl, but I was taken to a rather posher bus than the average and driven to the RAF transit hotel. The home-made sign outside the rather ramshackle building read: 'Fawlty Towers'. You can always rely on the British military's sense of humour.

I reported to reception. There was a huge intake of breath. I had forgotten about the 'Equivalent Military Rank' concept. I was head of a recognised formation. I was a Commanding Officer. My rank equivalent was full Colonel. I was important.

Suddenly, the rules changed. A car was found, with driver. I was to be taken to the Riyadh Sheraton, several floors of which had been leased to the RAF Movements team as senior officers' transit accommodation. I signed in and was delighted to hear that, as 'senior officer' in residence that night, I would be given the penthouse suite.

My kit bag and helmet were lovingly carried to the umpteenth floor and I was very soon installed in a suite of chambers not to be found outside Arabian Nights. Silk, satin and damask drapes covered hand-decorated walls, and luxuriant carpets and rugs climbed from the very floor to grip you snugly up to ankle height. Vaulted ceilings, carvings, mini-minarets, untold bowls of fruit, several rooms and the most deeply giving giant four-poster bed with an excess of yielding bolsters told me that I would sleep the sleep of a thousand sultans that night.

I couldn't believe my luck. This was the greatest luxury I had ever had to endure for my country. God, war was hell. I sank my teeth into a fresh, chilled peach, and felt all the stresses and strains slowly ebb from my body. Very soon, I would be…

It was then that the phone rang. I raised an eyebrow, then an elbow, then the receiver. It was Chris Russell. He was in the foyer. I invited him up. He appeared in full army combats, carrying his helmet. His desert boots were depositing sand on my exotic carpet. He didn't sit down.

'What's happening?' I prompted.

'I'm here to take you to Al Jubayl. The good news is that I've got a car. The bad news is that we've got to go back straight away, as there's a lot to do at base and there's no guarantee of being able to get you to Al Jubayl in time to open the station the morning after tomorrow.'

I looked around at my palatial quarters and in my head wished them a rather fond and premature farewell. Someone else would enjoy my temporary heaven for the night of his life.

*****

As we checked out, two sharp men-about-town, in full Saudi dress, noticed our uniforms and helmets and asked us where we were going. We told them we were off to Al Jubayl. Did they know which road would take us there? (It was difficult, as all the road signs were in Arabic, known to the ever urbane squaddie as 'wormspeak'.)

Thanks be to Allah, this was not to be a problem. They would drive their car in front of us and put us on the right road to Al Jubayl. Once we were on the road, it was a straight line journey of five hundred kilometres. They would be happy to help us.

As we left the hotel for our cars, I began to have niggling doubts. Here were two strong, fit men, with perfect teeth, comedy beards and rippling muscles, with plenty of room under their robes for a complete arsenal of weaponry, from scimitars to hand grenades, and they were going to drive us out of Riyadh, past the suburbs and out onto the lonely, moonlit road to our destination... I put the idea out of my mind. They seemed like nice boys.

Eventually, flashing brake lights told us to slow down. There was no other traffic. It was past midnight. We stopped directly behind their rather racy Porsche. They both stepped out, and each of them came to our windows. Ah well, if this was it, then Kismet.

Chris and I wound down our windows. A head-dress and face poked through on my side.

'Al Jubayl just down that road. You keep going, there is gas station on the way, very cheap!' grinned one of our potential murderers.

Chris's Saudi chimed in from the other side: 'Now, insh' Allah, you get to Al Jubayl safe and have good journey. And...'

We waited for the something special that his body language was implying.

'You fuck Saddam!'

'You fuck Saddam!' repeated my Saudi.

With such a blessing ringing in our ears, we set off through the long night to our destination.

*****

Driving down one of Saudi Arabia's smooth, straight, brand new eight-lane highways is an amazing experience. You see sand and stars. Occasionally stars and sand. If you are in a rented Toyota, at any speed over 120 km/h, which is compulsory if you want to get from Riyadh to Al Jubayl this week, you are forced to listen to a repeated, tinny, quasi-jingle that tells you that your speed is in excess of the arbitrary limit imposed by the authorities and ignored by every single driver in the country.

After three hours you don't notice the beeping any more. After six hours you've lost the will to live. Then a gas station appeared. Chris stopped and refuelled the car. It cost about the same as a Mars Bar. I reminded myself that we were NOT going to war over Iraq's co-incidental oil deposits.

Eventually we made it to Camp 4 at Al Jubayl. I was tired and had to lie down for an hour. My accommodation was a sandy room in a sandy Portakabin down a sandy road. I brushed sand off my biscuit mattress and lay down to dream of A thousand And One Nights in the penthouse suite of the Sheraton Hotel. All was well.

When I woke up, I put on my full combat uniform (it wasn't too hot!) and strolled around the camp till I found the BFBS sea container. It looked a bit battered and I was interested to see that a 'window' had been cut into the side with what must have been a giant can opener.

It didn't look at all soundproof. I walked in through the door at the end to see a familiar sight. Rising out from under the broadcasting desk, the camouflage covered arse of ace engineer, Peter 'Fook It' Ginn, busy doing what turned out to be the very last of the wiring. Within a couple of minutes he surfaced and told me we were hot to trot.

Using droit de seigneur for one of the few times in my life, I decided that I was going to be the one to open the station the next morning. I had also decided that, instead of using one-kilohertz tone to test the transmission chain, I would sit in the hot seat and do a pre-opening warm-up show, just to get used to the kit, the acoustics and the idiosyncrasies of having to brush and dust all the time because of the fine sand blowing through the open window. Peter went off for a tea and a biscuit, so I was left on my own to play some CDs and throw in some chat.

I guess I must have been on-air for about an hour when the studio door opened and a fully-kitted, armed to the teeth, roughy-toughy squaddie peered at me, as if he was examining a dog turd.

'BFBS?'

I smiled encouragingly, my chest bursting with pride.

'Yes,' I said. 'Official opening tomorrow.'

'You took your time,' he said, in a monotone, and shut the door behind him.

I was really chuffed. Translated into civvy speak, the squaddie had just informed me that he was over the moon that BFBS was actually here, live, alongside him and his mates.

There were two more visitors that evening. One was Lt Col Robert Gaylord of AFN, whom I had the opportunity to thank for letting our own Alton Andrews loose on his radio station. Robert was well into radio and we had a chat about the difference between what HQ thinks is going on and what actually happens in the field. He too was a pragmatist.

My next visitor was none other than Brigadier Patrick Cordingley, the charismatic 'Desert Rats' Commander. We knew each other slightly and he bounded over for a real soldier's handshake. When I had regained the use of my hand, I beckoned him to sit and we chatted about him coming over for the station opening and doing an interview.

He said that there were things he clearly couldn't talk about but that I should ask the questions anyway. After a few notes and guidelines, he asked if there was anything he should or shouldn't do. I was aware from an informal briefing that the lads on the front line were a bit hacked off because of the shortage of water. Could he mention that, or was it sensitive? Yes, he could mention it, as it had now been sorted. Anything else?

'Yes', I said, with some emphasis. 'You are a very important senior officer. When you say 'Charge!' your men will charge. They will respect you and follow your every order. But if you tell me that their morale is high, they will snigger and point fingers at the radio. That's what Colonel Blimps do. Please, Patrick, do not say 'morale is high'.'

Patrick looked a bit puzzled, but his face soon emerged into mood positive and he left me with, 'I'll try to remember that one.'

After the rehearsal, I wandered over to the cookhouse – good food – had coffee in the BFBS studio, then turned in for the night.

*****

I was up at 0600 military and the station was due to open at 0900. The guest list was quite impressive. As Head of BFBS Radio, I would open the station and play in the first song. I had decided on 'Love Shack' by the B52s. Live music would be supplied by the Band of the Royal Scots, playing directly outside the window of the BFBS container, using a crossed pair of microphones to pick up their songs.

Sir Harry Secombe would appear with his 'minder', CSE boss Les Austin. Then Brigadier Patrick would take centre stage, we'd busk it until 1200 and then all go off for some non-alcoholic drinks and non-pork canapés (warm Coke and cheese and onion crisps).

I watched as the Royal Scots set up their stands, organised their music and started rehearsing. Suddenly I felt very, very scared. The date was 15th December. The band was playing Christmas Carols. In Saudi Arabia.

I remember our verbal agreement with the Saudis as being 'experimental transmissions on a non-interference basis', but if they heard their airwaves being polluted by references to mangers, baby Jesus, Christian men rejoicing and herald angels, then our time in Saudi was not going to be very long.

I had words with the bandmaster. It was worse than I thought. They had bussed in from far too far away to go back. The bus had gone. The only parts they had brought with them were Christmas carols. No, they couldn't play standards by ear. Not all in the same key.

You know that moment when the cartoon light bulb above your head goes 'click' and the word of the day is suddenly 'Eureka!'? Well, I had thought of the solution. It was based on the premise that no local rural Saudis had ever heard any western Christmas carols and so if we played 'Hark the Herald Angels Sing' and called it 'Summer Serenade', then honour would be satisfied, as long as nobody actually sang any words.

The bandmaster and I had a great time turning Christmas carol titles into innocuous 'Happy Memory' pseudonyms and nobody was any the wiser. Sir Harry was brilliant, as ever, and did the full range of noises from his unique trademark repertoire. The Royal Scots played cheerfully, and in tune, and really added to the atmosphere of the opening. And then came Brigadier Patrick.

It was Patrick who actually caused the only accident and injury of the morning. I asked him several questions about his Desert Rats and what they were up to. He gave me the best answers he could and talked his troops up so well, without false flattery, I would have been proud to serve under him, even though my capacity was as a cowering jelly in the corner. He was really enjoying the interview and I could feel this massive wave of powerful and positive enthusiasm, grit and determination coming through.

It was then that he suddenly gripped my knee.   Very hard.

'I'm sorry, Peter. I *have* to say it!'

Oh dear. Through the wincing, I knew what was going to happen.

'Perhaps I shouldn't – but it *is* true. I have never in my life seen morale *so* high. We are ready for anything!'

You might imagine that the pain in my knee was a small price to pay. Patrick didn't even know he'd done it. We parted on very friendly terms. The next time we were destined to meet would be at the Great Yorkshire Show, by which point he was a recently-retired Major-General. He still behaved with the enthusiasm of a man decades younger. A real star.

My time was over. I was driven back to Riyadh, very proud of what our engineers had built, and very proud of the broadcasting staff, who very soon would be involved in a real shooting war.

The next two days passed in a dream – at times a bad one involving a Hercy bird - but lunchtime on the third day saw me marching up to the big house at Chalfont Grove to see the MD, Alan Protheroe.

I was really showing off. I still had evidence of sand on my combats; I was wearing army boots and helmet and was red-eyed and unshaven. I slumped down in one of his green leather chairs and he brought me over a tonic. We had a good chat. Colonel A.H. Protheroe appeared well chuffed. So was I.

*****

My job now was to monitor staff movements, detach various individuals and make sure that the output was the best that it could be. While the short wave transmissions on BBC frequencies were being broadcast from BFBS London, we, like the BBC, had in effect 'banned' certain records from being played.

Those songs included 'Eve of Destruction' from Jeff Wayne's 'War Of The Worlds' and, slightly more obtusely, 'The Air That I Breathe'. I felt that, from the distance of the UK, it would be a bit cold-blooded to be playing such songs, especially when we would be examining casualty lists on a daily basis to make sure that we weren't playing a record 'from Trooper Mike Wilkinson at Blackadder Camp for everyone at No 21, Maple Close, Edgbaston' when Trooper Wilkinson had just trodden on a land mine.

However, once the BFBS station was 'live and local' and our presenters were at the same risk of being hit by the same Scud missiles as the rest of the soldiery, then the rules changed. Military humour ruled. All of the banned records were not only played, but highlighted as 'The Saddam Hit List', which was updated every day.

Various personnel came and went. Dusty Miller found time to have a heraldic shield made to represent 'Jack's Shack', as the studio had become known. A Saudi-funded truck came round every day, taking orders from each unit for $5000.00 of 'things you might need', which is how Dave Boyle ended up not only with a pool table for the newly acquired offices, but a genuine reason for its purchase: in the case of a Scud attack, you dived under it. It appeared on the manifest as an air raid shelter.

My favourite cabaret was when I put Jonathan 'Knocker' Bennett in charge. I had given him the usual spiel of calling me 24/7 if he needed anything. He took me at my word. On one memorable occasion I was just digesting a late supper at home in High Wycombe, when the phone rang. It was Knocker.

'Boss, we're under attack,' he told me, a bit out of breath. 'There've been a few Scuds flying over. Wait one - I think another's coming over. I'll just shut the studio door.'

Yes, that would have saved his life. I think even he realised that after a few more minutes of clearly being still very much on the planet.

The second time was even funnier. Again, wee small hours and the phone went. I picked up the receiver. A strange noise emanated from the other end. It made no sense at all but had the spirit of apprehension about it.

'Achhhhfnyyaw snarrrrr hphhhhmphh smchnurrrr fnah!' it pleaded.

Suddenly I knew what it was.

'Knocker, for Christ's sake take off that bloody gas mask and talk to me.'

Someone on the staff had put the rumour around that there was to be a gas attack that night. I never did find out who it was, but everybody there with him remained a suspect.

*****

Eventually the Iraqis were knocked out by a pincer movement that caught them straight in the nads. The coalition forces made a triumphant entrance into Kuwait.

Charly Lowndes, a jeep, a dish and a BFBS transmitter beat the Yanks to Kuwait, and on our limited resources, BFBS was the first English language service out of the liberated country. We had won the war.

Although I'd really only had a walk-on part, I was very proud of what we had done. A fighting war was one feather in the cap.

The ultimate triumph, though, was still to win the Cold War. By now, the Berlin Wall was down, communist rule in Germany had been swept aside, and I had seen it happen, just as I'd seen the Wall going up in August 1961.

It was now the spring of 1991. It would be another three years before my destiny as a Cold War victor was to be fulfilled.

Chapter 26

The Big Five Oh

Back in leafy Bucks, there were to be further developments. By this time David Hatch had become the Vice-Chairman of SSVC's Board of Management. David was coming to the end of his tenure as Managing Director, BBC Network Radio, but would retain a senior role at Aunty, as special advisor to the incoming Director-General, John Birt.

As it turned out, he also became my special advisor. I could never stop thanking David for everything he did for me. He suggested that, in order to make my mark, I should hold a drinks party. He had an idea that he might be able to book the Holy of Holies in Broadcasting House, the BBC's Principal Shrine, the Director-General's council chamber, for this great event. Alan Protheroe thought this was a good idea, too.

David went away, organised the whole thing, including invitations to all the great and good, all the catering and even the special security and passes for the evening. About two hundred guests were invited, some of whom really glowed in the dark. We had a wonderful time in this beautiful, oak pannelled, tall-ceilinged room, hung with portraits of the great and the good, and the party was declared a rip-roaring success.

Two days later I received a letter from David, copied to the Board, telling me what a great idea of mine it had been to stage the party, how forceful I was in getting him to help organise it, how I had nagged him and nagged him until he was forced to give in, and how I'd clearly made a host of new contacts and, together with my staff, had helped raise the profile BFBS within the upper echelons of the BBC.

It seemed my Guardian angel was packing heat – and he wasn't going to disappear any time soon. It certainly improved the confidence of this quiet and occasionally shy broadcaster.

It wasn't too long before my mindset, as Assistant Director (Radio), was given a new direction. Alan Protheroe decided he no longer wished to subsume the role of Director of Broadcasting. The situation was complicated by the presence of an Assistant Director (Television), Gordon Randall, a formidable professional whom Alan had coaxed out of semi-retirement to update the SSVC TV operation. Gordon was about to hand in his dinner pail, so whoever became the new Director of Broadcasting would be responsible for the TV operation as well. Oh yes, and overall boss of Combined Services Entertainment.

One day, Colin Rugg and I were summoned to the big house. Rosemary sat us down in her office and, after a suitable period of waiting, Colin was decanted through into Alan's parlour. We hadn't the faintest idea why we were there. Both of us were back-cataloguing over past crimes and misdemeanours but we couldn't find anything on our radar that warranted this sudden call to arms.

After a while, Colin emerged. His face was red and, unusually, he didn't connect. He muttered a cryptic line, 'Don't worry, it's not bad news,' before I went in.

Alan was in his most dangerous position – arms behind his back, gazing out of the huge floor to ceiling windows onto the rolling sward of the lawn. He didn't immediately turn around when I went in. I stood by a chair but didn't sit down. Alan spoke, still without turning.

'We are going to make some vital and drastic changes,' he said. 'Part of those changes includes you.'

At the 'you', he swivelled round, fixed me with a hard look that would have received the approval of Judge Jefferies, and indicated that I should sit. A bit like the Woodhouse woman of TV fame telling her dogs to 'sit-t-t-t!', I sat.

Alan then proceeded to draw up a sketch map of a brighter, more engaging, vibrant, exciting, brain-straining, delightful, multi-coloured, multimedia world of the new BFBS Radio and SSVC

TV, where both would use the common resource of talent to become so much larger than the sum of their parts. He went on for quite some time, but I was a willing audience, as he had the power of eloquence and the ability to twist the spoken language around his little finger.

Finally he stopped, and fixed on me a steady, but neutral stare. I had not realised it, but he was just about to hand me Excalibur.

'Peter,' he almost declaimed, 'I have today appointed Colin Rugg as Assistant Managing Director, as well as Director of Engineering.'

He waited for this significant bombshell to explode. As the debris and smoke cleared away, he continued, almost with a messianistic tremor in his voice.

'And I am appointing you Director of Broadcasting'.

Nah. He was having a laugh. Let's think. Three years earlier, I was a jobbing producer, quite low down in the pecking order – about fortieth out of the then ninety in succession to the throne - and now here was this funny little Welshman telling me I was God.

I half-grinned, not wanting to spoil the impact of what Alan was saying, but just because the whole scene had become surreal. The rest of the meeting dissolved into a maelstrom of confused thoughts and cross-purpose conversations, but the following day I received confirmation from the Personnel department that I was now indeed monarch of all that I surveyed. Gulp – again.

*****

I now began a series of trips to visit the staff and assess the output of each of our radio stations overseas. This meant not very exotic trips to Germany, reasonably interesting trips to Cyprus and Gibraltar, and then some amazing journeys to Belize, Brunei and the Falklands. Oh yes – and Las Vegas.

I made a total of five visits to the kingdom of 'Lost Wages', home of 'tight slots' and subdued sin, and fell totally in love with the place. I should say that my reasons for going to Vegas were always professional, for it was, and is, the home of the annual conference to end all conferences, the National Association of Broadcasters convention, where the great and the good, the hucksters and the shysters, the brilliant and the demented demonstrate their wares, their ambitions, their dreams, and their ideas against a sea of mild danger, scantily clad ladies, free drinks and a million ways of being parted from your money.

Over a time I compiled a list of what to do or not to do rules for a successful Vegas visit.

1. On arrival in your hotel bedroom, hang your brain on a hook behind the door. You won't be needing it.

2. Check your bed. If it's a four-poster with a mirror inside the bed ceiling, change your room immediately. There is nothing worse than waking up in a strange bed and seeing the disgusting reflection of a horizontal, naked you, only feet away from your face.

3. Eat in casinos. The food is nourishing, cheap and is served quickly. They need you back at the tables as soon as possible.

4. Play the cheap slots. Even though the return rate is about 99% (in the UK it's about 70%), it takes quite a long time for you to lose. A bucket full of nickels is still permission to sit at a machine and feed it all night. If you are a drinker, you will still be eligible for 'Carktails', breathlessly delivered to your seat by a

pneumatic Californian blonde in a quasi-Playboy costume waiting for her prince to come. The drinks are free; the tip is a dollar.

5. Wear a watch. There are no clocks or windows on the casino floor, which is open for business 24/7. You need to know when you're tired. I have seen well-upholstered blue rinsers slide off their stools, snoring by the time they've hit the deck. Adrenalin and margueritas are not best companions.

6. Don't worry about crime. If you are a decrepit pensioner taking a stroll down the main drag, with a roll of greenbacks clearly sticking out of your pocket, you are perfectly safe. If you are a single girl, you are perfectly safe. You will not see a policeman all night. This is for a very good reason. Las Vegas is a town whose entire philosophy is to extract as much money from you in return for giving you some fun. It is inevitable that you will lose money. That is why Las Vegas is huge, powerful, and an enduring people magnet. So, if anybody gets in the way of Las Vegas legally removing your money, that person will be stopped. The police know this too, and are quite happy to pick up the pieces after the body has been discovered in the dark alleyway. Nobody appears to worry too much about being robbed or raped. It may not be moral but it's part of the Vegas contract.

7. You will have to work very hard to be caught up in a scandal. Vegas is for gambling. Reno is for brothels. Vegas tips its cap to some frisson of assumed sexuality by providing little Latinos with pencil moustaches who tout flyers up and down the strip. All of them advertise 'I will dance naked in your room holding your hand for $50', complete with a sugary portrait of a nubile and a telephone number. Reports indicate that this is what they do. They even bring their own music, courtesy of a boogie box. Anything further than hand holding instantly brings security to deal with the number of teeth you might like to consider losing if you persist in inappropriate behaviour. There is an apocryphal story concerning one dumb traveller who asked for *two* dancing girls. Apart from the cacophony of two competing boogie-boxes, there was the greater problem of each girl holding a hand, leaving him no hands to engage in whatever he might have had in mind...

8. Choose your meals carefully. The best nosh of the day is breakfast. An American breakfast is an exercise in cornucopian delights. Where else could you have a huge plate containing bacon, waffles, grits, gravy, eggs, steaks, tomatoes, fries, fried bread, toast, butter, pancakes, jams, fruit compotes, maple syrup, beans, accompanied by all the cawfee you can drink, and then get up from your table and have it all over again? Nobody does anything more than grazing at lunchtime, and the evening is given over to the locals making culinary boasts to each other about who can eat their own body weight in steak in the shortest

time. Breakfast is the only real meal of the day.

9. Know which foods to avoid and which foods will disappoint. After a million cowboy movies, the coffee myth is the worst. American cawfee tastes weak, has no body and its decaf version is only hot coloured water. If you put two drops of milk in it, it goes a pasty grey-white. Europeans just shake their heads. But there's no escape. Tea is a mystery to the USA. They know what it is, but can't believe people drink it. All dairy products are suspect. American milk is not sterilised, it's neutralised. It's white and tastes of nothing. Consequently, butter – only available in rock-hard tublets – tastes of nothing, and as for their cheese – always advertised as the generic 'cheese': it comes out of a tube and tastes of nothing. Bread is white, sliced and tastes of nothing. It does, though, serve as a cold compress in case of a cut or graze, as it is always served cold from the fridge and is invariably damp.

10. Go to a show. Vegas has the best shows on the planet. I can guarantee that if you suddenly went there tonight, you'd be able to find at least one of your favourite artistes performing in the most luxurious of surroundings. Vegas *is* a show and they very much like you to be part of it. As I mentioned, I went five times...

Now, where was I? Oh yes. I went to Vegas for professional reasons and learned a hell of a lot from the positive, chin-jutting, dynamic American approach to broadcasting. Yes, we are divided by culture and language, but there still remain acres of common ground. I sat through an entire

Apple launch lecture/cabaret one year and brought a phrase back with me - 'the sigma curve of isoquant' – which was Apple's current position.

I asked an Apple minion to explain this phrase to me.

The Greek letter sigma starts with a small curve at the bottom, then shoots upwards and slightly away for a long distance before ending in another tiny curve. So, a sigma curve indicates a powerful status change, a sudden climb, a breaking of tradition.

'Iso' is another Greek word, meaning (for these purposes) 'measurable'.

'Quant' is from the Latin 'quantum', meaning 'a measure of', and, by extension, a large measure - a quantity.

Put it all together and, rather prosaically, it means 'a bloody big and important step-change.'

But 'the sigma curve of iso-quant' is pure Starship Enterprise poetry. It enthrals and it motivates. It's perfect Yankee bullshit. And it works.

When I got back from Vegas that year, I tried it on Alan Protheroe. He had the grace to dry his eyes on his handkerchief after he'd stopped laughing. He quite liked the slogan from the next year, though: 'Think globally – act locally.'

Sometimes those Americans can hit the nail on the head. This was tailored for our operation. We used it, and did it, a lot in the years leading up to the global goal.

'By the year 2000,' I had sloganized back in 1994, 'BFBS will be available to every serviceman and woman in the world.' And that was before streaming had even started.

*****

The Gulf War may have been over – at least part one was - but we were conscious that BFBS needed to prove further to the MOD that we were ready to be placed on the Orbat.

I took on a Gulf War veteran, Phil Collins, as 'Broadcast Liaison Officer' (an unfortunate title, as he became universally known as 'the BLO job'). He had been commissioned after making his way through the ranks so was a member of the khaki mafia who knew both sides of the divide between officers and NCOs, and thus knew how to play one off against the other.

His companion in arms was a REME Warrant Officer called David Bailey – I know: Phil Collins and David Bailey… – who set up 'Punch FM' to broadcast at the Royal Tournament, and who went on to produce and present for BFBS.

Phil and David discovered a piece of magic called the UIN – unit identification number – and discovered that, pre-SKC merger, BFBS actually had a UIN, which somehow had not been withdrawn on privatisation. I was quite alarmed when they used this hooky UIN to requisition an Army three-ton truck, which they painted in UN white, plus a host of ancillary kit, uniforms, tools, spares and a considerable amount of material, all backed up in ledger form and countersigned by all the right elements of the Quartermaster staff.

Alan Protheroe and I attended the launch of 'Gladys II' (Gladys I was a British Liberation Army mobile forces broadcasting unit from 1944), which included the breaking of a bottle of champagne on the front bumper.

Gladys was used on the front line with the ACE Mobile Force (Land) in Northern Norway, buried in ice, broadcasting to Royal Marines on exercise. She also went over to Germany but her biggest triumph was her journey to all the old wartime Forces Broadcasting stations to coincide with the opening of the 'BFBS 50' anniversary exhibition at the National Army Museum.

Rory Higgins, an accomplished broadcaster with a very dry sense of humour and a passing resemblance to George Orwell, became 'CO' of the '1st FMBU, BFPO 786' – the Field Mobile Broadcasting Unit, BFBS UK, aka. 'Gladys' – and took her around Italy, France, Austria and Germany, where her presence ensured large crowds and lots of goodwill.

Meanwhile, back at base, we were busy organising the 50th anniversary event at the National Army Museum. Alan Grace, our retired Head of Broadcast Administration, had become the de facto Head of BFN/BFBS Archives and he helped assemble a variety of kit and memorabilia for this BFBS showcase. Alan Protheroe used his good offices, and those of the rest of the SSVC Board, to arrange the presence of a royal guest of honour - our patron, Princess Margaret.

One the morning of the great event of 1993 – fifty years since the opening of the first Forces Broadcasting station in an Algerian harem – we were all a little nervous, as the men in black with sniffer dogs covered every inch of the site ahead of the royal visitation, and eventually pronounced us 'clean'.

We were aware that Princess Margaret operated her own code of conduct and expected others to know, almost by telepathy, what she, and we, were supposed to do next.

Outside, MD, Alan Protheroe, and SSVC chairman, General Sir Geoffrey Howlett, waited for the royal car. Inside, our front line was represented by me, as Director of Broadcasting, and my chum, Assistant Managing Director, Colin Rugg.

There we stood, a couple of chancers, rubbing our shoes on the backs of our trouser legs to add a bit of shine, giggling like schoolboys and wondering out loud how deep to bow, what *not* to say and whether we could get away with a curtsy.

Suddenly the glass doors swung open and Chairman, MD and the Royal Presence marched purposefully towards us.

Colin was introduced to the Princess.

'Ee hya na smeen farquar smiddle nya Haquer?' she implied. It sounded very posh, but English it wasn't. Colin peered at her for an instant. She was smiling.

'Yes, ma'am,' he said, remembering to rhyme it with 'ham', not 'harm'.

Princess Margaret seemed satisfied, and suddenly she was standing right in front of me.

She gave me the expression specially reserved for a corgi that had peed on the carpet. I was duly introduced. I stepped forward and managed a bow that would have gone down well with the Japanese Imperial Navy.

This is where we move into slow motion. I was in mid-bow as she spoke to me. As with Colin, what I heard was not strictly English – apart from the last two words.

'Hengyop strah canna smeo thragacanthus *older people*?'

As I emerged from the bow, I could hear that her expression had softened. This was a real person who had asked a real question, and she wanted an answer. As she was royal, an answer was compulsory. The only clues I had were the words 'older people'.

Remember, I was still emerging from a bow as she was speaking. Holding the bow for a second, I answered her with what started as a low mutter, timing my response so that my head was facing hers with my last words.

'Bimble yay a snerd farquar *younger people*, ma'am!' I ended triumphantly.

She smiled, extended a handful of light, easily breakable porcelain fingers, gave my sweaty hand the most perfunctory of wobbles, and moved on.

I noticed a Protheroe eyebrow and a sardonic grin in the background, but I seemed to have passed muster.

Princess Margaret was due to shimmy up to the Long Gallery, where a lunchtime drinks party was to be held in her honour. The pre-visit letter of advice from the Lord Napier & Ettrick (turned out to be the same bloke) advised that 'Her Royal Highness does not consume alcohol before luncheon,' – my, how we laughed – 'but would favour a chilled tonic, in a suitable glass, with fresh ice and a slice of lemon. The lemon should appear whole on the salver, and there should be a sharp knife so that she might cut an appropriate slice herself.'

It would be fair to say in our defence, Your Honour, that everything was checked. The temperature of the tonic, the clarity of the ice, the cleanliness of the glass, the appropriate size of the silver-handled knife, the spotlessness of the fresh lemon, the strength of the waiter's hold on his tray and the sheen of the freshly ironed linen napkin, providing a resting place for all of the above. Two BFBS staff had been assigned to clear a way for the waiter, so that no accident might keep Princess and tonic apart.

The moment of truth arrived. HRH had the usual knot of admirers around her when she indicated that, for her, the bar should now be opened. A quiet snapping of fingers summoned the waiter, whose radar was first class. He almost floated to the side of the presence, where he held out the tray with some flourish and a very steady, sturdy hold.

The Princess poured the tonic, picked up the knife and dented the lemon. Suddenly her Hanoverian mouth tightened. She poked at the lemon again, this time with some vigour. The waiter's face began to go red as HRH attempted to slice into the lemon with genuine force.

The knife was silver. It was ornamental, dummy. The blade was blunt. Luckily, the situation was saved by the appearance of a real cutting knife, and very soon the sparkling of laughter joined the sparkling of tonic. Somewhere in the bowels of the National Army Museum, someone was receiving fifty lashes and a P45.

My only other encounter of note during the celebration came when I spotted my very first boss in BFBS, Peter Buckle, the misanthrope martinet who had sent the 'Next time, don't send a bloody recruit' signal to Ian Woolf after I'd been on station in Singapore for a week in 1971.

I recognised him after twenty-two years and walked over to say hello. He looked me up and down, and offered his hand with much greater reluctance than Princess Margaret had shown.

'Ah, Peter,' he almost spat. 'I note you're still with BFBS after all these years. You're something to do with administration now, aren't you?'

I decided not to give him the pleasure. He carried his own prison around with him.

'That's right, Peter,' I smiled broadly. 'You remembered. I was always *so* good at admin.'

He almost winced, and just walked away. Sad, really.

*****

The final highlight of the BFBS 50 celebration was a Forces' Broadcasting appearance at the Royal Tournament. It was kept well under wraps, and almost in the shadow of a second royal visit. Following the 'surprise' at the Tournament, the SSVC VIP contingent would repair to a private area, where we would be met by Prince Edward, who would then join us for a special dinner.

The evening of the great event arrived and I took my place with the SSVC/BFBS top nobs in the expensive seats. The chairman, Sir Geoffrey Howlett, was host, wearing the most amazing red velvet Edwardian smoking jacket. Alan Protheroe was more formally dressed, apart from the usual crooked smile. I was bemused.

Just before the start of the evening proper, a familiar voice rang out through Earls Court. Richard Astbury. Asters. He was commentating on the early days of Forces' Broadcasting and explaining the role of a truck called Gladys. Suddenly a 1940s Army lorry coughed, spluttered and kangarooed its way into the huge sawdust arena. Stabs of light nailed Gladys II, right in the centre.

Asters then introduced some of the famous names whose careers had begun in the Forces' Broadcasting family: the actor, Nigel Davenport, who had started out with BFN Hamburg;

David Jacobs, DJ with Radio SEAC in Ceylon; Peter Donaldson, BBC Radio 4's chief newsreader, formerly with BFBS in Aden; Patrick Lunt of BBC Radio 2, once a BFBS Cologne DJ; Sarah Kennedy, once of BFBS Singapore and now an award-winning radio & television presenter.

Each, in turn, was helped down from the truck's tailboard by our very own engineer, 'Corporal' Roger Dunn, wearing 1940s army uniform, and each received a cheer and a round of applause from the audience as they waved their way to the edge of the arena.

They had clearly saved the best until last. Asters introduced the man who had once read the news for BFBS in the Falkland Islands when he was Commander British Forces there -the man who had, as Gulf War Commander, demanded that a BFBS radio station be installed in the Gulf so he could talk to his troops. It was of course, General Sir Peter de la Billière. He leapt off the truck with a huge grin and was nearly knocked over by the wall of noisy appreciation coming from the ranks. It would be fair to say that this was the moment when BFBS and the Army top brass came together.

After the show was over, we all trooped down to the private area to be introduced to Prince Edward, who arrived with a small party. He was knowledgeable and charming, and obviously hugely interested in the broadcasting aspect of our operation. He had only recently set up his own media company, Ardent Films.

Sadly, this is where the visit became slightly unstuck. Protocol demanded that the Prince should sit next to our senior representative. This, of course, was General Sir Geoffrey Howlett, whose principal conversation revolved around killing people, 1940s cricket and its virtues, and raising bantams. None of these seemed to engage the good Prince, who nodded, smiled politely, and even tried to join in, but eventually made enough signals for his equerry to remember another important engagement.

But the evening had been fun, and had put the seal of approval on our own, sometimes shaky, operation. We had been given the total establishment tick in the box. We were now utterly kosher, recognised by royalty and generals, as well as our wonderful and unique audience. Morale was high and the future looked rosy. But there were of course, shadows in the sunlight.

*****

Alan Protheroe's undisputedly cavalier leadership - 'I've never bothered with budgets in my life!' - and his unreconstructible contrariness made for some exciting Board of Management meetings, at which we directors were 'in attendance' (so 'speak when you're spoken to'), but the world was changing.

It became clear that Alan was about to hand in his dinner pail after the 50th anniversary and it seemed, from large clues being dropped at board meetings, that Air Vice-Marshal David Crwys-Williams – another Welshman – would be taking over. Alan whispered in my ear that David's style of management would be rather different. How right he was. But first of all we had to give Mr. Protheroe a proper send off.

A dinner was suggested at the Bull Hotel, near Gerrards Cross, with its private dining room. I was asked to provide some entertainment, which became a radio-style 'This Is Your Life', featuring a host of digs about Bugs Bunny (Alan had two very prominent porcelain front teeth), Welshness, the Army, the BBC, 'the *only* way', cigarettes and eloquence. Colin Rugg played the role of engineer and span in taped inserts.

The whole thing was delightfully scurrilous and went down well. I'd brought my guitar along and, as an encore, we got to sing 'Goodnight Big Al' to the tune of 'Goodnight Irene'. The sound of knights of the realm, Group Captain Sir Gordon Pirie and General Sir Geoffrey Howlett, attempting to sing after four courses and lots of wine and brandy was an amazing thing and I think it would be fair to say that a good time was had by all – apart from one huge breach of protocol between the life Vice-Chairman, Sir Gordon, and me.

It started off quite innocuously. After the pud had been cleared, the smokers among us lit up. My cigarette caused a comment from Sir Gordon, two stops down the table from me.

'Ah, David!' he began.

I was used to it. He always called me David, even after I'd reminded him, many times, that I was Peter. Eventually I gave in and answered to the name he preferred. It was easier.

Sir Gordon looked at me over his half-moon spectacles, his bald, shiny pate gleaming in the chandelier's light and his large frame bisected at nipple level by a giant cummerbund.

'I used to smoke, you know, David!' He looked proudly around him, then back at me. He frowned slightly to emphasise the point he was making.

'I used to smoke forty Peter Stuyvesant a day. One day I gave up. Just like that.'

He paused slightly, for dramatic effect, then spoke in capital letters: '*I AM A NON SMOKER.*'

I looked at him squarely, and in a quiet voice, which still carried, as his statement had ensured total silence around the table, I replied steadily.

'No, Sir Gordon. You are *not* a non-smoker. You are an *ex*-smoker.'

This was said quietly, respectfully, but also with some degree of confidence. I was gambling on him taking it the right way.

There was a distinct 'he's for it now!' frisson in the room. Even Big Al looked nervous. A low rumbling emanated from the almost shaking frame of the good Sir Gordon. His eyebrows described several acrobatic manoeuvres and his breathing seemed to be coming in gulps. His cheeks became ruddier than usual and he placed both hands, palms down, on the tablecloth with a resounding slap.

'Oh, my, David, you've got me there! *Ex*-smoker – not *non*-smoker. You're right of course, David – well done!'

There then followed the obligatory accolade, which Sir Gordon used to emphasise approval.

'I salute you!'

The evening was a triumph. Alan Protheroe enjoyed it all and wasn't in the least bit offended. Sir Gordon had rubber-stamped it and David Crwys-Williams wrote me a very nice letter saying he'd nearly wet himself laughing.

*****

Little did I know that my glory days were now coming to an end and that changes at the top were about to return me to full-time membership of the Escape Committee.

Whereas Alan was insight, intuition and inspiration, David was precise, pernickety (to me, then, at least) and patronising. He had a patrician drawl, which sounded very elegant, and occasionally masked his otherwise excellent sociability and sense of humour. I really tried hard to work to his methodology but it wasn't destined to be an easy ride.

With Alan, I had been used to going into the office, suggesting we go from A to B, and describing the pros and cons of doing it. This usually ended with Alan saying 'It's the only way!' and me going and doing it.

With David, the process was agonisingly cerebral and inclusive. All directors had to be involved in a discussion about what was best for the SSVC corporation, rather than each individual division (Radio, TV, CSE and, by this point, the British Defence Film Library). The route map from A to B was declared too simplistic: we had to effectively model A to B via C, D, E and 3.2, purple and dy by dx. In the end, we invariably seemed to end up on the original A to B journey. I found this very frustrating and was rapidly losing interest. Which is not a good thing to be indicating to a new boss.

My swan song as a Cold War warrior was much on my mind. I was born in Berlin during the 1948 Airlift. I was there when the Wall went up on 13th August 1961 and I was there a couple of days after it had come down on 3rd October 1989. I had even watched the 'wallpeckers' carve out my own individual chunk of personal Berlin Wall, glue it to a thin disc from a tree's trunk and felt tip the crude slogan, 'Berlin 89/90', in large, rough letters.

After the fall of the Wall, the Russians had stayed on in Berlin, as they had no barracks to go back to, so there were still Allied Forces from the USA, UK and France in occupation of the no longer divided city. We learned that the Russians would be pulling out in 1994 and that meant the end of our BFBS Berlin operation.

David was kind enough to allow me the honour of closing down the station. There would be a huge celebration and the end of BFBS's live and local broadcasting would effectively coincide with the end of the Cold War, which the Allies appeared to have won.

I say 'appeared' because, as they were yet to find out, the momentum for victory had been provided by me and thirteen tanks.

Chapter 27

For You The War Is Over

1994. The year my life as a Cold War warrior came to an end. The year I could hang up my weapon, which I had been trained to use at BFN, then at RIAS (Rundfunk im Amerikanischen Sektor - Radio in the American Sector), SFB (Sender Freies Berlin - Radio Free Berlin), and finally, for the last twenty-five years, at BFBS.

My weapon was a genuine WMD. It was small but packed a powerful punch in the right hands. Its range could be local or global, it could influence troop movements, morale, or topple nations. I used it as my weapon of choice. It was, of course, the microphone.

I had first encountered it in the fifties, as a ten-year-old, when I was asked by the then Forces Broadcasting organisation in Berlin, BFN, to do a rugby report from the giant Maifeld, a grassed parade ground of stupendous size at the far end of the Olympic Stadium. I sat on the huge stone steps not far from where Hitler used to review his troops, trying to make sense of this alien game and its odd rules. Somehow I managed to do a credible report, but purists would have noticed that all of it took place within the last five minutes of the match.

The next time I broadcast in Berlin, it was to sing nursery rhymes for an English learning project. A small choir of a dozen of us spotty Herberts, all about 10 years old, was corralled into a studio, where we dutifully sang songs about Georgy Porgy and Old Mother Hubbard. We sang with some gusto, as we had been paid in advance. Five Deutschmarks each. I felt really grown up as I patted the coins in my shirt pocket. I felt really tiny and stupid when the engineer stopped the recording because some idiot was patting coins in his shirt pocket and had ruined the recording. Our teacher administered the necessary bollocking and the session continued. At least I was now a professional broadcaster, as well as being a young Cold War warrior.

The Sender Freies Berlin broadcasts were much later on, when I was with BFBS. My opinion was sought on the implications of the fall of the Wall and I was chosen as a spokesman because I worked for a proper broadcasting organisation, and they knew I spoke German and had grown up in Berlin. I asked them if I could do the interview in English, as my German was rather rusty. They didn't like this at all so, catching the mood, I said I could probably manage the Berlin dialect. They then had a committee meeting to see if the use of Berlin dialect was within the rules. After much toing and froing, it was determined that no German would be allowed to deviate from 'Hochdeutsch' – High German – but a strange foreign broadcaster could besmirch the language of Bismarck and Goethe with his own take.

Unfortunately, the Irish inside me had become a little tetchy at all of this equivocation, so when 'spokesman said' gave me the results of the Berlin jury, I was a little peeved. I decided to give it the *real* dialect - the one that makes dustmen cringe at the noise it makes. We had an interesting interview, with loads of gratuitous grunting from me contrasting with the highly polished questions prepared by the SFB Central Editorial Questioning Unit (Foreign Languages Division). Eyebrows were raised but the interview was live so there wasn't much they could do about it.

But now this was all going to come to an end. My career as a Cold War warrior had started in the British Military Hospital in Spandau; thence to Plonerstrasse in the rather upmarket Grunewald; on to Kastanienallee in Charlottenburg; a spell in the 'Englische Siedlung' (the English Ghetto) around Dickensweg, and later Heerstrasse. Then we moved down to Ahornallee and our final territorial claim to Berlin was Churchill House apartments on Karolingerplatz. My folks had finally left Berlin in 1979, by which point Dad was one of the longest serving Brits in the divided city, with thirty-three years before the mast.

My career with BFBS had begun as a volunteer in the old BFBS studio in the roof of 46 Army Education Centre in Brooke Barracks, Spandau; then Summit House, on Theodor- Heuss-Platz; and finally, we were to say goodbye forever from the warders' block of the former Spandau Prison next to Smuts Barracks - where those thirteen tanks were accommodated. At last, me and thirteen tanks were to be the closest we had ever been.

A large party of SSVC/BFBS employees made the journey to what used to be West Berlin – now of course, just Berlin – but one of the most delightful guests of honour was not a colleague, but a listener. Heidi Brauer had grown up in East Berlin, where she had risked life and limb by listening to BFBS from 'over the Wall'. Yes, even having BFBS on your radio dial was verboten in the East during the Cold War.

Heidi arrived at the BFBS Berlin closing ceremony with a small number of cassettes containing recordings of old BFBS programmes that she had taped and then wrapped in foil and buried in her garden so the Stasi couldn't find them. She had smuggled them out of the East in the family car when the Brauers were expelled from the wonderful GDR and we actually got to hear an excerpt of one of my programmes from the late seventies. I sounded like a complete twit.

We assembled in the studios for the farewell thrash. A number of BFBS presenters were around – Aidan

Donovan, Alan Phillips, Baz Reilly and more - bringing with them shed loads of memories and audio, covering the history of BFBS Berlin.

Finally it was time for me to take to the hot seat and say goodbye. I had wondered how to close. The easy bit was the 'thank you for listening'; the hard bit, given our very loyal but unofficial German audience, was how to say 'goodbye'. Usually, this would be 'Auf wiedersehen' – literally, 'to the again-seeing' or 'till we meet again'.

But we didn't *want* to meet again under these circumstances. We were saying farewell as occupying powers, however friendly we might have been for many of those forty-nine years. Also, BFBS had a reputation for its informality and friendliness so I didn't want to say goodbye in a pompous or portentous way. When it came to it, I contented myself with a simple 'tchüß!' – best translated as 'Cheers!' – which seemed to fit the bill.

No sooner had I closed the microphone for the last time than the engineers arrived to strip out the studios. As folk – Berliners, military, TV crews, colleagues - milled around, saying nice things, I had to get out of that building as quickly as possible.

From the new NAAFI complex, standing where Rudolf Hess's one-man prison had reared its ugly head until it was reduced to rubble the day after the Wall came down, I looked across to where the old BFBS Berlin studio used to be – the one where I had started my trade. The ghosts of many people, programmes and memories flitted past, to disappear along with a whole way of life. Berlin was no longer a magic and mystical city. It was just another major city with a bit of a past.

Some days later I would be walking past a sweat-shirt seller's huge rack at the Kaiser Wilhelm Gedächtniskirche, and noting the slogan on every one of these shirts: 'Gib uns unsere Mauer wieder zurück, aber diessmal 2 Meter höher!' – 'Give us our Wall back, but this time 2 metres higher!' I asked the seller who was buying these shirts. Was it the tourists? He grinned, in a typical Berlin way - an ironic grin. No, it wasn't mainly the tourists. Mostly locals.

'Ach,' I said, interested. 'Ossies oder Wessies?' – 'East or West Berliners?'

He caught my accent, and my drift. A broad grin. 'Beide!' he laughed. 'Both!'

The West Berliners had lost a lot of the subsidies required to keep the city as a showcase island of capitalism in an ocean of communism. National Service exemption was cancelled, as was eternal student status. The East Berliners lost cradle to grave welfare, employment in non-jobs and a whole hierarchy based on communism's tokens of approval, advancement and status. So a lot of people wanted the Wall back.

My head said I was glad it was gone. But, as I tried to explain to Heidi later on that day, my heart still liked the old Berlin, where I had played, grown up and mixed with a cosmopolitan community who treated liberty as a goal, a destination - not as a parroted slogan. My personal Berlin was actually being deconstructed by my simply being in this new city where freedom had arrived, thank you, and we could all get on with being tetchy little wage-slaves, bickering about tiny things going wrong and living pasteurised lives in a mundane setting. I suddenly felt very sad.

The mood became even worse when we drove down to the Berlin Officers' Club for a farewell reception. The MD, David Crwys-Williams, was the principal speaker, and he gave his usual brilliant talk about what Berlin had contributed to the BFBS and SSVC story. His eloquence, oratory and superb control of his brief ensured that the audience got its money's worth, and I was glad for him and us.

But very sorry for myself. More than BFBS, the Officers' Club was *my* personal stamping ground. My mis-spent youth had been mis-spent here. More rum and Cokes than had been strictly necessary had passed through my system here; I had drunk, laughed, swum, eaten, loved and cried here over many years; I had made one or two life-long friends.

And here I was, in a crowd of arrivistes, of people who had little or no connection with *my* Berlin. It was like the daft major who had patronised me all those years ago with, 'Peter, you'll really enjoy Berlin – there's *so* much to see and do.' I felt like screaming.

We had a few hours to spare the next day. I broke away from the main party and went, secretly, to see my never-changing girlfriend, the oldest ally in my life - Queen Nefertiti, cool and aloof, in her bullet proof glass cabinet, a stab of light igniting her soul after all those centuries. She calmed me, soothed me, and reminded me that in the same way she was always in my thoughts. Thanks to her, the old Berlin, *my* Berlin, would always be at the forefront of my mind, no matter how the external shapes and circumstances changed. I left the museum totally recharged and gave up on the negative thoughts. I had been the lucky one. I had lived this life. I was unique. I was blessed. The rest was just background noise. It was time to let go.

Back in the UK, I examined the record. I had personally been on duty from 1948 – 1994 in, or close to, Berlin. The twenty-one Soviet Army Divisions had been held at bay, thanks to me and thirteen tanks. (And, of course, a few walk-on extras, but many of those had only managed a couple of years before scuttling back to safety.)

I remembered once talking to a rather boozy old colonel, who had once commanded a battalion on the outskirts of Kladow, up by the East German border, at the time of the airlift. He had been given sealed packets of orders. The final one was a personal package that contained a Top Secret message. In the event of the Soviets invading, overpowering any resistance and entering his married quarter, he was to shoot his family first, then himself. It was not a pleasant idea to dwell on, but the threat was very real to the people there at the time.

There were many cases of clinical depression amongst the allied forces and their families in West Berlin, who felt that they were imprisoned on a small island, surrounded by certain death. Many used to use the military train or the autobahn 'corridor' to go down to the 'Zone' – the former British occupation zone, which offered delights such as the Kiel Yacht Club and the services' leave centres and where it was even possible to see some authentic German life in the wild, too.

I could see all the angst and the tension, but I guess my version was both fatalistic and logical. The safest place to be is in the eye of the storm. If that isn't the case, then when the atomic bomb explodes, it'll be right on top of you and you won't feel a thing. Especially after a drink or two.

*****

Back in the UK, not that I knew it at the time, I had fewer than five years left with the old firm. Gradually, I was ossifying into an administrator and getting further and further away from front line broadcasting. We moved closer and closer to a more formal privatisation and, by 1996, the idea of having to slim down the organisation was taking hold.

If we were to win a competitive tender to provide Forces' Broadcasting, we had to cut costs – and everyone knows what that means. Many of our staff came with the impedimenta of the 'jobs for life' culture of our civil service history. I began to examine the whole staff picture and realised, with some horror, that of the eighty-five UK-based (permanent) staff we employed worldwide, at least seventeen would have to go. Their number would include many old friends and colleagues.

I knew that the MD was expecting some changes but even he was surprised at how keen I was to back this swingeing proposition.

The only real joy left to me was my increasingly close relationship with our Chairman, David Hatch, who had acquired a well-deserved CBE and was to go on to become Chairman of the National Consumer Council, then Chairman of the Parole Board of England and Wales, and finally a very hearty knight of the realm.

David did not tolerate fools, as I was to find out during the preliminary negotiations to establish whether or not BFBS, as well as other SSVC activities, could be put out to competitive tender in order to make a profit.

Representatives from one of the big four predatory financial houses arrived one day. Used to the ways of Mammon, they didn't really listen to our pleas about the integrity and suitability of public service broadcasting. One gentleman in particular seemed to have developed a tin ear, until David gave him both barrels.

The whole idea of privatisation was tied up with BFBS's historic ability to access BBC programming on an unspoken 'grace and favour' basis. We did pay an annual subscription to the BBC Transcription Service as 'danegeld', but acquiring rights to carry BBC material was often as simple as this:

During the first Gulf War, we wanted to carry long simulcasts of BBC Radio 4's special 'Gulf FM' channel, which broadcast plenty of in-depth reportage, background and comment. I phoned Jenny Abramsky, Head of BBC Radio, on David's advice.

'Would it be OK to carry chunks of Gulf FM on BFBS?' I asked – a bit tentatively. Jenny was a pocket rocket, with the sharpest mind at the BBC at that time.

'And give us more listeners at a stroke, including overseas?' she chided. 'What kind of a question is that? Help yourselves! Anything and everything you want!'

I pointed out to Mr Financial House Predator that this was based on a long and historic relationship dating back to the Second World War.

'Oh!' said Predator. 'I'm sure any new company could come to a similar arrangement with the BBC. I don't see this as a showstopper.'

A quiet voice came from the top end of the table. David Hatch, former Managing Director, BBC Network Radio and by this point special advisor to John Birt, the BBC's formidable Director-General, entered the negotiations.

'I think you may have to revise that opinion,' he said, in a voice that betrayed only the very slightest bit of polite but ice-cold contempt.

'And why is that?' frowned Predator.

David looked him in the eye 'because some relationships are built on more than financial considerations. I can tell you now – and I speak with the BBC D-G's authority – that we will refuse absolutely to simply hand over any broadcasting rights for nothing to any profit-making organisation placed to take over from BFBS. What we give to BFBS is non-transferable and, if you insist on pursuing the rights issue, we will price them so high in the market that the MOD will run a mile rather than pay what we might ask for.'

There was a silence, after which I told Predator about the very low subscription fee we paid and what the likely rates for a commercial company might be. But that was a mouse's squeak compared to the wrath of David.

It was a broadside. Even I was terrified at the sheer momentum, venom and accuracy with which Big Dave had blown Predator out of the water. It took my breath away. The man in the white hat still lived. I could have hugged him. Predator disappeared and after that it was generally conceded that the moneymen wouldn't be sniffing BFBS's bum again in a hurry.

I wrote a note to David, thanking him for the spectacular attack. His reply was typically generous – even though this was a handwritten and private letter:

'Lovely Fellow,

I said no more than I should and less well than I ought. It seemed to me an impertinence that these arrivistes, ignorami, and self-interested berks should dare to tinker with something precious. I was actually rather angry that things had been allowed to reach the point where a debate was necessary! I'm glad you think I made a difference. It's my belief that we squeezed them in a rather effective sandwich. I did the heart and soul bit at the front end, and you did   the numbers (rights) at the other end. They got both barrels but didn't expect us to fire that way round! We won, and rightly so. To laughs and chats.

Yours, D.'

*****

David and I would make many trips overseas before my dinner pail was handed to me. I used to refer to these jaunts as 'Fat Bastards On Tour'. They were always a mixture of attending formal meetings and meals, and getting down with the local population, the BFBS crew, and any other waifs and strays we came across.

In the Falklands, we had dinner with the Governor, where we spent time trying to persuade him to open an ostrich farm. (Really. The idea was that he could then grow the feathers for the gubernatorial plumed hat and sell on the surplus to other Governors and High Commissioners around the world. His wife joined in with the joke, until we gradually managed to at least think of this as a viable idea. Well, almost.)

We had travelled down to the Falklands with a parallel VIP party. Unbeknown to us, the army's Adjutant-General, Lt Gen Sir Alex Harley, was making a state visit and we kept bumping into each other in various places, mainly VIP lounges, but more importantly, on the beach at Sea Lion Island, home to a very weighty and very smelly colony of elephant seals, who made a lot of noise and chased us around a bit. David, by this time, was Chairman of the National Consumer Council, as well as a Justice of the Peace. He and I must have made for quite a sight as we ran around the beach, dodging the local wildlife. How we kept straight faces I will never know.

When we got back from our Falklands adventures, I was not totally surprised to receive a very nice letter from David. The sort of letter that reminds you that Spike Milligan wasn't the only one who could squeeze laughter from a stone.

'Dear Peter,

A most extraordinary thing has happened – a load of photographs have arrived from the General and he has written comments and jokes on the backs!! It's most unnerving. He was clearly following us around; no wonder I felt nervous when I couldn't *see* him. If you look at the photos it quickly becomes clear where he was hiding: some of his disguises are really magnificent. Some are less good: he makes a lousy sea-lion, but his penguin is brilliant. The best is the sheep-shearing shed with POW [Prisoners of War] on it. Who on earth would have realised that the rusty oil-drum was a four-star General? It's quite superb.

'It's probably time I came clean and told you the truth. The General is my common-law wife & followed me to the Falklands believing I was having an affair with a variety of aquatic animals (actually it was originally only small goldfish). Pictures of elephant seals and penguins haven't helped my case, and he's suing for divorce. My only hope is that he'll be true to form and be late to court.

'My mind is beginning to go. I can still smell penguin shit, but I vaguely recall a nice young man came with us on the trip and took lots of photographs. Whatever happened to him or them? Must go: the General needs help with his shoe-laces. He threads beads on them but makes the odd mistake: last week a couple of hand grenades actually went off. Nurse needs me, bye bye. See you at Brown's [the Mayfair hotel where we held board meetings]. I'll be arriving by ostrich [deleted] *taxi* – sorry. Let's go to the Falklands sometime.

Yours, Colonel Arbuthnot (Mrs) Retd.'

*****

While David was around, and especially as Chairman, I felt that carrying on was still just about viable. Relations between the MD and me were not good – but that was not his fault. I was sulking, contrary and becoming idle. But Mr Hatch, later Sir David, was a great chum, and kept me sane.

One hot summer's day, after a board meeting and marquee lunch at SSVC HQ in Chalfont Grove, I was standing quietly with David on top of a little grassy knoll that looked down over the scuttling staff going about their business. It was one of those moments where there was no need to speak – so I did.

'I'm going to be fifty this year,' I volunteered.

David caught the message, and returned the volley.

'I've just turned sixty,' he said, not with any great emotion.

'Does it feel any different?' I said, instantly regretting asking such a daft question. We tended not to do small talk.

'Oh yes,' said David, his eyes lighting up with that brilliant sense of comic mischief. 'Being sixty is great.

You can tell people to fuck off, and they do.'

I couldn't top that. Meanwhile, the trips continued. David was convinced that the scenes of these journeys were actually scripted by me in advance, as no normal human behaviour could come near some of that exhibited on our 'Fat Bastards' tours.

On a visit to Cyprus, we paid a courtesy visit to a nameless civil servant from the upper echelon of the Sovereign Base Area Administration. This rather stiff and upright Dickensian gentleman was dressed in the perennial uniform of the UK civil servant in an 'ot country: white long-sleeved shirt, neutral tie, long white shorts, white knee length stockings and black Oxford lace-ups - what I remember calling 'the maggot look'. He expatiated on SBA law at some length. We were a bit peckish and tried to hurry him along but he had an agenda, and kept to it.

David's response, when we got back to the UK, had the maggot bang to rights.

'I suppose for me a strange highlight was watching the "civil servant" with his Treaty, leafing through, quoting annexes, drinking tea from cup and saucer, behaving for all the world as though in Whitehall. No wonder we acquired an empire: the refusal to adjust a life-style and manner must have seemed so very, very confident.'

We enjoyed the luxury of being able to stand back from the situation, just having a laugh at other people taking themselves too seriously.

The most memorable trip of all was the Far East Special, where we were to visit our two outposts of Hong Kong and Brunei.

Hong Kong had two BFBS stations, one at HMS Tamar (later renamed Prince of Wales Barracks), on Hong Kong Island, and the other at RAF Sek Kong, which was also home to a Gurkha battalion. Our trip saw us getting down and dirty in the local food parlours, which included an oil drum café (you sat on the drums and ate from the tops of them) in Yuen Long, and an unspeakably characterful bar in the Wanchai district. We even managed a full-day exploration of the New Territories, using only short haul rickety old local buses.

We then flew to Brunei, the Muslim sultanate on the island of Borneo, home to more Gurkhas and a small BFBS station near the border with Sarawak. The flight, courtesy of the very dry Royal Brunei Airways was a bit tedious – no Cointreau for David; I was used to tonic water and when we touched down at Bandar Seri Begawan's optimistically named 'International Airport', the sheer glumness of the Western-hating officials was tangible. David was dog-tired and I guess it wasn't the best of ideas for him to slam his suitcase down in front of the Brunei customs youth, with just perhaps a spot of peevishness.

You know how it is with tiny countries. Their airport metal detectors go off at the sensing of a tooth filling, and their customs officials all wear loads of gold braid, medal ribbons, badges and giant caps with stellar insignia.

'Why you do that?' hissed the nastier looking of the two customs men. 'You sram soocase down like "bang!" You no do tha' in fuckin' Heathrow, hey?'

David shrugged. Bit tired. Not registering. Didn't see a problem. The large sign above my head slid into focus. The large white sign with the big, red, bold, accusing letters, which read:

'THE PENALTY FOR IMPORTING DRUGS INTO BRUNEI IS DEATH.'

I suddenly saw a vivid and immediate connection between angry young customs official and us dangling from the end of a rope.

'Er, he not mean trouble,' I mollified. 'He very tired. In England he is judge, very important man. He no break law of wonderful Brunei country.'

I think I got a few brownie points for good intentions, but honour had by no means yet been satisfied.

'He no do that a' fuckin' Heathrow!' exclaimed our No. 1 charmer. 'Now you come with me!'

He led us to a small room. A very quiet room. With a lock on the door. It went 'click'. A comment, not a noise.

'Now you open suitcase!' he gestured to both of us.

We looked at each other. This, according to the script in my head, was where the little package of white powder would be 'discovered'. Ah well, it had been a good innings.

Our friend handled our suitcases in typical 'I'm a bolshie customs man having a bad day' mode.

Everything out and strewn all over the floor. Meanwhile, I was trying to be nice to the other customs officer, and actually sensing a bit of give. I was glad to notice that no little packets of white powder had been discovered.

'My friend very important man from London,' I tried again. 'He is judge, friend of Queen, and works with big boss of BBC.'

Ah, we seemed to be getting somewhere. My confidence grew.

'There is a man here to meet us who can tell you who he is. Can you take me to Arrivals to see him?'

There was a short interchange. This could just add to the cabaret value of a boring shift – an extra audience. Nasty official grunted a reluctant 'yes', and I set off with less horrid official to the Arrivals gate.

When we got there, I was delighted to see the large frame of Dusty Miller, our BFBS Brunei Station Manager. Standing next to him was a British Army captain, wearing jungle combats with rather unusual insignia. I jabbered out the nature of our problem.

Dusty looked concerned. The captain simply took over completely.

He machine-gunned the customs man with a barrage of joined-up 'local', not unkind in tone, but with the no-nonsense delivery which marks out leaders of men.

Customs listened, wide-eyed, as our captain explained. At the end of the oration, friendlier customs turned to us, clearly with a complete change of heart, and said, with some respect, 'You should all now come with me, please.'

We went back to the locked room, where David was looking very fed up indeed. He was briefly introduced to our new friend, the captain, who then delivered his speech once again for the benefit of horrid customs man. At the end there was a look of utter astonishment and a very, very reluctant order to us from our potential nemesis.

'You go now! Yes, you go! And you not do that with your fuckin' suitcase at Heathrow!'

The door was miraculously unlocked, and all four of us breathed the sultry Brunei air of comparative freedom.

David chatted to the captain, who just by chance had been waiting at Arrivals for his complement of jungle training recruits from the very quiet regiment based in Hereford that tends to dare, and win.

'What did you say to the guy?' asked David, with some admiration. 'I mean, he suddenly changed his tune – just like that?'

'Not too difficult,' said our boys' own hero, with a slightly self-conscious grin. 'I just told him you two were part of my unit.'

Yes, for a brief and wonderful instant, two chronically unfit and overweight broadcasters had been elevated to the ranks of the SAS.

We had a wonderful cabaret in Brunei. Capping it all was the legendary 'Meal with Special Tea', available from a local Chinese restaurant in the small oil town of Seria, where the British garrison was based. The 'special tea' was Carlsberg, served in a teapot so as not to inflame the sensibilities of the more devout Muslims.

However, on the night of the BFBS dinner, we had a problem. Although it was the end of Ramadan, the moon had not yet been sighted, thus the end of the Muslim fasting period was not yet confirmed. No moon: no party, and certainly no 'special tea'.

(To give you an idea of how important this sighting was, the local 'Brunei Times' newspaper carried two TV schedules. One, headlined 'If the moon is sighted', showed the usual fare – loads of old re-runs of 'I Love Lucy' and other US classics. The second schedule showed little more than news headlines and readings from the Koran, under the headline, 'If the moon is not sighted'...)

We waited at the BFBS station. As it got dark, we went outside and looked up. Disappointment. The sky was completely overcast. There would be no sighting. And no special tea. Suddenly there was a commotion. A local cleaner on the station threw down his broom and proclaimed, 'Moon is sighted!'

We needed to check this out so we contacted the Garrison HQ. Apparently we weren't the only ones tapping our feet and waiting for the end of Ramadan. The Sultan, having looked at the reluctant sky, had scrambled planes from his own Royal Brunei Air Force to break cloud cover and report back once they had seen the moon, which of course was very clear in the sky once the clouds had been left below. Once the radio report had been received, the moon had been sighted and it was time for Ramadana-ding-dong party time. The special tea was on.

David and I ended our travel trail with a series of campaign medals, huge grins and some of the best memories of my life. But things were about to change.

Chapter 28

All Good Things…

My career as a Cold War warrior had a shaky start. I have a tendency to over-complicate, with sometimes appalling consequences.

On one occasion, at primary school, I was asked to pronounce the word 'idiosyncrasy'. It came out 'idiossy n,crassy', as I applied my usual multi-layered approach to the problem. Similarly in secondary school, where an internal exam paper in science asked for a 'non-aqueous solvent'. To my convoluted thinking, 'non-aqueous' meant 'dry' (don't ask), and 'solvent' meant something that absorbed something else. So what is dry and absorbs something else? Of course. Blotting paper.

You can see why I was never invited to join the secret service. Wood for the trees? No chance. In Berlin, I used to be very, very careful whenever I used our telephone. My finger, gingerly and hesitantly, would describe an arc on the old fashioned dial, while I held my breath. The reason for this? In the centre of the dial, in big white letters on a blazing red background, was the slogan *'Not Secure'*. I thought it meant the dial would fall off if you used it too vigorously…

Which was a pity, because in addition to my principal Cold War warrior qualification – being there, being in Berlin as a token target – I could have offered so much more.

As a peacemaker, for example. I went to school with every regiment in the British Army, and could copy almost any dialect or accent. I had to do this to stop other kids from beating me up.

As a recruiter, too. My first 'best friend' was a high-ranking Canadian official's son, Robert Grande, who watched my back during critical moments in the playground. He left behind him a trail of mayhem on my account.

Had I not gone into the world of broadcasting, I could quite clearly have made a career in the spy game. I had a unique ability to walk into any empty pub first and still be served last. Catching the bartender's eye was virtually impossible for me. Everything from a winning smile to the loud offer of a bribe was ritually ignored or rejected. I would always be in the rear party. Also, in the pub, I could easily inveigle myself into a small group of chums, but they tended to ignore me - so much so that on one occasion, my pals were telling a story about me that was less than complimentary. They hadn't even realised I was there.

As a fighter, I was second to none. My method was subversion, and using the other person's strength against him was my favoured weapon. Why have a fight when you could sub-let the combat to someone else? I always felt this was a moral way of fighting, as I made it a rule to let sleeping dogs lie, so if anyone wanted to fight me, they were automatically in the wrong. The Royal Marine in Malta who had to be taken out with double Fernet Brancas got what he deserved. This was another complex piece of McD logic – but it worked for me.

Finally, in much of my Cold War fighting phase, I had the added weapon of drink. I could drink most people under the table. I was a happy drunk, then usually a happy sleeping drunk. In those days I was never argumentative or hostile – just keen to keep a collection of besh friendsh to whom I could offer drinks, laughs and cabaret.

In my club days, we even had a song that expressed it all. It went to a familiar tune:

'I don't want to go to Oxford

I don't want to have to work.

I'd rather hang around

Theodor Heuss Platz Underground

Living off the earnings of a Consul-General's daughter.

I don't want Glenfiddich up me arsehole

I don't want me Myers shot away

I'd rather stay in *Ber*lin

In bloody, bloody *Ber*lin

And sublimate me fuckin' life away.'

(The reference to the Consul-General's daughter refers to one Sara Edwards, who was adopted by our gang as principal mascot and young lady we'd quite like to if we had the nerve.)

Well, it was better, in the late sixties, than all that miserable hippie whingeing. It was part of the glue that kept us together.

*****

But I digress. All of these attributes had somehow conspired to get me to the top of the tree in my chosen field. I was only the fifth Director of BFBS and I had overseen some amazing changes in stations, numbers and the whole approach of the network to its listeners and viewers.

In 1997 I had to implement those redundancies. Seventeen of our tight-knitted band of eighty-five staff lost their jobs. It hurt them, but it wasn't a bed of roses for me, either. However, it went with the territory, and it was necessary, so eventually I learned to live with it.

A colleague who survived the cut asked me, 'How do you feel about all these redundancies?'

I tried to reply as honestly as I could.

'It takes away everything you always thought about your own permanence. As they're trooping out of the gates, I feel like a Japanese guard on duty right at the end of the war. Where should I be aiming my rifle when the enemy comes to liberate the camp? There are always consequences and I feel it won't be long before David comes knocking at my door.'

I became very fatalistic about it. There was nothing more I could do. I had been what the present day pundits call an 'Agent of Change'. The changes had happened and I was now tainted with the stain of 'yesterday'.

I have to say I made it very easy for the MD to hand me my P45. I'd become lazy, apathetic and lost interest almost completely in the old BFBS.

When the call came to see the MD, I felt almost a sense of relief. Now that the corporation had finished its changes, and been broken up into various businesses and scrap heaps, the need for all divisional directors was now over. They would all be going, including me. It was an elegant solution, one that I felt had been helped along in part by my guardian angel, the Chairman, Sir David Hatch.

I listened with something bordering on amusement as David read me my marching orders, which he did, I have to say, with some compassion and warmth. I had nothing to blame him for. Had it not been for the changes that he orchestrated, BFBS and SSVC would not be alive today. At the end of the death sentence, he asked me if I had any requests.

This was late autumn, 1998. I asked for two favours.

Firstly, that I could go on 5th April, as it was the end of a tax year. It would also give me a few extra weeks to get my post-employment affairs in order.

Secondly, could I personally announce my own redundancy at the Station Managers' annual conference, due to take place soon in Germany? I was surprised but quite delighted when David agreed.

We discussed the succession and agreed that Charles Foster would take over as Controller, BFBS Radio, and that Steve Mylles would continue as Controller, BFBS TV. Marc Tyley, who was also huge on the radar, would stay as Station Manager in Germany, where he was doing an excellent job of running our biggest overseas network.

With all that in mind, I went away to do my sums and see what the art of the possible was likely to be. In the next few weeks I was told that I would probably be re-employed on a very loose contract to oversee a trial of BFBS Radio on a number of military bases in the UK and that I would also be used to organise and participate in training courses. So, at least the next couple of years were looking good!

Plus, it seemed that I would be getting a more than healthy annual stipend based on the civil service pension scheme, which some of the longer-serving BFBS staff had retained from the old, pre-SSVC, MOD days. Boring it may have been, but with the added years in the formula, it meant an 'annual compensatory payment' that was well above the average working wage. With the kids now out of our hair, I calculated we'd be better off than we'd ever been.

With all of this going on in the background, I managed to keep news of my redundancy at Board level.

I kept my powder dry in the run-up to, and even during the Station Managers' conference in Germany.

The conference was held in the small 'North Rhine West Phailure' town of Lübekke. The venue was an imposing building called Church House, then the home of the British military chaplaincy, but formerly the headquarters of the Hitler Youth. The symbol, 'HJ' – 'HItlerjugend' remained in the middle of the front gate.

The upper echelons of the BFBS Radio hierarchy had three nights in that historic building, much to the consternation of some of the more reserved padres. Most of us enjoyed arguing and drinking so the evenings turned out to be very entertaining indeed. We dined in the Officers'

Wardroom, which was a replica of the wardroom on the Bismarck, and spent our days planning staff postings, drawing up new schedules, looking at new initiatives and picking at the entrails of what had gone wrong in the past.

By the time the final evening came along, I was very nearly sorry I was going – but I knew in my heart of hearts that my energy had gone.

I told them quietly, as we sat in the anteroom after dinner.

It came as a genuine shock to everyone.

The first part of the shock was, I would like to think, that I was actually leaving. Secondly, there was disbelief that it would be so soon. Then, finally, I very much enjoyed watching each member of my team realise that my departure would have consequences for them, too.

Did I know what the succession was going to be?

Yes I did, and here it was.

I explained as best I could, that these had been my suggestions, which David had ratified. I think one or two people might not have believed this but, whether they did or not, what I'd told them was fact and precisely what was going to happen. Some nice noises here heard, and I felt suitably consoled.

A few weeks later, we all met in the BFBS network centre in Chalfont, which had been opened less than two years before – my last major project – and there were drinks and dead things on sticks and speeches and prezzies and then it was time for me to hang up my dinner pail and become a boulevardier and tap dancer after decades of wage slavery. I felt almost light-headed.

*****

Looking back, I wish I'd had more stamina. I wish I'd had more talent. I wish I'd had steadier nerves. But I was me, and I got to where I was by honest means.

Now, many years later, I look back and I am delighted with the result.

I still treasure the letter David Hatch wrote to me after my departure as director.

'Certainly BFBS Radio is in thriving condition. All its constituent parts are moving forward positively: it's like an enormous well-drilled army. It's a pleasure to be involved in it all as we *expand* into new areas and arenas – retreating is so disheartening. The fact is, and it is an incontrovertible fact, BFBS thrives because you, my friend, were a wise and canny forward-thinker. You sowed seeds here, there and everywhere with one hand, as the other was forced to pull out the plugs in other places. You saw that unless radio became fleet of foot, technically global, where the fighting was, flexible enough to be both big and small, but consistent in its high standards, it could wither as funding froze. It's enjoying the sun because you toiled in the rain and cold. It's your BFBS, which is why I want you always to feel a part of it, if that is your wish.'

I can tell you that this was a wonderful tonic and, as a result, I did continue to put time and effort into BFBS, quite happy no longer to have the heavy responsibilities of previous times.

Sadly, we lost David Hatch in 1997, after a short but not entirely humour-free battle with pancreatic cancer. At his memorial service, John Cleese, a former partner in crime, spoke of his visit to David during the latter's final days at home. The familiar Monty Python voice filled the vaults and crannies of All Souls church at the Langham, as he spoke in hushed tones about how gone to the Hatch residence to see the very ill David and found his old friend sitting in his favourite armchair.

'He was wearing a grin, and a T-shirt,' said Cleese. 'And I had to laugh out loud at the slogan. It said simply '*Going Underground*'.

At the funeral, on a suitably Irish day, David's coffin was given pride of place in the village church, as a crowd of the great and the good (and us lesser mortals) trooped in to hear a simple service featuring some kind and loving words.

Ben Hatch, David's eldest son, was due to read a poem, according to the order of service. When it was his turn, he stood next to the coffin, patted it in an almost absent-minded way, then threw away his prepared script.

'I won't do that,' he said, levelly. 'I want to talk about my Dad.'

Ben is a writer, and a fine observer, and he had soon conjured before us a living David, a capricious, Cointreau-drinking, argumentative, loving, funny, endearing, contrary, incompetent, brilliant Dad, a Dad who we all recognised as our David.

At the end Ben confessed, 'By the way, Dad ended up having the last laugh. Everybody sniggered when he said he wanted to be buried in his pink suit. But I saw him just before the lid went on.'

He patted the coffin again. 'Pink suit.'

It was a magic moment. We buried David just up the hill from the church. The rain helped hide the tears – not that anybody cared. We'd lost a giant.

*****

And that, perhaps, is a suitable point at which to end the story of a rather nervous kid who kept twenty-one Soviet armoured divisions at bay for much of his lifetime, won the Cold War with just thirteen tanks (and a few extras), became a famous DJ with an audience of twenty million on 'Family Favourites', had an award-winning radio show, appeared in 'Billboard' and on the cover of 'Rolling Stone', was Tommy Vance's producer for a number of years and employed broadcasters of the calibre of John Peel, Tony Blackburn, Johnnie Walker and David Rodigan. Oh, and did the last interview with Peter Sellers *and* recorded a single on Tamla Motown.

Yeah, that's right. Me.

Mine's a tonic– ice and lemon.

Cheers.

EPILOGUE (SWANSONG)

Dateline: Wednesday 15th January 2014

'IS THERE ANY POINT IN TAKING OUT A YEAR'S SUBSCRIPTION TO GARDENERS' WORLD?'

Well, it seemed a good icebreaker. I was sitting in the oncology suite at Inverness's Raigmore Hospital, just about to have my fortune read.

I already knew I had cancer of all the "L"s - lung, liver, lights. An aggressive form. The first diagnosis, from Dr. Stuart and a video team of specialists the week before, gave me a window of one to two years before my appointment with the Grim Reaper. This baby was inoperable, terminal, and the only treatment was chemotherapy.

Now I was sitting with Dr Marion and her team, Kate, Linda, and Leslie, and at least I'd got a half-smile out of them with the gardening crack.

Marion gave me the updated news. A small cell lung cancer was the highlight. The new prognosis was a little eye watering. No treatment. I might manage 6 weeks. With chemo, if successful, an 80% chance of about a year.

When you are told something like that, the mind goes into overdrive thinking about the consequences.

Luckily, Moo is totally catered for. Also I had achieved several ambitions in work, home, and play. I worked for a great firm - BFBS - in a job I loved, with many fulfilling years as Director, and then in another field, when I became Chairman of the British Wireless for the Blind Fund.

I'd always thought about eternity. In fairly short order, I'd be enjoying a celestial brandy with Terry James, a Cointreau with David Hatch, a pint of Guinness with Dave Boyle, a glass of cassis with Uncle Bill, a claret with 'Udson, a Keo with Pete Johnson ('moi cocker'), a pink gin with Roy ffoulkes, a JD with Jourdan Griffiths - one of my college mates - and mine would be a Myers' Rum and Coke.

How do I know? The wedding feast. Now, did Jesus turn wine into water, or water into wine? (Clue: the liquid got darker!)

As you can surmise, I rather believe in the Afterlife. A case of nearer my God to thee!

*****

On 1ˢᵗ June 2010, Moo and I moved to our beautiful home, called, rather exotically, but also prosaically, 'Ardhachaidh' - Gaelic for 'Our Home' - a delightful bungalow with one-and-a-half uncarved acres of prime Scottish field in Latheronwheel, near Wick, on the Moray Firth coast.

As global nomads for much of our lives, we had both determined that the UK would be our eventual home and, by a process of argument, attrition, compromise and curiosity, we ended up with Scotland as our target. Several visits narrowed the location down to Caithness and further ructions of fate pitched us up at Ardhachaidh.

Here, under duress at first, I learnt the gentle art of gardening - ditch-digging, path laying, gravel-humping, muscular landscaping - until we'd beaten parts of the field into an ornamental garden, a vegetable patch, a rose arbour, an apple orchard, several grass-pathed walkways and a profusion of scattered trees and bushes.

I planted so many trees that I felt like Her Queen! About halfway through this labour of love, I turned from a townie into a straw-sucking agrophile, and could even keen an eye at the weather and go "aarr", knowledgeably, in all the right places.

After a few years of shelf-stacking for Marks and Sparks (saved money on a gym subscription!) and working as a lecturer in radio production at Amersham and Wycombe College - truly an exciting and pleasant experience - it was good to settle into another period where I was able to say, 'I enjoy what I do, and I do what I enjoy.' In that sense, I have been so very lucky!

*****

I told my German (!) GP, Doctor Bert Martens, that it was my overriding desire not to have to spend my declining years slowly festering in the draughty "Bide a Wee" nursing home with de-sensitised staff, sipping thin gruel in my wingback chair as I stared out of the window at the inspiring sight of the Wick Gasworks. Every cloud, etc!

Sadly, I probably won't get to hide my own Christmas presents - no time for dementia - and I was told I should go out with a full complement of marbles, which is another positive outcome. And I should still have most of the other bits that make me me!

At the beginning of February 2014, the entire family, with kids, piled in from the West Country, Australia and America.

Olly the Firefighter and Allison the Doula, with offspring Daisy, Molly and Lucy made it through Philadelphia blizzards to be with us, as did Paddy the Financial Wizard and Helen the Financier from the warmth of Brisbane. From Axminster, Mandy the Youth Worker, Richard the Piemaker, and daughters Tabitha and Jessie made the cut, as did Alex the Carer, Emma the Consultant, and their two little twinklers, Sebastian and Robbie Roo. Enough backgrounds, generations and ages to make for a very lively few days, culminating in a group photo - all seventeen of us, with the Dynasty Chief front centre, wearing a wonderful London Tube t-shirt - the iconic map, framed by the slogan, 'I'M GOING UNDERGROUND'. We laughed a lot.

I went through four chemo cycles. The only side effect (five pages of dire prognostications in the handbook!) was the hiccups. I felt a bit of a fraud. Mind you, the chemo's main agent is platinum based. Suddenly, I was worth a lot more.

It's been an exciting journey. As we go to press, I peer with curiosity over the rim of the unknown. (If I've already been planted, then 'I peered with curiosity over the rim of the unknown.') Pretentious, moi?

Thanks for giving me the airtime. I do value you, and we've had fun.

And don't forget, you should always cry at a wedding and laugh at a funeral. At least with a funeral you know where the bugger's going!

PMcD.

Printed in Great Britain
by Amazon.co.uk, Ltd.,
Marston Gate.